An Index to Musical Festschriften

AND SIMILAR PUBLICATIONS

by Walter Gerboth

Brooklyn College of the City University of New York

W · W · NORTON & COMPANY · INC ·
NEW YORK

FIRST EDITION

 Published simultaneously in Canada by George J. McLeod Limited, Toronto. *Library of Congress Catalog Card No. 68-12182*. Printed in the United States of America.

SBN 393 02134 3

1 2 3 4 5 6 7 8 9 0

Contents

Preface

THE PRESENT INDEX is a revised and enlarged version of the one that originally appeared in *Aspects of Medieval and Renaissance Music: A Birthday Offering to Gustave Reese.** It has been revised to include corrections of typographical errors and a few articles inadvertently omitted, and it has been enlarged to include: 1) Festschriften published after the first compilation was completed (roughly from 1964 through 1967), and 2) additional Festschriften that were published earlier, but which were located in a public institution after the first compilation was completed. In particular, the coverage of material in Slavic languages and musical articles in non-musical Festschriften has been expanded.

The process of compilation uncovered a number of references to musical *Festschriften* that were never published. These include collections in honor of Ludwig Schiedermair (70th birthday), Max Schneider (75th), Hermann Stephani (70th), Willi Kahl (50th), Karl Gustav Fellerer (50th), Antoine-Elisée Cherbuliez (70th), and Richard Münnich (70th). Whenever it was possible to obtain microfilm copies of the typescripts and place them in an institutional library they have been indexed. Conversely, published *Festschriften* which could not be located in an institutional library, and which could not be obtained and placed in one, have not been indexed.

The index is organized in three sections: I) a list of the *Festschriften*, II) a classified list of the musical articles and complete musical compositions in the *Festschriften*, and III) an index by author and subject to the articles in section II.

A typical entry in section I contains the following information: name of the person being honored (initials if it is an institution); title and editors of the publication; if it is part of a series, title and volume of the series; place of publication, publisher, and date of publication; number of pages; the term "bibliog" if the publication contains a bibliography of the works of the person being honored, and the names

* Ed. by Jan La Rue [et al] New York: W. W. Norton & Company, Inc., 1966.

of the compilers of the bibliography if they are given; the term "biog" if the publication contains articles about the life or work of the person being honored, and the names of the authors of such articles. The following is a sample entry.

SCHENK Festschrift für Erich Schenk. (*Studien zur Musikwissenschaft, Beihefte der Denkmäler der Tonkunst in Österreich* 25) Graz: Böhlau, 1962 ◇ 652p bibliog biog (G. Roncaglia)

The number of pages, and the bibliographical and biographical information are given only for the musical *Festschriften.* The editors, authors, and compilers listed there are not listed anywhere else in the index.

A typical entry in section II contains the following information: item number; author; title; symbol for the *Festschrift* and page numbers; information about publication of the articles in other sources, summaries in other languages, etc. The following is a sample entry.

86 Handschin, Jacques. Der Geist des Mittelalters in der Musik. HANDSCHIN 70–81; orig. in *Neue Schweizer Rundschau* 20 (1927)

Most of the articles in section II are grouped according to the standard historical eras. Each article is listed only once. Articles that could appropriately appear in several categories are usually placed in a historical era whenever possible. An article about wind instruments in the Renaissance, for example, would be found under the heading "Renaissance era: Instruments and instrumental music." Cross references are made for articles about several individuals, for historical articles about several eras, and for articles that give equal emphasis to several of the categories used. Complete musical compositions, whether included in the *Festschriften* separately or as part of an article, have been listed individually with the identifying symbol ♪.

For the compilation of the index many references were consulted. There were five chief sources of information: 1) A basic list of musical Festschriften was compiled from existing bibliographies such as Willi Kahl's and Wilhelm-Martin Luther's *Repertorium der Musikwissenschaft* (Kassel 1953) and James B. Coover's *Festschriften, a Provisional List of those Proposed for Indexing* (1958). 2) Library catalogues, chiefly those of Columbia University Library, New York Public Library, and the Library of Congress, were searched under various catchwords. 3) Lists of current publications, especially those in *Jahrbuch der Musikbibliothek Peters* and *Music Library Association Notes,* were scanned. 4) The bibliographies in the Festschriften also yielded many references to additional articles. Persons who are subjects of

Festschriften, it would seem, write busily for those of their colleagues. 5) Published indexes of Festschriften in other fields were also used. The most important, both for their musical yield and for good coverage of related fields, are:

Golden, Herbert H. and Seymour O. Simches. Modern French Literature and Language, a Bibliography of Homage Studies. Cambridge, Mass.: Harvard Univ. Press, 1953. ["Concerned primarily with studies of French literature and language from 1500 to the present."]

——. Modern Iberian Language and Literature, a Bibliography of Homage Studies. Cambridge, Mass.: Harvard Univ. Press, 1958

——. Modern Italian Language and Literature, a Bibliography of Homage Studies. Cambridge, Mass.: Harvard Univ. Press, 1959

International Committee of Historical Sciences. Bibliographie internationale des travaux historiques publiés dans les volumes de mélanges. Paris: Librairie Armand Colin, 1955 & 1965. [Tome I: 1880–1939; Tome II: 1940–1950 avec compléments au tome Ier]

Marcus, Jacob R. and Albert T. Bilgray. An Index to Jewish Festschriften. Cincinnati: Hebrew Union College, 1937

Metzger, Bruce Manning. Index of Articles on the New Testament and the Early Church Published in Festschriften. (Journal of Biblical Literature, Monograph Series 5) Philadelphia: Society of Biblical Literature, 1951

Rave, Paul Ortwin and Barbara Stein. Kunstgeschichte in Festschriften, allgemeine Bibliographie kunstwissenschaftlicher Abhandlungen in den bis 1960 erscheinen Festschriften. Berlin: Gebr. Mann, 1962

Rounds, Dorothy. Articles on Antiquity in Festschriften. Cambridge, Mass.: Harvard Univ. Press, 1962

Williams, Harry F. An Index of Medieval Studies Published in Festschriften, with Special Reference to Romance Material. Berkeley: Univ. of California Press, 1951.

Many persons assisted me in the preparation of this index. Professor Gustave Reese gave me much helpful advice and encouragement when the index was in its formative stages (although he had no notion then where it would first appear), and the unstinting efforts of Professors Jan La Rue and Hans Lenneberg were most helpful in preparing the first compilation for publication. Mr. Thor E. Wood's assistance and generosity must be especially mentioned. For a time we worked jointly on the index. When this was no longer possible, he continued to supply useful information and advice. I am equally grateful to the many others, particularly the members of the editorial staff at W. W. Norton & Company, who have been helpful. While the index is infinitely better for their assistance, the responsibility for its present form, its idiosyncrasies and limitations, and any errors, is solely mine.

W. G.

Brooklyn College
January 1968

I

List of Festschriften

AALL Festskrift til Anathon Aall på 70–årsdagen hans 15. August 1937. Oslo: H. Aschehoug, 1937

ABERT Gedenkschrift für Hermann Abert von seinen Schülern; hrsg. von Friedrich Blume. Halle/Saale: M. Niemeyer, 1928 ◇ 189p bibliog (E.T. Laaff) biog (F. Blume)

ABRAHAMS Jewish Studies in Memory of Israel Abrahams by the Faculty and Visiting Teachers of the Jewish Institute of Religion. New York: Jewish Inst. of Rel., 1927

ADLER Studien zur Musikgeschichte. Festschrift für Guido Adler zum 75. Geburtstag. Wien: Universal, 1930 ◇ 224p bibliog

ADN Festschrift zum 15. Neuphilologentage in Frankfurt am Main, 1912 [Im Auftrag des Vorstandes des Allgemeinen deutschen Neuphilologen-Verbandes hrsg. von M. Banner, F. J. Curtis, M. Friedwagner] Frankfurt/Main: Knaver, 1912

ADORNO/60TH Zeugnisse. Theodor W. Adorno zum 60. Geburtstag. Im Auftrag des Instituts für Sozialforschung; Max Horkheimer, ed. Frankfurt am Main: Europaische Verlagsanstalt, 1963

ALBRECHT Hans Albrecht in memoriam. Gedenkschrift mit Beiträgen von Freunden und Schülern; hrsg. von Wilfried Brennecke und Hans Haase. Kassel: Bärenreiter, 1962 ◇ 290p bibliog (M. Geck) biog (A. A. Abert, H. Haase)

ALMEIDA Estudos e ensaios folclóricos em homenagem a Renato Almeida; organizando pelo professor Antonio Jorge Dias. (*International Folklore Congress, São Paolo,* 1954) Rio de Janeiro: Ministério das Relações Exteriores, Seção de Publicações, 1960

ALONSO Homenaje a Amado Alonso. (*Nueva revista de filología hispánica* 7) Colegio de México, 1953

AMMANN Ammann-Festgabe; besorgt vom Seminar für vergleichende Sprachwissenschaft an der Universität Innsbruck anlässlich der Feier d. 25jähr. Dienstjubiläums . . . (*Innsbrucker Beiträge zur Kulturwissenschaft* 1 & 2) Innsbruck: Sprachwiss. Seminar d. Univ., 1953–1954

ANDERLUH Lied und Brauch aus der Kärntner Volksliedarbeit und Brauchforschung. [Anton Anderluh, dem Volksliedforscher und -pfleger, zur Vollendung seines 60. Lebensjahres dargebracht] (*Kärntner Museumsschriften* 8) Klagenfurt: Landesmuseum für Kärnten, 1956 ◇ 167p bibliog (F. Koschier) biog (G. Graber, G. Mittergradnegger, H. Pommer, E. Zenker-Starzacher)

ANDERSON Holberg blandinger; udg. af Holbergsamfundet af 3. december 1922. [Vilhelm Anderson, 75th Birthday] København: Gyldendal, 1939

ANDERSON, A. Kring konst och kultur. Studier tillägnade Amos Anderson 3. IX. 1948. Helsingfors: Söderström, 1948

ANDERSSON, O./85TH Studier i musik och folklore. (*Skrifter Utgiva av Svenska Litteratursällskap et i Finland* 408) Åbo: 1964 ◇ 425p bibliog (A. Forslin)

ANDLER Mélanges offerts à M. Charles Andler par ses amis et ses élèves. (*Publ. de la faculté des lettres de l'université de Strasbourg* 21) Strasbourg: Librairie Istra/London: Oxford, 1924

ANDREAE Volkmar Andreae. Festausgabe aus Anlass seines Rücktrittes nach 43jähriger erfolgreicher Tätigkeit als künstlerischer Leiter der Tonhalle-Gesellschaft Zürich und verantwortlicher Chef des Tonhalle-Orchesters, 1906–1949; hrsg. vom Vorstand der Tonhalle-Gesellschaft Zürich. Zürich: Tonhalle-

Gesellschaft, 1949 ◇ 109p biog (H. v. Gonzenbach, W. de Boer, R. Wittelsbach, C. Vogler, M. Auer, H. Odermatt, F. Brun, B. Walter)

ANDRIESSEN, W. Willem Andriessen, 1887–1964. Gedenkboek onder redactie van Prof. Dr. K. Ph. Bernet Kempers . . . 's-Gravenhage: Kruseman's Uitgeversmaatschappij N. V., 1964 ◇ 123p biog (M. Aleven-Vranken, S. Swaap, C. L. Walther Boer, H. Andriessen, W. Paap, P. Frenkel, P. Niessing, J. Odé, J. v. d. Boogert, N. Steier-Wagenaar, K. P. Bernet Kempers, J. A. Abbing)

ANGLÉS Miscellánea en homenaje a Monseñor Higinio Anglés. Barcelona: Consejo Superior de Investigaciones Científicas, 1958–1961 ◇ 1054p in 2 v bibliog

ANSERMET Hommage à Ernest Ansermet. Lausanne: Marguerat, 1943 ◇ 138p

APEL/70TH "To Willi Apel on His Seventieth Birthday." (*Musica Disciplina* 17, 1963, 7–237) Rome: American Institute of Musicology, 1963

ASAF'EV Pamiati akademika Borisa Vladimirovicha Asaf'eva. Sbornik statei o nauchno-kriticheskom nasl'edii. [In Memory of Academician Boris Vladimirovich Asaf'ev. Collection of Articles on the Scientific-Critical Heritage] Moskva: Izdat'elstvo Akademii Nauk SSSR, 1951 ◇ 94p biog (R. Glière, I. E. Grabar, D. Kabalevsky, T. N. Livanova, V. A. Vasina-Grossman, E. M. Orlova)

ATL Thüringische Studien. Festschrift zur Feier des 250jährigen Bestehens der Thüringischen Landesbibliothek Altenburg; hrsg. von deren Leiter Dr. Franz Paul Schmidt. Altenburg: O. Bonde, 1936

AUBIN Syntagma Friburgense. Historische Studien Hermann Aubin dargebracht zum 70. Geburtstag am 23. 12. 1955. (*Schriften des Kopernikuskreises* 1) Lindau, Konstanz: Thorbecke, 1956

AUBIN/T Deutscher Osten und slawischer Westen. Tübinger Vorträge; hrsg. von Hans Rothfels und Werner Markert. [Hermann Aubin zum 70. Geburtstage 23. Dezember 1955] (*Tübinger Studien zur Geschichte und Politik* 4) Tübingen: J. C. B. Mohr, 1955

BADT Festschrift Kurt Badt zum siebzigsten Geburtstage: Beiträge aus Kunst- und Geistesgeschichte. Berlin: W. de Gruyter, 1961

BAG Festschrift zur Vierhundertjahrfeier des Alten Gymnasiums zu Bremen, 1529–1928. Bremen: G. Winter [1928]

BALDELLÓ En homenaje a Mosén Francisco de Paula Baldelló. (*Anuario Musical* 19, 1964, 1–241) Barcelona: Consejo Superior de Investigaciones Científicas, Institut Español de Musicología, 1966 ◇ biog (A. Llopis)

BALDENSPERGER Mélanges d'histoire littéraire générale et comparée offerts à Fernand Baldensperger. Paris: H. Champion, 1930

BALZER Księga pamiątkowa ku czci Oswalda Balzera. Lwów: Gubrynowicz, 1925

BARBEAU Hommage à Marius Barbeau. (*Les Archives de folklore* 2) [Montréal]: Editions Fidés, 1947

BARBLAN/60TH Studi di musicologia in onore di Guglielmo Barblan in occasione del LX compleanno. (*Historiae Musicae Cultores—Biblioteca; Collectanea Historiae Musicae* 4) Firenze: Leo S. Olschki, 1966 ◇ 316p biog (F. Mompellio) bibliog (A. Z. Laterza)

BARTH Antwort. Karl Barth zum siebzigsten Geburtstag am 10. Mai 1956. Zollikon-Zürich: Evangelischer Verlag, [1956]

BARTÓK/40TH Sonderheft Béla Bartók. (*Musikblätter des Anbruch* 3/5, Mar. 1921, 87–104) Wien: Universal, 1921 ◇ biog. (B. Bartók, C. Gray, O. Bie, Z. Kodály, F. Petyrek)

BARTÓK/E Erkel Ferenc és Bartók Béla emlékére; szerk. Szabolcsi Bence és Bartha Dénes. (*Zenetudományi Tanulmányok* 2) Budapest: Akadémiai Kiadó, 1954 ◇ 560p bibliog biog (J. Demény) summaries in English

BARTÓK/L Liszt Ferenc és Bartók Béla emlékére; szerk. Szabolcsi Bence és Bartha Dénes. (*Zenetudományi Tanulmányok* 3) Budapest: Akadémiai Kiadó, 1955 ◇

560p bibliog (A. Szöllösy) biog (B. Bartók Jr, J. Demény, Z. Kodály, D. Legány, E. Lendvai, B. Szabolcsi) summaries of most articles in English, French & German

BARTÓK/S Studia memoriae Belae Bartók sacra; [adiuvantibus Z. Kodály et L. Lajtha curant B. Rajeczky et L. Vargyas] Budapestini: Aedes Academiae Scientiarum Hungaricae, 1956 [2d ed, 1957; 3d ed, 1959] ◇ 544p biog (S. Drăgoi)

BARTÓK/T Béla Bartók, A Memorial Review; Including Articles on his Life and Works Reprinted from *Tempo*, a Chronological Listing of Works, Bartók on Records. New York: Boosey & Hawkes, 1950 ◇ 95p bibliog discog (F. F. Clough, G. J. Cuming) biog (B. Bartók Jr, D. Dille, R. Hawkes, M. Seiber, S. Veress, G. Oláh, J. Weissmann)

BASTIAN Adolf Bastian als Festgruss zu seinem 70. Geburtstage, 26. Juni 1896, gewidmet von seinen Freunden und Verehrern. Berlin: D. Reimen, 1896

BATTISTI Per Cesare Battisti [Città di Castello: Soc. *Leonardo da Vinci*, 1917]

BAUMSTARK Festschrift Anton Baumstark zum sechzigsten Geburtstag am 4. August 1932 gewidmet von seinen Freunden und Schülern; hrsg. von A. Rücker. (*Oriens Christianus; Halbjahrshefte für die Kunde des Christlichen Orients* 3/7, Jg.29) Leipzig: O. Harrassowitz, 1932

BECHER Dem Dichter des Friedens, Johannes R. Becher, zum 60. Geburtstag. Berlin: Aufbau, 1951

BÉEN Juhlakirja jonka ovat omistaneet hovisaarnaaja Isaac Béen'ille hänen kuusikymmenvuotispäivänään kuudentena kesäkuuta MCMXLVIII ystävät suomessa/Festskrift tillägnad hovpredikanten Isaac Béen pa hans sextioärsdag den sjätte juni MCMXLVIII av vänner i Finland. Helsingissä/Helsingfors: 1948

BELLA/80TH Ján Levoslav Bella k 80. narozeninám Seniora Slovenské Hudby. (*Universita Komenského v Bratislave, Filozoficka Faculta. Sbornik*, ročník 2, čislo 8, 1924) Bratislava: 1924 ◇ 166,36p biog (D. Orel) autobiog bibliog (D. Orel, A. Hořejš)

BENZ Gegenwart im Geiste. Festschrift für Richard Benz. Hamburg: C. Wegner, 1954

BERNET KEMPERS Feestaflevering ter gelegenheid van de zestige verjaardag van Prof. Dr. K. Ph. Bernet Kempers . . . (*Orgaan K.N.T.V., Officieel Maandblad van de Koninklijke Nederlandsche Toonkunstenaars Vereeniging* 12, Sept. 1957, 1–61) Amsterdam, 1957

BESSELER Festschrift Heinrich Besseler zum sechzigsten Geburtstag; hrsg. vom Institut für Musikwissenschaft der Karl-Marx-Universität. Leipzig: VEB Deutscher Verlag für Musik, 1961 ◇ 538p bibliog

BEZZENBERGER Festschrift Adalbert Bezzenberger zum 14. April 1921 dargebracht von seinen Freunden und Schülern. Göttingen: Vandenhoeck & Ruprecht, 1921

BGGK Zur Feier des Wohlthäterfestes im berlinischen Gymnasium zum grauen Kloster, Sonnabend, den 20. Dezember 1856 . . . ladet ein . . . der Director Dr. Friedrich Bellermann. Berlin: Nauck, 1856

BIANCHI Studi in onore di Lorenzo Bianchi. Bologna: Zanichelli, 1960

BICK Die Österreichische Nationalbibliothek. Festschrift hrsg. zum 25jährigen Dienstjubiläum des Generaldirektors Univ.-Prof. Dr. Josef Bick von . . . Josef Stummvoll. Wien: H. Bauer-Verlag, 1948

BIEHLE Festschrift Johannes Biehl zum sechzigsten Geburtstage überreicht; hrsg. von Erich M. Müller. Leipzig: Kistner & Siegel, 1930 ◇ 107p bibliog biog (H. Biehle, D. H. Schöttler)

BINZ Festschrift Gustav Binz, Oberbibliothekar der Öffentlichen Bibliothek der Universität Basel, zum 70. Geburtstag am 16. Januar 1935 von Freunden und Fachgenossen dargebracht. Basel: B. Schwabe, 1935

BISHOP Miscellanea Musicologica. (*Adelaide Studies in Musicology* 1) Adelaide: Libraries Board of South Australia in association with the University of Adelaide, 1966 <> 255p bibliog (W. Gallusser) biog (H. Basten)

BJØRNDAL Norsk folkemusikk; utg. som festskrift til 70-årsdagen Arne Bjørndal. Bergen: Nord- og Midnordland sogelag, I komm. hja A.s Lunde, 1952

BJØRNSON Bjørnstjerne Bjørnson. Festskrift i anleding af hans 70 års fødelsdag. København: Gyldendal, 1902

BLECH Leo Blech, ein Brevier; anlässlich des 60. Geburtstages hrsg. und eingeleitet von Walter Jacob. Hamburg, Leipzig: Prismen [1931] <> 64p bibliog biog (W. Jacob, K. Holy, H. Rüdel, R. Albert, F. Schorr)

BLUME/F Festschrift Friedrich Blume zum 70. Geburtstag: hrsg. von Anna Amalie Abert und Wilhelm Pfannkuch. Kassel: Bärenreiter, 1963 <> 426p bibliog

BLUME/S Syntagma musicologicum, gesammelte Reden und Schriften; hrsg. von Martin Ruhnke. Kassel: Bärenreiter, 1963 <> 904p

BOAS Boas Anniversary Volume. Anthropological Papers Written in Honor of Franz Boas . . . Presented to Him on the Twenty-fifth Anniversary of His Doctorate, Ninth of August, 1906. New York: G. Stechert, 1906

BÖMER Westfälische Studien; Beiträge zur Geschichte der Wissenschaft, Kunst und Literatur in Westfalen. Alois Bömer zum 60. Geburtstag gewidmet, Leipzig: K. W. Hiersemann, 1928

BOLLERT Festschrift Martin Bollert zum 60. Geburtstage. Dresden: W. Jess, 1936

BOLLERT/80TH Festschrift Martin Bollert zum achtzigsten Geburtstag am 11. Oktober 1946; dargebracht von Freunden und Mitarbeitern. Dresden: [VEB Landesdruckerei Sachsen] 1956

BONSDORFF Borgå stift och dess herde. Festskrift tillägnad Biskop Max von Bonsdorff 23 augusti 1952. (*Lutherska Litteraturstiftelsens Svenska Publikationer* 6) Helsingfors: Förbundet för Svenskt Församlingsarbete i Finland, 1952

BORREN Hommage à Charles van den Borren. Mélanges. Anvers: N. V. de Nederlandsche Boekhandel, 1945 <> 360p bibliog (R. Wangermée) biog (S. Clercx)

BORREN/75TH [Issue dedicated to Charles van den Borren on the occasion of his 75th birthday] (*Revue belge de musicologie* 3, Fasc.4, 1949, 206–246) <> bibliog biog (A. v. d. Linden)

BORREN/80TH Hommage à Charles van den Borren à l'occasion de son quatre-vingtième anniversaire. (*Revue belge de musicologie* 8, 1954, 61–140).

BORREN/90TH Liber amicorum Charles van den Borren. Anvers: Impr. Lloyd Anversois, 1964 <> 226p

BOSSE/50TH 50 Jahre Gustav Bosse Verlag. Streiflichter aus der Verlagsarbeit; statte einer Festschrift hrsg. von Erich Valentin. Regensburg: Gustav Bosse, 1963. <> 161p bibliog

BOTKIN/65TH Folklore and Society. Essays in Honor of Benjamin A. Botkin; ed. by Bruce Jackson. Hatboro, Penna.: Folklore Associates, 1966 <> 192p bibliog biog (B. Jackson)

BOUCHÉ Hommage au Docteur Georges Bouché. Bruxelles: Éditions du Parthenon, 1956

BOYER Mélanges publiés en l'honneur de M. Paul Boyer. (*Institut d'études slaves. Travaux* 2) Paris, 1925

BREDIUS Feest-Bundel, Dr. Abraham Bredius aangeboden den achttienden April 1915. Amsterdam: Gebroeders Binger, 1915

BREITKOPF Breitkopf & Härtel. Gedenkschrift und Arbeitsbericht von Oskar von Hase. 4. Aufl. Leipzig: Breitkopf & Härtel, 1917–1919

BRITTEN Tribute to Benjamin Britten on His Fiftieth Birthday; ed. by Anthony

Gishford. London: Faber & Faber [1963] ◇ 195p biog (M. Rostropovich, C. Curzon, A. Copland)

BRODY Geist und Werk aus der Werkstatt unserer Autoren zum 75. Geburtstag von Dr. Daniel Brody. Zürich: Rhein-Verlag, 1958

BROWN Essays and Studies in Honor of Carleton Brown. New York: New York Univ. Press, 1940

BRUUN Kristendom og norskdom. Festskrift til Christopher Bruun . . . Oslo: Steen, 1920

BU Festschrift zur Feier des 450jährigen Bestehens der Universität Basel; hrsg. von Rektor und Regenz. Basel: Helbing & Lichtenhahn, 1910

BURCKHARDT Dauer im Wandel. Festschrift zum 70. Geburtstag von Carl J. Burckhardt; hrsg. von Hermann Rinn & M. Rychner. München: G. D. W. Callweg [1961]

BUSH Tribute to Alan Bush on his Fiftieth Birthday, A Symposium. London: Workers' Music Assn., 1950 ◇ 63p bibliog biog (J. Ireland, H. Murrill, R. Boughton, W. Mellers, H. Eisler, W. Sahnow, E. H. Meyer, M. Rostal, T. Russell, D. Ellenberg, E. J. Dent)

BUSZIN Cantors at the Crossroads. Essays on Church Music in Honor of Walter E. Buszin; Johannes Riedel, editor. St. Louis, Mo.: Concordia, 1967 ◇ 238p bibliog (J. Riedel) biog (J. Riedel)

CAIX In memoria di Napoleone Caix e Ugo Angelo Canello. Miscellanea di Monnier, 1886
filologia e linguistica per G. Ascoli, C. Avolio . . . ; Firenze: Successori Le

CAMPBELL, Å. Arctica. Essays presented to Åke Campbell, 1 May, 1956; ed. by Arne Furumark [et al.] (*Studia Ethnographica Upsaliensia* 11) Uppsala: 1956

CARÍAS Homenaje tributado por el pueblo hondureño por medio del soberano Congreso Nacional, al . . . Tiburcio Carías Andino. [Tegucigalpa, 1945]

CASADESUS Hommage à Francis Casadesus, pour ses quatre-vingts ans, 2 décembre 1870–2 décembre 1950. [Paris, 1950] ◇ 79p

CASE Studies in the Literature of the Augustan Age. Essays Collected in Honor of Arthur Ellicott Case. Ann Arbor: Augustan Reprint Society, 1952

CASELLA [Special number for his 60th birthday] (*Rassegna musicale* 16, 1943, 129–208) ◇ bibliog biog (G. de Chirico, M. Mila, G. Gavazzeni, A. Mantelli, G. Rossi-Doria, E. Zanetti, F. d'Amico, D. Alderighi, M. Labroca)

CASTIGLIONI Studi in onore di Carlo Castiglioni, Prefetto dell'Ambrosiana. (*Fontes Ambrosiani* 32) Milano: A. Giuffrè, 1957

CCZ Der kölner Dom. Festschrift zur Siebenhundertjahrfeier, 1248–1948; hrsg. vom Zentral-Dombau-Verein. Köln: Baldwin Pick, 1948

CHABANEAU Mélanges Chabaneau. Festschrift Camille Chabaneau zur Vollendung seines 75. Lebensjahres 4. März 1906. (*Romanische Forschungen* 23) Erlangen: Junge, 1907

CHAMARD Mélanges d'histoire littéraire de la renaissance offerts à Henri Chamard, professeur honoraire à la Sorbonne, par ses collègues, ses élèves et ses amis. Paris: Nizet, 1951

CHWOLSON Recueil des travaux rédigés en mémoire du jubilé scientifique de M. Daniel Chwolson (1846–1896). Berlin: S. Calvary, 1899

CHYBIŃSKI/50TH Księga pamiątkowa ku czci profesora Dr. Adolfa Chybińskiego ofiarowana przez uczniów i przyjaciól z okazji pięćdziesiątej rocznicy urodzin i dwudziestej piątei rocznicy jego pracy naukowej (1880–1905–1930). [A Memorial Volume in Honor of Prof. Dr. Adolf Chybiński, Offered by his Friends and Pupils on the Occasion of his 50th Birthday and the 25th Anniversary of his Scholarly Activity) Kraków: Nakładem Autorów, 1930 ◇ 187p

CHYBIŃSKI/70TH Księga pamiątkowa ku czci Prof. Adolfa Chybińskiego w 70-

lecie urodzin. Rozprawy i artykuły z zakresu muzykologii [A Memorial Volume in Honor of Prof. Adolf Chybiński on his 70th Birthday. Studies and Articles in the field of Musicology] Kraków: Polskie Wydawnictwo Muz., 1950 <> 380p bibliog (K. Michałowski) biog

CIAN A Vittorio Cian i suoi scolari dell'Università di Pisa (1900–1908). Pisa: F. Mariotti, 1909.

CLOSSON Mélanges Ernest Closson. Recueil d'articles musicologiques offerts à Ernest Closson à l'occasion de son 65e anniversaire. Bruxelles: Société Belge de Musicologie, 1948 <> 210p bibliog (A.-M. Regnier, A. van der Linden) biog (C. van den Borren)

COHEN Mélanges d'histoire du théâtre du moyen-âge et de la renaissance offerts à Gustave Cohen . . . par ses collègues, ses élèves et ses amis. Paris: Nizet, 1950

COLOMBO Albo di onoranze internazionale a Cristoforo Colombo, iniziato da Angelo de Gubernatis e Cecilio Vallardi pel glorioso ricordo del quarto centenario della scoperta dell'America. Milano: Casa Editrice Dottor Francesco Vallardi, 1892

CORBINIANUS Wissenschaftliche Festgabe zum zwölfhundertjährigen Jubiläum des heiligen Korbinian; hrsg. von D. Dr. Joseph Schlecht. München: A. Huber, 1924

CORTESE Scritti storici [di] G. Ceci . . . [et al.] Nozze Cortese–De Cicco, Napoli XXII Aprile MCMXXXI. Napoli: Riccardo Ricciardi, 1931

CRESCINI Miscellanea di studi critici in onore di Vincenzo Crescini. Cividale: Stagni, 1927

CROZET Mélanges offerts à René Crozet à l'occasion de son soixante-dixième anniversaire . . . ; ed. par Pierre Gallais et Yves-Jean Riou. Poitiers: Société d'Études Médiévales, 1966

CU Cologne. Universität. Concordia decennalis, deutsche Italienforschung. Festschrift der Universität Köln zum 10jährigen Bestehen des Deutsch-Italienischen Kulturinstituts Petrarcahaus 1941. Köln: Balduin Pick [1941]

CU/F Festschrift zur Erinnerung an die Gründung der alten Universität Köln im Jahre 1388. Köln: K. Schroeder, 1938

CURTIUS, L./60TH Corolla. Ludwig Curtius zum 60. Geburtstag dargebracht. Stuttgart: W. Kohlhammer, 1937

CUYPERS Hubert Cuypers 80 jaar. [Amsterdam: Huldigingscomité Hubert Cuypers, 1953?] <> 93p biog

ČYŽEVŚKYJ Festschrift für Dmytro Čyževśkyj zum 60. Geburtstag am 23. März 1954. (*Berlin, Freie Universität, Osteuropa-Institut, Slavistische Veröffentlichungen* 6) Wiesbaden: Harrassowitz, 1954

DAMDK Deutsche Akademie für Musik und darstellende Kunst in Prag. Festschrift, 1920–1930; hrsg. vom Kuratorium der Deutschen Akademie . . . Prag: 1931 <> 106p biog (F. Wien-Claudi, F. F. Finke)

DAVISON Essays on Music in Honor of Archibald Thompson Davison by His Associates. Cambridge, Mass.: Harvard Univ., Dept. of Music, 1957 <> 374p bibliog (J. M. Coopersmith)

DEBUSSY Numéro spécial consacré à la mémoire de Claude Debussy. (*La Revue musicale* 12, Dec. 1920, 97–216, suppl. 1–32) <> biog (A. Suarès, A. Cortot, L. Laloy, E. Vuillermoz, R. Peter, D. E. Inglebrecht, R. Godet, G. J. Aubry, H. Lesbroussart, M. de Falla, L. Dunton-Green, A. Casella, L. Saminsky)

DEGERING Mittelalterliche Handschriften, paläographische, kunsthistorische, literarische und bibliotheksgeschichtliche Untersuchungen. Festgabe zum 60. Geburtstage von Hermann Degering. Leipzig: K. W. Hiersemann, 1926

DENYN Gedenkboek Jef Denyn, stadtsbeiaadier en meester van den toren.

Mechelen: Beiaardschool [1947] <> 329p bibliog biog (P. Verheyden, K. Lefévere, S. Nees, J. Casparie, J. Rottiers, A. Geudens, G. Clement, N. Johnston, L. Reypens)

DESDERI/70TH A Ettore Desderi nel suo 70. compleanno. Bologna: Conservatorio di Musica "G. B. Martini," 1963 <> 206p bibliog biog (H. O. Boehm, A. Bonaccorsi, A. Bonsanti, A. Damerini, E. Galanti, E. Greco, F. Perrino, P. Rattalino, M. Rinaldi, W. Sandelewski, F. Sartori, O. Siegl, L. F. Tagliavini, A. Toni, K. Walter)

DEUTSCH/80TH Festschrift Otto Erich Deutsch zum 80. Geburtstag am 5. September 1963; hrsg. von Walter Gerstenberg, Jan LaRue und Wolfgang Rehm. Kassel: Bärenreiter, 1963 <> 392p bibliog (O. Schneider)

DRUMMOND Studies in Speech and Drama in Honor of Alexander M. Drummond. Ithaca, N.Y.: Cornell Univ. Press, 1944

DUKAS Hommage à Paul Dukas. (*La Revue musicale,* numéro spécial, May/June 1936, 321–456, suppl. 1–32) <> bibliog (G. Samazeuilh) biog (P. Valéry, R. Brussel, G. Samazeuilh, E. Dujardin, J. G. Ropartz, M. Emmanuel, O. Messiaen, E. Schneider, G. Marcel, A. George, R. Dumesnil, J. Rouché, A. Boschot, A. Boll)

DUSSAUD Mélanges syriens offerts à Monsieur René Dussaud . . . par ses amis et ses élèves. Paris: P. Geuthner, 1939

EHMANN/60TH Musik als Lobgesang. Festschrift für Wilhelm Ehmann; hrsg. von Gerhard Mittring und Gerhard Rödding. Darmstadt: Tonkunst Verlag Karl Merseburger, 1964 <> 151p bibliog & discog (F. Haasemann) biog (D. Wilm, E. Nievergelt, T. Kuusisto)

EINSTEIN [Essays for Alfred Einstein and Curt Sachs on their 60th Birthdays] (*Musical Quarterly* 27, 1941, 263–413) bibliog & biog (E. Hertzmann)

EINSTEIN/C Collectanea historicae musicae I. (*Biblioteca historiae musicae cultores* 2) Florentiae: L. S. Olschki, 1953 <> 210p bibliog

EITREM Serta Eitremiana. Opuscula philologica S[amson] Eitrem septuagenario XXVIII. Dec. MCMXLII oblata. Oslo: Brøgger, 1942

EK Nordiska folkminnesstudier. Tillägnade Sverker Ek. (*Folkminnen och Folktankar* 24, 1937) Malmö: Lund, 1937

EMANUELE Studi pubblicati dalla regia università di Torino nel IV centenario della nascita di Emanuele Filiberto, 8 Luglio 1928. Torino: F. Villarboito [1928]

EMMANUEL Maurice Emmanuel. (*La Revue musicale,* numéro spécial 206, 1947, 1–128) <> bibliog biog (R. Bernard, E. Estaunié, R. Jardillier, R. Dumesnil, R. Schwab, L. Aubert, V. Basch, G. Migot, C. Koechlin, S. Demarquez, P. Le Flem, G. Samazeuilh, J. Chailley, M. B. d'Harcourt, F. Raugel, S. Baud-Bovy, O. Messiaen, E. Jacques-Dalcroze, A. Fornerod, H. Classens)

EMSHEIMER/60TH Studia ethnomusicologica eurasiatica. (*Musikhistoriska Museets Skrifter* 1) Stockholm: Musikhistoriska Museet, 1964 <> 107p biog (C. -A. Moberg)

ENGEL A Birthday Offering to Carl Engel; comp. and ed. by Gustave Reese. New York: G. Schirmer, 1943 <> 233p bibliog biog (P. L. Atherton, J. Erskine, N. Peterkin, H. Spivacke)

ENGEL/70TH Festschrift Hans Engel zum siebzigsten Geburtstag; hrsg. von Horst Heussner. Kassel: Bärenreiter, 1964. 464p bibliog

ERDMANN Minnesskrift af forna lärjungar tillägnad professor Axel Erdmann på hans sjuttioårsdag den 6. febr. 1913. Upsala: Almquist & Wiksell, 1913

ESSEN Festgabe für Otto von Essen zum 65. Geburtstag 20. Mai 1963. (*Zeitschrift für Phonetik, Sprachwissenschaft und Kommunikationsforschung* 16:1–3) Berlin: Akademie-Verlag, 1963

FABRA Miscellània Fabra; recull de treballs de lingüística catalana i romànica dedicats a Pompeu Fabra pels seus amics i deixebles amb motiu del 75e aniversari de la seva naixença. Buenos Aires: Coni, 1943

FALLETTI Studi di storia e di critica dedicati a Pio Carlo Falletti dagli scolari celebrandosi il XL anno del suo insegnamento. Bologna: N. Zanichelli, 1915

FAURÉ Gabriel Fauré. (*La Revue musicale*, numéro spécial, Oct. 1922, 193–308, suppl. 1–47) ◇ bibliog biog (E. Vuillermoz, M. Ravel, R. Chalupt, C. Koechlin, F. Schmitt, J. J. Roger-Ducasse, A. Cortot, N. Boulanger)

FDH Festschrift der neuphilologischen Sektion des Freien Deutschen Hochstifts zur Begrüssung des zweiten allgemeinen deutschen Neuphilologentages am 31. Mai und 1. Juni 1887. Frankfurt/Main: Mahlau & Waldschmidt, 1887

FÉDEROV/65TH Mélanges offerts à Vladimir Féderov à l'occasion de son soixante-cinquième anniversaire 5 Août 1966; ed. par Harald Heckmann et Wolfgang Rehm. (*Fontes Artis Musicae* 13, 1966, 1–152) Kassel: Bärenreiter, 1966 ◇ bibliog (B. Bardet) biog (F. Blume, K. Vötterle)

FEICHT Instytut Muzykologii Uniwersytetu Warsawskiego. Studia Hieronymo Feicht septuagenario dedicata; red. naczelny prof. dr. Zofia Lissa . . . Kraków: Polskie Wydawnictwo Muzyczne, 1967 ◇ 486p bibliog (H. Drabik) biog

FELLERER Festgabe zum 50. Geburtstag von Karl Gustav Fellerer am 7. Juli 1952. Köln: Unpublished typescript [1952?] ◇ 104, 23p bibliog (K. Weiler)

FELLERER/60TH Festschrift Karl Gustav Fellerer zum sechzigsten Geburtstag am 7. Juli 1962 überreicht von Freunden und Schülern; hrsg. von Heinrich Hüschen. Regensburg: Gustav Bosse, 1962 ◇ 593p bibliog (K. W. Niemöller, J. P. Fricke)

FELLERER/60THM Musicae sacrae ministerium. Beiträge zur Geschichte der kirchenmusikalischen Erneuerung im XIX. Jahrhundert. Festgabe für Karl Gustav Fellerer zur Vollendung seines 60. Lebensjahres am 7. Juli 1962; unter Mitarbeit seiner Schüler und Freunde hrsg. von Johannes Overath. (*Schriftenreihe des Allgemeinen Cäcilien-Verbandes für die Länder der deutschen Sprache* 5, 1962) Köln: 1962 ◇ 319p

FELLERER/60THS Karl Gustav Fellerer zum 60. Geburtstag Überreicht von den Mitgleidern der Arbeitsgemeinschaft für Rheinische Musikgeschichte; hrsg. von Herbert Drux . . . (*Beiträge zur Rheinischen Musikgeschichte* 52; *Studien zur Musikgeschichte des Rheinlandes* 2) Köln: Arno Volk, 1962 ◇ 307p

FEUILLERAT Essays in Honor of Albert Feuillerat; ed. by Henri M. Peyre. (*Yale Romanic Studies* 22) New Haven, Yale Univ. Press, 1943

FGA Festschrift zur Feier des 25jährigen Bestehens der Frankfurter Gesellschaft für Anthropologie, Ethnologie und Urgeschichte. Frankfurt/Main: H. Bechhold, 1925

FINKE Miscellania Heinrich Finke d'historia i cultura catalana. (*Analecta sacra Tarraconensia, anuari de la Biblioteca Balmes* 11) Barcelona, 1935

FINKE/100TH Zur Erinnerung an den 100. Geburtstag Heinrich Finkes, 1855 13. Juni 1955. (*Spanische Forschungen der Görresgesellschaft*, Reihe 1, *Gesammelte Aufsätze zur Kulturgeschichte Spaniens* 11–13) Münster Westfalen: Aschendorffsche Verlagsbuchhandlung, 1955–1957

FISCHER/E Dank an Edwin Fischer [hrsg. im Einverständnis mit Lina Gerlieb . . . und . . . Dr. Walter Strebi . . . von Hugo Haid] Wiesbaden: F. A. Brockhaus, 1962 ◇ 164p bibliog discog biog (W. Löffler, H. Isenstein, P. Badura-Skoda, J. Schmidt-Voigt)

FISCHER/W Festschrift Wilhelm Fischer zum 70. Geburtstag überreicht im Mozartjahr 1956 [hrsg. von Hans Zingerle] (*Innsbrucker Beiträge zur Kulturwissenschaft*, Sonderheft 3) Innsbruck: Sprachwissenschaftliches Seminar der Univ. Innsbruck, 1956 ◇ 177p

FOCK Aus Wissenschaft und Antiquariat. Festschrift zum 50jährigen Bestehen der Buchhandlung Gustav Fock. Leipzig, 1929

FOERSTER/90TH J. B. Foerster. Jeho životni pouť a tvorba, 1859–1949; ed. Josef Bartoš . . . [et al.] Praha: Národní Hudební Vydavatelství Orbis, 1949 <> 423p bibliog (J. Fiala, O. Fric) biog (J. Bartoš, V. Holzknecht, J. Bachtík, O. Jeremiáš, M. Očadlík, F. Pala, C. Sychra, J. Plavec, A. Pražák, V. Nikodem, A. J. Patzaková; letters from: A. Dvořák, E. H. Grieg, P. I. Tchaikovsky, O. Ostričil, L. Janáček, J. Suk, A. Jirásek, K. Kovařovic, J. V. Sládek, A. Sova, O. Březina, F. X. Šalda, J. Vrchlický, R. Rolland)

FORSELL Boken om John Forsell; utg. av operan på John Forsells 70-årsdag den 6, nov. 1938. Stockholm: P. A. Norstedt, 1938 <> 112, 57p biog (A. Engberg, A. Söderblom, H. Brenguiér, H. Meissner, E. Stiebel, G. Lundequist, D. Hesse, M. Ohlson, P. Brunius, O. F. Wennberg, R. Hylten-Cavallius, A. Kletbeck, E. Ljungberger, F. Gustavson, A. de Wahl, H. Eneroth, A. Lindenbaum)

FRANK Mélanges de linguistique et de littérature romanes à la mémoire d'István Frank. (*Annales Universitatis Saraviensis; hrsg. von der Philosophischen Fakultät* 6) Saarbrücken: 1957

FREIDUS Studies in Jewish Bibliography and Related Subjects, in Memory of Abraham Solomon Freidus. New York: Kohut Foundation, 1929

FREY/60TH Kunstgeschichtliche Studien. Dagobert Frey zum 23. 4. 1943 von seinen Kollegen, Mitarbeitern und Schülern; hrsg. von Hans Tintelnot. Breslau: Gauverlag-NS-Schlesien, 1943

FRIEDLAENDER Festgabe zum siebzigsten Geburtstage Max Friedlaenders; hrsg. von Rudolf Schwartz. (*Jahrbuch der Musikbibliothek Peters* 28/2, 1922, 1–78) <> bibliog (G. Schünemann) biog (J. Bolte)

FRIEND Late Classical and Medieval Studies in Honor of Albert Mathias Friend Jr; ed. by Kurt Weitzmann . . . Princeton: Princeton Univ. Press, 1955

FÜRNBERG Louis Fürnberg; ein Buch des Gedenkens zum 50. Geburtstag. Berlin: Dietz [1959]

FURTWÄNGLER Wilhelm Furtwängler im Urteil seiner Zeit [hrsg. im Einverständnis mit Frau Elisabeth Furtwängler von Dr. Martin Hürlimann] Zürich: Atlantis [1955] <> 296p bibliog discog biog (F. Thiess, A. Cortot, E. Fischer, Y. Menuhin, E. Preetorius, O. Kokoschka, P. Hindemith, W. Riezler, J. von Kalckreuth, J. Marx, F. Hamel, M. Conrad, L. Dieckmann, H. Grohe, M. Brockhaus, P. Wackernagel, B. Paumgartner, H. Schmidt, F. Sedlak, A. Nowakowski, O. Erhardt, D. Schmedes, G. Samazeuilh, M. Hürlimann)

GAMIO Estudios antropologicos publicados en homenaje al doctor Manuel Gamio. México, D. F.: Dirección General de Publicaciónes, 1956

GARMAN Studies in Philosophy and Psychology by former Students of Charles Edward Garman in Commemoration of Twenty-five Years of Service as Teacher of Philosophy in Amherst College. Boston/New York: Houghton, Mifflin, 1906

GAUCHAT Festschrift Louis Gauchat. Aarau: H. R. Sauerländer, 1926

GEIGER Beiträge zur Literatur- und Theatergeschichte. Festschrift Ludwig Geiger. Berlin: B. Behr, 1918

GERSTENBERG/60TH Festschrift Walter Gerstenberg zum 60. Geburstag; im Namen seiner Schüler hrsg. von Georg von Dadelsen und Andreas Holschneider. Wolfenbüttel: Möseler, 1964 <> 175p

GESSLER Miscellanea J. Gessler. 's-Gravenhage: Martinus Nijhoff, 1948

GEWANDHAUS Festschrift zum 175jährigen Bestehen der Gewandhauskonzerte, 1781–1956. Leipzig: Deutscher Verlag für Musik, 1956 <> 107p hist (O. Gerster, R. Fischer, M. Butting, F. Konwitschny, H. J. Moser, W. Vetter, H. Keller, R. Petzoldt, D. Wolf)

GILDERSLEEVE Studies in Honor of Basil L. Gildersleeve. Baltimore: Johns Hopkins Press, 1902

GLAUNING Otto Glauning zum 60. Geburtstag. Festgabe aus Wissenschaft und Bibliothek; hrsg. von Heinrich Schreiber. Leipzig: Hadl, 1938

GOTTRON Prof. Dr. Adam Gottron . . . zum 75. Geburtstag am 11. Oktober 1964. (*Mainzer Zeitschrift. Mittelrheinisches Jahrbuch für Archäologie, Kunst und Geschichte* 60/61, 1965/1966) Mainz: Verlag des Mainzer Altertumsvereins, 1966

GRAT Mélanges dédiés à la mémoire de Félix Grat. Paris: Pecquer-Grat, 1946

GRÉGOIRE Pankarpeia. Mélanges Henri Grégoire. (*Annuaire de l'Institut de Philologie et d'Histoire Orientales et Slaves* 9–12) Bruxelles, 1949–1953

GREGOR Zum 65. Geburtstage von Hofrat Prof. Dr. Joseph Gregor. (*Das Antiquariat* 9/15–18, 1953, 225–242)

GRÜNWALD Festschrift zur Feier des 50. Geburtstags Richard Grünwalds; hrsg. von der deutschen Zitherkonzert-Gesellschaft. Düsseldorf: D. Zitherk.-Ges., 1927 ◇ 66p biog (F. Stichenoth, J. Brandlmeier, W. Gfeller, J. Schletter, J. Baltes, K. Lohmann, W. Altmann)

GSHG Festschrift 75. Jahre Stiftliches Humanistisches Gymnasium M. Gladbach. M. Gladbach, 1952

GÜNTHER Festschrift Carl Günther. Basel: National-Zeitung AG, 1956

GUGITZ Kultur und Volk, Beiträge zur Volkskunde aus Österreich, Bayern und der Schweiz. Festschrift für G. Gugitz zum 80. Geburtstag; hrsg. von Leopold Schmidt. (*Veröffentlichungen des Österreichischen Museums für Volkskunde* 5) Wien: Horn, Berger, 1954

GURLITT Festheft Wilibald Gurlitt zum siebzigsten Geburtstag. (*Archiv für Musikwissenschaft* 16/1–2, 1959, 1–259)

GUTBIER Unserem Ehrenmitglied Staatsarchivrat I. R. Dr. Ewald Gutbier zur Vollendung des 70. Lebensjahres gewidmet. (*Verein für Hessische Geschichte und Landeskunde. Zeitschrift* 68) Kassel: Bärenreiter, 1957

HAAS Festgabe Joseph Haas von seinen Schülern, Mitarbeitern und Freunden, nebst einem Verzeichnis seiner Werke, zum 60. Geburtstag am 19. März 1939; hrsg. von M. Gebhard, O. Jochum und H. Lang . . . Mainz: Schott [1939] ◇ 131p bibliog biog (K. Laux)

HAAS/75TH Joseph Haas-Heft. (*Zeitschrift für Musik* 115, 1954, 129–149) ◇ biog (K. G. Fellerer, W. Zentner, H. Lang, E. Valentin)

HAEBLER Wiegendrucke und Handschriften. Festgabe Konrad Haebler zum 60. Geburtstage; dargebracht von Isak Collijn. Leipzig: K. W. Hiersemann, 1919

HALPHEN Mélanges d'histoire du moyen âge dédiés à la mémoire de Louis Halphen. Paris: Presses Universitaires, 1951

HAMM Adolf Hamm. Errinnerungsschrift; hrsg. von Paul Sacher. Basel: 1942 ◇ bibliog (E. Refardt, A. Müry) biog (P. Sacher, A. Hiebner, O. Moppert, E. Thurneysen, E. Refardt, A. Geering, J. Cron, H. Zehnter)

HAMMARSTEDT Etnologiska studier tillägnade Nils Edvard Hammarstedt. (*Föreningen för svensk kulturhistoria, Böcker* 2) Stockholm, 1921

HANDSCHIN Gedenkschrift Jacques Handschin. Aufsätze und Bibliographie; [hrsg. von der Ortsgruppe Basel der Schweizerischen Musikforschenden Gesellschaft; zusammengestellt von Hans Oesch] Bern, Stuttgart: Paul Haupt [1957] ◇ 397p bibliog

HANDSCHIN/I In memoriam Jacques Handschin; ediderunt H. Anglés, G. Birkner, Ch. van den Borren, Fr. Benn, A. Carapetyan, H. Husmann, C.-A. Moberg. Argentorati: P. H. Heitz, 1962 ◇ 200p bibliog (C. Stroux)

HANDSCHIN/M "To the memory of Jacques Handschin." (*Musica Disciplina* 10, 1956, 1–209) Rome: American Institute of Musicology, 1956

HANSELMANN Festschrift zum 60. Geburtstag von Professor Dr. phil. Heinrich Hanselmann. Erlenbach/Zürich: Rotapfel Verlag, 1945

HANSEN Festskrift til museumforstander H. P. Hansen, Herning, på 70-årsdagen den 2. oktober 1949. København: Rosenkilde og Bagger, 1949

HARNACK Fünfzehn Jahre Königliche- und Staatsbibliothek dem scheidenden Generaldirektor Exz. Adolf von Harnack überreicht von den wissenschaftlichen Beamten der preussischen Staatsbibliothek. Berlin: Preuss. Staatsbibl., 1921

HASKIL Clara Haskil; mit Beiträgen von Pierre Fournier, Ferenc Fricsay, Rafael Kubelik, Igor Markevitch, Peter Rybar. Bern/Wien/Stuttgart: Scherz [1961] ◇ 169p discog biog (R. Wolfensberger)

HAUVETTE Mélanges de philologie, d'histoire et de littérature offerts à Henri Hauvette. Paris: Presses Françaises, 1934

HELD Festschrift für Hans Ludwig Held; eine Gabe der Freundschaft und des Dankes zum 65. Geburtstag dargebracht 1. August 1950. München: K. Alber, 1950

HERRLIN Festskrift tillägnad Axel Herrlin den 30. mars 1935. Lund: C. Blom, 1935

HERRMANN Hugo Herrmann, Leben und Werk. Festschrift zum 60. Geburtstag am 19. 4. 1956 . . . ; hrsg. von Armin Fett. Trossingen: M. Hohner, 1956 ◇ 85p bibliog biog (A. Fett, H. J. Moser, B. Stürmer, R. Sonner, W. M. Berten)

HERTZ Philologische Abhandlungen. Martin Hertz zum 70. Geburtstage von ehemaligen Schülern dargebracht. Berlin: W. Hertz, 1888

HEWARD Leslie Heward, A Memorial Volume; ed. by Eric Blom. London: Dent, 1944 ◇ 89p bibliog discog biog (S. H. Nicholson, E. Warr, W. D. Suddaby, B. Johnson, A. Boult, V. Hely-Hutchinson, H. Costley-White, S. Goddard, C. Armstrong-Gibbs, E. J. Moeran, J. Harrison, W. H. Bell, M. Mukle, B. Marx, A. Goldsbrough, J. Barbirolli, P. Jones, H. Proctor-Gregg, A. N. Harty, G. D. Cunningham, M. Tookey, N. Stanley, E. Ansermet, H. Unger, E. de Selingcourt, W. K. Stanton, C. Gray, M. Johnstone, E. Irving, G. Sharp, E. Blom)

HEWITT Essays on German Language and Literature in Honor of Theodore B. Hewitt; ed. by J. Alan Pfeffer. (*Buffalo University Studies* 20/1) [Buffalo, 1952]

HILBER J. B. Hilber. Festgabe zu seinem 60. Geburtstage 2. Januar 1951 überreicht von seinen Freunden. Altdorf: Schweizer Kirchenmusikverlag, 1951 ◇ 100p bibliog biog (A. Schönenberger, P. Schaller, H. Lemacher, O. Eberle, F. A. Herzog, W. Hauser)

HIRSCH "This the forty-fifth number of The Music Review is offered as a small tribute to Paul Hirsch on his seventieth birthday, 24 February, 1951." (*Music Review* 12, 1951, 1–86) Cambridge: W. Heffer & Sons, 1951 ◇ bibliog (O. Hirsch) biog (J. Christie, P. H. Muir)

HIRTH Festschrift für Friedrich Hirth zu seinem 75. Geburtstag 16. April 1920. Berlin: Österheld, 1920

HOBOKEN Anthony van Hoboken. Festschrift zum 75. Geburtstag; hrsg. von Joseph Schmidt-Görg. Mainz: Schott, 1962 ◇ 162p biog (J. Schmidt-Görg)

HOEPFFNER Mélanges de philologie romane et de littérature médiévale offerts à Ernest Hoepffner . . . par ses élèves et ses amis. (*Publications de la faculté des lettres de l'université de Strasbourg* 113) Paris: Société d'Édition Les Belles Lettres, 1949

HOFMANN [Special number in honor of Dr. Josef Hofmann's golden jubilee] (*Overtones* 8, Nov. 1937, 5–31) Philadelphia: Curtis Inst., 1937

HOFMEISTER Tradition und Gegenwart. Festschrift zum 150jährigen Bestehen des Musikverlages Friedrich Hofmeister. Leipzig: VEB F. Hofmeister, 1957 ◇ 102p hist

HOLMES Holmes Anniversary Volume. Anthropological Essays presented to William Henry Holmes in Honor of His Seventieth Birthday, December 1, 1916, by his Friends and Colaborers. Washington: [J. W. Bryan] 1916

HOLTZMANN Kritische Beiträge zur Geschichte des Mittelalters. Festschrift für Robert Holtzmann zum sechzigsten Geburtstag. Berlin: E. Ebering, 1933

HOMMEL Eranion. Festschrift für Hildebrecht Hommel . . . ; hrsg. von Jürger Kroymann unter Mitwirkung von Ernst Zinn. Tübingen: M. Niemeyer, 1961

HORACE Études horatiennes, recueil publié en l'honneur du bimillénaire d'Horace. (*Travaux de la faculté de philosophie et lettres de l'université de Bruxelles* 7) Bruxelles, 1937

HOSTINSKÝ/60TH Profesoru Dru. Otakaru Hostinskému k sedesátým narodzeninám 2. ledna 1847–1907. (*Česká Mysl*, ročník 8, čislo 1, 1907) Praha: 1907 ◇ 112p bibliog biog (Z. Nejedlý, J Máchal, B. Matějka, F. Krejči, F. Cáda, F. Drtina, A. Novák)

HOWARD Festschrift zum 50. Geburtstag Walther Howards am 8. Mai 1930; hrsg. vom Walther Howard-Bund. Berlin-Hermsdorf: Verlag für Kultur und Kunst, 1930 ◇ 62p biog (E. Ulrich, A. Heymann, W. Schönberg, H. Pflieger-Haertel, M. Scholle)

HOYOS SÁINZ Homenaje a Don Luis de Hoyos Sáinz. Madrid: 1949

HUBER Kurt Huber zum Gedächtnis. Bildnis eines Menschen, Denkers und Forschers dargestellt von seinen Freunden; hrsg. von C. Huber. Regensburg: Habbel, 1947 ◇ 172p bibliog biog (K. Vossler, C. Huber, O. Ursprung, W. Riezler, A. Wenzl, H. Maier, G. Schischkoff, T. Georgiades, K. Pauli, I. Köck, M. Li, C. Orff)

HUC Hebrew Union College Jubilee Volume (1875–1925). Cincinnati: Hebrew Union College, 1925

HUCKL Library [Hebrew Union College, Klau Library] Dedication Issue, ". . . the occasion for this Festschrift-type issue." (*Studies in Bibliography and Booklore* 5, 1961) Cincinnati: 1961

HUDSON Folklore Studies in Honor of Arthur Palmer Hudson. Chapel Hill: The North Carolina Folklore Society, 1965

HUGUET Mélanges de philologie et d'histoire littéraire offerts à Edmond Huguet par ses élèves, ses collègues et ses amis. Paris: Boivin, 1940

JAHN, J. Festschrift Johannes Jahn zum xxii November MCMLVII; hrsg. vom Kunsthistorischen Institut der Karl-Marx-Universität, Leipzig. Leipzig: VEB E. A. Seeman, 1958

JAHNN Hans Henry Jahnn. Im Auftrag der Freien Akademie der Künste in Hamburg aus Anlass von Hans Henny Jahnns 60. Geburtstag von Rolf Italiaander zusammengestellt. Hamburg-Wandsbek: Hanseat. Druckanst., 1954

JAKOBSON For Roman Jakobson. Essays on the Occasion of his Sixtieth Birthday, 11 October, 1956; [ed. by Morris Halle & others] The Hague: Mouton, 1956

JASPERS Offener Horizont. Festschrift für Karl Jaspers. München: R. Piper [1953]

JBMV Aus der Welt des Barock, dargestellt von Richard Alewyn . . . Stuttgart: J. B. Metzlersche Verlagsbuchhandlung, erschienen im 275. Jahr ihres Bestehens [1957]

JEANROY Mélanges de linguistique et de littérature offerts à M. Alfred Jeanroy. Paris: E. Droz, 1928

JENKINSON Essays presented to Sir Hilary Jenkinson; ed. by J. Conway Davies. London: Oxford, 1957

JEPPESEN Natalicia musicologica Knud Jeppesen septuagenario collegis oblata; redig. curaverunt Bjørn Hjelmborg & Søren Sørensen. Hafniae: Wilhelm Hansen, 1962 ◇ 318p bibliog (J. P. Jacobsen)

JÖDE Fritz Jöde, Leben und Werk; eine Freundesgabe zum 70. Geburtstag im

Auftrage der Fritz Jöde-Stiftung zusammengestellt und hrsg. von Reinhold Stapelberg. Trossingen: Hohner; Wolfenbüttel: Möseler [1957] ◇ 221p bibliog biog (R. Stapelberg, H. Mersmann, W. Burmeister, H. R. Franzke, L. Kestenberg. H. Scheel, E. Zuckmeyer, H. Erpf, J. Müller-Blattau, H. M. Sambeth, W. Jansen, K. Lorenz, G. Maasz, J. Thiel, F. Wartenweiler, H. Alm, C. Bresgen, E. Österreicher, A. Junge, E. Auwärter, H. J. Moser, E. Valentin)

JOHNER Der kultische Gesang der abendländischen Kirche; ein gregorianisches Werkheft aus Anlass des 75. Geburtstages von Dominicus Johner; in Verbindung mit zahlreichen Mitarbeitern hrsg. von Dr. Franz Tack. Köln: J. P. Bachem, 1950 ◇ 126p biog (H. Lemacher)

JUCHOFF Aus der Welt des Bibliothekars. Festschrift für Rudolf Juchoff zum 65. Geburtstag; hrsg. von K. Ohly and Werner Krieg. Köln: Greven [1959]

KAHL Festgabe zum 60. Geburtstag von Willi Kahl am 18. Juli 1953. Köln: [Unpublished typescript] ◇ 146p bibliog (J. Hein)

KAHLE Studien zur Geschichte und Kultur des Nahen und Fernen Ostens. Paul Kahle zum 60. Geburtstag überreicht von Freunden und Schülern aus dem Kreise des orientalischen Seminars der Universität Bonn; hrsg. von W. Heffening und W. Kirfel. Leiden. E. J. Brill, 1935

KALLEN Aus Mittelalter und Neuzeit. Gerhard Kallen zum 70. Geburtstag dargebracht von Kollegen, Freunden und Schülern; hrsg. von Josef Engel und Hans Martin Klinkenberg. Bonn: P. Hanstein, 1957

KARABECEK Festschrift Josef Ritter von Karabecek zum siebzigsten Geburtstage gewidmet von seinen Schülern . . . Wien: Hälder, 1916

KIENZL Festschrift zum sechzigsten Geburtstage des Meisters Wilhelm Kienzl; hrsg. von Hilde Hagen [Hermann Schilling, pseud.] 2. Aufl. Graz: Leuschner & Lubensky, 1917. ◇ 63p biog (F. Weingartner, J. Schuch, F. Hirth)

KINKELDEY [. . . Otto Kinkeldey in Honor of His Seventieth Birthday, November 27, 1948] (*Music Library Assn. Notes*, ser. 2/6, Dec. 1948, 27–121) ◇ biog (C. S. Smith)

KINKELDEY/80TH A Musicological Offering to Otto Kinkeldey upon the Occasion of His 80th Birthday. (*Journal of the American Musicological Society* 13, 1960, 1–269)

KITTO Classical Drama and Its Influence. Essays Presented to Prof. H. D. F. Kitto; ed. by M. J. Anderson. New York: Barnes & Noble/London: Methuen, 1965

KLOSE Friedrich Klose zum 80. Geburtstag 29. November 1942; hrsg. von der Bibliothek Walter Jesinghaus, Lugano. [Lugano, 1942] ◇ 114p bibliog biog (G. Becker, G. Geierhaas, H. Suter, F. Grüninger, M. Hohl, F. de Quervain, H. Knappe, A. Oetiker)

KML Festschrift zum 75jährigen Bestehen des Königl. Konservatoriums der Musik zu Leipzig am 2. April 1918. Leipzig: C. F. W. Siegel, 1918 ◇ 80p

KOCZIRZ Festschrift Adolph Koczirz zum 60. Geburtstag; hrsg. von Robert Haas und Joseph Zuth. Wien: E. Strache [1930] ◇ 56p

KODÁLY/60TH Emlékkönyv Kodály Zoltán hatvanadik születésnapjára/Mélanges offerts à Zoltán Kodály à l'occasion de son soixantième anniversaire; szerk. Gunda Béla/Réd. par Béla Gunda. Budapest: Kiadja a Magyar Néprajzi Társaság/Edition de la Société Ethnographique Hongroise, 1943 ◇ 372p bibliog (J. Bartók) biog (S. Veress)

KODÁLY/70TH Emlékkönyv Kodály Zoltán 70. születésnapjára; szerk. Szabolcsi Bence és Bartha Dénes. (*Zenetudományi Tanulmányok* 1) Budapest: Akadémiai Kiadó, 1953 ◇ 766p bibliog (A. Szöllösy) biog (F. Szabó, A Tóth, L. Vargyas, B. Szabolcsi)

KODÁLY/75TH Zenetudományi tanulmányok Kodály Zoltán 75. születésnapjára;

szerk. Szabolcsi Bence és Bartha Dénes. (*Zenetudományi Tanulmányok* 6) Budapest: Akadémiai Kiadó, 1957 <> 763p biog (A. Molnár, B. Szabolcsi, J. Kovács)

KODÁLY/80TH Zoltano Kodály octogenario sacrum. Budapest: Akadémiai Kiadó, 1962; also appeared as *Studia musicologica* 3. <> 399p bibliog (L. Eösze, F. Bónis) biog (L. Eösze, E. Martinov, A. Molnár, B. Szabolcsi, C. Mason)

KONWITSCHNY Vermächtnis und Verpflichtung. Festschrift für Franz Konwitschny zum 60. Geburstag. Leipzig: Deutscher Verlag für Musik, 1961 <> 94, 32p discog biog (H. Pischner, H. Heyer, E. Krause, F. Zschoch) incl. a 45rpm phonodisc of *Fidelio* & *Egmont* overtures conducted by K.

KORRODI Freundesgabe für Eduard Korrodi zum 60. Geburtstag. Zürich: Fretz & Wasmuth [1945?]

KRÁL Sborník prací filologických dvornímu radovi professoru Josefu Královi k šedesátým narozeninám. V Praze: B. Stýlbo, 1913

KRAUS Festschrift Walther Kraus zum 60. Geburtstage. (*Wiener Studien, Zeitschrift für klassische Philologie* 75) Wien: O. Höfels, 1962

KRETSCHMER Festschrift für Univ.-Prof. Hofrat Dr. Paul Kretschmer. Beiträge zur griechischen und lateinischen Sprachforschung. Wien: Deutscher Verlag für Jugend und Volk, 1926

KRETZSCHMAR Festschrift Hermann Kretzschmar zum siebzigsten Geburtstage überreicht von Kollegen, Schülern und Freunden. Leipzig: C. F. Peters, 1918 <> 184p bibliog (G. Adler)

KRISTENSEN Festskrift til Evald Targ Kristensen på hans halvtredsårsdag son mindesamler den 31. december 1917; udg. af foreningen Danmarks folkeminder ved Gunnar Knudsen. (*Danmarks Folkeminder* 17, 1917) København: Schønberske, 1917

KROHN Juhlakirja Ilmari Krohn'ille 8. IX. 1927. Helsinki; 1927 <> 183p

KROYER Theodor Kroyer. Festschrift zum sechzigsten Geburtstage am 9. September 1933 überreicht von Freunden und Schülern; hrsg. von H. Zenck, H. Schultz, W. Gerstenberg. Regensburg: G. Bosse, 1933 <> 182p

KUBELIK Jan Kubelik. Vydalo r. 1942 k uctěni památky Mistra Jana Kubelíka . . . ; [ed.] J. Dostál. Praha: Školní Nakladatelství pro Čechy a Moravu, 1942. <> 167p biog (J. Dostál, N. Kubát, K. Koval, A. Kvapilova, K. Procházka, O. Haša, A. Holeček, K. Moravec, M. Hýsek, K. Otáhal)

KUHNERT Von Büchern und Bibliotheken. Dem ersten Direktor der Preussischen Staatsbibliothek geheimen Regierungsrat Dr. Phil. Ernst Kuhnert als Abschiedsgabe dargebracht von seinen Freunden und Mitarbeitern. Berlin: Struppe und Winckler, 1928

KURTH Anschauung und Deutung. Willy Kurth zum 80. Geburtstag. Berlin: Akademie-Verlag, 1964

LACH Robert Lach, Persönlichkeit und Werk, zum 80. Geburtstag überreicht von Freunden und Schülern . . . Wien: [Musikwissenschaftliches Institut der Univ. Wien] 1954 <> 31p bibliog biog (E. Schenk, W. Graf, L. Nowak, R. Meister, H. Jancik)

LAMPRECHT Studium Lipsiense. Ehrengabe Karl Lamprecht dargebracht aus Anlass der Eröffnung des Königlichen Sächsischen Instituts für Kultur- und Universalgeschichte bei der Universität Leipzig von Schülern aus der Zeit seiner leipziger Wirksamkeit. Berlin: Weidmann, 1909

LAMPROS Eis mnemen Spyridonos Lamproy. Athenais: 1935

LAURENCIE Mélanges de musicologie offerts à M. Lionel de la Laurencie. (*Publ. de la Société Française de Musicologie* 2/3 & 4) Paris: E. Droz, 1933 <> 294p

LEEMANS Études archéologiques, linguistiques et historiques dédiées à M. le Dr.

C. Leemans à l'occasion du cinquantième anniversaire de sa nomination aux fonctions de Directeur du Musée Archéologique des Pays-Bas. Leiden: E. Brill, 1885

LEFORT Mélanges L. Th. Lefort. (*Le Muséon, revue d'études orientales* 59, 1946) Louvain, 1946

LEFRANC Mélanges offerts à M. Abel Lefranc par ses élèves et ses amis. Paris: E. Droz, 1936

LEIDINGER Festschrift für Georg Leidinger zum 60. Geburtstag am 30. Dezember 1930. München: H. Schmidt [1930]

LEIP Hans Leip, Leben und Werk; [aus Anlass von Hans Leips 65. Geburtstag am 22. Sept. 1958 von R. Italiaander zusammengestellt] Hamburg: Freie Akademie der Künste, 1958

LEITE Miscelânea scientífica et literária dedicada ao doutor J. Leite de Vasconcellos. Coimbra: Imprensa da Universidade, 1934

LEMACHER Musikalisches Brauchtum. Festschrift für Heinrich Lemacher; hrsg. von seinen Freunden und Schülern. (*Schriftenreihe des Allgemeinen Cäcilien-Verbandes für Deutschland, Österreich und die Schweiz* 1/3) [Köln, 1956] ◇ 93p bibliog biog (W. Hammerschlag, A. Schneider)

LEMONNIER Mélanges offerts à M. Henri Lemonnier par la Société de l'Histoire de l'Art Français, ses amis et ses élèves (*Archives de l'art français*, nouv. période 7) Paris: E. Champion, 1913

LENZ Homenaje a la memoria del Dr. Rodolfo Lenz. (*Universidade de Chile, Anales de la Facultad de Filosofía y Educación, Sección de Filología,* T.2, Cuaderno núm. 1, 1937–1938) Santiago: 1937

LEVY Mélanges Isidore Levy. (*Annuaire de l'Institut de Philologie et d'Histoire Orientales et Slaves* 13, 1953) Bruxelles, 1955

LEXA Diatribae quas amici, collegae, discipuli Francesco Lexa, quinque et septuaginta annos nato, DDD; ed. curavit Zbyněk Žába. (*Archiv orientální* 20) Praha, 1952

LGR Festgabe zum 25jährigen Jubiläum des Gymnasiums und Realgymnasiums zu Landsberg a. W. dargebracht von ehemaligen Lehrern und Schülern. Landsberg a. W.: F. Schoeffer, 1885

LICHTENBERGER Mélanges Henri Lichtenberger; hommage de ses élèves et ses amis, juin 1934. Paris: Stock, 1934

LILIENCRON Festschrift zum 90. Geburtstage Sr. Exz. des Wirklichen geheimen Rates Rochus Freiherrn von Liliencron überreicht von Vertretern deutscher Musikwissenschaft. Leipzig: Breitkopf & Härtel, 1910 ◇ 463p

LIPATTI Hommage à Dinu Lipatti. Genève: Labor et Fidés, 1951 ◇ 95p bibliog discog biog (M. Lipatti, E. Ansermet, N. Boulanger, C. J. Burckhardt, J. Chapuis, A. Cortot, H. Gagnebin, A. Honegger, W. Legge, N. Magaloff, I. Markevitch, F. Martin, R.-A. Mooser, P. Sacher, B. Siki)

LÖFSTEDT Eranos Löfstedtianus. Opuscula philologica einaro Löfstedt, A. D. XVII Kal. Iul. anno MCMXLV dedicata. (*Eranos; Acta philological Suecana* 43, 1945), Gotoburgi, 1945

LOTH Mélanges bretons et celtiques offerts à M. J. Loth. Rennes: Plihon, 1927

LÜTZELER Der Mensch und die Künste. Festschrift für Heinrich Lützeler. Düsseldorf o. J.: 1962

LUICK Neusprachliche Studien. Festgabe Karl Luick zu seinem sechzigsten Geburtstage dargebracht von Freunden und Schülern. (*Die neueren Sprachen,* Beiheft 6) Marburg/Lahn: N. G. Elwert, 1925

LUMBROSO Raccolta de scritti in onore di G. Lumbroso, 1844–1925. (*Aegyptus, pubblicazioni,* ser. scientifica 3) Milano, 1925

LYDENBERG Bookmen's Holiday. Notes and Studies Written and Gathered in Tribute to Harry Miller Lydenberg. New York: New York Public Library, 1943

MAHRENHOLZ Musicologica et liturgica. Gesammelte Aufsätze von Christhard Mahrenholz als Festgabe zu seinem 60. Geburtstag am 11. August 1960; hrsg. von Karl Ferdinand Müller. Kassel: Bärenreiter, 1960 ◇ 685p bibliog biog

MAIER/75TH Tanz und Brauch aus der musikalischen Volksüberlieferung Kärntens. Roman Maier, dem Sammler und Pfleger von Kärntnerlied- und Kärntnertanzgut, zur Vollendung seines 75. Lebensjahres dargebracht. (*Kärntner Museumsschriften* 19) Klagenfurt: Verlag des Landesmuseums für Kärnten, 1959 ◇ 176p biog (G. Moro, A. Anderluh, F. Koschier)

MALMBERG Festskrift till Bertil Malmberg den 13. augusti 1949. Stockholm: Bonnier, 1949

MARINUZZI L'Orchestra [in onore Gino Marinuzzi 1882–1945] Firenze: G. Barbera, 1954 ◇ 200p biog (I. Pizzetti)

MARIOTTI Miscellanea storico letteraria a Francesco Mariotti nel cinquantesimo anno della sua carriera tipografica. Pisa: E. Pacini, 1907

MARTINENCHE Hommage à Ernest Martinenche. Études hispaniques et américaines. Paris: Éditions d'Artrey [1939?]

MARTINŮ Bohuslav Martinů. Sborník vzpomínek a studií; redig. Zdeněk Zouhar. Brno: Krajské Nakladatelství, 1957 ◇ 155, 20p bibliog biog (K. Martinů, M. Martinů, J. Macek, J. Kunc, A. Balatka, V. Talich, P. Bořkovec, I. Krejčí, J. Novák, S. Novák, I. Popelka, R. Pečman, Z. Mrkos, J. Trojan, Z. Zouhar)

MARX, K./70TH Festschrift Karl Marx zum 70. Geburtstag dargebracht von seinen Schülern: Heinrich Deppert . . . [et al] Stuttgart: Ichthys, 1967 ◇ 119p bibliog (H. Deppert, W. Wöhler) biog (W. Wöhler, G. Küntzel, J. F. Doppelbauer, M. Gümbel, R. Zillhardt)

MASPERO Mélanges Maspero. (*Institut Français d'Archéologie Orientale du Caire, mémoires* 66–68) Le Caire, 1935–1940

MASSON Mélanges d'histoire et d'esthétique musicales offerts à Paul-Marie Masson . . . par ses collègues, ses élèves et ses amis. Paris: R. Masse [1955] ◇ 194, 222p in 2v bibliog biog

MATTHIAS Mátyás Király [Matthias Corvinus] emlékkönyv [1440–1940] születésének ötszázéves fordulójára. Budapest: Franklin Társulat [1940?]

MAUERSBERGER Kirchenmusik heute. Gedanken über Aufgaben und Probleme der Musica sacra. [Rudolf Mauersberger zur Vollendung seines 70. Lebensjahres] hrsg. von Hans Böhm. Berlin: Union, 1959 ◇ 186p bibliog biog (T. Schrems, G. Raphael, S. Stuligrosz, K. Thomas, M. Mitzenheim)

MAYER/S Scritti in memoria di Sally Mayer (1875–1953), saggi sull'ebraismo italiano. Milano: Fondazione S. Mayer, Scuola Superiore di Studi Ebraici, 1956

MAYER/T Aus Verfassungs- und Landesgeschichte. Festschrift zum 70. Geburtstag von Theodor Mayer dargebracht von seinen Freunden und Schülern. Lindau/Konstanz: J. Thorbecke [1955]

MEDTNER Nicholas Medtner, a Tribute to His Art and Personality. London: D. Dobson, 1955 ◇ 238p bibliog discog biog (A. Medtner, M. Salaman, A. Swan, E. Newman, M. Ritchie, J. Yasser, A. Laliberté, E. Blom, L. Sabaneiev, G. Abraham, A. Alexander, E. Karnitzka, G. Conus, M. Dupré, A. Robertson, T. Makushina, O. Slobodskaya, K. S. Sorabji, C. Raybould, L. Collingwood, D. Laberge, C. Glover, J. Isserlis, A. Jarosy, I. Ilyin, E. Prehn, R. Holt, K. Klimov, V. Pohl, I. Dobroven)

MEIER/70TH Volkskundliche Gaben. John Meier zum siebzigsten Geburtstage dargebracht. Berlin: W. de Gruyter, 1934

MEIER/85TH Angebinde John Meier zum 85. Geburtstag am 14. Juni 1949 dargeboten von basler und freiburger Freunden und Kollegen. Lahr: M. Schauenburg [1949]

MEINHOF Festschrift Meinhof. Glückstadt: J. J. Augustin, 1927

MENDELSSOHN Gedenkbuch für Moses Mendelssohn; hrsg. vom Verbande der Vereine für jüdische Geschichte und Literatur in Deutschland. Berlin: Poppelauer, 1929

MENÉNDEZ PIDAL Homenaje ofrecido a Ramón Menéndez Pidal. Miscelánea de estudios linguisticos, literarios e históricos. Madrid: Hernando, 1925

MENÉNDEZ PIDAL/E Estudios dedicados a Menéndez Pidal. Madrid: Consejo Superior de Investigaciones Científicas, 1952–1957

MENÉNDEZ Y PELAYO Homenaje a Menéndez y Pelayo en al año vigésimo de su profesorado. Madrid: Suárez, 1899

MENGELBERG Willem Mengelberg. Gedenkboek 1895–1920. 's-Gravenhage: Nijhoff, 1920 ◇ 290p bibliog biog

MERCATI Studi storici in memoria di Mons. Angelo Mercati, Prefetto dell'Archivio Vaticano; raccolti a cura della Biblioteca Ambrosiana. (*Fontes Ambrosiani* 30) Milano: A. Giuffrè, 1956

MERSMANN Musikerkenntnis und Musikerziehung. Dankesgaben für Hans Mersmann zu seinem 65. Geburtstage; hrsg. von Walter Wiora. Kassel: Bärenreiter, 1958 ◇ 224p bibliog

MICHAËLIS DE VASCONCELLOS Miscelânea de estudos em honra de d. Carolina Michaëlis de Vasconcellos, professora da faculdade de letras da Universidade de Coimbra. (*Revista da Univ. de Coimba* 11) Coimbra, 1933

MICHELS Perennitas. Beiträge zur christlichen Archäologie und Kunst . . . P. Thomas Michels OSB zum 70. Geburtstag; hrsg. von Hugo Rahner SJ und Emmanuel von Severus OSB. (*Beiträge zur Geschichte des alten Mönchtums und des Benediktinerordens*, Supplbd. 2) Münster: Verlag Aschendorff, 1963

MIES Beiträge zur Musikgeschichte der Stadt Köln. Zum 70. Geburtstag von Paul Mies in Verbindung mit Heinrich Hüschen, Willi Kahl und Klaus Wolfgang Niemöller; hrsg. von Karl Gustav Fellerer. (*Beiträge zur rheinischen Musikgeschichte* 35) Köln: Volk, 1959 ◇ 80p

MILFORD Essays Mainly on the Nineteenth Century Presented to Sir Humphrey Milford. London: Oxford, 1948

MIRBT Begegnungen und Wirkungen. Festgabe für Rudolf Mirbt und das deutsche Laienspiel; hrsg. von Hermann Kaiser. Kassel: Bärenreiter [1956]

MIRBT/70TH Darstellendes Spiel . . . ; hrsg. in Verbindung mit dem Kuratorium Darstellendes Spiel von Paul Amtmann und Hermann Kaiser. Kassel: Bärenreiter, 1966

MOBERG Studier tillägnade Carl-Allan Moberg 5 juni 1961. (*Svensk tidskrift för musikforskning* 40, 1961) Stockholm, 1961 ◇ 407p bibliog (M. Tegen)

MOHLBERG Miscellanea liturgica in honorem L. C. Mohlberg. (*Bibliotheca ephemerides liturgicae* 22, 23) Roma: Edizioni Liturgiche, 1948–1949

MOMMSEN Commentationes philologiae in honorem Theodori Mommseni scripserunt amici. Berolini: apud Weidmannos, 1877

MONTE CASSINO Casinensia. Miscellanea di studi cassinesi pubblicata in occasione del XIV centenario della fondazione della Badia di Monte Cassino. Sora: [Stab. tipogr. P. C. Camustro] 1929

MONTEMEZZI Omaggio a Italo Montemezzi; a cura di Luigi Tretti e Lionello Fiumi. (Numero unico ed. a cura del Comitato onoranze a Italo Montemezzi in collaborazione con la rivista mensile *Vita veronese*) Verona, 1952 ◇ 79p biog (G. Silvestri, L. Fiumi, L. Tretti, L. Ceolari, U. Cattini, L. Spezzaferri)

MORNET Mélanges d'histoire littéraire offerts à Daniel Mornet, professeur honoraire à la Sorbonne, par ses anciens collègues et ses disciples français. Paris: Nizet, 1951

MOSER Festgabe für Hans Joachim Moser zum 65. Geburtstag 25. Mai 1954; hrsg. von einem Freundeskreis. Kassel: Hinnenthal, 1954 <> 170p bibliog (H. Wegener)

MOSER/70TH Musik in Zeit und Raum, ausgewählte Abhandlungen. Berlin: Merseburger, 1960 <> 358p

MÜLLER VON ASOW Festschrift Erich H. Müller von Asow, Dr. Phil., Ritter des Ordens der Krone von Rumänien, zum fünfzigsten Geburtstag überreicht von Hermann Ambrosius. Salzburg. [Unpublished typescript] 1942 <> 307p bibliog (H. Müller von Asow) biog (J. Pilz)

MÜLLER-BLATTAU Festgabe für Joseph Müller-Blattau zum 65. Geburtstag. (*Annales Universitatis Saraviensis, Philosophische Fakultät* 9/1, 1960, 1–112) Saarbrücken: 1960 [2d ed. 1962]

MÜLLER-BLATTAU/70TH Zum 70. Geburtstag von Joseph Müller-Blattau; im Auftrage des Musikwissenschaftlichen Instituts der Universität des Saarlandes hrsg. von Christoph-Hellmut Mahling. (*Sarrbrücker Studien zur Musikwissenschaft* 1) Kassel: Bärenreiter, 1966 <> 340p biog (H. Reutter, K. Vötterle)

MÜNNICH Festschrift Richard Münnich zum achtzigsten Geburtstage. Beiträge zur Musikästhetik, Musikgeschichte, Musikerziehung. Leipzig: Deutscher Verlag für Musik [1957] <> 152p bibliog (H. Grossmann) biog (A. Krauss)

MÜNNICH/70TH Festschrift zum siebzigsten Geburtstag von Richard Münnich dem Künstler, Forscher und Pädagogen überreicht von Freunden und Schülern am 7. Juni 1947. Weimar: [Unpublished typescript] 1947 <> 95p biog (H. Kirmsse)

MÜNNICH/80THM Münnich-Festschrift. Richard Münnich zum achtzigsten Gebertstage überreicht von Freunden und Schülern. Berlin: [Unpublished typescript] 1957 <> 157p

MUEREN Miscellanea musicologica Floris van der Mueren. Gent: L. van Melle, 1950 <> 262p bibliog (R. Roemans) biog (A. Stubbe)

MURATORI Miscellanea di studi muratoriani; atti e memorie del *Convegno di studi storici in onore di L. A. Muratori* tenuto in Modena, 14–16 aprile 1950. Modena: Aedes Muratoriana, 1951

MURATORI/M Miscellanea di studi muratoriani. (*Atti e memorie della Regia Deputazione di Storia Patria per le Provincie Modenesi* 7/8) Modena: Società Tipografica Modenese, 1933

NAVARRE Mélanges offerts à M. Octave Navarre par ses élèves et ses amis. Toulouse: E. Privat, 1935

NEF Festschrift Karl Nef zum 60. Geburtstag dargebracht von Schülern und Freunden. Zürich/Leipzig: Hug. 1933 <> 219p bibliog (E. Mohr)

NEILSON Essays Contributed in Honor of President William Allen Neilson; ed. Caroline B. Bourland . . . (*Smith College Studies in Modern Languages* 21/1–4, 1939/40) Northampton, Mass. [1939–1940]

NEJEDLÝ/50TH Sborník prací k padesátým narozeninám Profesora Dra Zdeňka Nejedlého, 1878–1928. Praha: Fr. Borový, 1928 <> 303p bibliog (A. J. Patzaková)

NEJEDLÝ/50THP Padesát let Zdeňka Nejedlého; [ed. B. Belohlávek] Praha: Ludka Mandause, 1928 <> 249p biog (J. Goll, F. S. Šalda, V. Novotný, Gamma, P. Levit, A. J. Patzaková, M. Novák, J. Kohn, Q. Hodura, J. B. Foerster, O. Zich, J. Bartoš, Z. Hostinská, E. Rádl, P. Maxa, J. Kratochvíl, Landová-Štychová, R. Fibish, F. Famíra, F. Táborský)

NEJEDLÝ/70TH O Zdeňku Nejedlém. Stati a projevy k jeho sedemdesátinám; [ed.] V. Pekárek. Praha: Orbis, 1948 <> 298p bibliog (V. Pekárek) biog (K. Gottwald, B. Maslarić, A. Gundurov, P. Mocálov, V. Kopecký, L. Svoboda, J. Duriš, A. Zápotocky, L. Koubek, Z. Popel, J. Gallas, A. Kolman, L. Kopříva, V. Vacek, F. Jungman, J. Ulrich, J. Charvát, A. Kurš, A. J. Pacákova, M. Očadlík, A. Waisar, Q. Hadura, O. Chlup, M. Matoušek, J. Teichman, V. Nezval, A. Matějček, F. Pujman, B. Markalous-John, B. Vomáčka, V. Vydra, E. F. Burian, J. Škoda, K. Hanuš, K. Popelka)

NEJEDLÝ/75TH Zdeňku Nejedlému k 75. narozeninám. (*Masarykova Universita, Brno, Czechoslovakia, Filosofická Faculta, Sborník prací* ročník 2, číslo 2–4) Brno: 1953 <> 356p biog (M. Novák, J. Kolejka)

NEUMANN Salvatore Di Giacomo, ein neapolitanischer Volksdichter in Wort, Bild und Musik. Festgabe für Fritz Neumann von Karl Vossler. Heidelberg: Carl Winter, 1908

NEUSS Wilhelm Neuss zum 80. Geburtstag 24. Juli 1960. (*Spanische Forschungen der Görresgesellschaft*, Reihe 1, *Gesammelte Aufsätze zur Kulturgeschichte Spaniens* 16) Münster Westfalen: Aschendorffsche Verlagsbuchhandlung, 1960

NEWMAN Fanfare for Ernest Newman; ed. by Herbert Van Thal. London: A. Barker, 1955 <> 191p biog (N. Cardus, St. J. Nixon, J. F. Russell, P. Vincent)

NIESSEN Mimus und Logos, eine Festgabe für Carl Niessen. Emsdetten: Lechte, 1952

NIKANDER Kulturhistoria och folklivforskning. Festskrift tillägnad Gabriel Nikander 19 21/5 34. (*Budklaven* 13, 1934) Helsingfors: 1934

NIKISCH Arthur Nikisch, Leben und Wirken; Heinrich Chevalley, hrsg. Berlin: Bote & Bock, 1922 <> 220p biog (F. Pfohl, H. Chevalley, S. Stražnicky, L. Wolff, H. Freiherrn, L. von Stoedten, H. Zöllner, D. Danielson, A. van Raalte, A. Moszkowski)

NORWOOD Studies in Honor of Gilbert Norwood. (*The Phoenix, Journal of the Classical Assn. of Canada*, Supplementary v.1) [Toronto: Univ. of Toronto Press, 1952]

NOVÁK/60TH Sborník na počest 60. narozenin Vítězslava Nováka; redig. Boleslav Vamáčka a Stanislav Hanuš. Praha: Hudební Matice Umélecké Besedy, 1930 <> 92p bibliog (O. Šourek) biog (J. Suk, V. Stěpán, R. Veselý, O. Šín, J. Křička, I. Ballo, F. Pala, H. Doležil, J. Kunc, V. Stěpán, A. Cmíral, B. Vomáčka, A. Strettiová-Šourková)

NOWAK/60TH Bruckner-Studien. Leopold Nowak zum 60. Geburtstag; hrsg. von Franz Grasberger. Wien: Musikwissenschaftlicher Verlag, 1964. <> 152p bibliog (A. Ziffer) biog (A. van Hoboken)

OGG Historical Essays 1600–1750 Presented to David Ogg; ed. by H. E. Bell and R. L. Ollard. London: Adam & Charles Black, 1963

OIKONOMOS Eis mnemen Georgiou P. Oikonomou. (*Archaiologike ephemeris*, 1953/1954) Athenais: 1955

OLDMAN "Tribute to C. B. Oldman on his seventieth birthday, 2 April 1964. (*Music Review* 25, May 1964, 85–157) Cambridge: W. Heffer & Sons, 1964 <> bibliog (U. Sherrington)

OLSEN Til Sparre Olsen på 50-års dagen, 25. april 1953; [red. Reidar Kjellberg, Inge Krokann og Dag Winding Sørensen. Oslo] Gyldendal [1953?] <> 121p bibliog (Ø. Gaukstad) biog (T. Fischer, L. Greni, O. M. Sandvik, A. Vaa, I. Krokann)

OPPENHEIM Aus fünf Jahrtausenden morgenländischer Kultur. Festschrift Max Freiherrn von Oppenheim zum 70. Geburtstage gewidmet von Freunden und Mitarbeitern. (*Archiv für Orientforschung*, Beiband 1) Berlin, 1933

OREL Alfred Orel; Aufsätze und Vorträge zu seinem 50. Geburtstage gesammelt und hrsg. von Freunden und Schülern. Wien/Berlin: Paver, 1930 <> 174p bibliog

OREL/70TH Festschrift Alfred Orel zum 70. Geburtstag überreicht von Kollegen,

Freunden und Schülern; hrsg. von Hellmut Federhofer. Wien/Wiesbaden: R. M. Rohrer [1960] <> 212p bibliog (I. Orel) biog (F. Racek)

ØRJASAETER Festskrift til Tore Ørjasaeter på 70-årsdagen 8. mars 1956. Oslo: O. Norlis, 1956

ORTIZ Miscelanea de estudios dedicados a Fernando Ortiz por sus discipulos, colegas y amigos. La Habana, 1956

OSTHOFF Festschrift Helmuth Osthoff zum 65. Geburtstage; hrsg. von Lothar Hoffmann-Erbrecht und Helmut Hucke. Tutzing: H. Schneider, 1961 <> 237p bibliog (W. Osthoff)

OSTRČIL Památce Otakara Ostrčila [ed. A. J. Patzaková] Praha: Vydal Melantrich A. S. péčí Společnosti Otakara Ostrčila, 1935. <> 146p biog (A. Ostrčil, J. Ostrčil, J. Ostrčilová, A. Kulhánek, Z. Wirth, V. Pospíšil, B. Zafouk, K. B. Jirák, J. B. Foerster, F. X. Svoboda, F. Vach, H. Malina, J. Kvapil, M. Doležil, J. Zelinka, E. Němeček, K. Hába, O. Jeremiáš, F. Kysela, V. Hofman, F. Zelenka, Vojta Novák, J. Munclingr, A. Nordenovă, J. Šafář, M. Zunová, V. Podrabský, Z. Čančiková, M. Očadlík, J. Bartoš, F. Pala, J. Mařánek, J. Plavec, M. Sachs, Hanus Thein, A. Waisar, A. Rektorys, V. Helfert, Z. Nejedlý)

OSTROGORSKY Mélanges Georges Ostrogorsky. (*Recueil de Travaux de l'Institut Français d'Études Byzantines* 8:2) Beograd: 1963–1964

PANOFSKY De artibus opuscula XL. Essays in Honor of Erwin Panofsky; ed. by Millard Meiss. [New York] New York Univ. Press, 1961

PAULER Gedenkschrift für Ákos von Pauler; mit Unterstützung der Ungarischen Wissenschaftlichen Akademie und der P. Pázmány-Universität Budapest, hrsg. von der Ungarischen Philosophischen Gesellschaft; unter Mitwirkung von Julius Kornis zusammengestellt von Ludwig Prohászka. Berlin/Leipzig: W. de Gruyter, 1936

PAULS Aus Schleswig-Holsteins Geschichte und Gegenwart. Eine Aufsatzsammlung als Festschrift für Volquart Pauls; hrsg. von Fritz Hähnsen, Alfred Kamphausen, Harry Schmidt. Neumünster: Wachholtz, 1950.

PAUMGARTNER Wissenschaft und Praxis, eine Festschrift zum 70. Geburtstag von Bernhard Paumgartner. [Die Herausgabe besorgte Dr. Eberhard Preussner] [Zürich, Freiburg i. Br.] Atlantis Verlag, [1957?] <> 160p bibliog biog (O. F. Schuh)

PEDRELL Al maestro Pedrell, escritos heortásticos. Tortosa: Orfeó Tortosí, 1911 <> 332, 60p in 2v bibliog biog (J. J. de Urríes, R. Chabás, M. Urgellés, C. Rofas, A. Gasco, R. Catarineu, G. E. Campa, M. D. Calvocoressi, A. Galli, E. L. Chávarri, R. Goberna, A. Serrano, V. Ripollés, R. Ortiz, R. Mitjana, M. Morera y Galicia, F. Lliurat, A. Amorós, S. Guinot, F. de P. Viñaspre, A. Bonaventura, J. J. Nin, F. Ortiz y San Pelayo, H. Collet, F. Mestre y Noé)

PEDROLLO Per Arrigo Pedrollo. [Vicenza] La scuola di Arzignano [1953] <> 47p bibliog (R. Cevese) biog (R. Cevese)

PETERSON-BERGER Wilhelm Peterson-Berger. Festskrift den 27. februari 1937 [red. av E. Arbman, S. Beite, G. Morin, E. Rosenborg. Stockholm] Natur och Kultur [1937] <> 302p bibliog (T. Fredbärj) biog (B. Bergman, O. Rabenius, S. Beite, I. Oljelund, C. Berg, J. A. Selander, H. G. Pihl, F. Ege, F. H. Törnblom, J. Norrby, G. Berg, S. E. Svensson, T. Fogelquist, B. Carlberg, R. G. Berg, E. W. Olson, L. Wahlberg)

PEUCKERT Festschrift für Will-Erich Peuckert zum 60. Geburtstag dargebracht von Freunden und Schülern. [Berlin] E. Schmidt [1955]

PFITZNER Hans Pfitzner, ein Bild in Widmungen anlässlich seines 75. Geburtstages im Auftrag seiner Freunde und Verehrer; hrsg. von Walter Abendroth. Leipzig: Heling [1944] <> 126p biog (W. Abendroth, F. Schütz, J. Marx, W. Matthes,

Z. Diemer, V. Junk, O. Krauss, L. Schrott, W. Preetorius, E. Ernst, M. Fischer, V. v. Falkenhayn-Groeben, H. v. Besele, H. Unger, M. Brockhaus, H. Franck, G. Frommel, J. Müller-Blattau, E. Betz, W. Gieseking, M. Strub, F. Wührer, J. Ritt, R. Ockel)

PHILIPP Franz Philipp 70 Jahre. Das Bild eines deutschen Musikers in Zeugnissen von Zeitgenossen [hrsg. von der Franz-Philipp-Gesellschaft e. V.] Gedruckt als Gabe seiner Freunde zum 70. Geburtstag, 24. August 1960 ◇ 202p bibliog biog (J. Amann, H. A. Berger, H. Berl, W. M. Berten, M. Ganter, F. Grüninger, J. Hatzfeld, F. Hirtler, J. Lechthaler, O. zur Nedden, K. Preisendanz, H. E. Rahner, F. Ruh, H. Ruh, H. Schorn, W. Schwarz, B. Steinert, K. E. Wiemann, E. Zimmermann)

PINIŃSKI Księga pamiątkowa ku czci Leona Pinińskiego. Lwów: Naktadem Komiteto Redakcyjnego, 1936

PIPPING Festskrift tillägnad Hugo Pipping på hans sextioårsdag den 5 november 1924. (*Svenska litteratursällskapet i Finland, Helsingfors. Skrifter*, 175) Helsingfors: 1924

PIPPING, R. Hyllningsskrift tillägnad Rolf Pipping på hans sextioårsdag den 1 juni 1949. (*Åbo Akademi, Turku, Finland. Acta Academiae Aboensis Humaniora* 18, 1949) Turku: 1949

PIZZETTI La Città dannunziana a Ildebrando Pizzetti, saggi e note; [a cura di Manlio La Morgia. Pescara, Comitato Centrale Abruzzese per le Onoranze a Ildebrando Pizzetti, dist. Milano: G. Ricordi] 1958 ◇ 338p

PLAVEC/60TH Sborník Pedagogické Fakulty University Karlovy k šedesátým narozeninám Prof. Dr. Josefa Plavce. Praha: Universita Karlova, 1966 ◇ 405p bibliog (J. Vrchotová-Pátová, F. M. Hradil, J. Snížková, J. Petr) biog (F. Voves, J. Šamko, J. Snížková, E. Špriňarová, F. Pala, V. Ljubimov, K. V. Štěpka)

POPPEN Weg und Werk, eine Festgabe zum 70. Geburtstag von Prof. Dr. Hermann Meinhard Poppen, geb. 1. Jan. 1885; unter Mitwirkung von H. Haag hrsg. von O. Riemer. (*Evangelische Kirchenmusik im Baden, Hessen, Pfalz.* 32/1, Jan. 1955, 1–31 ◇ bibliog biog (C. Mahrenholz, K. Dürr, W. Lieb, H. Haag, G. Hees, W. Fortner, S. Hermelink, K. M. Ziegler, O. Riemer)

PRETZEL Festgabe für Ulrich Pretzel zum 65. Geburtstag dargebracht von Freunden und Schülern; hrsg. von Werner Simon . . . [et al.] Berlin: Erich Schmidt Verlag, 1963

PRICE In Honorem Lawrence Marsden Price. Contributions by His Colleagues and by His Former Students. (*University of California. Publications. Modern Philology* 36) Berkeley: Univ. of Calif. Press, 1952

PUIG I CADAFALCH Societat Catalana d'Estudios Històries. Miscellanea Puig i Cadalfalch. Barcelona: Institut d'Estudis Catalans, 1947–1951

PUSTET Bohatta, Hanns. Liturgische Drucke und liturgische Drucker. Festschrift zum 100jährigen Jubiläum des Verlages Friedrich Pustet, Regensburg: Kösel & Pustet [1926] ◇ 74p

PUTNAM Essays offered to Herbert Putnam by His Colleagues and Friends on His Thirtieth Anniversary as Librarian of Congress, 1 April 1929; ed. by William Warner Bishop and Andrew Keough. New Haven: Yale Univ. Press, 1929

QC Twenty-fifth Anniversary Festschrift (1937–1962); ed. by Albert Mell. Flushing, N.Y.: Queens College Department of Music, 1964 ◇ 91p

RAABE Von deutscher Tonkunst. Festschrift zu Peter Raabes 70. Geburtstag; in Gemeinschaft mit dreiundzwanzig Fachgenossen hrsg. von Alfred Morgenroth. Leipzig: Peters [1942] ◇ 247p bibliog biog (Alfred Morgenroth)

RACEK/60TH (*Sborník Prací Filosofické Fakulty Brněnské University*, Ročník XIV, *Řada Uměnovědná* (*F*) Č. 9) Brno: 1965 ◇ 522p bibliog (T. Straková) biog (C. v. d. Borren)

RAMUZ Hommage à C.-F. Ramuz. Lausanne: Porchet, 1938

RASPE Festschrift zum 50jährigen Amtsjubiläum Gustav Heinrich Carl Raspes, vom Lehrer-Collegium des Friedrich Franz-Gymnasium zu Parchim gewidmet. Parchim, 1883

RAVEL Maurice Ravel. (*La Revue musicale*, numéro spécial, Apr. 1925, 1–112, suppl. 1–4) ◇ bibliog biog (A. Suarès, T. Klingsor, R. Manuel, E. Vuillermoz, A. Casella, H. Gil-Marchex, A. Hoérée, R. Chalupt, A. Coeuroy, H. Prunières, Colette)

RAVEL/H Hommage à Maurice Ravel. (*La Revue musicale*, numéro spécial, Dec. 1938, 1–284, 4p) ◇ biog (H. Bidou, A. Suarès, E. Vuillermoz, A. Boll, A. Honegger, G. Marnold, S. Lifar, G. Marcel, H. Gil-Marchex, A. Hoérée, M. Babaian, A. Mirambel, D. E. Ingelbrecht, T. Klingsor, R. Dumesnil, R. Chalupt, P. Landormy, R. Allard, V. Jankélévitch, F. Goldbeck, B. Crémieux, M. Dauge)

REESE/65TH Aspects of Medieval and Renaissance Music. A Birthday Offering to Gustave Reese; ed. by Jan La Rue, assoc. eds. Martin Bernstein, Hans Lenneberg, Victor Yellin. New York: W. W. Norton, 1966 ◇ 891p bibliog (F. Freedman) biog (F. Blume)

REFARDT Musik in der Schweiz, ausgewählte Aufsätze [zum] 75. Geburtstag Edgar Refardts; hrsg. im Auftrag der Ortsgruppe Basel der Schweizerischen Musikforschenden Gesellschaft von Hans Ehinger und Ernst Mohr. Bern: P. Haupt, 1952 ◇ 160p

REFARDT/85TH Edgar Refardt zum 85. Geburtstag am 8. August 1962. (*Schweizerische Musikforschende Gesellschaft, Mitteilungsblatt* 33, Aug. 1962) ◇ 30p bibliog (H. P. Schanzlin)

REGER Max Reger. Festschrift aus Anlass des 80. Geburtstages des Meisters am 19. März 1953; hrsg. vom Max-Reger-Archiv Meiningen in Verbindung mit dem Rat des Bezirkes Suhl. Leipzig: F. Hofmeister [1953] ◇ 90p biog (J. Haas, K. Hasse, H. Unger, H. J. Moser, A. Kalkoff, G. Wehmeyer, H. Poppen, H. Grabner, F. Stein, A. Schmid-Lindner)

RENIER Scritti varii di erudizione e di critica in onore di Rodolfo Renier. Torino: Bocca, 1912

RICORDI . . . R. stabilimento Tito di Gio. Ricordi e Francesco Lucca, G. Ricordi & C., Mailand . . . (*Internationale Musik- und Theaterausstellung*, 1892, Wien) [Milano] G. Ricordi, 1892 ◇ 168p

RICORDI/C—Casa Ricordi, 1808–1958; Profile storico a cura di Claudio Sartori. Itinerarie grafice editoriale. Milano: Ricordi, 1958 ◇ 116p

RICORDI/100TH 1808–1908. 1° centenario della Casa Editrice Ricordi. (*Ars et Labor* [*Gazzetta Musicale di Milano*], suppl. straordinario nov. 1908) Milano: G. Ricordi, 1908 ◇ biog (E. A. Marescotti, et al.)

RICORDI/100THR Fascicolo dedicato al centenario della ditta Ricordi & C. di Milano. (*Il Risorgimento Grafico* 5:10, 1908, [22 unnumbered p] 169–184) Milano: 1908 ◇ biog

RIDGEWAY Essays and Studies presented to William Ridgeway . . . on his Sixtieth Birthday, 6 August 1913; ed. by E. C. Quiggin. Cambridge: Univ. Press, 1913

RIEMANN Riemann-Festschrift. Gesammelte Studien; Hugo Riemann zum sechzigsten Geburtstag überreicht von Freunden und Schülern. Leipzig: M. Hesse, 1909 ◇ 524p bibliog (H. Sočnik) biog

RIEMANN/70TH [Hugo Riemann zum 70. Geburtstag] (*Zeitschrift für Musik-*

wissenschaft 1/10, July 1919, 569–628) Leipzig: 1919 ◇ biog (A. Einstein, W. Gurlitt, R. Steglich, G. Becking)

ROBINSON Studies Presented to Daniel Moore Robinson on his Seventieth Birthday; ed. by George E. Mylonas. St. Louis: Washington Univ., 1951

RÖDER 1846–1896. Festschrift zur 50jährigen Jubelfeier des Bestehens der Firma C. G. Röder, Leipzig. Leipzig: Röder, 1896 ◇ 16, 88p

RÖDER/75TH Zur Westen, Walter von. Musiktitel aus vier Jahrhunderten. Festschrift anlässlich des 75jährigen Bestehens der Firma C. G. Röder, Leipzig. [Leipzig: Röder, 1921] ◇ 115p

ROMAGNOLI Omaggio alla memoria del Romagnoli. (*Dioniso, bollettino dell'Istituto Nazionale del Dramma Antico*, n.s. 11, 1948, 65–141) Siracusa, 1948

ROSENFELD Paul Rosenfeld, Voyager in the Arts; ed. by Jerome Mellquist and Lucie Wiese. New York: Creative Age, 1948 ◇ 284p biog (W. Schuman, M. Graf, A. Frankenstein, C. Chávez, E. Carter, C. Ives, A. Copland, C. Mills, E. Bloch, E. Varèse, R. Harris, D. Diamond, L. Engel)

ROSENHEIM Festschrift für Jacob Rosenheim anlässlich der Vollendung seines 60. Lebensjahres. Frankfurt/Main: J. Kauffmann, 1931

ROTHACKER Konkrete Vernunft. Festschrift Erich Rothacker; hrsg. von Gerhard Funke. Bonn: H. Bouvier, 1958

ROUSSEL Albert Roussel. (*La Revue musicale*, numéro spécial, Apr. 1929, 1–112, suppl. 1–32p) Paris, 1929 ◇ biog (R. Chalupt, M. Brillant, G. Aubry, A. George, P. Le Flem, H. Prunières, P.-O. Ferroud, H. Gil-Marchex, A. Hoérée, N. Boulanger)

ROUSSEL/M A la mémoire d'Albert Roussel. (*La Revue musicale*, 18, Nov. 1937, 289–374, suppl. 1–4) ◇ biog (R. Bernard, A. Cortot, M. Emmanuel, G. Samazeuilh, C. Delvincourt, R. Chalupt, R. Dumesnil, J. Weterings, P. Collaer, F. Goldbeck)

ROY Essays in Anthropology Presented to Rai Bahadur Sarat Chandra Roy; ed. by J. P. Mills, K. P. Chattopadhayay, B. S. Guha . . . Lucknow: Maxwell [1941?]

RUBIÓ I LLUCH Homenatge a Rubió i Lluch. (*Estudis universitaris catalans* 21–22; *Analecta sacra Tarraconensia* 12) Barcelona, 1937

RUDBECK Rudbeck studier. Festskrift vid Uppsala Universitets minnesfest til högtidlighållande av 300-årsminnet av Olof Rudbeck d. Ä:s födelse. (*Upplands fornminnesförening Uppsala, tidskrift* 44 Bilaga, 1930) Uppsala: Almquist & Wiksell, 1930

SACHS see EINSTEIN

SACHS/C The Commonwealth of Music, in honor of Curt Sachs; ed. by Gustave Reese and Rose Brandel. Glencoe: The Free Press, 1964 ◇ 374p biog (L. Schrade, H.-H. Draeger)

SALÉN Strandblomster, en bukett överräckt till Sven Salén med anledning av hans sextioårsdag den 7 november 1950. [Stockholm] Fågel [1950]

SALÉN/70TH Om visor och låtar. Studier tillägnade Sven Salén den 7 november 1960. (*Skrifter utgivna av Svenskt Visarkiv* 2) Stockholm: Svenskt Visarkiv, 1960

SAMUEL Bingkisan budi; een bundel opstellen aan Dr. Philippus Samuel van Ronkel door vrienden en leerlingen aangeboden op zijn tachtigste verjaardag, 1. Augustus 1950. Leiden: A. W. Sijthoff, 1950

SANDBERGER Festschrift zum 50. Geburtstag Adolf Sandberger überreicht von seinen Schülern. München: Ferdinand Zierfuss, 1918 ◇ 295p

SANDVIK Festskrift til O. M. Sanvik, 70 års dagen 1875–9. Mai 1945. Oslo: H. Aschehoug, 1945 ◇ 268p bibliog (Ø. Gaukstad) biog (S. Olsen, A. Sandvold)

SANTANGELO Siculorum Gymnasium. Studi in onore di Salvatore Santangelo. (*Siculorum Gymnasium. Rassegna della Facoltà di Lettere e Filosofia dell'Università di Catania* 8, 1956) Catania, Sicily: 1956

SARMIENTO Homenaje a Domingo Faustino Sarmiento en el cincuentenario de su muerte. (*Humanidades, filosofía y educación* 26) [La Plata] Universidad Nacional de La Plata, 1938

SCHÄFER Ter herinnering aan Dirk Schäfer, 25. November 1873–16. Februari 1931. Amsterdam-Sloterdijk: Maatschappij tot verspreiding van goede en goedkoope lectuur, 1932 ◇ 112p bibliog discog biog (J. Koning, H. van Loon, W. Zonderland, M. J. Brusse, H. Mooy, A. de Wal, L. Couturier)

SCHAEFER Festschrift zum 70. Geburtstage vom Moritz Schaefer zum 21. Mai 1927; hrsg. von Freunden und Schülern. Berlin: Philo, 1927

SCHAUINSLAND Festschrift zum 70. Geburtstage 30. Mai 1927 und 40jährigen Dienstjubiläum 31. Mai 1927 des Herrn Professor Dr. H. H. Schauinsland. Bremen: Heilig & Bartels, 1927

SCHENK Festschrift für Erich Schenk. (*Studien zur Musikwissenschaft, Beihefte der Denkmäler der Tonkunst in Österreich* 25) Graz. Böhlau, 1962 ◇ 652p bibliog biog (G. Roncaglia)

SCHERING Festschrift Arnold Schering zum sechzigsten Geburtstag; in Verbindung mit Max Schneider und Gotthold Frotscher hrsg. von Helmuth Osthoff, Walter Serauky, Adam Adrio. Berlin: A. Glas, 1937 ◇ 274p bibliog (K. Taut)

SCHEURLEER Gedenkboek aangeboden aan Dr. D. F. Scheurleer op zijn 70sten verjaardag. Bijdragen van vrienden en vereerders op het gebied der muziek. 's-Gravenhage: Nijhoff, 1925 ◇ 396p bibliog (A. J. de Mare) biog (W. N. F. Sibmacher Zijnen)

SCHIEDMAIR/60TH Beethoven und die Gegenwart. Festschrift des Beethovenhauses Bonn. Ludwig Schiedermair zum 60. Geburtstag; hrsg. von A. Schmitz. Berlin/Bonn: Dümmler, 1937 ◇ 342p

SCHIEDMAIR/80TH Studien zur Musikgeschichte des Rheinlands. Festschrift zum 80. Geburtstag von Ludwig Schiedermair; in Verbindung mit der Arbeitsgemeinschaft für rheinische Musikgeschichte und dem Verein Beethovenhaus, Bonn; hrsg. von Willi Kahl, Heinrich Lemacher und Joseph Schmidt-Görg. (*Beiträge zur rheinischen Musikgeschichte* 20) Köln: Volk, 1956 ◇ 155p bibliog E. Wagner)

SCHLOSSER Festschrift für Julius Schlosser zum 60. Geburtstage. Zürich: Amalthea, 1927

SCHMALZ Oskar Friedrich Schmalz und der heimatliche Jodelgesang; hrsg. Eidgenössischer Jodlerverband und Bernisch-Kantonaler Jodlerverband. [Oskar Friedrich Schmalz zu seinem siebzigsten Geburtstag, 1881–1951]. Thun: F. Weibel, 1951 ◇ 124p biog (B. Kaiser, H. Holzer, K. Grunder, J. Berger)

SCHMID In memoriam Ernest Fritz Schmid, 1904–1960; ein Gedenkblatt für seine Angehörigen und Freunde. [Recklingshausen: Bauer, 1961] ◇ 42p bibliog biog (H. Endrös, W. Fischer, W. Gerstenberg, L. Nowak)

SCHMIDT Festschrift; Publication d'hommage offerte au P. W. Schmidt; hrsg. von W. Koppers. Wien: Mechistaristen-Congregation, 1928

SCHMIDT-GÖRG Festschrift Joseph Schmidt-Görg zum 60. Geburtstag; Gemeinsam mit seinen Kollegen, Schülern und Freunden im Auftrag des Beethovenhauses hrsg. von Dagmar Weise. Bonn: Beethovenhaus, 1957 ◇ 408p bibliog biog (L. Schiedermair)

SCHMIDT-GÖRG/70TH Colloquium Amicorum. Joseph Schmidt-Görg zum 70. Geburtstag; hrsg. von Siegfried Kross und Hans Schmidt. Bonn: Beethovenhaus, 1967 ◇ 461p bibliog biog (A. & E. v. Hoboken)

SCHMITZ Festheft Arnold Schmitz zum siebzigsten Geburtstag; hrsg. von Wilibald Gurlitt and Hans Heinrich Eggebrecht . . . (*Archive für Musikwissenschaft* 19/20:3–4, 1962/1963, 1–306) Wiesbaden: Franz Steiner Verlag GMBH, 1963

SCHNEIDER/60TH Festschrift Max Schneider zum 60. Geburtstag überreicht von Kollegen, Freunden und Schülern; hrsg. von H. J. Zingel. Halle, Eisleben-Lutherstadt: E. Schneider, 1935 ◇ 160p bibliog (H. Ludwig) biog (A. Schering, H. Hoffmann)

SCHNEIDER/80TH Festschrift Max Schneider zum achtzigsten Geburtstage; in Verbindung mit Franz von Glasenapp, Ursula Schneider und Walther Siegmund-Schultze hrsg. von Walther Vetter. Leipzig: Deutscher Verlag für Musik [1955] ◇ 363p

SCHNÜTGEN Alexander Schnütgen, dem treuen Hüter der Tradition, zum 70. Geburtstag 1. Juli 1953. (*Annalen des Historischen Vereins für den Niederrhein* 153–154) Düsseldorf: L. Schwann, 1953

SCHOECK/50TH Othmar Schoeck. Festgabe der Freunde zum 50. Geburtstag; hrsg. von Willi Schuh. Erlenbach-Zürich: Eugen Rentsch Verlag, 1936 ◇ 133p biog (V. Andreae, H. Bärlocher, F. Brun, H. Corrodi, K. H. David, H. Hesse, H. Hubacher, E. Isler, W. Schuh)

SCHÖNBERG/50TH Arnold Schönberg zum fünfzigsten Geburtstage 13. September 1924. (*Musikblätter des Anbruch* 6, Sonderheft Aug./Sept. 1924, 269–342 ◇ bibliog biog (W. Klein, P. Bekker, E. Stein, R. Kolisch, P. von Klenau, H. Eisler, H. Scherchen, D. J. Bach, P. A. Pisk, A. Berg)

SCHÖNBERG/60TH Arnold Schönberg zum 60. Geburtstag, 13. September 1934. [Wien: Universal, 1934] ◇ 75p biog (H. Jone, H. Jalowetz, E. Buschbeck, A. Webern, A. Hába, T. Wiesengrund-Adorno, E. Wellesz, E. Stein, E. Steuermann, O. Adler, A. Zemlinsky, J. Koffler, P. Stefan, W. Reich, K. Schulhofer, J. Polnauer, H. Brock, A. Berg, D. J. Bach)

SCHÖNBERG/70TH Homage to Schönberg. (*Modern Music* 21, 1944, 131–145) biog (E. Krenek, L. Harrison, K. List)

SCHÖNBERG/75TH [Arnold Schönberg Jubilee Issue.] (*The Canon, Australian Journal of Music* 3, Sept. 1949, 83–96) ◇ biog (D. Newlin, R. Liebowitz, F. Stiedry, P. A. Pisk, O. Klemperer, R. Kolisch, K. McIntyre)

SCHOLTE Verzamelde opstellen geschreven door oud-leeringen van professor Dr. J. H. Scholte. Amsterdam: J. M. Meulenhoff, 1947

SCHRADE Musik und Geschichte. [Leo Schrade zum sechzigsten Geburtstag]/ Music and History [Leo Schrade on the Occasion of His Sixtieth Birthday] Köln: Volk [1963] ◇ 206p

SCHRADE/D Leo Schrade. De scientia musicae studia atque orationes. Zum Gedächtnis der Verfassers hrsg. im Auftrag der Schweizerischen Musikforschenden Gesellschaft, Ortsgruppe Basel, von Ernst Lichtenhahn. Bern/Stuttgart: Paul Haupt, 1967. ◇ 623p bibliog biog

SCHRADE/M Leo Schrade in memoriam. Bern/München: Francke, 1966 ◇ 30p biog (P. Sacher, R. Stamm, E. Lichtenhahn, A. Schmitz)

SCHREIBER Volkstum und Kulturpolitik, eine Sammlung von Aufsätzen gewidmet Georg Schreiber zum 50. Geburtstag; hrsg. von H. Konen und J. P. Steffes. Köln: Gilde, 1932

SCHREIBER Georg Schreiber zum 80. Geburtstag 5. Januar 1962. (*Spanische Forschungen der Görresgesellschaft*, Reihe 1, *Gesammelte Aufsätze zur Kulturgeschichte Spaniens* 19–20) Münster Westfalen: Aschendorffsche Verlagsbuchhandlung, 1962

SCHREKER Franz Schreker zum 50. Geburtstag, 23. März 1928. (*Musikblätter des Anbruch* 10, Sonderdruck aus dem Märzheft 1928, 81–118) Wien: Universal,

1928 ◇ biog (A. Maril, F. L. Hörth, O. Erhardt, R. St. Hoffman, W. Gmeindl, G. Schünemann)

SCHREMS Musicus—Magister. Festgabe für Theobald Schrems zur Vollendung des 70. Lebensjahres; hrsg. von Georg Paul Köllner. Regensburg: F. Pustet, 1963 ◇ 226p biog (G. P. Köllner, R. Mauersberger, J. Stadler, H. Schrems)

SCHRIJNEN Donum natalicum Schrijnen. Versameling van opstellen door oudleerlingen en bevriende vakgenooten opgedrangen aan Mgr. Prof. Dr. Jos. Schrijnen bij gelegenheid van zijn zestigsten verjaardag, 3. Mei 1929. Nijmegen-Utrecht: Dekker & Van de Vegt, 1929

SCHÜTZ Festschrift Julius Franz Schütz; unter Mitwirkung der Steiermärkischen Landesbibliothek hrsg. und redig. von Berthold Sutter. Graz, Köln: Böhlau, 1954

SCHWARBER Festschrift Karl Schwarber. Beiträge zur Schweizer Bibliotheks- Buch- und Gelehrtengeschichte zum 60. Geburtstag am 22. Nov. 1949 dargebracht. Basel: Schwabe, 1949

SCHWEITZER/60TH Albert Schweitzer, mannen och hans gärning. Vänners hyllning till Lambarenesjukhusets 25-åriga tillvaro; utg. av Greta Lagerfelt. Uppsala: Lindblads, 1938 ◇ biog (E. Bangert, H. Ekman)

SCHWEITZER/70TH Albert Schweitzer Jubilee Book; ed. by A. A. Roback with the Cooperation of J. S. Bixler and George Sarton. Cambridge, Mass: Sci-Art Publishers [1945] ◇ biog (A. Ehlers)

SCHWEITZER/80TH Ehrfurcht vor dem Leben. Albert Schweitzer, eine Freundesgabe zu seinem 80. Geburtstag. Bern: Haupt [1955] ◇ biog (E. Bangert)

SCHWEITZER/80F Hommage à Albert Schweitzer [pour son quatre-vingtième anniversaire le 14 janvier 1955. Paris] Diffusion Le Guide [1955] ◇ biog (P. Casals, A. Cortot, A. Honegger, R. Minder)

SCHWEITZER/85TH Albert Schweitzer, Mensch und Werk, eine kleine Festgabe zu seinem 85. Geburtstag von Willy Bremi [u.a.] hrsg. im Auftr. des Hiffsvereins für das Albert Schweitzer-Spital in Lambarene. Bern/Stuttgart: Paul Haupt, 1959

SEEBACH Ehrengabe dramatischer Dichter und Komponisten Sr. Exzellenz dem Grafen Nikolaus von Seebach zum zwanzigjährigen Intendanten-Jubiläum. [Leipzig: K. Wolff] 1914

SEEMAN/75TH Festschrift zum 75. Geburtstag von Erich Seeman; hrsg. von Rolf Wilhelm Brednich. (*Jahrbuch für Volksliedforschung* 9) Berlin: Walter de Gruyter & Co., 1964 ◇ 181p bibliog (R. H. Brednich)

SEIDL/AN Anton Seidl, A Memorial by His Friends. New York: Scribner, 1899 ◇ 259p biog (H. T. Finck)

SEIDL/AR Musik und Kultur. Festschrift zum 50. Geburtstag Arthur Seidls; hrsg. von Bruno Schuhmann. Regensburg: G. Bosse [1913] ◇ 273p biog (B. Schuhmann)

SEIFFERT Musik und Bild. Festschrift Max Seiffert; in Verbindung mit Fachgenossen, Freunden und Schülern hrsg. von Heinrich Besseler. Kassel: Bärenreiter, 1938 ◇ 160p bibliog (T. Schneider)

SEIFFERT/70THA (*Archiv für Musikforschung* 3:1, 1938, 1–128) Leipzig: 1938 ◇ biog (Max Schneider)

SHAW G. B. S. 90. Aspects of Bernard Shaw's Life and Work . . . ; ed. by S. Winsten. London: Hutchinson, 1946

SIEBS Festschrift Theodor Siebs zum 70. Geburtstag 26. August 1932; hrsg. von Walther Steller. (*Germanistische Abhandlungen* 67) Breslau: M. & H. Marcus, 1933.

SIEVERS Germanica. Eduard Sievers zum 75. Geburtstage 25. November 1925. Halle/Saale: M. Niemeyer, 1925

SILVA Studi in onore di Pietro Silva. Firenze: F. Le Monnier [1957]

SINGER Festgabe Samuel Singer überreicht zum 12. Juli 1930 von Freunden und Schülern; hrsg. von Harry Maync unter Mitwirkungen von Gustav Keller und Marta Marti. Tübingen: Mohr, 1930

SJÖGREN Emil Sjögren in memoriam. Stockholm: Lundholm [1918] ◇ 90p biog (B. Sjögren, S. Elmblad, W. Peterson-Berger, G. Norlén, N. Söderblom)

SMEND Festschrift für Friedrich Smend zum 70. Geburtstag dargebracht von Freunden und Schülern. Berlin: Merseburger [1963] ◇ 100p bibliog (R. Elvers)

SÖHNGEN Gestalt und Glaube. Festschrift für Vizepräsident Professor D. Dr. Oskar Söhngen zum 60. Geburtstag am 5. Dezember 1960; hrsg. von einem Freundeskreis. Witten: Luther-Verlag/Berlin: Merseburger [1960]

SPG Festschrift zur Feier des 350jährigen Bestehens des protestantischen Gymnasiums zu Strassburg; hrsg. von der Lehrerschaft des protestantischen Gymnasiums. Strassburg: Heitz, 1888

STÄBLEIN/70TH Festschrift Bruno Stäblein zum 70. Geburtstag; hrsg. von Martin Ruhnke. Kassel: Bärenreiter, 1967 ◇ 326p bibliog (B. Mogge)

ŠTĚDROŇ "Univ. prof. dr. Bohumíru Štědroňovi, CSc., mositeli vyznamenání Za vynikajicí práci, k jeho šedesátinám věnůjí kolegové, spolupracovníci a žaci." (*Sborník Prací Filosofické Fakulty Brněnské University, Ročník* XVI, Řada Hudebněvědná (H), Č. 2) Brno: 1967 ◇ 171p bibliog (M. Štědroň)

STEIN Festschrift Fritz Stein zum 60. Geburtstag überreicht von Fachgenossen, Freunden und Schülern; hrsg. von H. Hoffmann und Fr. Rühlmann. Braunschweig: H. Litolff, 1939 ◇ 213p bibliog (K. von Pein)

STEINECKE "Diesen vierten Band seinem Gedächtnis . . . zu widmen." (*Darmstädter Beiträge zur Neuen Musik* 4, 1961, 1–128) Mainz: B. Schott's Söhne, 1962

STEUBEN Festschrift zur Feier des zweihundertjährigen Geburtstages von Baron Friedrich Wilhelm von Steuben. (*Deutsch-amerikanische Geschichtsblätter, Jahrbuch der deutsch-amerikanischen historischen Gesellschaft von Illinois* 30, 1930, 4–181) Chicago, 1930

STRAUBE Karl Straube zu seinem 70. Geburtstag; Gabe der Freunde. Leipzig: Koehler & Amelang, [1943] ◇ 387p biog (F. A. Beyerlein, J. N. David, W. Furtwängler, W. Gurlitt, K. Matthaei, H. Mitteis, F. Münch, G. Ramin, M. Schneider, B. Schwarz, K. Thomas)

STRAUSS, F. Festschrift Dr. Franz Strauss zum 70. Geburtstag. Tutzing: Hans Schneider, 1967 ◇ 160p biog (G. Bodechtel, F. Grasberger, R. Hartmann, B. Hauptmann, E. Hilbert, G. K. Kende, L. Kusche, K. Overhoff, S. v. Scanzoni, S. Konrad)

STRAVINSKY/70TH Igor Strawinsky zum siebzigsten Geburtstag. (*Musik der Zeit, eine Schriftenreihe zur zeitgenössischen Musik*) London/Bonn: Boosey & Hawkes, 1952 ◇ 78p bibliog discog biog (H. H. Stuckenschmidt, G.-F. Malipiero, A. Honegger, W. Grohmann, T. Karsavina, I. Markevitch, F. Ballo, H. Boys, G. von Einem, C. Stuart, A. Cortot, E. Ansermet, W. Egk, E. W. White, F. Fricsay, P. Sacher, E. Zanetti, M. See, H. Mersmann)

STRAVINSKY/75TH [In Honor of Stravinsky's 75th birthday] (*The Score & I.M.A. Magazine* 20, June 1957, 1–76) ◇ biog (R. Craft, H. Boys, R. Sessions, R. Gerhard, M. Perrin, D. Drew)

STRAVINSKY/80TH Special Issue for Igor Stravinsky on His 80th Anniversary. (*Musical Quarterly* 48, 1962, 287–384) ◇ bibliog (C. D. Wade) biog (P. H. Lang, B. Schwarz, E. T. Cone)

STRAVINSKY/80TH/W Igor Strawinsky, eine Sonderreihe des Westdeutschen Rundfunks zum 80. Geburtstag; hrsg. von Otto Tomek. Köln: Westdeutscher Rundfunk, 1963 ◇ 86p biog (L. Schrade, P. Souvtchinsky, H. Kirchmeyer, A. von

Milloss, K. H. Ruppel, J. Cocteau, H. Lindlar, H. Curjel, R. Schubert, R. Vlad, P. Boulez, P. Sacher, O. F. Schuh)

STRECKER Studien zur lateinischen Dichtung des Mittelalters. Ehrengabe für Karl Strecker zum 4. September 1931; hrsg. von W. Stach und H. Walther. Dresden: W. und B. v. Baensch Stiftung, 1931

STRICH Weltliteratur. Festgabe für Fritz Strich zum 70. Geburtstag; im Verbindung mit W. Henzen hrsg. von W. Muschg und E. Staiger. Bern: Francke, 1952

STRÖMBÄCK Folkloristica. Festskrift till Dag Strömbäck 13 augusti 1960. (*Saga och Sed, Kungl. Gustav Adolfs Akademiens Årsbok,* 1960) Uppsala: 1961

STUMMVOLL Festschrift für Josef Strummvoll, Alios Kisser, Ernst Trenkler zum 50. Geburtstage dargebracht von Kollegen, Freunden und Mitarbeitern; zusammengestellt von Michael Stickler und Bruno Zimmel in Zusammenarbeit mit Walter Kreig. (*Das Antiquariat* 8/13–18, Aug. 15, 1952, 1–94)

STUTEN In memoriam Jan Stuten 15 Aug. 1890–25. Febr. 1948; im Auftrag von M. Steiner hrsg. durch W. Teichert und F. Wörsching. Dornach, Schweiz, 1949 ◇ 56p bibliog (F. Wörsching) biog (L. F. Edmunds, F. Wörsching, W. Teichert, H. O. Proskauer)

SUBIRÁ/80TH En homenaje al Excmo. Sr. D. José Subirá en su 80 aniversario. (*Anuario Musical* 18, 1963, 1–239) Barcelona: Consejo Superior de Investigaciones Científicas, Institut Español de Musicología, 1965 ◇ bibliog (J. M. Llorens) biog (J. M. Llorens)

SUCHIER Forschung zur romanischen Philologie. Festgabe für Hermann Suchier zum 15. März 1900. Halle: M. Niemeyer, 1900

SUFL Mélanges 1945. (*Publications de la faculté des lettres de l'université de Strasbourg* 104–108) Paris: Les Belles Lettres, 1946–1947

SUIDA Studies in the History of Art Dedicated to William E. Suida on His Eightieth Birthday. New York: Phaidon, 1959

SWINDLER [Dedicated to Mary H. Swindler] (*American Journal of Archeology* 50/2, 1946, 217–340)

TEGNÉR Studier tillegnade Esias Tegnér den 13 januari 1918. Lund: C. W. K. Gleerups Förlag, 1918.

THOMPSON Studies in Folklore in Honor of Distinguished Service Professor Stith Thompson. (*Indiana University Publications, Folklore Series* 9) Bloomington: Indiana Univ. Press, 1957

TIEMANN Libris et litteris. Festschrift für Hermann Tiemann zum 60. Geburtstag am 9. Juli 1959; hrsg. von C. Voigt & E. Zimmermann. Hamburg: Maximilian Gesellschaft, 1959

TILLYARD see WELLESZ/TILLYARD

TIPPETT/60TH Michael Tippett. A Symposium on His 60th Birthday; ed. by Ian Kemp. London: Faber & Faber, 1965 ◇ 242p bibliog biog (E. W. White, B. Britten, S. Wanamaker, A. Bliss, P. Heyworth, P. R. Fricker, H. Schmidt-Isserstedt, A. Bush, N. Brainin, M. Kitchin, P. Pears, A. Copland, H. Hartog, N. Del Mar, B. Hepworth, Y. Menuhin, I. Berlin, D. Ayerst, S. Morrison, J. Amis, P. Rainer, A. Hopkins, A. Deller, W. Bergmann, R. Donington, W. Mann, P. Evans, W. Mellers, A. Ridout, C. Mason, A. Milner)

TITCHENER Studies in Psychology, Contributed by Colleagues and Former Students of Edward Bradford Titchener. Worcester, Mass.: L. N. Wilson, 1917

TODD Todd Memorial Volumes. Philological Studies ed. by John D. Fitzgerald and Pauline Taylor. New York: Columbia Univ. Press, 1930

TRIER Festschrift für Jost Trier zu seinem 60. Geburtstag am 15. Dezember 1954; hrsg. von Benno von Weise und Karl Heinz Borck. Meisenheim: A. Hain, 1954

TYLOR Anthropological Essays Presented to Edward Burnett Tylor in Honour of His 75th Birthday, Oct. 2, 1907. Oxford: Clarendon Press, 1907

UNIVERSAL 25 Jahre neue Musik. Jahrbuch 1926 der Universal-Edition; hrsg. von Hans Heinsheimer and Paul Stefan. Wien: Universal [1926] ◇ 279p

UUTF Festskrift utgiven av Teologiska fakulteten i Upsala, 1941, till 400-årsminnet av Bibelns utgivande på svenska, 1541. Upsala: A.-B. Lundquist/Leipzig: O. Harrassowitz [1941]

VARONA Y PERA Homenage a Enrique José Varona y Pera en el cincuentenario de su primer curso de filosofía. La Habana: Molina, 1935

VECCHIO Studi filosofico-giuridici dedicati a Giorgio del Vecchio nel XXV anno di insegnamento, 1904–1929. Modena: Società Tipografica Modenese, 1930–1931

VERMEYLEN Gedenkboek A. Vermeylen. 's-Gravenhage: Nijhoff [1932]

VIANEY Mélanges de philologie, d'histoire et de littérature offerts à Joseph Vianey. Paris: Presses Françaises, 1934

VIRGIL Virgilio nel medio evo. (*Studi medievali*, n.s.5) Torino: G. Chiantore, 1932

VIVES Joseph Vives zum goldenen Priesterjubiläum 20. Oktober 1963. (*Spanische Forschungen der Görresgesellschaft*, Reihe 1, *Gesammelte Aufsätze zur Kulturgeschichte Spaniens* 21) Münster Westfalen: Aschendorffsche Verlagsbuchhandlung, 1963

VNB Festschrift der Nationalbibliothek in Wien; hrsg. zur Feier des 200jährigen Bestehens des Gebäudes. Wien: Österreichische Staatsdruckerei, 1926

VORSTIUS Bibliothek, Bibliothekar, Bibliothekswissenschaft. Festschrift Joris Vorstius zum 60. Geburtstag dargebracht; unter Mitarbeit von W. Göber, H. Kunze und E. Paunel hrsg. von H. Roloff. Leipzig: Harrassowitz, 1954

WAESBERGHE Organicae voces. Festschrift Joseph Smits van Waesberghe angeboten anlässlich seines 60. Geburtstages 18. April 1961. [Amsterdam: Instituut voor Middeleeuwse Muziekwetenschap, 1963] ◇ 180p bibliog

WAGNER Festschrift Peter Wagner zum 60. Geburtstag gewidmet von Kollegen, Schülern und Freunden; hrsg. von K. Weinmann. Leipzig: Breitkopf & Härtel, 1926 ◇ 237p

WAHLE Funde und Forschungen. Eine Festgabe für Julius Wahle zum 15. Februar 1921, dargebracht von Werner Deetjen, Max Friedlaender . . . Leipzig: Inselverlag, 1921

WALEY Arthur Waley Anniversary Volume. (*Asia Major* 7, London 1959, 1–227)

WALZEL Vom Geiste neuer Literaturforschung. Festschrift für Oskar Walzel; hrsg. von Julius Wahle und Viktor Klemperer. Wildpark-Potsdam: Athenaion [1924]

WARTENWEILER Gespräch und Begegnung. Gabe der Freunde zum 70. Geburtstag von Fritz Wartenweiler; hrsg. von den Freunden schweizerischer Volksbildungsheime zum 20. August 1959. Zürich: Rotapfel, 1959

WEBERN Anton Webern zum 50. Geburtstag. (*23, eine wiener Musikzeitschrift* 14. Feb. 1934, 1–25) ◇ biog (W. Reich)

WEBERN/R Anton Webern. (*Die Reihe* 2) Wien: Universal [1955]; [English edition] Bryn Mawr: Presser [1958] ◇ 100p bibliog biog (F. Wildgans, H. Eimert, K. Stockhausen, P. Boulez, C. Wolff)

WEINGARTNER Festschrift für Dr. Felix Weingartner zu seinem siebzigsten Geburtstag; hrsg. von der Allgemeinen Musikgesellschaft, Basel, 2. Juni 1933. [Basel: H. Oppermann, 1933] ◇ 167p bibliog (I. Schaefer) biog (E. Bienenfeld, R. Petit, A. Cortot, O. Maag, L. D. Green, E. von Sauer, C. B. Oldman, A. Botstiber, F. Hirt, A. Müry, B. Paumgartner, J. Homberg, W. Merian, H. Oppermann)

WELLESZ/80TH Essays Presented to Egon Wellesz; ed. by Jack Westrup. Oxford: Clarendon Press, 1966 ◇ 188p

WELLESZ/TILLYARD Studies in Eastern Chant, v.1; ed. by Miloš Velimirović. London: Oxford Univ. Press, 1966 ◇ 134p bibliog

WICHMANN Juhlakirja Yrjö Wichmannin kuusikymmenenvuotipäiväksi. (*Suomalais-ugrilainen Seura, Helsingfors. Suomalais-ugrilaisen Seura Toimituksia* 58) Helsinki: 1928

WILCOX Studies in Honor of John Wilcox by Members of the English Department, Wayne State University. Detroit: Wayne State Univ. Press, 1958

WILMANNS Beiträge zur Bücherkunde und Philologie, August Wilmanns zum 25. März 1903 gewidmet. Leipzig: O. Harrassowitz, 1903

WILMOTTE Mélanges Maurice Wilmotte. Paris: Champion, 1910

WIORA/60TH Festschrift für Walter Wiora zum 30. Dezember 1966; hrsg. von Ludwig Finscher und Christoph-Hellmut Mahling. Kassel: Bärenreiter, 1967. ◇ 678p bibliog (H. Kühn)

WK Festschrift zur 900-Jahr-Feier des Klosters [Weingarten] 1056–1956; ein Beitrag zur Geistes- und Gütergeschichte der Abtei. Weingarten: Abtei, 1956

WLH Kirchenmusik, Vermächtnis und Aufgabe, 1948–1958. Festschrift zum zehnjährigen Bestehen der westfälischen Landeskirchenmusikschule in Herford; hrsg. von Wilhelm Ehmann. [Darmstadt-Eberstadt: K. Merseburger, 1958?] ◇ 109p bibliog (W. Ehmann) discog hist (H. Henche, W. Ehmann, F. Ehmann)

WÖLFFLIN Festschrift Heinrich Wölfflin zum siebzigsten Geburtstage. Dresden: W. Jess, 1935

WOLF Musikwissenschaftliche Beiträge. Festschrift für Johannes Wolf zu seinem sechzigsten Geburtstag; hrsg. von W. Lott, H. Osthoff und W. Wolffheim. Berlin: M. Breslauer, 1929 ◇ 221p

WOOD Sir Henry Wood; Fifty Years of the Proms . . . London: British Broadcasting Corp. [1944] ◇ 64p biog (W. W. Thompson, T. Burke, C. B. Rees, A. Bax, B. Shore, Solomon, G. Baker, R. Hill, F. Dobson, C. E. M. Joad, J. Agate, S. Sitwell)

WOSSIDLO Volkskundliche Beiträge. Richard Wossidlo am 26. Januar 1939 zum Dank dargebracht von Freunden und Verehreren und dem Verlag. Neumünster: K. Wachholtz, 1939

WROTH Essays honoring Lawrence C. Wroth. Portland, Maine: [Anthoensen] 1951

ZAHN Festgabe für Theodor Zahn. Leipzig: A. Deichert 1928

ZOBELTITZ Von Büchern und Menschen. Festschrift Fedor von Zobeltitz zum 5. Oktober 1927 überreicht von der Gesellschaft der Bibliophilen. Weimar: Gesellschaft der Bibliophilen, 1927

ZODER [Raimund Zoder zum 75. Geburtstag] Geleitet von Karl M. Klier, Leopold Nowak, Leopold Schmidt. (*Jahrbuch des österreichischen Volksliedwerkes* 6) Wien, 1957 ◇ 227p bibliog (M. Kundegraber) biog (K. Lugmayer)

ZUCKER Festschrift für Friedrich Zucker zum 70. Geburtstag. Berlin: Akademie-Verlag, 1954

ZWEIBRÜCKEN Zweibrücken, 600 Jahre Stadt, 1352–1952. Festschrift zur 600-Jahrfeier; im Auftrag der Stadtverwaltung Zweibrücken hrsg. Zweibrücken: Historischer Verein, 1952

II

Classified Listing of Articles

GENERAL AND LOCAL HISTORY

1a Andersson, Otto. Instrumenthistorien såsom vetenskap. ANDERSSON, O./85TH 1–6; orig. in *Budklaven* 4 (1925) 33–40

1b Besseler, Heinrich. Das Wesen der Musik in heutiger Sicht. WIORA/60TH 27–30

1c Bösken, Franz. Beiträge zur Geschichte der Kirchen- und Schulmusik im Emsland. FELLERER/60THM 147–195

1d Borren, Charles van den. Musique expérimentale à travers les âges. HANDSCHIN/I 186–190

1e Dalhaus, Carl. Historismus und Tradition. MÜLLER-BLATTAU/70TH 46–58

2 Dent, Edward J. The Universal Aspect of Musical History. ADLER 7–11

2a Doflein, Erich. Historismus und Historisierung in der Musik. WIORA/60TH 48–56

3 Einstein, Alfred. Die deutsche Musiker-Autobiographie. FRIEDLAENDER 57–66

3a Grout, Donald J. "Adaptation" as a Hypothesis in the History of Music. WIORA/60TH 73–78

4 Hutschenruyter, Wouter. Componeerende gekroonde hoofden. SCHEURLEER 169–175

5 Kamieński, Lucian. Musikhistorische Grenzforschungen. SEIDL/AR 223–233

5a Kümmel, Werner F. Der Historiker Heinrich v. Sybel als Schüler Siegfried Wilhelm Dehns. ENGEL 200–220

6 Liess, Andreas. Prolegomena zu einer Weltmusikgeschichtsschreibung. OREL/70TH 103–111

6a Linden, Albert van der. Les manuels scolaires d'histoire de Belgique et l'histoire de la musique. BORREN/75TH 231–241

7 Łobaczewska, Stefania. Z zagadnień metodycznych historii muzyki. [Concerning a Methodical History of Music] CHYBIŃSKI/70TH 120–145

8 Lorenz, Alfred. Neue Gedanken zur Klangspaltung und Klangverschmelzung. SCHERING 137–150

8a Mahling, Christoph-Hellmut. Zur Soziologie des Chorwesens. MÜLLER-BLATTAU/70TH 192–200

9 Mersmann, Hans. Zur Stilgeschichte der Musik. FRIEDLAENDER 67–78

10 Moser, Hans Joachim. De mari interno quasi vinculo musico gentium accolentium. MOSER/70TH 252–254; orig. in *Atti del Congresso Internazionale di Musica Mediterranea e del Convegno dei Bibliotecari Musicali* (Palermo 1959)

11 ——. Historie, Historik, und Historismus. MOSER/70TH 8–9; orig. in *Musik und Kirche* 23 (1953)

12 ——. Ist Tradition Schlamperei? MOSER/70TH 244–247

13 ——. Neuralgische Punkte der Musikgeschichte. MOSER/70TH 9–12; orig. in *Neue Musikzeitung* 4 (1950)

13a ——. Zur Musikbegabung der Althessen. GUTBIER 125–130

14 Mueren, Floris van der. Pourquoi l'histoire universelle se désintéresse-t-elle de l'histoire de la musique? FELLERER/60TH 368–376

15 Ochlewski, Tadeusz. Z dziejów pracy wydawniczej prof. A. Chybińskiego [From the Published Works of Prof. A. Chybiński] CHYBIŃSKI/70TH 380–389

16 Orel, Alfred. Der Wandel der Musik im Spiegel ihrer Niederschrift. OREL 23–32

17 Pannwitz, Rudolf. Betrachtung über den Wert der Geschichte. SEIDL/AR 137–151

17a Quaglia, Mario. La "Cappella Puerorum Cantantium" del Duoma di Asti. DESDERI/70TH 119–122

17b Refardt, Edgar. Anfänge des Musiklebens im Aargau. GÜNTHER 208–216

17c Schrade, Leo. Diabolus in musica. SCHRADE/D 537–555; orig. in *Melos* 26 (1959) 361–373

17d ——. Eine Einführung in die Musikgeschichtsschreibung älterer Zeit. SCHRADE/D 17–34; orig. in *Musikerziehung* 7 (1930) 3–13

18 Siegmund-Schultze, Walther. Zum Problem Wort und Ton. BESSELER 465–474

18a Trojan, Jan. Zur Problematik des sog. Archaismus in der Musik. ŠTĚDROŇ/60TH 129–136, summary in Czech at end of article

18b Waesberghe, Joseph Smits van.

Der Niederländer in seinen sprachlichen, tänzerischen und musikalischen Äusserungen. BALDELLÓ 185–199
19 Westphal, Kurt. Französische und deutsche Musikentwicklung. MERSMANN 164–170
19a Wiora, Walter. Lex und Gratia in der Musik. MÜLLER-BLATTAU/70TH 330–340
20 Wolff, Hellmuth Christian. Geschichte und Wertbegriff. BLUME/F 398–405
21 Wustmann, Rudolf. Individualismus als musikgeschichtlicher Begriff. LAMPRECHT 214–224

ANTIQUITY: GENERAL

21a Behn, Friedrich. Wagen oder Musikinstrument? JAHN, J. 13–16
22 Bielefeld, Erwin. Ein boiotischer Tanzchor des 6. Jh. v. Chr. ZUCKER 27–35
23 Gerlach, Hermann. Die musikalische Proportion. RASPE 1–7
24 Kraiker, W. Aus dem Musterbuch eines pompejanischen Wandmalers. ROBINSON I, 801–807
25 Landsberger, Benno. Die angebliche babylonische Notenschrift. OPPENHEIM 170–178
25a Stauder, Wilhelm. Ein Musiktraktat aus dem zweiten vorchristlichen Jahrtausend. WIORA/60TH 157–163
26 ——. Zur Frühgeschichte der Laute. OSTHOFF 15–25
26a Zagiba, Franz. Von der keltischen Carnyz I zum Alphorn. WIORA/60TH 609–612

ANTIQUITY: EGYPT

27 Baillet, Auguste, & Jules Baillet. La Chanson chez les Egyptiens. MASPERO I/i, 121–135
28 Borchardt, Ludwig. Die Rahmentrommel im Museum zu Kairo. MASPERO I/i, 1–6
29 Closson, Ernest. Une nouvelle série des hautbois égyptiens antiques. ADLER 17–25
30 Sainte-Fare Garnot, Jean. L'Offrande musicale dans l'ancienne Egypte. MASSON I, 89–92
31 Hickmann, Hans. L'Essor de la musique sous l'Ancien Empire de l'Egypte pharaonique (2778–2423 av. J.-C.) ORTIZ II, 831–836
32 ——. Le Jeu de la harpe dans l'Egypte ancienne. LEXA 449–456
33 ——. Musikerziehung im alten Ägypten. MERSMANN 55–63
33a ——. Pharaonic jingles. SACHS/C 45–70
33b ——. Sonderformen antiker Becken. WIORA/60TH 193–195
34 Pasini, Francesco. A propos d'une contradiction de Diodore de Sicile. RIEMANN 185–189
35 Sachs, Curt. Die altägyptischen Namen der Harfe. KRETZSCHMAR 127
36 ——. Zweiklänge im Altertum. WOLF 168–170
37 Schott, S. Der Gott des Harfenspiels. MASPERO I/ii, 457–462
38 Skalska-Zunova, M. Konstruktsii arfy i igra na arfe v drevnem Egipte [The Construction and Playing of Egyptian Harps] LEXA 457–481
39 Stracmans, M. Osiris-Dionysos et les chants des harpistes. LEFORT 207–214

ANTIQUITY: GREECE AND ROME

See also no. 2082f

40 Abert, Hermann. Antike Musikerlegenden. LILIENCRON 1–16
41 ——. Der gegenwärtige Stand der Forschung über die antike Musik. FRIEDLAENDER 21–40
42 Adams, S. M. Salamis Symphony; The *Persae* of Aeschylus. NORWOOD 46–54
43 Barbour, J. Murray. The Principles of Greek Notation. KINKELDEY/80TH 1–17
44 Bell, H. I. A Musical Competition in the Third Century B.C. LUMBROSO 13–22
45 Bodley, Nicholas B. The Auloi of Meroë, a Study of the Greek-Egyptian Auloi found at Meroë, Egypt. SWINDLER 217–240
46 Boyance, Pierre. Les Muses et l'harmonie des sphères. GRAT 3–16
46a Crocker, Richard L. Aristoxenus and Greek Mathematics. REESE/65TH 96–110
46b Dahlhaus, Carl. Ein vergessenes Problem der antiken Konsonanztheorie. WIORA/60TH 164–169
47 Düring, Ingemar. Studies in Musical Terminology in 5th-Century Literature. LÖFSTEDT 176–197
48 Eitrem, Sam. Opferaufzug und Opfermusik auf korinthischen Amphoriskos. OIKONOMOS 25–34
49 Fairclough, H. Rushton. The

Connection between Music and Poetry in Early Greek Literature. GILDERSLEEVE 205–227
50 Fischer, Wilhelm. Das Grablied des Seikilos, der einzige Zeuge des antiken weltlichen Liedes. AMMANN I, 153–165
51 Guhrauer, Heinrich. Zur Frage der Mehrstimmigkeit in der griechischen Musik. HERTZ 169–188
52 Hommel, Hildebrecht. Das Apollonorakel in Didyma. Pflege alter Musik im spätantiken Gottesdienst. SMEND 7–18
53 Huchzermeyer, Helmut. Die Bedeutung und Stellung der Musik in der griechischen Tragödie. GSHG 63–71
53a Hunger, Herbert & Egert Pöhlmann. Neue griechische Musikfragmente aus ptolemäischer Zeit in der Papyrussammlung der Österreichischen Nationalbibliothek. KRAUS 51–78
54 Jan, Karl von. Die Musikinstrumente der Griechen und Römer. LGR 24–30
55 Kuiper, K. Woord en lied. MENGELBERG 135–138
56 Lachmann, Robert. Die Weise vom Löwen und der pythische Nomos. WOLF 97–106
56a Lippmann, Edward A. The Place of Music in the System of Liberal Arts. REESE/65TH 545–559
57 Lohmann, Johannes. Der Ursprung der Musik. GURLITT 148–173
58 Paribeni, R. Cantores graeci nell'ultimo secolo della repubblica in Roma. LUMBROSO 287–292
59 Regnier, Anne-Marie. Un Type de concours musical dans l'antiquité. Les Épreuves musicales aux jeux pythiques et la signification des concours dans la Grèce archaïque et la période classique. BORREN 260–282
60 Roussel, Louis. Bel canto et Sophocle. NAVARRE 371–374
61 Sachs, Curt. Lituus und Karnyx. LILIENCRON 241–246
62 ——. Muses and Scales. DAVISON 3–8
63 ♪ Seikilos' song. AMMANN I, 161
64 Six, J. Het geluid van de Salpinx. MENGELBERG 139–141
65 Vaněk, Ferd. Byla řecká hudba vícehlasá? Příspěvek k řešení staré otázky. [Was Greek Music Polyphonic? A Contribution to the Solution of an Old Question] KRAL 215–224
66 Vetter, Walther. Zur Erforschung der antiken Musik. SCHNEIDER/60TH 137–146
67 Vogel, Martin. Harmonikale Deutung eines pythagoreischen Spruches. SCHMIDT-GÖRG 377–382
67a Werner, Eric. Greek Ideas on Music in Judeo-Arabic Literature. SACHS/C 71–96
67b Wille, Günther. Singen und Sagen in der Dichtung des Horaz. HOMMEL 169–184
68 Wilmanns, August. Über Vitruv V. 4. MOMMSEN 254–261

ANTIQUITY: JEWISH MUSIC

See also nos. 67a, 106d, 169, 192a

69 ♪ Aschkenazy chant. *Waj'chullu haschomajim.* JOHNER 48
70 Binder, Abraham Wolfe. *V' shomru,* a Century of Musical Interpretations. ABRAHAMS 53–65
71 Büchler, A. Zur Geschichte des Tempelcultus in Jerusalem. CHWOLSON 1–41
72 Gerson-Kiwi, Edith. Halleluia and Jubilus in Hebrew-Oriental Chant. BESSELER 43–49
72a ——. "Justus ut Palma." STÄBLEIN/70TH 64–73
73 Idelsohn, Abraham Zevi. Collections of and Literature on Synagogue Song. FREIDUS 388–403
74 ——. Songs and Singers of the Synagogue in the Eighteenth Century, with Special Reference to the Birnbaum Collection of the Hebrew Union College Library. HUC 397–424
75 ♪ Nadel, Arno. *L' dovid mismaur!* SCHAEFER xiii–xvi
76 ♪ Peissachowitsch, J. Benno. *Mah nômar l'fonecho jôschëw morôm.* ROSENHEIM 451–458
76a Werner, Eric. An Early Compendium of Ashkenazic Synagogue Music. HUCKL 110–121
77 Yasser, Joseph. The Magrepha of the Herodian Temple: A Five-fold Hypothesis. KINKELDEY/80TH 24–42
78 ♪ Yemenite Chant. *Wajikro mauschah.* JOHNER 49

MIDDLE AGES: GENERAL

See also nos. 56a, 405, 407, 439c, 747a, 2130a, 2187

79 Anglés, Higinio. Musikalische Beziehungen zwischen Deutschland

und Spanien in der Zeit vom 5. bis 14. Jahrhundert. GURLITT 5–20
80 ——. Musikalische Beziehungen zwischen Österreich und Spanien in der Zeit vom 14. bis 18. Jahrhundert. SCHENK 5–14
80a ——. Die Rolle Spaniens in der mittelalterlichen Musikgeschichte. SCHREIBER I, 1–24
80b ——. Sakraler Gesang und Musik in den Schriften Gregors des Grossen. WELLESZ/80TH 33–42
81 Borren, Charles van den. De verschillende betekenissen van het woord *Gothiek*, wat de beoordeling van de kunstwerken, in het bijzonder de muzikale, betreft. MUEREN 177–182
82 Chailley, Jacques. La Musique médiévale vue par le XVIIIe et le XIXe siècle. MASSON I, 95–103
82a Durán Gudiol, Antonio. La capilla de música de la Catedral de Huesca. BALDELLÓ 29–55
82b Dworzyńska, Wiesława. Kultura muzyczna Warsawy w okresie średniowiecza i renesansu. FEICHT 190–197
83 Evans, Seiriol. Ely Almonry Boys and Choristers in the Later Middle Ages. JENKINSON 155–163
83a Gerson-Kiwi, Edith. Der Sinn des Sinnlosen in der Interpolation sakraler Gesänge. WIORA/60TH 520–528
83b Günther, Ursula. Die Musiker des Herzogs von Berry. APEL/70TH 81–95
84 Gurlitt, Wilibald. Ars musica. ROTHACKER 373–376
85 Handschin, Jacques. Die Anfänge des Kirchengesanges in der Schweiz. HANDSCHIN 188–191; orig. in *Neue Zürcher Zeitung* 939 (1934)
86 ——. Der Geist des Mittelalters in der Musik. HANDSCHIN 70–81; orig. in *Neue Schweizer Rundschau* 20 (1927)
87 ——. Mittelalterliche Kulturprobleme der Schweiz. HANDSCHIN 175–187; orig in *Neue Zürcher Zeitung* 211, 219, & 226 (1931)
88 ——. Die religiöse Lyrik des Mittelalters. HANDSCHIN 150–160; orig. in *Neue Zürcher Zeitung* 393 & 406 (1933)
89 Kolsrud, Oluf. Korsongen i Nidarosdamen. SANDVIK 83–122
90 Komorzynski, Egon. Die Sankt-Nikolausbruderschaft in Wien (1288 bis 1782). FISCHER/W 71–74
90a Maróthy, János. A középkori tömegzene alkalmai és formái—The Occasions and Forms of Popular Music in the Middle Ages. KODÁLY/70TH 439–494
90b Messenger, Ruth Ellis. De nominibus Domini. BUSZIN 15–20
90c Meyer-Baer, Kathi. Music in Dante's *Divina Commedia*. REESE/65TH 614–627
91 Moberg, Carl Allen. Die hl. Birgitta von Schweden und die Musik. FELLERER/60TH 336–349
92 Moser, Hans Joachim. Die Entstehung des Durgedankens, ein kulturgeschichtliches Problem. MOSER/70TH 13–31; orig. in *SIMG* 15 (1913/1914)
93 Müller, Hermann. Zur Musikauffassung des Mittelalters. KRETZSCHMAR 96–100
94 Norlind, Tobias. Säng och harpenspel under vikingatiden. SANDVIK 173–183
95 Orel, Alfred. Das Erwachen des nordischen Geistes. OREL 10–22
95a Querol, Miguel. Notes sobre la música en la Iglesia Latina de los siglos III–VI. BALDELLÓ 155–166
96 Radó Polykarp. Mittelalterliche liturgische Handschriften deutscher, italienischer und französischer Herkunft in den Bibliotheken Südosteuropas. MOHLBERG II, 349–392
97 Raugel, Félix. Notes pour servir à l'histoire musicale de la Collégiale de Saint-Quentin depuis les origines jusqu'en 1679. BESSELER 51–58
97a Reaney, Gilbert. The Performance of Medieval Music. REESE/65TH 704–722
98 ——. Terminology and Medieval Music. BESSELER 149–153
99 Ribera, Julián. Origen árabe de algunas voces románicas relacionadas con la música: *segrel*, *travador*, etc. MICHAËLIS 646–657
100 Rubió y Lluch, A. El Sentiment poétic de la música en el Dante i en fra Lluis de Leon. MICHAËLIS 35–54
101 Sachs, Curt. Primitive and Medieval Music: A Parallel. KINKELDEY/80TH 43–49
102 Salmen, Walter. Die internationale Wirksamkeit slawischer und magyarischer Musik vor 1600. AUBIN 235–242
103 Schering, Arnold. Über Musikhören und Musikempfinden im Mittelalter. FRIEDLAENDER 41–56
104 Schmid, Hans, & Ernest Waeltner. *Lexicon musicum latinum*, ein Unter-

nehmen zur Erforschung der musikalischen Fachsprache des Mittelalters. WAESBERGHE 145–148
104a Schmidt-Görg, Joseph. Zur Musikanschauung in den Schriften der hl. Hildegard. LÜTZELER 230–237
104b Schrade, Leo. Die Darstellung der Töne an den Kapitellen der Abteikirche zu Cluny, ein Beitrag zum Symbolismus in mittelalterlicher Kunst. SCHRADE/D 113–151; orig. in *Deutsche Vierteljahrsschrift für Literaturwissenschaft und Geistesgeschichte* 7 (1929) 229–266
105 Szabolcsi, Bence. Die ungarischen Spielleute des Mittelalters. ABERT 154–164
106 Ursprung, Otto. Freisings mittelalterliche Musikgeschichte. CORBINIANUS 245–278
106a Vogel, Martin. Musica falsa und falso bordone. WIORA/60TH 170–176
106b Waesberghe, Joseph Smits van. Singen und Dirigieren der mehrstimmigen Musik im Mittelalter. Was Miniaturen uns hierüber lehren. CROZET 1345–1354
106c Wellesz, Egon. Über die Zusammenhänge zwischen dem Gesang der Ost- und Westkirche. MICHELS 155–159
106d Werner, Eric. The Genesis of the Liturgical Sanctus. WELLESZ/80TH 19–32
107 ——. *If I speak in the tongues of men . . . :* St. Paul's Attitude toward Music. KINKELDEY/80TH 18–23
108 Wiora, Walter. Elementare Melodietypen als Abschnitte mittelalterlicher Liedweisen. ANGLÉS II, 993–1009
109 Wolf, Johannes. Neue Quellen zur mittelalterlichen Musikgeschichte. HARNACK 218–226
110 Zagiba, Franz. Die *Conversio Bagoariorum et Carantanorum* als musikgeschichtliche Quelle. Beitrag zur Geschichte der Musik in Bayern und Österreich im Frühmittelalter. ANGLÉS II, 1023–1051

MIDDLE AGES: BYZANTINE CHANT
See also nos. 158, 186a

111 Baumstark, A. Ein Formaltyp antiken Kultgesangs in christlicher Liturgie des Morgen- und Abendlandes? SCHRIJNEN 788–806
112 Borgia, Nilo. L'ultima eco del canto bizantino nella magna Graecia. LAMPROS 162–169
112a Dévai, Gábor. Akathistos-Prooemia in Byzantine Musical Manuscripts in Hungary. WELLESZ/TILLYARD 1–8
113 Di Salvo, Bartolomeo. Le antiche raccolte musicali bizantine. HANDSCHIN/I 97–106
113a Dragoumis, Markos. The Survival of Byzantine Chant in the Monophonic Music of the Modern Greek Church. WELLESZ/TILLYARD 9–36
113b Engberg, Gudrun. Greek Ekphonetic Neumes and Masoretic Accents. WELLESZ/TILLYARD 37–49
114 Handschin, Jacques. Byzantinische Musik. HANDSCHIN 304–305; orig. in *Neue Zürcher Zeitung* 939 (1934)
115 ——. Kirchengesang aus dem Osten. HANDSCHIN 296–299; orig in *Neue Zürcher Zeitung* 1094 (1935)
116 ♪ Hieronymus Tragodistes. *O pascha to mega.* JEPPESEN 105
116a Jakobson, Roman. Methodius' Canon to Demetrius of Thessalonica and the Old Church Slavonic Hirmoi. RACEK/60TH 115–121
116b ♪ Laskaris, John. *Te ten oraiō* (Ms. Athens. Natl. Lib. 2406). REESE/65TH 827–831
117 Levy, Kenneth. The Slavic Kontakia and their Byzantine Originals. QC 79–87
117a Milojković-Djurić, Jelena. Papadika u Hilandarskom neumskom rukopisu broj 311 [Papadika in the Neumatic Manuscript 311 from Chilander] OSTROGORSKY 273–285, summary in English
117b ——. A Papadike from Skoplje. WELLESZ/TILLYARD 50–56
117c ♪ Prooemium no. 1 (Ms. Budapest. Natl. Széchényi Lib. Oct. Graec. 9, f47v–48r). WELLESZ/TILLYARD 4–5
117d ♪ Prooemium no. 2 (Ms. Budapest. Natl. Széchényi Lib., Oct. Graec., f48r–49r). WELLESZ/TILLYARD 6–8
117e Raasted, Jørgen. Some Reflections on Byzantine Musical Style. WELLESZ/TILLYARD 57–66
117f Stefanović, Dimitrije. Codex Peribleptos. OSTROGORSKY 393–398
117g —— and Miloš Velimirović. Peter Lampadarios and Metropolitan Serafim of Bosnia. WELLESZ/TILLYARD 67–88
117h ♪ Sticheron no. 5 (Ms. Athens. Natl. Lib. 2147, f14, 84v). WELLESZ/TILLYARD 128–129

117i ♪ Sticheron no. 20 (Ms. Athens. Natl. Lib. 2147, f23). WELLESZ/TILLYARD 125–126
117j ♪ Sticheron no. 22 (Ms. Athens. Natl. Lib. 2147, f24r). WELLESZ/TILLYARD 126–127
117k Stöhr, Maria. Reflections on Transcribing the Hirmoi in Byzantine Music. WELLESZ/TILLYARD 89–94
118 Strunk, Oliver. The Antiphons of the Oktoechos. KINKELDEY/80TH 50–67
118a ——. H. J. W. Tillyard and the Recovery of a Lost Fragment. WELLESZ/TILLYARD 95–103
119 ——. St. Gregory Nazianzus and the Proper Hymns for Easter. FRIEND 82–87
119a Tillyard, H. J. W. The Rediscovery of Byzantine Music. WELLESZ/80TH 3–6
119b Trypanis, C. A. On the Musical Rendering of the Early Byzantine Kontakia. WELLESZ/TILLYARD 104–107
119c Velimirović, Miloš. Byzantine Composers in Ms. Athens 2406. WELLESZ/TILLYARD 7–18
119d ——. Ioakeim Monachos toi Harsianitos kai thomestikos serbias [Article is in English] OSTROGORSKY 451–458
119e ——. Two Composers of Byzantine Music: John Vatatzes and John Laskaris. REESE/65TH 818–831
119f ——. Unknown Stichera for the Feast of St. Athanasios of Mount Athos. WELLESZ/TILLYARD 108–129
120 Wellesz, Egon. Zum Stil der Melodien der Kontakia. ANGLÉS II, 965–975

MIDDLE AGES: AMBROSIAN, MOZARABIC, ETC. CHANT

121 Anglés, Higinio. Die Sequenz und die Verbeta im mittelalterlichen Spanien. MOBERG 37–47
121a Baroffio, Giacomo. Die mailändische Überlieferung des Offertoriums *Sanctificavit*. STÄBLEIN/70TH 1–8
122 Brou, Louis. Deux mauvaises lectures du Chanoine Ortiz dans l'édition du bréviaire mozarabe de Ximénes *Lauda, capitula*. ANGLÉS I, 175–190
123 Caglio, Ernesto Moneta. I Responsori *Cum infantibus* della liturgia Ambrosiana. CASTIGLIONI 481–576
124 Cattaneo, Enrico. I Canti della frazione e communione nella liturgia ambrosiana. MOHLBERG II, 147–174
125 ♪ *Congratulamini mihi* (Ambrosian chant). CASTIGLIONI 575–578
126 Fleischauer, Günter. Zur Geschichte des Knabengesanges im ausgehenden Altertum. SCHNEIDER/80TH 11–15
126a Gołos, Jerzy. Antyfonarz ambrozjański Biblioteki Jagiellońskiej w Krakowie [An Ambrosian Antiphonary in the University Library in Cracow] FEICHT 129–136
127 Haapanen, Toivo. Vieraita vaikutuksia Suomen vanhimmassa musiikkulttuurissa [Foreign Influences in the Earliest Finnish Music Culture] KROHN 25–40, German summary iii
128 Marstrander, Petter. De første kristenmenigheters gudstjenesteliv [The First Christian Congregation's Divine Service] SANDVIK 148–164
128a Peacock, Peter. The Problem of the Old Roman Chant. WELLESZ/80TH 43–47
129 Rajeczky, Benjámin. Mittelalterliche ungarische Musikdenkmäler und das neue Volkslied. KODÁLY/80TH 263–269
130 Schmidt-Görg, Joseph. Ein handschriftliches neu-gallikanisches Graduale aus dem Jahre 1852. FELLERER/60TH 474–480
130a Stäblein, Bruno. Zur archaischen Ambrosianischen (Mailänder) Mehrstimmigkeit. DESDERI/70TH 169–174
130b Weakland, Rembert G. The Performance of Ambrosian Chant in the 12th Century. REESE/65TH 856–866
131 Werner, Eric. Eine neuentdeckte mozarabische Handschrift mit Neumen. ANGLÉS II, 977–984
131a Zagiba, Franz. Einige grundlegende Fragen des Cyrillomethodianischen liturgischen Gesanges. RACEK/60TH 403–415

MIDDLE AGES: GREGORIAN CHANT

See also nos. 72a, 111, 248, 288a, 532e, 756, 773, 838a, 1314, 1369h, 1379, 1460, 1737, 1839, 2036a, 2044, 2105c, 2187, 2196, 2647, 2667a

131b Anglés, Higinio. Problemas que plantea el canto gregoriano en su historia y en su valor oracional y artistico musical. BALDELLÓ 13–27
132 ——. Sul mensuralismo nelle

melodie gregoriane. JOHNER 19–24 (text in Italian & German)
133 Bárdos, Kornél. Az Eperjesi graduál. I: Gregorián kapcsolatok [The Eperges Gradual. I: Connections with Gregorian Chant] KODÁLY/75TH 165–198, German summary 754
134 Beyssac, G. M. Versus ad Christe. HANDSCHIN/I 73–86
135 Bomm, Urbanus. Hymnus Seraphicus—das Sanctus als Zugang zum Choralverständnis. JOHNER 36–39
136 ——. Vom Sinn und Wert der Editio Vaticana. SCHREMS 63–75
137 Closson, Ernest. L'Elément celtique irlandais dans le chant liturgique. MUEREN 63–65
138 Dijk, S. J. P. van. Papal Schola versus Charlemagne. WAESBERGHE 21–30
139 Dreimüller, Karl. Ein niederrheinisches Antiphonar. JOHNER 76–83
140 Drinkwelder, Erhard. Drei Missale-Hss. deutscher Herkunft in der Batthyány-Bibliothek zu Karlsburg (Siebenbürgen). WAGNER 44–54
141 Falvy, Zoltán. Zur Frage von Differenzen der Psalmodie. SCHENK 160–173
142 Fellerer, Karl Gustav. Cod. XXVII, 84 der Chorbibliothek der Frauenkirche in München. Ein Beitrag zur Geschichte der Choralbegleitung. WAGNER 55–68
143 ——. Zu den Cantus ecclesiastici missae der kölner und münsterischen Tradition im 19. Jahrhundert. JOHNER 24–28
143a ——. Zu den Gesängen des Kölner Missale 1506. STÄBLEIN/70TH 47–51
143b ——. Zur Chorallehre des Geronimo Romero de Avila. SCHREIBER I, 265–268
144 Ferretti, Paolo Maria. I Manoscritti musicali gregoriani dell'Archivio di Montecassino. MONTE CASSINO I, 187–204
144a Fischer, Kurt von. Neue Quellen zum einstimmigen Ordinariumszyklus des 14. und 15. Jahrhunderts aus Italien. BORREN/90TH 60–68
145 Fischer, Wilhelm. Die Herkunft des *Ite, missa est* V. toni. OREL/70TH 67–72
146 Freistedt, Heinrich. Introitspsalmodie in aachener Handschriften des ausgehenden Mittelalters. SCHIEDERMAIR/80TH 29–33
147 Gaisser, Hugo Athanas. Die Antiphon *Nativitas tua* und ihr greichisches Vorbild. RIEMANN 154–166
148 Galley, Eberhard. Miniaturen aus dem kölner Klarissenkloster; ein Kapitel rheinischer Buchmalerei des 14. Jahrhunderts. JUCHHOFF 15–28
149 Gennrich, Friedrich. Die *Laudes sancte crucis* der Hs. Darmstadt, Hessische Landesbibliothek 2777. WAESBERGHE 45–58
150 ♪ *Glorietur letabunda* (Modena, Arch. d. Duomo. *Capit. O.I.* 16) MURATORI 536
151 Haberl, Ferdinand. Der Choral des Messpropriums vom Feste des heiligen Johannes Baptista. HILBER 41–45
152 ——. Das Choralcredo im vierten Modus in seiner unterschiedlichen Gestalt. JOHNER 28–34
153 ——. Die Gradualien des dritten Modus und ihre musikalische Struktur. SCHREMS 76–99
154 Handschin, Jacques. Saint-Maurice et Saint-Gall. HANDSCHIN 192–197; orig. in *Formes et couleurs* 1 (1943)
155 ——. Zur Biographie Hermanns des Lahmen. HANDSCHIN 170–174; orig. in *Neue Zürcher Zeitung* 661 (1935)
156 Hesbert, René-Jean. Un antique offertoire de la pentecôte: *Factus est repente*. WAESBERGHE 59–69
157 ——. L'Office de la commémoraison des défunts à Saint-Benoît-sur-Loire au XIIIe siècle. MOHLBERG II, 393–421
157a Hucke, Helmut. Tractusstudien. STÄBLEIN/70TH 116–120
157b Huglo, Michel. Les chants de la *Missa Greca* de Saint-Denis. WELLESZ/80TH 74–83
158 ——. La Tradition occidentale des mélodies byzantines du Sanctus. JOHNER 40–46 (text in French and German)
158a Husmann, Heinrich. Das Einseidelner Graduale-Sakramentar St. Paul/Kärnten 25. 2. 25 (Seine Stellung und Bedeutung). FEICHT 89–95
159 ——. Das Graduale von Ediger, eine neue Quelle der rheinischen Augustinerliturgie. FELLERER/60TH 224–234
160 ——. Zur Überlieferung der Thomas-Offizien. WAESBERGHE 87–88
161 Jachimecki, Zdzislaw. Symbolismus in der Motivik des ersten gregorianischen Credo. ADLER 42–44
161a ——. W kole zagadnień *Bogurodzicy* [On the Thorny Problem

of *Bogurodzica*] PINIŃSKI I, 403–410
162 Jammers, Ewald. Einige Anmerkungen zur Tonalität des gregorianischen Gesanges. FELLERER/60TH 235–244
163 ——. Problème der rheinischen Choralgeschichte. SCHIEDERMAIR/80TH 46–53
164 ——. Wort und Ton bei Julian von Speyer. JOHNER 93–101
164a Kojimi, Shin. Die Ostergradualien "Haec Dies" und ihr Verhältnis zu den Tractus des II. und VIII. Tons. SCHMIDT-GÖRG/70TH 146–178
165 Kreps, Joseph. Antiphonaires monastiques des XIXe et XXe siècles. JOHNER 83–90 (text in French & German)
166 ——. Les Antiphonaires monastiques de 1934 et 1943. MUEREN 115–125
167 Krohn, Ilmari. Der tonale Charakter gregorianischer Rezitative. ADLER 33–44
168 Kunzelmann, Adalbero. Die gregorianischen Eigenmelodien des Augustinereremitenordens. JOHNER 90–93
169 Levi, Leo. Sul rapporto tra il canto sinagogale in Italia e le origini del canto liturgico cristiano. MAYER/S 139–193
169a Lipphardt, Walther. Das Hymnar der Metzer Kathedrale um 1200. STÄBLEIN/70TH 160–177
170 Kunz, Lucas. Der Introitus *Gaudeamus*. JOHNER 34–36
171 ——. Zur symmetrischen Struktur der Psalmen. ANGLÉS I, 453–464
172 Lach, Robert. Gregorianische Choral- und vergleichende Musikwissenschaft. WAGNER 133–145
173 Lassaulx, Hubert von. Der gregorianische Choral als liturgische Musik. JOHNER 14–18
174 Lipphardt, Walther. Die Antiphonen der Sonntagsvesper in der altrömischen Liturgie. JOHNER 53–63
175 Lohr, Ina. Zur Wiederbelebung der geistlichen Monodie des Mittelalters im heutigen Chorkonzert. NEF 157–164
176 Mittler, Placidus. Die neumierten Gesänge des Siegburger Lektionars. SCHMIDT-GÖRG/70TH 250–259
177 Moberg, Carl Allan. Gregorianische Reflexionen. ANGLÉS II, 559–583
178 Moragas, Beda M. Transcripció musical de dos himnes. ANGLÉS II, 591–595
178a Morawski, Jerzy. Sekwencje "Grates nunc omnes" w polskich zabytkach chorałowych [The Sequence "Grates nunc omnes" in Ancient Polish Chant] FEICHT 120–128
179 Müller, Ewald. Ein Kapitel aus der *Medulla choralis* der deutschen Franziskaner-Rekollektenprovinzen vom Jahre 1670 über das gute Psallieren. JOHNER 104–106
180 Pulikowski, Juljan. Pontificale lwowskie z XIV wieku pod wzgledem muzycznym [The Lwow Pontifical of the 14th Century with regard to Music] CHYBIŃSKI/50TH 1–14
181 Rajeczky, Benjámin. Adatok a magyar gregoriánumhoz [Contributions to the Hungarian Gregorian Chants] KODÁLY/70TH 279–286
181a ——. Sur le "Kyrie ungaricum" du manuscrit no. 1267 de al Biblioteka Jagiellońska. FEICHT 137–142
181b ——. Über die Melodie Nr. 773 der *Monumenta Monodica* I. STÄBLEIN/70TH 191–194
181c Ritscher, M. Immaculata. Zur Musik der heiligen Hildegard. SCHMIDT-GÖRG/70TH 309–326
182 Roeseling, Kaspar. Das Gloria der 10. Messe und seine melodische Form. KAHL 18–25
183 Schmidt, Hans. Die Tractus des zweiten Tones in gregorianischer und stadtrömischer Überlieferung. SCHMIDT-GÖRG 283–302
184 Stäblein, Bruno. Eine Hymnusmelodie als Vorlage einer provenzalischen Alba. ANGLÉS II, 889–894
185 ——. Zur Geschichte der choralen *Pange lingua* Melodie. JOHNER 72–75
186 ——. Zwei Textierungen des Alleluia *Christus resurgens* in St. Emmeram, Regensburg. WAESBERGHE 157–167
186a Strunk, Oliver. The Latin Antiphons for the Octave of the Epiphany. OSTROGORSKY 417–426
187 Suñol, Gregorio María. Font de bellesa. PEDRELL 283–291
187a Toussaint, Georg. Neue Quellen zur Geschichte des Chorstifts Kiedrich. SCHMITZ 257–264
188 Ursprung, Otto. Die Psalmen im heiligen Gesang. JOHNER 47–53
189 Vecchi, Giuseppe. S. Geminiano nella lirica della liturgia modenese. MURATORI 524–538
190 Vives, José. Oficio rítmico mariano en el leccionario de Solsona. ANGLÉS II, 959–963
190a Waesberghe, Joseph Smits van.

"De glorioso officio . . . dignitate apostolica . . . " (Amalarius): Zum Aufbau der Gross-Alleluia in den päpstlichen Ostervespern. WELLESZ/80TH 48–74
190b ——. Die Geschichte von Glastonbury (1082) und ihre Folgen. SCHMIDT-GÖRG/70TH 372–378
191 Wagner, Peter. Romanische und germanische Choraltradition. KROHN 143–148
191a Weiss, Günther. Zur Rolle Italiens im frühen Tropenschaffen. Beobachtungen zu den Vertonungen der Introitus-Tropen *Quem nascei mundo* und *Quod prisco vates.* STÄBLEIN/70TH 287–293
192 Werder, Ernestine. Jacopone da Todi im Licht der neueren Forschung. GAUCHAT 1–21
192a Werner, Eric. Zur Textgeschichte der Improperia. STÄBLEIN/70TH 274–286

MIDDLE AGES: GREGORIAN CHANT. TROPES & SEQUENCES

193 ♪ *Alleluia. Christus resurgens.* WAESBERGHE 163–165
194 ♪ *Alleluia. Psalle modulamina.* WAESBERGHE 163–165
195 ♪ *Alleluia. Rex regum summe.* WAESBERGHE 163–165
195a Angles, Higinio. Die volkstümlichen Melodien in den mittelalterlichen Sequenzen. WIORA/60TH 214–220
196 Brenn, Franz. Die Sequenzen des Graduale von St. Katharinenthal. OREL/70TH 23–42
197 Ewerhart, Rudolf. Eine Gangolf-Sequenz aus Trier. FELLERER 28–33
198 Fellerer, Karl Gustav. Der Semifigurato-Vortrag der Hymnen und Sequenzen im 18. Jahrhundert. MOBERG 135–143
199 Handschin, Jacques. Gesungene Apologetik. MOHLBERG II, 75–106, & HANDSCHIN 117–149
200 ——. Zur Notker-Frage. HANDSCHIN 166–169; orig. in *Neuer Zürcher Zeitung* 356 (1927)
200a Hoppin, Richard H. *Exultantes collaudemus:* a Sequence for Saint Hylarion. REESE/65TH 392–405
201 Husmann, Heinrich. Das Alleluia *Multifarie* und die vorgregorianische Stufe des Sequenzengesanges. SCHNEIDER/80TH 17–23
202 ——. Alleluia, Sequenz und Prosa im altspanischen Choral. ANGLÉS I, 407–415
203 ——. *Ecce puerpera genuit.* BESSELER 59–66
203a ——. Eine Palimpsest-Jahrestabelle in der Handschrift Stiftsbibliothek St. Gallen 381. ENGEL 188–191
203b ——. Ein Prosar-Tropar aus St. Frambould in Senlis (Bibliothèque Sainte-Geneviève ms. 1297). WIORA/60TH 229–230
204 ——. Die Sequenz *Duo tres;* zur Frühgeschichte der Sequenzen in St. Gallen und St. Martial. HANDSCHIN/1 66–72
205 ——. Sinn und Wesen der Tropen; veranschaulicht an den Introitustropen des Weihnachtsfestes. GURLITT 135–147
206 Ilmoniemi, K. Arvi. Kaksi sekvenssitutkielmaa [Two Sequence Studies] KROHN 55–81, German summary iv
207 Irtenkauf, Wolfgang. Die Alleluia-Tropierungen der Weingartner Handschriften. WK 345–361
208 Jaeggi, Oswald, Zum Tropus *Psalle ludens thalia.* JOHNER 63–66
209 Lausberg, Heinrich. Zum altfranzösischen Assumptionstropus *Quant li solliez.* TRIER 88–147
210 ♪ *Psalle modulamina laudis canora.* BERNET KEMPERS 53
210a Rönnau, Klaus. *Regnum tuum . solidum.* STÄBLEIN/70TH 195–205
211 ♪ St. Katharinenthal Gradual Sequences. OREL/70TH 36–42
211a Schlager, Karl-Heinz. Ein beneventanisches Alleluia und seine Prosula. STÄBLEIN/70TH 217–225
212 Schmidt-Görg, Joseph. Die Sequenzen der heiligen Hildegard. SCHIEDERMAIR/80TH 109–117
212a Stäblein, Bruno. "Psalle symphonizando." WIORA/60TH 221–228
213 ——. Die Schwanenklage; zum Problem Lai-Planctus-Sequenz. FELLERER/60TH 491–502
213a ——. Die Sequenzmelodie "Concordia" und ihr geschichtlicher Hintergrund. ENGEL 364–392
214 ——. Das sogenannte aquitanische *Alleluia Dies sanctificatus* und seine Sequenz. ALBRECHT 22–26
215 ——. Der Tropus *Dies sanctificatus* zum Alleluia *Dies sanctificatus.* SCHENK 504–515
215a Thannabaur, Peter Josef. Anmer-

kung zur Verbreitung und Struktur der Hosanna-Tropen im deutschsprachigen Raum und den Ostländern. STÄBLEIN/70TH 250–259
216 Waesberghe, Joseph Smits van. Die Imitation der Sequenztechnik in den Hosanna-Prosulen. FELLERER/60TH 485–490
217 ——. Over het ontstaan van sequens en prosula en beider oorspronkelijke uitvoeringswijze. BERNET KEMPERS 50–57
218 Wiora, Walter. Jubilare sine verbis. HANDSCHIN/I 39–65

MIDDLE AGES: LITURGICAL DRAMA

219 Aebischer, Paul. Un ultime écho de la *Procession des Prophètes.* Le *Cant de la Sibilla* de la nuit de Noël à Majorque. COHEN 261–270
219a Brandel, Rose. Some Unifying Devices in the Religious Music Drama of the Middle Ages. REESE/65TH 40–55
219b Chailley, Jacques. Du drame liturgique aux prophètes de Notre-Dame-la-Grande. CROZET 835–841
220 Falvy, Zoltán. Un *Quem queritis* en Hongrie au XIIe siècle. KODÁLY/80TH 101–107
221 Kettering, Heinz. Die essener Osterfeier. FELLERER 23–27
222 Lach, Robert. Das mittelalterliche Musikdrama im Spiegel der Kunstgeschichte. KOCZIRZ 17–20
223 Lipphardt, Walther. Das Herodesspiel von Le Mans nach den Handschriften Madrid Bibl. Nac. *288 und 289* (11. und 12. Jhd.) WAESBERGHE 107–122
223a ♪ *Planctus Iudei* (Ms. Orléans 201, 191–193). CROZET 884
223b Romeu Figueras, José. La canción popular navideña, fuente de un misterio dramático de técnica medieval. BALDELLÓ 167–184
223c ♪ *Sponsus* play (Ms. Paris. Bibl. Nat. f. lat. 1139), Ursprung ed. SEIFFERT/70THA 84–88
223d Stäblein, Bruno. Zur Musik des Ludus de Antichristo. MÜLLER-BLATTAU/70TH 312–327
224 Ursprung, Otto. Hildegards Drama *Ordo virtutum,* Geschichte einer Seele. ANGLÉS II, 941–958
224a ——. Das Sponsus-Spiel. SEIFFERT/70THA 80–95
225 ♪ *Versus ad Herodem faciendum.* WAESBERGHE 110–112
226 Waesberghe, Joseph Smits van. Das nürnberger Osterspiel. SCHMIDT-GÖRG 303–308
226a Wagenaar-Nolthenius, Helene. Der *Planctus Iudei* und der Gesang jüdischer Märtyrer in Blois anno 1171. CROZET 881–885
227 ——. Structuur en melodiek van het Danielspel. WAESBERGHE 169–174

MIDDLE AGES: TROUBADOR & TROUVÈRE SONGS

228 Anglés, Higinio. Gacian Reyneau am Königshof zu Barcelona in der Zeit von 139 . . . bis 1429. ADLER 64–70
229 ——. Die volkstümlichen Melodien bei den Trouvères. MÜLLER-BLATTAU 11–18
230 Aubry, Pierre. Refrains et rondeaux du XIIIe siècle. RIEMANN 213–229
231 Beck, Jean-Baptiste. Der Takt in den Musikaufzeichnungen des XII. und XIII. Jahrhunderts, vornehmlich in den Liedern der Troubadours und Trouvères. RIEMANN 166–184
232 Bédier, Joseph. Les Chansons du Comte de Bretagne. JEANROY 477–495
233 Catel, Jean. *Le Jeu de Robin et Marion,* pastourelle d'Adam le Bossu, adaptée à la scène moderne. VIANEY 59–75
234 Chailley, Jacques. La Nature musicale du *Jeu de Robin et Marion.* COHEN 111–117
234a ——. Notes sur les troubadours, les versus et la question Arabe. FRANK 118–128
234b ♪ Ernoul le Viel de Gastinois. [Works] APEL/70TH 28–56
235 Gennrich, Friedrich. Wer ist der Initiator der *Modaltheorie?* Suum cuique. ANGLÉS I, 315–330
236 Hoepffner, Ernest. Les Intermèdes musicaux dans le jeu provençal de Sainte-Agnès. COHEN 97–104
237 Jeanroy, Alfred. Les Chansons pieuses du ms. fr. *12483* de la Bibliothèque Nationale. WILMOTTE I, 245–266
238 Karp, Theodore. Modal Variants in Medieval Secular Monophony. SACHS/C 118–129
239 ——. The trouvère Ms. Tradition. QC 25–52
239a Machabey, Armand. Comment déterminer l'authenticité d'une chanson médiévale? CROZET 915–920

239b Maillard, Jean. Lais & chansons d'Ernoul de Gastinois. APEL/70TH 21–56
239c ——. Problèmes musicaux et littéraires du Descart. FRANK 388–409
240 Nef, Karl. Gesang und Instrumentenspiel bei den Troubadours. ADLER 58–63
240a Pokorný, František. De influzu, quem in drama liturgicum cantus Kyrialis Exercebat. ŠTĚDROŇ/60TH 53–70, summary in Czech at end of article
241 Schläger, Georg. Über Musik und Strophenbau der französischen Romanzen. SUCHIER 115–160, Anh. i-xxvii
242 ♪ Trouvère songs. MÜLLER-BLATTAU 14–18
242a VanderWerf, Hendrik. Recitative Melodies in Trouvère Chansons. WIORA/60TH 231–240

MIDDLE AGES: MINNE- AND MEISTERGESÄNGE

243 Aarburg, Ursula. Verzeichnis der im Kolmarer Liedercodex erhaltenen Töne und Leiche. BESSELER 127–136
244 Andel, G. G. van den. Über die Melismen in mittelhochdeutschen Liedern. SCHOLTE 106–109
244a Bell, Clair Hayden. The Meistersingerschule at Memmingen and Its "Kurtze Entwerffung." PRICE 1–90
244b Collaer, Paul. Moyen-âge et traditions populaires. WIORA/60TH 205–213
245 ♪ *Diu frow ob allen frowen.* RIEMANN 261
246 Enke, Heinz. Der *hofedon* des Meister Boppe. SCHNEIDER/80TH 31–48
247 ♪ *Ich will dich bitten.* RIEMANN 260–261
248 Jammers, Ewald. Minnesang und Choral. BESSELER 137–147
249 ♪ Laufenberg, Heinrich. *Wilkom lobes werde/Bis grüst, maget reine.* LILIENCRON 231–240
249a Lomnitzer, Helmut. Kritisches zu neueren Neidhart-Übertragungen. ENGEL 231–244
250 ♪ *Maria můter reinû maît.* RIEMANN 259–266
250a Mohr, Wolfgang. Vortragsform und Form als Symbol im mittelalterlichen Liede. PRETZEL 128–138
251 Müller-Blattau, Wendelin. Melodietypen bei Neidhart von Reuenthal. MÜLLER-BLATTAU 65–74
252 Runge, Paul. *Maria můter reinû maît.* RIEMANN 256–267
253 ——. Der Marienleich Heinrich Laufenbergs *Wilkom lobes werde.* RIEMANN 228–240
254 Waesberghe, Joseph Smits van. Über den Ursprung der Melodie *Nun siet uns wellekommen.* SCHENK 496–503
255 Wolf, Johannes. Zwei Tagelieder des XIV. Jahrhunderts. DEGERING 325–327
256 Wustmann, Rudolf. Die Hofweise Walthers von der Vogelweide. LILIENCRON 440–463
256a Zatočíl, Leopold. Závišova píseň ve světle Minnesangu a její předloha [The Song of Záviš in the Light of Minnegesang and a Proposal] NEJEDLÝ/75TH 110–126, summaries in German & Russian at end of article

MIDDLE AGES: LATIN, SPANISH, ETC. SONGS

257 Batlle y Prats, Luis. Juglares en la corte de Aragon y en el municipio de Gerona en el siglo XIV. MENÉNDEZ PIDAL/E V, 165–184
258 ♪ *Carmina Burana.* Selections. BESSELER 101–126
259 Corbin, Solange. Comment on chantait les classiques latins au moyen âge. MASSON I, 107–113
260 Jammers, Ewald. Nichtmodale Interpretation einiger lateinischer Achtsilber. KAHL 26–34
261 Lipphardt, Walther. Einige unbekannte Weisen zu den *Carmina Burana* aus der zweiten Hälfte des 12. Jahrhunderts. BESSELER 101–126
262 López-Aydillo, Eugenio. El Siglo XIII en los cancioneros gallego portugueses. MENÉNDEZ PIDAL III, 619–631
263 Müller-Blattau, Joseph. *In Gottes Namen fahren wir.* SCHNEIDER/60TH 65–73
263a Mužik, Frantisek. Závišova píseň [Song of Záviš] RACEK/60TH 167–182, summary in German
264 Nunes, J. J. Un Ramo de flores colhido na antiga lirica galego-portuguesa. JEANROY 337–347
265 Pais, Dezső. Árpád- és Anjou-kori mulattatóink [Minstrels of the Arpad and Anjou Periods] KODÁLY/70TH 95–110

266 Pelaez, Mario. La Leggenda della Madonna della Neve e la *Cantiga de Santa Maria*, N. CCCIX di Alfonso el Sabio MENÉNDEZ PIDAL I, 215–223
267 Ribera, Julián. De música y métrica gallegas. MENÉNDEZ PIDAL III, 7–35
268 Salmen, Walter. A középkori magyar vándorzenészek külföldi útjai [Medieval Hungarian Minstrels in Foreign Countries] KODÁLY/75TH 159–163, German summary 751–754
269 ——. Zur Geschichte der Ministriles im Dienste geistlicher Herren des Mittelalters. ANGLÉS II, 811–819
270 Spanke, Hans. Klangspielereien im mittelalterlichen Liede. STRECKER 171–183
270a ♪ Záviš. *Jižt mne vše radost ostává.* RACEK/60TH 177–179

MIDDLE AGES: POLYPHONY TO 1300

271 Anglés, Higinio. Die Mehrstimmigkeit des Calixtinus von Compostela und seine Rhythmik. BESSELER 91–100
272 ——. La Música anglesa dels segles XIII-XIV als països hispànics. FINKE 219–233
273 Apel, Willi. Bemerkungen zu den Organa von St. Martial. ANGLÉS I, 61–70
274 ——. Imitation in the Thirteenth and Fourteenth Centuries. DAVISON 25–38
275 ♪ *L'autre jour/Hier matinet/Ite missa est.* HANDSCHIN/I 168[c]
275a ♪ *Beata nobis gaudia* (13th-century conductus). SCHRADE/D 198
276 Belaiev, Victor. Early Russian Polyphony/Rannee russkoe mrogogolosie. BARTÓK/S 307–336 (text in English & Russian)
276a ♪ *Benedicamus Domino* (Ivrea, Bibl. Capitolare, *Ms. LXVIII*). SCHMITZ 253
277 Birkner, Günter. Notre Dame-Cantoren und -Succentoren vom Ende des 10. bis zum Beginn des 14. Jahrhunderts. HANDSCHIN/I 107–126
278 ♪ Calixtinus codex. Selections. BESSELER 95–100
279 Chailley, Jacques. Fragments d'un nouveau manuscrit d'Ars Antiqua à Châlons-sur-Marne. HANDSCHIN/I 140–149
280 ——. Sur la rythmique des proses victoriennes. FELLERER/60TH 77–81
280a Dittmer, Luther A. The Lost Fragments of a Notre Dame Manuscript in Johannes Wolf's Library. REESE/65TH 122–133
281 Fischer, Kurt von. Das Kantorenamt am Dome von Siena zu Beginn des 13. Jahrhunderts. FELLERER/60TH 155–160
281a ♪ *Gaude, felix Francia* (13th-century conductus) Paris, B.N. lat. 15139 SCHRADE/D 199–204
282 Geering, Arnold. Retrospektive mehrstimmige Musik in französischen Handschriften des Mittelalters. ANGLÉS I, 307–311
283 Handschin, Jacques. Die Schweiz welche sang. Über mittelalterliche Cantionen aus schweizerischen Handschriften. NEF 102–133
283a Harrison, Frank Lloyd. Polyphony in Medieval Ireland. STÄBLEIN/70TH 74–78
284 Hibberd, Lloyd. Giraldus Cambrensis on Welsh Popular Singing. DAVISON 17–23
284a Hofmann-Brandt, Helma. Eine neue Quelle zur mittelalterlichen Mehrstimmigkeit. STÄBLEIN/70TH 109–115
285 Hughes, Anselm. The Topography of English Mediaeval Polyphony. HANDSCHIN/I 127–139
285a Hughes, David G. The Sources of *Christus Manens.* REESE/65TH 432–434
286 Husmann, Heinrich. Ein dreistimmiges Organum aus Sens unter den Notre-Dame Kompositionen. BLUME/F 200–203
286a ——. The Practice of Organum in the Liturgical Singing of the Syrian Churches of the Near and Middle East. REESE/65TH 435–439
287 ——. St. Germain and Notre-Dame. JEPPESEN 31–36
288 ——. Zur Stellung des Messpropriums der österreichischen Augustinerchorherren. SCHENK 261–275
288a Köllner, Georg Paul. Eine Mainzer Choralhandschrift des 15. Jahrhunderts als Quelle zum "Crucifixum in carne." SCHMITZ 208–212
288b ♪ *Lectio: Surge Illuminare, Jerusalem (Ivrea, Bibl. Capitolare,* Ms. *LXVIII*). SCHMITZ 254–256
288c ♪ *Lectio: Vidi supra montem (Ivrea, Bibl. Capitolare,* Ms. *LXVIII*). SCHMITZ 253–254
289 Ludwig, Friedrich. Die liturgischen Organa Leonins und Perotins.

RIEMANN 200–213
290 ——. Mehrstimmige Musik des 12. oder 13. Jahrhunderts im Schlettstädter St. Fides-Codex. KRETZSCHMAR 80–84
291 ——. Über den Entstehungsort der grossen Notre-Dame Handschriften. ADLER 45–49
292 Machabey, Armand. Remarques sur le Winchester Troper. BESSELER 67–90
292a Monterosso, Raffaello. Un' "auctoritas" dactasca in un madrigale dell'Ars Nova. BARBLAN/60TH 185–193
293 ♪ *O miranda/Salve Mater salutifera/Kyrie.* HANDSCHIN/I 168[a]
293a Osthoff, Wolfgang. Die Conductus des Codex Calixtinus. STÄBLEIN/70TH 178–186
294 ♪ *Pato linis oculum/In seculum.* HANDSCHIN/I 168[b]
294a Petrobelli, Pierluigi. Due mottetti francesi in una sconosciuta fonte Udinese. BARBLAN/60TH 201–214
295 ♪ *Plus joliment/Quant li douz/Portare.* HANDSCHIN/I 168[a]
296 ♪ *Psallat chorus/Eximine Pater/Aptatur.* HANDSCHIN/I 168[c]
297 ♪ *Reple sacro flamine/Reple tuorum corda.* HANDSCHIN/I 168[a]
298 ♪ *Res nova mirabilis/Virgo decus castitatis/Alleluia.* HANDSCHIN/I 168[b]
299 Rokseth, Yvonne. Le Contrepoint double vers 1248. LAURENCIE 5–13
300 ——. Danses cléricales du XIIIe siècle. SUFL III, 93–126
301 ♪ *Rondeaux,* 13th-century. SUFL III, 120–126
301a Sanders, Ernest H. The Question of Perotin's Oeuvre and Dates. WIORA/60TH 241–249
301b Schrade, Leo. Ein neuer Fund früher Mehrstimmigkeit. SCHMITZ 238–256
301c ——. Political Compositions in French Music of the 12th and 13th Centuries (The Coronation of French Kings). SCHRADE/D 152–211; orig. in *Annales Musicologiques* I (1953) 9–68, 409
301d ——. Unknown Motets in a Recovered Thirteenth-Century Manuscript. SCHRADE/D 212–240; orig. in *Speculum* 30 (1955) 393–412
302 ♪ *Se je chant/Bien doi/Et sperabit.* HANDSCHIN/I 168[d]
303 ♪ *Serena virginum/Manere.* HANDSCHIN/I 168[d]
304 Spiess, Lincoln Bunce. An Introduction to the Pre-History of Polyphony. DAVISON 11–15
304a ♪ *Spiritus et alme* (Évreux, Ms. Lat. *17*). FRANK 378
305 Stäblein, Bruno. Modale Rhythmen im Saint Martial Repertoire? BLUME/F 340–362
306 Stimming, Albert. Altfranzösische Motette in Handschriften deutscher Bibliotheken. CHABANEAU 89–103
306a Strohm, Reinhart. Ein Zeugnis früher Mehrstimmigkeit in Italien. STÄBLEIN/70TH 239–249
306b Tischler, Hans. The Arrangements of the *Gloria Patri* in the Office Organa of the *Magnus Liber Organi.* STÄBLEIN/70TH 260–265
306c ——. Perotinus Revisited. REESE/65TH 803–817
306d Thurston, Ethel. A Comparison of the St. Victor Clausulae with their Motets. REESE/65TH 785–802
307 Wagner, Peter. Ein versteckter Discantus. WOLF 207–213
308 Wallin, Nils L. Hymnus in honorem Sancti Magni comitis Orchadiae: Codex Upsaliensis *C 233.* MOBERG 339–354
309 ♪ Winchester Troper. *Dies sanctificatus.* BESSELER 82–83
310 ♪ ——. *Fulgens praeclara.* BESSELER 86–90
311 ♪ ——. *Ymera/Dies.* BESSELER 84–96
312 Wolf, Johannes. Eine neue Quelle zur mehrstimmigen kirchlichen Praxis des 14. bis 15. Jahrhunderts. WAGNER 222–237

MIDDLE AGES: POLYPHONY AFTER 1300

See also nos. 273, 274, 312

313 ♪ Alanus, Johannes. *Sub Arturo/Fons citharizancium/In omnem terram.* BESSELER 169–174
314 Anglés, Higinio. Els Cantors i organistes Franco-Flamencs i Alemanys a Catalunya els segles XIV–XVI. SCHEURLEER 49–62
315 ——. El Músic Jacomí al servei de Joan I i Martí I durant els anys 1372–1404. RUBIO 613–625
316 ——. Una nueva versión del credo de Tournai. BORREN/80TH 97–99
317 ♪ Bartolino da Padua. *La Biancha selva.* ANGLÉS I, 277–280
317a Becherini, Bianca. Le insegne Viscontee e i testi poetici dell'Ars Nova. BORREN/90TH 17–25

318 Borren, Charles van den. Le *Fragment de Gand.* WOLF 198–206
319 ♪ Ciconia, Johannes. *Regina gloriosa.* BORREN/80TH 68–70
320 Dart, Thurston. Une Contribution anglaise au manuscrit de Strasbourg? BORREN/80TH 122–124
320a ♪ *Deduto sey a quel che may non fusti* (vocal & instr. versions). BORREN/90TH 157–164
320b Eggebrecht, Hans Heinrich. Machauts Motette Nr. 9. SCHMITZ 281–293
321 Fischer, Kurt von. Drei unbekannte Werke von Jacopo da Bologna und Bartolino da Padua? ANGLÉS I, 265–281
321a ——. Die Lauda "Ave Mater" und ihre Verschiedenen Fassungen. SCHMIDT-GÖRG/70TH 93–99
321b ——. Eine neue süddeutsche Quelle des frühen 15. Jahrhunderts. STÄBLEIN/70TH 52–56
321c ——. Ein neues Trecento-fragment. WIORA/60TH 264–268
321d ——. Reply to N. E. Wilkins' Article on the Codex Reina. APEL/70TH 75–77
322 ♪ Ballade (Gent fragment). WOLF 203–206
323 Ghisi, Federico. Gli Aspetti musicali della lauda fra il XIV e il XV secolo, prima metà. JEPPESEN 51–58
323a Gümpel, Karl-Werner. Der Toledaner Kapellmeister Bartolomé de Quevedo und sein Kommentar zu der Extravagante "Docta Sanctorum" Johanns XXII. VIVES 294–308
324 Günter, Ursula. Das Wort-Ton-Problem bei Motetten des späten 14. Jahrhunderts. BESSELER 163–178
325 Haapanen, Toivo. Dominikanische Vorbilder im mittelalterlichen nordischen Kirchengesang. SCHEURLEER 129–134
325a Hoppin, Richard H. Reflections on the Origin of the Cyclic Mass. BORREN/90TH 85–92
326 ♪ Jacopo da Bologna. *Gridavan tuti: viva sachomano.* ANGLÉS I, 266–267
327 ♪ ——. *Nel prato pien de fiori.* ANGLÉS I, 269–272
328 Krings, Alfred. Zur Rhythmik einiger Balladen der Handschrift Chantilly *1047.* KAHL 35–42
328a Li Gotti, Ettore. Il petrarchismo della poesia musicale e il gusto del popolaresco in Italia agli inizi del sec. XV. SANTANGELO 249–260
329 Machabey, Armand. *O potores.* MASSON I, 149–153
329a Main, Alexander. Lorenzo Masini's Deer Hunt. SACHS/C 130–162
330 ♪ *O potores.* MASSON I, 151–152
331 Pedrell, Felipe. Jean I d'Aragon, compositeur de musique. RIEMANN 229–240
332 Pirro, André. Musiciens allemands et auditeurs français au temps des rois Charles V et Charles VI. ADLER 71–77
333 Pirrotta, Nino. Due sonetti musicali del secolo XIV. ANGLÉS II, 651–662
333a ——. On Text Forms from Ciconia to Dufay. REESE/65TH 673–682
333b ——. Paolo da Firenze in un nuovo frammento dell'Ars Nova. HANDSCHIN/M 61–66
334 —— & Ettore Li Gotti. Paolo tenorista, fiorentino *extra moenia.* MENENDEZ PIDAL/E II, 577–606
335 ——. Scuole polifoniche italiane durante il sec. XIV: di una pretesa scuola napoletana. EINSTEIN/C 11–18
335a Plamenac, Dragan. Faventina. BORREN/90TH 145–164
336 Reaney, Gilbert. The Development of the Rondeau, Virelai and Ballade Forms from Adam de la Hale to Guillaume de Machaut. FELLERER/60TH 421–427
337 ——. Modes in the Fourteenth Century, in particular in the Music of Guillaume de Machaut. WAESBERGHE 137–143
337a ——. A Postscript to the Manuscript Chantilly, Musée Condé 1047. HANDSCHIN/M 55–60
338 Reichert, Georg. Wechselbeziehungen zwischen musikalischer und textlicher Struktur in der Motette des 13. Jahrhunderts. HANDSCHIN/I 151–169
339 ♪ *Renart le nouvel.* RIEMANN 215–229
340 Riquer, Martín de. Don Enrique de Villena en la corte de Martín I. ANGLÉS II, 717–721
341 Rubio, Jordi. La Música del paradís a *l'Escala de contemplacio* de Fra Antoni Canals. ANGLÉS II, 769–774
342 Schrade, Leo. The Cycle of the *Ordinarium missae.* HANDSCHIN/I 87–96
342a ——. A Fourteenth-Century Parody Mass. SCHRADE/D 241–282; orig. in *Acta Musicologica* 27 (1955) 13–39
343 ——. Guillaume de Machaut and the *Roman de Fauvel.* ANGLÉS II, 843–850
344 ——. The Mass of Toulouse.

BORREN/80TH 84–96
344a ——. Philippe de Vitry, Some New Discoveries. SCHRADE/D 283–309; orig. in *Musical Quarterly* 42 (1956) 330–354
345 Stäblein, Bruno, & Hanna Harder. Neue Fragmente mehrstimmiger Musik aus spanischen Bibliotheken. SCHMIDT-GÖRG 131–141
345a Stevens, Denis. Polyphonic Tropers in 14th-century England. REESE/65TH 768–784
345b Wilkins, N. E. The Codex Reina: a Revised Description (Paris, Bibl. Nat., ms. n. a. fr. 6771). APEL/70TH 57–73
346 Young, Karl. The *Dit de la harpe* of Guillaume de Machaut. FEUILLERAT 1–20

MIDDLE AGES: THEORY & THEORISTS

347 Anglés, Higinio. Dos tractats medievals de música figurada. WOLF 6–12
348 Bragard, Roger. Boethiana; études sur le *De institutione musica* de Boèce. BORREN 84–139
349 Bronarski, Ludwik. Die *Quadripartita figura* in der mittelalterlichen Musiktheorie. WAGNER 27–43
349a Chailley, Jacques. Essai analytique sur la formation de l'Octoéchos latin. WELLESZ/80TH 84–93
350 ——. La Naissance de la notion modale au moyen âge. ANGLÉS I, 203–210
350a Dolch, Josef. Die "ars musica" in den Studienberichten Walthers von Speyer (984) und Hugo von St. Viktor (1127). MÜLLER-BLATTAU/70TH 59–68
351 Fellerer, Karl Gustav. Untersuchungen zur *Musica* des Wilhelm von Hirsau. ANGLÉS I, 239–252
352 ——. Zum Musiktraktat des Wilhelm von Hirsau. FISCHER/W 61–70
352a Gilles, Andrés. Un témoignage inédit de l'enseignement de Philippe de Vitry. HANDSCHIN/M 35–54
353 Hammerstein, Reinhold. Instrumenta Hieronymi. GURLITT 117–134
354 Handschin, Jacques. Der Organum-Traktat von Montpellier. ADLER 50–57
355 Hüschen, Heinrich. Der Einfluss Isidors von Sevilla auf die Musikanschauung des Mittelalters. ANGLÉS I, 397–406
356 ——. Regino von Prüm, Historiker, Kirchenrechtler und Musiktheoretiker. FELLERER/60TH 205–223
357 ——. Rutgerus Sycamber de Venray und sein Musiktraktat. SCHIEDERMAIR/80TH 34–45
357a Huglo, Michel. Règlement du XIIIe siècle pour la transcription des livres notés. STÄBLEIN/70TH 121–133
358 Kromolicki, Josef. Die Lehre von der Transposition in der Musiktheorie des früheren Mittelalters. KRETZSCHMAR 62–64
359 Kroyer, Theodor. Die *Musica speculativa* des Magister Erasmus Heritius. SANDBERGER 65–120
360 Lenaerts, René B. Oude en nieuwe muziek naar het *Speculum musicae*. MUEREN 127–132
361 Maas, Christian J. Een duistere passage bij Guido. BERNET KEMPERS 44–45
361a Machabey, Armand. Notions scientifiques disseminées dans les textes musicologiques du Moyen Âge. APEL/70TH 7–20
362 Moberg, Carl Allan. Die Musik in Guido von Arezzos Solmisationshymne. GURLITT 187–206
363 Müller, Hermann. Der Musiktraktat in dem Werke des Bartholomaeus Anglicus *De proprietatibus rerum*. RIEMANN 241–255
364 Omlin, P. Ephrem. Guido von Arezzo und der Johannes-Hymnus *Ut queant laxis*. HILBER 46–54
365 Pirrotta, Nino. Una arcaica descrizione trecentesca del madrigale. BESSELER 155–161
366 Rawski, Conrad H. Notes on Aribo Scholasticus. JEPPESEN 19–30
366a Reaney, Gilbert, André Gilles, & Jean Maillard. The "Ars Nova" of Philippe de Vitry. HANDSCHIN/M 3–34
366b Schrade, Leo. Das propädeutische Ethos in der Musikanschauung des Beothius. SCHRADE/D 35–75; orig. in *Zeitschrift für Geschichte der Erziehung und des Unterrichts* 20 (1930) 179–215
366c ——. Die Stellung der Musik in der Philosophie des Boethius als Grundlage der Ontologischen Musikerziehung. SCHRADE/D 76–112; orig. in *Archiv für Geschichte der Philosophie* 41 (1932) 368–400
367 Stellfeld, Bent. Prosdocimus de Beldomandis als Erneuerer der Musikbetrachtung um 1400. JEPPESEN 37–50

367a Vecchi, Giuseppe. Musica e scuola delle artes a Bologna nell'opera di Boncompagno da Signa (sec. XIII). STÄBLEIN/70TH 266–273

368 Wackernagel, Peter. Textkritisches zu Guido von Arezzo. HOLTZMAN 53–63

368a Waesberghe, Joseph Smits van. Eine merkwürdige Figur und ihr musik-geometrisches Geheimnis. STÄBLEIN/70TH 234–238

369 Waite, William G. Two Musical Poems of the Middle Ages. SCHRADE 13–34

370 Wolf, Johannes. *L'Arte del biscanto misurato secondo* el maestro Jacopo da Bologna. KROYER 17–39

371 ——. Der Choraltraktat des Cristoual de Escobar. SCHEURLEER 383–391

MIDDLE AGES: NOTATION

372 Anglés, Higinio. Die Bedeutung der Plika in der mittelalterlichen Musik. FELLERER/60TH 28–39

372a Beigański, Krzysztof. Fragment jednego z najstarszych zabytków diastematycznych w Polsce (dodatek do ms. 149 Bibl. Kapit. Gnieźnieńskiej = fr. 149) [A fragment of One of the Oldest Diastematic Relics in Poland (appendix to Gniezno, Bibl. Kapit., fr. 149)] FEICHT 95–119

372b Bergsagel, John D. An English Liquescent Neume. WELLESZ/80TH 94–99

372c Chwałek, Jan. Dwa fragmenty cheironomiczne nr 362 z Muzeum Diecezjalnego w Sandomierzu (XI/XIIw.) [Two chironomic fragments, Ms. 362 from the Diocesan Museum in Sandomierz (11/12th century)] FEICHT 77–88

373 Falvy, Zoltán. A Pray-kódex zenei paleográfiája [The Musical Paleography of the Pray Codex] BARTÓK/E 509–533, English summary 557–558

374 Fischer, Kurt von. Zur Entwicklung der italienischen Trecento-Notation. GURLITT 87–99

375 Gerstenberg, Walter. Eine Neumenhandschrift in der Dombibliothek zu Köln. KROYER 8–16

376 Hucke, Helmut. Die Neumierung des althochdeutschen Petruslieds. WAESBERGHE 71–78

376a Jammers, Ewald. Gedanken und Beobachtungen zur Geschichte der Notenschriften. WIORA/60TH 196–204

377 ——. Neumen im Lateinunterricht; Randbemerkungen zu einer St. Galler Handschrift. BOLLERT/80TH 64–68

377a ——. Rhythmen und Hymnen in einer St. Galler Handschrift des 9. Jahrhunderts. STÄBLEIN/70TH 134–142

377b——. Zur Entwicklung der Neumenschrift im Karolingerreich. GLAUNING I, 89–98

378 Koschmieder, Erwin. Zur Herkunft der slavischen Krjuki-Notation. ČYŽEVŠKYJ 146–152

379 Liuzzi, Fernando. Notazione musicale del sec. XI in un manoscritto dell'*Eneide*. VIRGIL 67–80

379a Machabey, Armand. Problèmes de notation musicale (Notations médiévales des manuscrits d'Évreux). FRANK 361–387

380 Mocquereau, André, & Gabriel M. Beyssac. De la transcription sur lignes des notations neumatique et alphabétique à propos du répons *Tua sunt*. RIEMANN 137–153

381 Riesemann, Oskar von. Zur Frage der Entzifferung altbyzantinischer Neumen. RIEMANN 189–199

382 Sablayrolles, Maur. Une Notation grégorienne espagnole. PEDRELL 301–306

383 Strunk, Oliver. A Cypriote in Venice. JEPPESEN 101–114

384 Tack, Franz. Die liquescierenden Neumen des Introitus in der Tradition des *Codex 339* von St. Gallen. JOHNER 66–72

385 Wagner, Peter. Zur mittelalterlichen Tonartenlehre. ADLER 29–32

386 Wellesz, Egon. Die Entwicklungsphasen der byzantinischen Notation. KOCZIRZ 41–46

387 ——. Die Epochen der byzantinischen Notenschrift. BAUMSTARK 277–288

MIDDLE AGES: INSTRUMENTS & INSTRUMENTAL MUSIC

See also nos. 26a, 80b

387a Andersson, Otto. Orglar och organister i Åbo Domkyrka intill slutet av 1600-talet. ANDERSSON, O./85TH 7–31; orig. in ANDERSON, A. 9–58

388 Anglés, Higinio. Die Instrumentalmusik bis zum 16. Jahrhundert in Spanien. JEPPESEN 143–164

388a Bösken, Franz. Die Musik in der Schornsheimer Kirche. Ein Beitrag zur Instrumentenkunde und Musikikonographie. GOTTRON 107–117

388b Bowles, Edmund A. The Symbolism of the Organ in the Middle Ages: a Study in the History of Ideas. REESE/65TH 27–39
389 Buhle, Edward. Das Glockenspiel in den Miniaturen des frühen Mittelalters. LILIENCRON 51–71
390 Cesari, Gaetano. Tre tavole de strumenti in un *Boezio* del X secolo. ADLER 26–28
391 Devoto, Daniel. La Enumeración de instrumentos musicales en la poesía medieval Castellana. ANGLÉS I, 211–222
392 Englehardt, Walther. Die musizierenden Engel des Münsterschatzes in Essen. SCHIEDERMAIR/80TH 14–16
392a Ghisi, Federico. An Angel Concert in a Trecento Sienese Fresco. REESE/65TH 308–313
392b Gieysztor, Aleksander. O dacie średniowiecznego dzwonu "pro pace" ze Słączna na Śląsku [Concerning the date of the medieval bell "pro pace" from Słączno in Silesia] FEICHT 143–147
393 Handschin, Jacques. Zur Behandlung des Mensurproblems im Mittelalter. BIEHLE 40–46, & HANDSCHIN 82–89
393a Harrison, Frank Lloyd. Tradition and Innovation in Instrumental Usage, 1100–1450. REESE/65TH 319–335
393b Kolsrud, Oluf. Les Inscriptions des cloches de l'église de Sauherad. EITREM 43–52
393c Mahling, Christoph-Hellmut. Das "Haus der Musikanten" in Reims. Versuch einer ikonographischen Deutung. WIORA/60TH 250–263
394 Mare, A. J. de. Afbeeldingen van muziekinstrumenten in het handschrift van Priester Laurentis Voltooid in 1366. SCHEURLEER 201–206
394a Minis, C. Über Rolands Horn, Burgers *Passio Rotolandi* und Konrads *Roland*. FRANK 439–453
395 Moberg, Carl Allen. Fistula und Fidhla; zur Kritik altschwedischer Musiknotizen. SCHENK 369–377
395a Pope, Isabel. King David and His Musicians in Spanish Romanesque Sculpture. REESE/65TH 693–703
395b Puccianti, Anna. La descrizione della *viella* e della *rubeba* in Girolamo di Moravia. BARBLAN/60TH 227–237
396 Rittmeyer-Iselin, Dora J. Das Rebec; ein Beitrag zur Geschichte unserer Streichinstrumente. NEF 210–219
397 Salmen, Walter. Zur Verbreitung von Einhandflöte und Trommel im europäischen Mittelalter. ZODER 154–161
397a Salvini, Joseph. Les orgues du Moyen Âge à Saint-Hilaire de Poitiers. CROZET 1389–1390
397b Sutkowski, Adam. Les sujets musicaux dans les miniatures médiévales en Pologne. CROZET 1341–1343
398 Werner, Joachim. Leier und Harfe im germanischen Frühmittelalter. MAYER/T I, 9–15

RENAISSANCE ERA: GENERAL

See also nos. 106a, 387a, 467a, 2621b

399 Adler, Guido. Über Textlegung in den Trienter Codices. RIEMANN 50–54
399a Adler, Israël. Une source hébraïque de 1602 relative à la musica reservata? FÉDEROV 9–15
400 Barblan, Guglielmo. I *Rognoni,* musicisti milanesi tra il 1500 e il 1600. HOBOKEN 19–28
401 Besseler, Heinrich. Grundsätzliches zur Übertragung von Mensuralmusik. SCHENK 31–38
402 ——. Umgangsmusik und Darbietungsmusik im 16. Jahrhundert. GURLITT 21–43
403 Birtner, Herbert. Renaissance und Klassik in der Musik. KROYER 40–53
404 Blume, Friedrich. Die Musik der Renaissance. BLUME/S 10–66; orig. in *MGG* 11, col. 224
405 Borren, Charles van den. Esquisse d'une histoire des tombeaux musicaux. SCHENK 56–67
406 ——. Le Madrigalisme avant le madrigal. ADLER 78–83
407 Cherbuliez, Antoine-Elisée. Musikpädagogische Beziehungen zwischen der Schweiz und Deutschland in älterer Zeit. MERSMANN 19–29
408 Clercx, Suzanne. D'une ardoise aux partitions du XVIe siècle. MASSON I, 157–170
409 Doorslaer, George van. L'Education artistique des anciens musiciens instrumentalistes. SCHEURLEER 89–97
409a Dürr, Walther. Auftakt und Taktschlag in der Musik um 1600. GERSTENBERG/60TH 26–36
410 Ehmann, Wilhelm. Das Musizierbild der deutschen Kantorei im 16. Jahrhundert. SEIFFERT 69–79
411 Federhofer, Helmut. Hohe und tiefe Schlüsselung im 16. Jahrhundert. BLUME/F 104–111

411a Fellerer, Karl Gustav. Monodie und Diminutionsmodelle. RACEK/60TH 79–85
411b ——. Zur Kontrapunkt-Literatur im 16. Jahrhundert. FÉDEROV 39–43
411c Fischer, Kurt von. Organal and Chordal Style in Renaissance Sacred Music: New and Little-known Sources. REESE/65TH 173–182
412 Gavel, H. De coro decorar; note sur l'ancien usage de chanter de mémoire dans les églises. MENÉNDEZ PIDAL I, 137–150
413 Gerstenberg, Walter. Zur Motette im 16. Jahrhundert. OREL/70TH 73–75
413a ♪ *Gratiarum Actio* (Cluny Museum, inscribed knives) SACHS/C 256
414 Gurlitt, Wilibald. Canon sine pausis. MASSON I, 117–123
415 Haraszti, Emile. Une Fête de paon à Saint-Julien de Tours. MASSON I, 127–145
415a Haydon, Glen. *Ave Maris Stella* from Apt to Avignon. STÄBLEIN/70TH 79–91
415b Horsley, Imogene. Fugue and Mode in 16th-century Vocal Polyphony. REESE/65TH 406–422
416 Huber, Kurt. Die Doppelmeister des 16. Jahrhunderts; eine methodologische Skizze. SANDBERGER 170–188
417 Jeppesen, Knud. Das isometrische Moment in der Vokalpolyphonie. WAGNER 87–100
418 Kahl, Willi. Das Geschichtsbewusstsein in der Musikanschauung der italienischen Renaissance und des deutschen Humanismus. ALBRECHT 39–47
419 Kinkeldey, Otto. Equal Voices in the *a cappella* Period. DAVIDSON 101–109
420 Kirsch, Winfried. Die Verbindung von Magnificat und Weihnachtsliedern im 16. Jahrhundert. OSTHOFF 61–74
421 Kroyer, Theodor. A cappella oder conserto? KRETZSCHMAR 65–73
422 ——. Zur Chiavetten-Frage. ADLER 107–115
423 Kurthen, Wilhelm. Über Choral und Polyphonie im 16. Jahrhundert. JOHNER 106–109
424 Lang, Paul Henry. Objectivity and Constructionism in the Vocal Music of the 15th and 16th Centuries. JEPPESEN 115–124
425 Lenaerts, René B. Niederländische polyphone Musik in der Bibliothek von Monserrat. SCHMIDT-GÖRG 196–201
425a ——. Zur Ostinato-Technik in der Kirchenmusik der Niederländer. STÄBLEIN/70TH 157–159
425b Lockwood, Lewis. On "Parody" as Term and Concept in 16th-century Music. REESE/65TH 560–575
426 ——. A View of the Early 16th-Century Parody Mass. QC 55–81
427 Lowinsky, Edward. Early Scores in Manuscript. KINKELDEY/80TH 126–173
428 Luther, Wilhelm Martin. Die nichtliturgischen Musikinkunabeln der göttinger Bibliothek. TIEMANN 130–148
429 Moser, Hans Joachim. Musikaliendruckerei auf der deutschen Ritterburg. MOSER/70TH 31–33; orig. in *ZfMW* 17 (1953)
430 Mueren, Floris van der. Hoe benaderen wij onze laat-middeleeuwsche muziek. VERMEYLEN 376–380
431 Novati, Francesco. Contributo alla storia della lirica musicale italiana popolare e popolareggiante dei secoli XV, XVI, XVII. RENIER 899–980
432 Pfister, Arnold. Vom frühesten Musikdruck in der Schweiz. BINZ 160–178
433 Pirro, André. Un Manuscrit musical du XVe siècle au Mont-Cassin. MONTE CASSINO I, 206–208
434 Prahács, Margit. A nemzeti kórus-stílusok kibontakozása/ L'Evoluzione degli stili corali nazionali. KODÁLY/60TH 72–83
435 Preussner, Eberhard. Solmisationsmethoden im Schulunterricht des 16. und 17. Jahrhunderts. STEIN 112–128
436 Reese, Gustave. Maldeghem and his Buried Treasure, a Bibliographical Study. KINKELDEY 75–117
437 ——. The Polyphonic Magnificat of the Renaissance as a Design in Tonal Centers. KINKELDEY/80TH 68–78
438 Römer, Ludwig. Zwölf französische Lieder aus dem 16. Jahrhundert. FDH 30–44
439 Sartori, Claudio. Nuove conclusive aggiunte alla *Bibliografia del Petrucci*. EINSTEIN/C 175–210
439a Schrade, Leo. Renaissance: the Historical Conception of an Epoch. SCHRADE/D 310–325; orig in. *Internat. Ges. f. Musikwiss. Kongress-Bericht Utrecht*, 1952, 19–32
439b Smith, Carleton Sprague. Table Blessings Set to Music. SACHS/C 236–282
439c Spiess, Lincoln Bunce. Inconsistency of Meaning in Certain Medieval and Renaissance Terms. BUSZIN 25–32
440 Springer, Hermann. Zur Musik-

typographie in der Inkunabelzeit. WILMANNS 173–180

440a Swaryczewska, Katarzyna. Przycznek do zagadnienia repertuaru muzycznego w okresie renesansu [A Note on the Problems of the Musical Repertoire in the Renaissance] FEICHT 148–156

441 Waesberghe, Joseph Smits van. Das Weihnachtslied *In dulci jubilo* und seine ursprüngliche Melodie. OSTHOFF 27–37

441a Weise, Georg. "Spätgotik" als Stilbezeichnung im Bereich der Musikgeschichte. FREY/60TH 315–344

442 Winternitz, Emanuel. The Curse of Pallas Athena: Notes on a *Contest between Apollo and Marsyas* in the Kress Collection. SUIDA 186–195

443 Wolff, Hellmuth Christian. Die Musik im alten Venedig. BESSELER 291–303

RENAISSANCE ERA: LOW COUNTRIES, FRANCE, & ITALY. 15TH CENTURY

See also nos. 314, 333a, 535a, 575a

444 Becherini, Bianca. Musica italiana a Firenze nel XV secolo. BORREN/80TH 201
109–121

445 Bridgman, Nanie. Fêtes italiennes de plein air au quattrocento. ALBRECHT 34–38

446 ♪ *Brunette ie vous ay amée/ Brunette au foral noir*. BRESSELER 199–

446a Clarke, Henry Leland. Musicians of the Northern Renaissance. REESE/ 65TH 67–81

447 Droz, Eugénie. Les Chansons de François Villon. LAURENCIE 29–32

448 ——. Les Formes littéraires de la chanson française au XVe siècle. SCHEURLEER 99–102

449 ♪ *Et in terra* (Copenhagen. Königl. Bibl. Ny kgl. Saml. *1848*fol.) JEPPESEN 81–86

450 ♪ *Faulx envieux tenez vous/()e qui vous ame*. BESSELER 195

451 Fédorov, Vladimir. Des Russes au concile de Florence, 1438–1439. ALBRECHT 27–33

452 Feldmann, Fritz. Alte und neue Probleme um Cod. *2016* des Musikalischen Instituts bei der Universität Breslau. SCHNEIDER/80TH 49–66

453 ♪ *Filles a marier* (Sevilla. Bibl. Col. Cod. *5-I-43*). BESSELER 201–202

454 ♪ *Funde preces* (Copenhagen. Kgl. Bibl. Ny kgl. Saml. *1848*fol.) JEPPESEN 95–97

455 Gerber, Rudolf. Die Hymnen des Apelschen Kodex (Mus. Ms. *1494* der Universitätsbibliothek, Leipzig). SCHERING 76–89

456 Gerson-Kiwi, Edith. Sulla genesi delle canzoni popolari nel '500. HANDSCHIN/I 170–184

456a Ghisi, Federico. Alcune canzoni a ballo del primo cinquecento. ENGEL 125–133

457 ——. Strambotti e laude nel travestimento spirituale della poesia musicale del quattrocento. EINSTEIN/C 45–78

458 Glahn, Henrik. Ein kopenhagener Fragment aus dem 15. Jahrhundert. JEPPESEN 59–100

459 Gmelch, Joseph. Unbekannte Reimgebetkompositionen aus Rebdorfer Handschriften. WAGNER 69–80

460 Gülke, Peter. Das Volkslied in der burgundischen Polyphonie des 15. Jahrhunderts. BESSELER 179–202

461 Handschin, Jacques. Zur Musikgeschichte des 15. Jahrhunderts. HANDSCHIN 113–116; orig. in NEUE ZÜRCHER ZEITUNG 2376 (1934)

461a Heartz, Daniel. A 15th-century Ballo: *Rôti Bouilli Joyeux*. REESE/65TH 359–375

462 Helm, Everett B. Heralds of the Italian Madrigal. EINSTEIN 306–318

462a Hewitt, Helen. A Chanson Rustique of the Early Renaissance: *Bon Temps*. REESE/65TH 376–391

463 Hoppin, Richard H. A Fifteenth-Century *Christmas Oratorio*, DAVISON 41–49

463a Jeppesen, Knud. The Manuscript Florence, Biblioteca Nazionale Centrale, Banco Rari 230: an Attempt at a Diplomatic Reconstruction. REESE/65TH 440–447

464 ——. Népi dallamelemek Octavio Petrucci frottolakiadványaiban (1504–1514)/Das Volksliedsgut in den Frottolenbüchern des Octavio Petrucci (1504–1514). KODÁLY/60TH 265–274

465 ——. Die Textlegung in der Chansonmusik des späteren 15. Jahrhunderts. KROHN 82–90

466 ——. Ein venezianisches Laudenmanuskript. KROYER 69–76

466a Kenney, Sylvia. W. Four Settings

of "Ave Regina Coelorum." BORREN/90TH 98–104
466b ——. In Praise of the Lauda. REESE/65TH 489–499
467 Linden, Albert van der. La Musique dans les chroniques de Jean Molinet. CLOSSON 166–180
467a Meier, Bernhard. Musikgeschichtliche Vorstellungen des Niederländischen Zeitalters. GERSTENBERG/60TH 98–106
467b ♪ *O Rosa Bella/In Pace* (quodlibet, Seville Chansonnier 27). SACHS/C 173–175
468 Parrish, Carl. A Curious Use of Coloration in the Pixérécourt Codex. DAVISON 83–90
469 Plamenac, Dragan. Browsing through a Little-Known Manuscript. KINKELDEY/80TH 102–111
469a ——. The Two-part Quodlibets in the Seville Chansonnier. SACHS/C 163–181
469b ♪ *Pour Prison/Passio Domini Nostri* (quodlibet, Seville Chansonnier 26). SACHS/C 169–170
470 ♪ *Rolet ara la tricoton/Maistre Piere/La tricotée.* BESSELER 198–199
471 ♪ *Salve Regina* (Copenhagen. Kgl. Bibl. Ny kgl. Saml. *1848*fol.). JEPPESEN 77–81
472 Schwartz, Rudolf. Zum Formproblem der Frottole Petruccis. KROYER 77–85
472a Seay, Albert. The 15th-century *Coniuncta:* a Preliminary Study. REESE/65TH 723–737
472b ♪ *Seule Esgarée/O Rosa Bella* (quodlibet, Seville Chansonnier 28). SACHS/C 177–180
473 Wolf, Johannes. Eine neue Quelle zur Musik des 15. Jahrhunderts. KROHN 151–162

RENAISSANCE ERA:
LOW COUNTRIES, FRANCE, & ITALY.
16TH CENTURY

See also nos. 314, 532e, 575a, 760a, 773a

474 Albrecht, Hans. Ein quodlibetartiges Magnificat aus der Zwickauer Ratsschulbibliothek. BESSELER 215–220
475 Becherini, Bianca. Tre incatenature del codice Fiorentino Magl. XIX. *164–65–66–67*. EINSTEIN/C 79–96
476 Borren, Charles van den. A propos d'un album musical de Marguerite d'Autriche. MASSON I, 173–181
477 ——. L'Enigme des *Credo de Village*. ALBRECHT 48–54
478 Bridgman, Nanie, & François Lesure. Une Anthologie historique de la fin du XVIe siècle: le manuscrit Bourdeney. ANGLÉS I, 161–172
478a Brown, Howard Mayer. Chansons for the Pleasure of a Florentine Patrician. REESE/65TH 56–66
479 Cauchie, Maurice. La Pureté des modes dans la musique vocale francobelge du début du XVIe siècle/Die Reinheit der Kirchentöne in der französisch-neiderländischen Chormusik des frühen 16. Jahrhunderts. KROYER 54–61
480 ♪ *Donna tu pure invecchi* (quodlibet). EINSTEIN/C 93–95
481 Dürr, Walther. Die italienische Canzonette und das deutsche Lied im Ausgang des XVI. Jahrhunderts. BIANCHI 71–102
482 Engel, Hans. Nochmals die Intermedien von Florenz 1589. SCHNEIDER/80TH 71–86
482a Fabbri, Mario. Una preziosa raccolta di musica sacra cinquecentesca: il "Codice 215" dell'Archivio del Duomo di Pistoia. BARBLAN/60TH 103–123
482b Ferand, Ernest T. Didactic Embellishment Literature in the Late Renaissance: a Survey of Sources. REESE/65TH 154–172
483 Finscher, Ludwig. Zur Cantus-Firmus-Behandlung in der Psalm-Motette der Josquinzeit. ALBRECHT 55–62
484 ♪ *Fortuna desperata* (quodlibet). EINSTEIN/C 89–91
485 Handschin, Jacques. Die Grundlagen des A cappella-Stils. HANDSCHIN 90–112; orig. in *Hans Häusermann und der Häusermannsche Privatchor* (Zürich 1929)
485a Hartog, J. De toonkunst die verbindt. BREDIUS 95–96
486 ♪ *Jam pris amour* (quodlibet). EINSTEIN/C 85–87
487 Jeppesen, Knud. Über italienische Kirchenmusik in der ersten Hälfte des 16. Jahrhunderts. KODÁLY/80TH 149–160
487a Kenton, Egon. A Faded Laurel Wreath. REESE/65TH 500–518
488 Kroyer, Theodor. Von der Musica Reservata des 16. Jahrhunderts. WÖLFFLIN 127–144

488a Lenaerts, René Bernard. Parodia, reservata-kunst en muzikaal symbolisme. BORREN/90TH 107–112
489 ——. Polyphonische missen op Nederlandse liederen. WAESBERGHE 101–105
489a Lesure, François. Some Minor French Composers of the 16th Century. REESE/65TH 538–544
490 Llorens Cisteró, José María. Miniaturas de Vincent Raymond en los manuscritos musicales de la Capilla Sixtina. ANGLÉS I, 475–494
491 Lovarini, Emilio. Una Poesia musicata del Ruzzante. CRESCINI 237–266
491a Müller-Blattau, Wendelin. Der Humanismus in der Musikgeschichte Frankreichs und Deutschlands. WIORA/60TH 296–303
492 ♪ *Nobis datus, nobis natus* (Toledo. Bibl. Cath. Cod. *25*). ADLER 114–115
492a Noske, Frits. Early Sources of the Dutch National Anthem (1574–1626). FÉDEROV 87–94
492b Pidoux, Pierre. Polyphonic Settings of the Genevan Psalter: Are They Church Music? BUSZIN 65–74
493 Renier, Rodolfo. Un Mazzetto di poesie musicali francesi. CAIX 271–288
494 Schering, Arnold. Tricinium. SCHEURLEER 279–281
495 Schmitz, Arnold. Italienische Quellen zur Figuralpassion des 16. Jahrhunderts. SCHNEIDER/60TH 92–102
496 ——. Zur motettischen Passion des 16. Jahrhunderts. GURLITT 232–245
497 Schneider, Max. Zur Geschichte des begleiteten Sologesangs. KRETZSCHMAR 138–140
497a Schrade, Leo. The Festivities at the Wedding of Francesco dei Medici and Bianca Cappello. SCHRADE/D 326–359; orig. (in French) in *Les fêtes de la renaissance I, Journées Internat. d'Études, Abbaye de Royaument* 1955. Paris (1956) 107–131
498 Thibault, Geneviève. Un Manuscrit de chansons françaises à la Bibliothèque Royale de la Haye. SCHEURLEER 347–358
499 Torri, Luigi. Quattro sonetti musicati per le nozze e in onore di Emanuele Filiberto e Margherita di Francia. EMANUELE 479–492
500 Weinmann, Karl. Parmensische Musiker aus der zweiten Hälfte des 16. Jahrhunderts. KRETZSCHMAR 169–171
501 Wolff, Hellmuth Christian. Die ästhetische Auffassung der Parodiemesse des 16. Jahrhunderts. ANGLÉS II, 1011–1017

RENAISSANCE ERA: GERMANY, SWITZERLAND, & SCANDINAVIA

See also nos. 491a, 529b, 814a, 1165a, 2146

502 Adler, Guido. Die Turbae einer deutschen Matthäuspassion von 1559. LILIENCRON 17–34
502a Blume, Friedrich. Geistliche Musik am Hofe des Landgrafen Moritz von Hessen. GUTBIER 131–140
502b Bork, Gerhard. Die mehrstimmigen lateinischen Magnificat-Kompositionen in der Kirchenordnung von Pfalz-Zweibrücken (Neuburg) aus dem Jahre 1570 (1557). FELLERER/60THS 39–54
502c Cuyler, Louise E. Music in Biographies of Emperor Maximilian. REESE/65TH 111–121
502d ——. Musical Activity in Augsburg and Its *Annakirche, ca.* 1470–1630. BUSZIN 33–43
502e Dürr, Walther. Die italienische Canzonette und das deutsche Lied im Ausgang des XVI. Jahrhunderts. BIANCHI 73–102
502f Federhofer-Königs, Renate. Ein musiktheoretisches Fragment aus der Abtei Feicht (Tirol). WIORA/60TH 177–181
503 Fellerer, Karl Gustav. Das kölner Provinzial-Konzil 1536 und die Kirchenmusik. KALLEN 327–336
504 ——. Die Mariensequenzen im freiburger Prosarium. SCHERING 61–67
505 Geering, Arnold. *Ein tütsche Musica des figurirten Gesangs* 1491. FELLERER/60TH 178–181
506 ♪ German monophonic songs (Vatican C. Bibl. Ap. Vat. Pal. lat. *1260*). SCHERING 259–274
507 Gerstenberg, Walter. Die deutsche Musik und der Osten. AUBIN/T 61–66
508 Glahn, Henrik. En ny kilde til belysning af det preussiske hofkapels repertoire på Hertug Albrechts tid [A New Source of the Repertoire of the Prussian Court in Prince Albert's Time] MOBERG 145–161
508a Gudewill, Kurt. Deutsche Liedtenores mit F-dur-Melodik und Oktavambitus. WIORA/60TH 269–277

509 Hammerich, Angul. Niederländische Musiker in Dänemark im 16.–17. Jahrhundert. SCHEURLEER 135–142
510 Hoffmann-Erbrecht, Lothar. Datierungsprobleme bei Kompositionen in deutschen Musikhandschriften des 16. Jahrhunderts. OSTHOFF 47–60
510a Hüschen, Heinrich. Hessische Gesangbuchdrucker und -verleger des 16. und 17. Jahrhunderts. ENGEL 166–187
510b Jenny, Markus. The Hymns of Zwingli and Luther, a Comparison. BUSZIN 45–63
511 Kahl, Willi. Die Musik an der alten kölner Universität um 1500. CU/F 473–501
512 Krohn, Ilmari. Den lutherske Koral i Finnland. SANDVIK 122–147
513 ♪ Lochamer Liederbuch. *Des klaffers Neiden.* SCHERING 154
514 Mahrenholz, Christhard. Auswahl und Einordnung der Katechismuslieder in den wittenberger Gesangbüchern seit 1529. SÖHNGEN 123–132
515 Marx, Hans Joachim. Der Tabulator-Codex des Basler Humanisten Bonifacius Amerbach. SCHRADE 50–70
516 ♪ *Matthäuspassion* (Vienna. Nat. Bibl. *16195*). ADLER 19–27, 32–34
517 Moberg, Carl Allan. En svensk Johannespassion från stormaktsiden. UUTF 1–32
518 Moser, Hans, Joachim. Das deutsche monodische Kunstlied um 1500. WAGNER 146–169
519 ——. Eine trienter Orgeltabulatur aus Hofhaimers Zeit. ADLER 84–86
520 Müller-Blattau, Joseph. Über Instrumentalbearbeitungen spätmittelalterlicher Lieder. SCHERING 151–165
521 ——. *Wach auff, mein hort!* Studie zur deutschen Liedkunst des 15. Jahrhunderts. ADLER 92–99
522 Nef, Karl. Die Musik an der Universität Basel. BU 297–336
523 Norlind, Todias, Die schwedische Hofkapelle in der Reformationszeit. WOLF 148–152
523a Pietsch, Gerhard. Die Jülich'sche Hochzeit 1585. FELLERER/60THS 166–189
524 Refardt, Edgar. Die Musik der basler Volksschauspiele des 16. Jahrhunderts. REFARDT 9–23; orig. in *Basler Nachrichten*, Sonntagsblatt 50–52 (1920)
524a Schneider, Marius. Zur Metrisierung des altdeutschen Liedes. WIORA/60TH 278–283
525 Senn, Walter. Beiträge zum deutschen Kirchenlied Tirols im 16. Jahrhundert. AMMANN II, 146–155
525a Southern, Eileen. Basse-dance Music in Some German Manuscripts of the 15th Century. REESE/65TH 738–755
526 Stevens, Denis. German Lute-Songs of the Early Sixteenth Century. BESSELER 253–257
526a Suppan, Wolfgang. "In der wyss, wer ich ein edler Falke." WIORA/60TH 651–657
527 Werner, Theodore W. Ein malerischer Winkel in der Altstadt Hannover. MÜLLER VON ASOW [226–230]
528 Wolf, Johannes. Deutsche Lieder des 15. Jahrhunderts. LILIENCRON 404–420
529 ——. Deutsche Lieder des 15. Jahrhunderts. SCHERING 259–274 (different from no. 528)

RENAISSANCE ERA:
IBERIAN COUNTRIES
See also nos. 82a, 391

529a Anglés, Higinio. Alfonso V d'Aragona mecenate della música ed il suo ménestrel Jean Boisard. BORREN/90TH 6–16
529b ——. Austausch deutscher und spanischer Musiker im 15. und 16. Jahrhundert. NEUSS 166–178
529b1 ——. El canto religioso popular en los manuales litúrgicos de la Tarraconense. SUBIRÁ/80TH 103–108
529c ——. Early Spanish Musical Culture and Cardinal Cisneros's Hymnal of 1515. REESE/65TH 3–16
530 ——. Die spanische Liedkunst im 15. und am Anfang des 16. Jahrhunderts. KROYER 62–68
530a ——. Un tractat de cant plà d'autor anònim del segle XVI. VIVES 277–293
531 Aubrun, Charles. Inventaire des sources pour l'étude de la poésie castillane au XVe siècle. MENÉNDEZ PIDAL/E IV, 297–330
532 Bohigas, Pere. Les Miniatures dels cantorials de Pedralbes. ANGLÉS I, 135–148
532a ♪ Cisneros Hymnal. Selections. REESE/65TH 14–16
532b Fischer, Kurt von. Ein singulärer Typus portugiesischer Passionen des 16. Jahrhunderts. SCHMITZ 180–185
532c Kastner, Santiago. Ursprung und Sinn des "medio registro." BALDELLÓ 57–69
532d Llordén, P. Andrés. Notas his-

tóricas de los maestros de capilla en la Catedral de Málaga (1583–1641). BALDELLÓ 71–93
532e Massenkeil, Günther. Eine spanische Choralmelodie in mehrstimmigen Lamentations-Kompositionen des 16. Jahrhunderts. SCHMITZ 230–237
532f Moll, Jaime. Notas para la historia musical de la corte del Duque de Calabria. SUBIRÁ/80TH 123–135
532g ——. La Princesa Juana de Austria y la música. Notas para su estudio. BALDELLÓ 119–122
533 Pfandl, Ludwig. Über einige spanische Handschriften der Münchener Staatsbibliothek. I. Das Original des Cancionero de la Sablonara. MENÉNDEZ PIDAL II, 531–544
534 Plamenac, Dragan. *Excerpta Colombiniana:* Items of Musical Interest in Fernando Colón's *Regestrum.* ANGLÉS II, 663–687
535 Pope, Isabel. Notas sobre la melodía del *Conde claros.* ALONSO 395–402
535a —— and Masakata Kanazawa. The Musical Manuscript Montecassino N879 [i.e. 871] BALDELLÓ 123–153
536 Restori, Antonio. Poesie spagñole appartenute a Donna Ginevra Bentivoglio. MENÉNDEZ Y PELAYO II, 455–485
537 Romeu Figueras, José. Las Canciones de raíz tradicional acogidas por Cáceres en su ensalada *La Trulla.* ANGLÉS II, 735–768
538 Schneider, Marius. Die Modustransformation in einer spanischen Melodiegestalt. FELLERER/60TH 481–484
539 ——. Studien zur Rhythmik im *Cancionero de Palacio.* ANGLÉS II, 833–835
540 Solar-Quintes, Nicholás A. Nuevos documentos sobre ministriles, trompetas, cantorcicos, organistas y Capilla Real de Felipe II. ANGLÉS II, 851–888
541 Trend, John Brande. Spanish Madrigals and Madrigal-Texts. ADLER 116–120

RENAISSANCE ERA: ENGLAND & SCOTLAND

542 ♪Bannatyne Ms. *Prise Me As Ye Think Cause Why.* BESSELER 264–265
543 Deutsch, Otto Erich. Cäcilia und Parthenia. OREL/70TH 43–46
543a Duckles, Vincent. The English Musical Elegy of the Late Renaissance. REESE/65TH 134–153
543b Ellingwood, Leonard. From Plainsong to Anglican Chant. BUSZIN 21–24
544 Kenney, Sylvia W. Ely Cathedral and the *Contenance angloise.* SCHRADE 35–49
545 Mishkin, Henry G. Irrational Dissonance in the English Madrigal. DAVISON 139–145
546 ♪Raitt Ms. *Greensleeves.* BESSELER 269
547 ♪——. *Who Shall my Malady Amend?* BESSELER 265–266
548 Rubsamen, Walter. Scottish and English Music of the Renaissance in a Newly-Discovered Manuscript. BESSELER 259–284
549 Tuttle, Stephen. Watermarks in Certain Manuscript Collections of English Keyboard Music. DAVISON 147–158
550 Vaughan Williams, Ralph. A Minim's Rest. MILFORD 113–116
550a Ward, John M. *Joan qd John* and Other Fragments at Western Reserve University. REESE/65TH 832–855
551 Wormald, Francis. The Solemn Entry of Mary Tudor to Montreuil-sur-mer in 1514. JENKINSON 471–479

RENAISSANCE ERA: HUNGARY & SLAVIC NATIONS

See also no. 82b.

552 Chybiński, Adolf. Nowe materyaly do dziejów królewskiej kapeli Rorantystów w Kaplicy Zygmuntowskiej na Wawelu [New Materials from the Sigismund Chapel on Wawel Hill concerning the History of the Royal Rorantist Collegium] BALZER I, 133–151
553 ——. Über die polnische mehrstimmige Musik des XVI. Jahrhunderts. RIEMANN 340–348
553a Cvetko, Dragotin. Testimonianza di Paolo Santonino sulle condizioni della musica in Slovenia verso la fine del secolo XV. DESDERI/70TH 29–36
554 ♪Eperjes gradual. 16th-century psalm settings. KODÁLY/75TH 210–264
555 Gombosi, Otto. Die Musikalien der Pfarrkirche zu St. Aegidi in Bártfa; ein Beitrag zur Geschichte der Musik in Oberungarn. WOLF 38–47
556 Haraszti, Emile. Les Rapports

italo-transylvains de *Il Transilvano* de Girolamo Diruta. LAURENCIE 73–84

557 ——. Zene és ünnep Mátyás és Beatrix idejében [Music and Festivities in the Time of Matthias and Beatrice] MATTHIAS II, 291–412

558 Kardos, Tibor. A magyár vígjáték kezedetei [The Beginnings of Hungarian Comedy] KODÁLY/70TH 133–168

558a Macůrek, Josef. Kpočátkům slavisticko-historických studií Zdeňka Nejedlého [Concerning the Beginning of the Slavic-Historical Studies of Zdenko Nejedlý] NEJEDLÝ/75TH 24–47, summaries in Russian & German

559 Orel, Dobroslav. Stilarten der Mehrstimmigkeit des 15. und 16. Jahrhunderts in Böhmen. ADLER 87–91

559a Protopopov, Vladimir. O polofonii cheshskoy shkoly XVI–nachala XIX veka [Concerning the Polyphony of the Czech School from the 16th Century to the Beginning of the 19th Century] RACEK/60TH 207–226

560 Rattay, Kurt. Das masurische Kirchenlied; ein aussterbendes Volksgut. ABERT 125–132

561 Salmen, Walter. Die internationale Wirksamkeit slawischer und magyarischer Musik vor 1600. AUBIN 235–242

562 Szabolcsi, Bence. Über das Fortleben antiker Metren in der ungarischen Lied- und Tansmusik. BESSELER 15–20

563 Szczepańska, Maria. Nieznana tabulatura lutniowa krakowska z drugiej połowy XVI stulecia [An Unknown Cracow Lute Tablature from the Second Half of the 16th Century] CHYBIŃSKI/70TH 198–217

564 ——. Nowe źródło do historji muzyki średniowiecznej w Polsce [A New Source for Medieval Music History in Poland] CHYBIŃSKI/50TH 15–56

564a Wessely, Othmar. Beiträge zur Geschichte der Hofkapelle Lajos' II. Jagello, Königs von Böhmen und Ungarn. STÄBLEIN/70TH 293–300

RENAISSANCE ERA: INSTRUMENTS & INSTRUMENTAL MUSIC

See also nos. 388, 532c, 532f, 797, 2569

565 Anglés, Higinio. Orgelmusik der Schola Hispanica vom XV. bis XVII. Jahrhundert. WAGNER 11–26

566 Bernoulli, Eduard. Volksinstrumente in Zeichnungen und Holzschnitten von Hans Holbein und Urs Graf. KRETZSCHMAR 18–21

567 Broder, Nathan. The Beginnings of the Orchestra. KINKELDEY/80TH 174–180

567a Ceci, Giuseppe. Maestri organari a Napoli dal XV al XVIII secolo. CORTESE 3–10

568 Dart, Thurston. Elisabeth Eysbock's Keyboard Book. ALBRECHT 84–87

569 Fellerer, Karl Gustav. Musikalische Bilddarstellungen des 15./16. Jahrhunderts zu Freiburg im Üchtland. SEIFFERT 80–82

570 Fischer, Kurt von. Zur Entstehungsgeschichte der Orgelchoralvariation. BLUME/F 137–145

571 Frotscher, Gotthold. Die Volksinstrumente auf Bildwerken des 16. und 17. Jahrhunderts. SEIFFERT 61–68

572 Gombosi, Otto. About Dance and Dance Music in the Late Middle Ages. EINSTEIN 289–305

573 ——. About Organ Playing in the Divine Service, circa 1500. DAVISON 51–68

573a Hammerstein, Reinhold. Ein altelsässischer Totentanz als musikgeschichtliche Quelle. MÜLLER-BLATTAU/70TH 97–100

574 Jeppesen, Knud. Ein altvenetianisches Tanzbuch. FELLERER/60TH 245–263

575 Kastner, Santiago. Organos antiquos en España y en Portugal (siglos XVI–XVIII). ANGLÉS I, 433–448

575a Klotz, Hans. Über die gegenseitigen Beziehungen zwischen der niederländerischen und rheinischen Orgelbaukunst in der Zeit der Renaissance und das Frühbarock. FELLERER/60THS 95–102

575b Kolneder, Walter. Die musikalisch-soziologischen Voraussetzung der Violinenentwicklung. SCHMIDT-GÖRG/70TH 179–196

576 Kretzschmar, Hermann. Musikgeschichtliche Stichproben aus deutscher Laienliteratur des 16. Jahrhunderts. LILIENCRON 116–137

577 Opieński, Henryk. Quelques considérations sur l'origine des ricercari pour luth. LAURENCIE 39–45

578 Sachs, Curt. Der Rhythmus der basse danse. LAURENCIE 57–59

579 Sander, Hans-Adolf. Ein Orgelbuch der breslauer Magdalenen-Kirche

aus dem 17. Jahrhundert; ein Beitrag zum Aufführungsbrauch des späten 16. und 17. Jahrhunderts. SCHNEIDER/60TH 74–83
579a Scharnagel, August. Die Orgeltabulatur C 119 der Proske-Musikbibliothek Regensburg. STÄBLEIN/70TH 206–216
580 Schneider, Max. Eine unbekannte Lautentabulatur aus den Jahren 1537–1544. WOLF 176–178
581 Tschernitschegg, Erich. Zu den Violintabulaturen im Germanischen Museum in Nürnberg. KOCZIRZ 38–41
582 Wallner, Bertha. Ein Instrumentenverzeichnis aus dem 16. Jahrhundert. SANDBERGER 275–286
583 ——. Urkunden zu den Musikbestrebungen Herzog Wilhelms V von Bayern. SCHEURLEER 369–377
584 Ward, John. The Lute Music of Ms Royal Appendix *58*. KINKELDEY/80TH 117–125
584a ——. Parody Technique in 16th-Century Instrumental Music. SACHS/C 202–228
584a[1] White, John R. The Tabulature of Johannes of Lublin. APEL/70TH 137–162
584a[2] Winternitz, Emanuel. Keyboards for Wind Instruments Invented by Leonardo da Vinci. REESE/65TH 883–888
584b ——. The School of Gaudenzio Ferrari and the Early History of the Violin. SACHS/C 182–200
585 Wolf, Johannes. Ein Lautenkodex der Staatsbibliothek Berlin. KOCZIRZ 46–50
585a Young, William. Keyboard Music to 1600. APEL/70TH 163–193

RENAISSANCE ERA: INDIVIDUAL COMPOSERS, PERFORMERS, ETC.

585b [Agricola] Picker, Martin. A Letter of Charles VIII of France Concerning Alexander Agricola. REESE/65TH 665–672
586 [Agrippa] Fellerer, Karl Gustav. Agrippa von Nettesheim und die Musik. GURLITT 77–86
587 [Aichinger] Kroyer, Theodor. Gregor Aichinger als Politiker. WAGNER 128–132
587a [Anerio] Llorens, José María. Felice Anerio, compositor pontificio, en los Códices Ottoboniani de la Biblioteca Vaticana. BALDELLÓ 95–109
588 ♪ Antico, Andrea. *Io uorei dio d'amore*. KRETZSCHMAR 139–140
588a [Antico] Plamenac, Dragan. The Recently Discovered Copy of A. Antico's Frottole Intabulate (1517). REESE/65 683–692
589 ♪ Arcadelt, Jacob. *Deh come trista dei*. EINSTEIN 316–318
590 [Aron] Wolf, Johannes. Ein Brief Pietro Arons an Giovanni del Lago. KUHNERT 65–70
[Ballard, Robert] See no. 662
591 [Barbireau] Fox, Charles W. Barbireau and Barbingant: A Review. KINKELDEY/80TH 79–101
592 [Bassano] Ferand, Ernest T. Die *Motetti, Madrigali, et Canzoni Francese . . . diminuiti . . .* des Giovanni Bassano (1591). OSTHOFF 75–101
593 [Bati] Ghisi, Federico. Luca Bati, maestro della cappella granducale di Firenze. BORREN/80TH 106–108
594 [Bertrand] Thibault, Geneviève. Anthoine de Bertrand, musicien de Ronsard et ses amis toulousains. LEFRANC 282–300
595 ♪ Besard, Jean-Baptiste. *Dolce mia vita*. RIEMANN 287–288
596 [Besard] Chilesotti, Oscar. Villanella a 3 voci dal *Thesaurus harmonicus* di J. B. Besard (1603). RIEMANN 287–288
597 [Boll] Kyhlberg, Bengt. Vem var orgelbyggaren Frantz Boll? Några biografiska notiser am en svensk 1600-talsmästare. MOBERG 209–213
598 [Boni] Droz, Eugénie. Guillaume Boni, de Saint-Flour en Auvergne, musicien de Ronsard. LEFRANC 270–281
599 [Borbonius] Hartmann, Karl-Günther. Nicolaus Borbonius in der Oden- und Motettenkomposition des 16. Jahrhunderts. ALBRECHT 81–83
600 [Bottrigari] Giazotto, Remo. *Il patricio* di Hercole Bottrigari dimostrato praticamente da un anonimo cinquecentista. EINSTEIN/C 97–112
601 [Brätel] Bente, Martin. Ulrich Brätel; über Leben und Werk des ersten württembergischen Hofkomponisten der Reformationszeit. ALBRECHT 63–74
602 [Bruck] Osthoff, Helmuth. Das *Te Deum* des Arnold Bruck. BLUME/F 252–257
603 [Burckard] Schering, Arnold. Musikalisches aus Joh. Burckards *Liber notarum* (1483–1506). WOLF 171–175

604 [Byrd] Dent, Edward J. William Byrd and the Madrigal. WOLF 24–30
604a —— Kerman, Joseph. Byrd, Tallis, and the Art of Imitation. REESE/65TH 519–537
605 [Camargo] Querol, Miguel. Nuevos datos para la biografía de Miguel Gómez Camargo. ANGLÉS II, 707–716
605a ♪ Cara, Marco. *Cantai mentre nel core* (frottola & keyboard transcription). REESE/65TH 690–691
606 [Carver] Fuller-Maitland, John A. A Scottish Composer of the 16th Century. SCHEURLEER 119–122
606a [Cerone] Fellerer, Karl Gustav. Zu Cerones musiktheoretischen Quellen. FINKE/100TH 171–178
607 [Claudin] Mantuani, Josef. Zu den Gemälden vom Meister der weiblichen Halbfiguren. VNB 591–608
608 [Clemens] Bernet Kempers, Karel P. Die Messe *En espoir* des Jacobus Clemens non Papa. SCHMIDT-GÖRG 10–20
609 —— ——. Zum Todesjahr des Clemens non Papa. FELLERER/60TH 46–50
610 [Cochlaeus] Schrade, Leo. Johannes Cochlaeus, Musiktheoretiker in Köln. SCHIEDERMAIR/80TH 124–132
610a [Coclico] Meier, Bernhard. The Musica Reservata of Adrianus Petit Coclico and Its Relationship to Josquin. HANDSCHIN/M 67–105
[Compère, Loyset] See No. 645
611 [Copus] Albrecht, Hans. Caspar Copus, ein fast unbekannter deutscher Komponist des 16. Jahrhunderts. ANGLÉS I, 1–9
612 ♪ Cornago, Johannes. *Qu'es mi vida.* ANGLÉS II, 701–702
613 [Cornago] Pope, Isabel. The Secular Compositions of Johannes Cornago. Part I. ANGLÉS II, 689–700
614 [Corteccia] Haydon, Glen. The Dedication of Francesco Corteccia's *Hinnario.* KINKELDEY/80TH 112–116
614a [Crema] Dardo, Gianluigi. Considerazioni sull'opera di Giovan Maria da Cream liutista del cinquecento. BARBLAN/60TH 61–77
615 ♪ Dufay, Guillaume. *Je vous pri/ Tant que mon argent dura/Ma tres doulce.* BESSELER 196–198
616 ♪ ——. *Seigneur Leon, vous soyés bienvenus.* BORREN/80TH 83
617 [Dufay] Besseler, Heinrich. Dufay in Rom. ANGLÉS I, 111–134
617a —— Gallo, F. Alberto. Citazioni da un trattato di Dufay. BARBLAN/60TH 149–152
618 —— Plamenac, Dragan. Une Composition inconnue de Dufay? BORREN/80TH 75–83
618a [Eccard] Heckmann, Harald. Johann Eccards Gelegenheitskompositionen. STÄBLEIN/70TH 92–100
618b [Erasmus of Hörtiz] Palisca, Claude. The *Musica* of Erasmus of Hörtiz. REESE/65TH 628–648
619 [Esquivel] Geiger, Albert. Juan Esquivel, ein unbekannter spanischer Meister des 16. Jahrhunderts. SANDBERGER 138–169
620 [Faber] Peters-Marquardt, Franz. War Heinrich Lychtenfels der spätere Musiktheoretiker Heinrich Faber? Biographische Skizze zu Heinrich Faber. ALBRECHT 75–80
620a ♪ Farmer, John. *A Hymn After Meat to the Magnificat Tune.* SACHS/C 263.
621 [Festa] Haydon, Glen. The Case of the Troublesome Accidental. JEPPESEN 125–130
622 ♪ Févin, Antoine de. *On a mal dit.* DAVISON 98–99
623 [Févin] Merritt, A. Tillman. A Chanson Sequence by Févin. DAVIDSON 91–99
623a ♪ Fiesco, Giulio. *Bacio soave.* REESE/65TH 484–487
623b ♪ ——. *Nov' angioletta.* REESE/65TH 478–482
623c [Fiesco] Kaufmann, Henry W. A. "Diatonic" and a "Chromatic" Madrigal by Giulio Fiesco. REESE/65TH 474–488
624 [Flecha] Anglés, Higinio. Mateo Flecha el Joven. KODÁLY/80TH 45–51
625 [Florentius de Faxolis] Seay, Albert. The *Liber musices* of Florentius de Faxolis. SCHRADE 71–95
626 [Fritzius] Federhofer, Helmut. Joachimus Fridericus Fritzius. SCHÜTZ 325–342
627 [Fritzsche] Gurlitt, Wilibald. Der kursächsische Hoforgelmacher Gottfried Fritzsche. SCHERING 106–124
628 ♪ Frosch, Johannes. *Qui de terra est.* ANGLÉS II, 1120–1121
628a [Gabrieli, A.] Müller-Blattau, Wendelin. Klangliche Strukturen im Satzbau des Psalmus Primus aus dem "Sieben Busspsalmen" von Andrea Gabrieli. MÜLLER-BLATTAU/70TH 212–220

629 [Gaforio] Bondioli, Pio. Per la biografia di Franchino Gaffurio da Lodi. EINSTEIN/C 19–24
630 —— Handschin, Jacques. Ein Autograph des Franchino Gafori. MÜLLER VON ASOW [64–77]
631 —— Hirsch, Paul. Bibliographie der musiktheoretischen Drucke des Franchino Gafori. WOLF 65–72
632 —— Sartori, Claudio. Il quarto codice di Gaffurio non è del tutto scomparso. EINSTEIN/C 25–44
633 [Glareanus] Kirsch, Ernst. Studie zum Problem des Heinrich Loriti (Glarean). SCHERING 125–136
634 ♪ Gonzago, Guglielmo. *Missa apostolorum. Kyrie.* KROYER 126–129
635 [Gonzaga] Cesari, Gaetano. L'Archivio musicale di S. Barbara in Mantova ed una Messa di Guglielmo Gonzaga/Das Musikarchiv zur Hl. Barbara in Mantua und eine Messe des Herzogs Wilhelm Gonzaga. KROYER 118–129
636 ♪ Gorzanis, Giacomo. *Passamezzo antico*, lute. FELLERER/60TH 436
637 ♪ ——. *Passamezzo moderno*, lute. FELLERER/60TH 437
638 [Gorzanis] Halbig, Hermann. Eine handschriftliche Lautentabulatur des Giacomo Gorzanis. KROYER 102–117
639 —— Reichert, Georg. Giacomo Gorzanis *Intabolatura di liuto* (1567) als Dur- und Molltonarten-Zyklus. FELLERER/60TH 428–438
640 [Gratius] Fellerer, Karl Gustav. Zur *Oratio de laudibus musicae disciplinae* des Orwin Gratius. KAHL 43–48
641 [Guerson] Ferand, Ernest T. Guillaume Guerson's Rules of Improvised Counterpoint (c.1500). ANGLÉS I, 253–263
642 [Guglielmo Ebreo] Kinkeldey, Otto. A Jewish Dancing Master of the Renaissance, Guglielmo Ebreo. FREIDUS 329–372. Reprinted by Dance Horizons (Brooklyn, 1966)
643 [Guilliaud] Cauchie, Maurice. Maximilien Guilliaud. KOCZIRZ 6–8
644 [Guyot de Châtelet] Clercx, Suzanne. Jean Guyot de Châtelet, succentor à la Cathédrale Saint-Lambert à Liège par José Quitin. BORREN/80TH 125–126
644a [Handl] Cvetko, Dragotin. Jacobus Gallus à Olomouc et à Prague (Contribution à biographie pour la période 1579–1591). RACEK/60TH 59–69
644b —— ——. Le problème du rythme dans les oeuvres de Jacobus Gallus. STÄBLEIN/70TH 28–32
645 [Hayne van Ghizeghem] Gombosi, Otto. Ghizeghem und Compère; zur Stilgeschichte der burgundischen Chanson. ADLER 100–106
646 [Hellinck] Lenaerts, René B. Les Messes de Lupus Hellinck du manuscrit 766 de Montserrat. ANGLÉS I, 465–474
647 [Herpol] Geering, Arnold. Homer Herpol und Manfred Barbarini Lupus. NEF 48–71
648 [Hofhaimer] Hoffmann-Erbrecht, Lothar. Paul Hofhaimer in Salzburg. BESSELER 211–214
649 —— Nowak, Leopold. Paul Hofhaymers *Nach willen dein* in den Lautentabulaturen des 16. Jahrhunderts; ein Vergleich. KOCZIRZ 25–29
649a ♪ Hooper, Edmund. *My God, O King, I'll Thee Extol.* SACHS/C 261
649b [Hubertus] Mischiati, Oscar. Uno sconosciuto frammento di codice polifonico quattrocentesco nella Biblioteca "G. B. Martini" di Bologna. BARBLAN/60TH 179–183
650 [Isaac] Jeppesen, Knud. *Choralis Constantinus* som liturgisk dokument. SANDVIK 52–82
650a —— Pätzig, Gerhard. Das Chorbuch Mus. ms. 40024 der Deutschen Staatsbibliothek Berlin. Eine wichtige Quelle zum Schaffen Isaacs aus der Hand Leonhard Pämingers. GERSTENBERG/60TH 122–144
651 —— Webern, Anton von. *Choralis Constantinus.* WEBERN/R 23–25; orig. in *DTÖ* 16/1
652 ♪ Iselin, Ludwig. Studententänze, lute. NEF 331–335
653 [Janequin] Cauchie, Maurice. Les Psaumes de Janequin. LAURENCIE 47–56
654 —— Chailley, Jacques. Le Chant de *l'Alouette* de Janequin et son modèle médiéval. CHAMARD 39–41
654a —— Merritt, A. Tillman. Janequin: Reworkings of Some Early Chansons. REESE/65TH 603–613
654b [Jhan of Ferrara] Johnson, Alvin. A Musical Offering to Hercules II, Duke of Ferrara. REESE/65TH 448–454
654c ♪ Josquin des Prez. *En l'ombre d'un buissonet*, à 3. BORREN/90TH 132–133
654d ♪ ——. *L'homme armé, canon et*

sic de singulis. BORREN/90TH 54

655 [Josquin] Borren, Charles van den. Une Hypothèse concernant le lieu de naissance de Josquin des Prez. SCHMIDT-GÖRG 21–25

656 —— Corbin, Solange. Les Textes musicaux de *l'Auto da alma;* identification d'une pièce citée par Gil Vincente. HALPHEN 137–143

656a —— Disertori, Benvenuto. Una storica mistificazione mensurale di Josquin des Prés: sue affinità con Leonardo da Vinci. BORREN/90TH 49–56

656b —— Fellerer, Karl Gustav. Josquins Missa "Faisant Regretz" in der Vihuela-Transkription von Mudarra und Narváez. NUESS 179–184

656c —— Osthoff, Helmuth. Ein Josquin-Zitat bei Henricus Isaac. BORREN/90TH 127–134

657 —— ——. Das Magnificat bei Josquin Desprez. GURLITT 220–231

658 —— Smijers, Albert. Een kleine bijdrage over Josquin en Isaac. SCHEURLEER 313–319

658a [Kepler] Werner, Eric. The Last Pythagorean Musician: Johannes Kepler. REESE/65TH 867–882

658b [Kerle] Haydon, Glen. The Hymns of Jacobus de Kerle. REESE/65TH 336–358

659 [Kugelmann] Spitta, Friedrich. Die Liedersammlung des Paul Kugelmann. RIEMANN 272–277

659a [La Rue] Rosenberg, Marianne. Symbolic and Descriptive Text Settings in the Sacred Works of Pierre de la Rue (c. 1460–1518). BISHOP 225–248

660 [Lampadius] Hermelink, Siegfried. Die *Tabula compositoria.* BESSELER 221–230

661 [Lasso] Boetticher, Wolfgang. Eine französische Bicinien-Ausgabe als frühmonodisches Dokument. FELLERER/60TH 67–76

661a —— ——. New Lasso Studies. REESE/65TH 17–26

661b —— Lesure, François. Les premiers rapports de Roland de Lassus avec la France. BORREN/75TH 242

661c —— Steinhardt, Milton. The *Missa si me tenes:* a Problem of Authorship. REESE/65TH 756–767

662 [Le Roy] Hofer, Philip. Adrian Le Roy and Robert Ballard, Printers of the Late Renaissance. LYDENBERG 475–482

662a [Lechner] Ameln, Konrad. Leonhard Lechner in His Time. BUSZIN 75–86

663 ♪ Legrant, Johannes. *Et in terra.* KROHN 158–162

664 [Leisentritt] Müller, Hermann. Germanische Choraltradition und deutscher Kirchengesang. WAGNER 170–175

665 [Leo X, Pope] Pirro, André. Léon X et la musique. HAUVETTE 221–234

666 —— Weinmann, Karl. Eine Komposition des Kardina's Joh. de Medici, des nachmaligen Papstes Leo X. SCHEURLEER 379–381

666a [Leopolita] Perz, Mirosław. Motety Marcina Leopolity [The Motets of Marcin Leopolita] FEICHT 155–189

[Lupus, Manfred Barbarini] See no. 647

667 ♪ Lurano, Filippo de. *Donna contra la mia voglia.* EINSTEIN 322–323

668 ♪ ——. *Donna questa a la mia voglia.* EINSTEIN 324–325

669 [Lurano] Ferand, Ernest T. Two Unknown Frottole. EINSTEIN 319–338

670 [Luther] Gerber, Rudolf. Zu Luthers Liedweisen. SCHNEIDER/60TH 26–39

671 —— Mahrenholz Christhard. Luther und die Kirchenmusik. MAHRENHOLZ 136–153; orig. in *Luther und die Kirchenmusik* (Kassel 1937)

672 —— ——. Zur musikalischen Gestaltung von Luthers Gottesdienstreform. MAHRENHOLZ 154–168; orig. in *Musik und Kirche* 5 (1933)

673 —— Moser, Hans Joachim. *Nun freut euch, lieben Christen gmein.* SÖHNGEN 137–144

674 [Maletty] Thibault, Geneviève. Les *Amours* de P. Ronsard, mises en musique par Jehan de Maletty (1578). LAURENCIE 61–72

675 [Macque] Clercx, Suzanne. Jean de Macque et l'évolution du madrigalisme à la fin du XVIe siècle. SCHMIDT-GÖRG 66–80

676 ♪ Marenzio, Luca. *Liquide perle amor.* OSTHOFF 80, 82–85

677 [Marenzio] Einstein, Alfred. Eine Caccia im Cinquecento. LILIENCRON 72–80

677a [Martini] Karp, Theodore. The Secular Works of Johannes Martini. REESE/65TH 455–473

677b ♪ Masini, Lorenzo. *A poste messe*

transcription). REESE/65TH 688–689
737 [Tromboncino] Gallico, Claudio. Un *Dialogo d'amore* di Niccolò da Correggio musicato da Bartolomeo Tromboncino. SCHENK 205–213
737a [Vaet] Steinhardt, Milton. Addenda to the Biography of Jacobus Vaet. SACHS/C 229–235
737b [Valenzola] Bussi, Francesco. Il cantore spagnolo Pietro Velenzola e i suoi madrigali Italiani. BARBLAN/60TH 17–34
738 [Vecchi] Hol, Joan C. Horatio Vecchi et l'évolution créatrice. SCHEURLEER 159–167
[Victoria, Tomás Luis de] See nos. 710, 719
739 [Vicentino] Zenck, Hermann. Nicola Vicentinos *L'Antica musica* (1555). KROYER 86–101
739a [Virdung] Krautwurst, Franz. Bemerkungen zu Sebastian Virdungs "Musica getuscht" (1511). STÄBLEIN/70TH 143–156
740 [Waelrant] Bogaert, Irène. De Waelrants te Antwerpen; biographische bijzonderheden over de drie Huibrechts en Raymond Waelrant. BORREN 72–83
741 [Walter] Schmitz, Arnold. Zu Johann Walters Choralpassion. SIEBS 445–461
742 —— Schröder, Otto. Zu Johann Walters Choralpassionen. SCHNEIDER/60TH 103–109
742a —— Stalmann, Joachim. Johann Walters Versuch einer Reform des gregorianischen Chorals. GERSTENBERG/60TH 166–175
742b ♪ Weck, Johannes. *Hopper dancz (Rôti bouilli)*. REESE/65TH 371
742c [Wert] MacClintock, Carol. New Light on Giaches de Wert. REESE/65TH 595–602
742d —— ——. Some Notes on the Secular Music of Giaches de Wert. HANDSCHIN/M 106–141
743 [Willaert] Lenaerts, René B. Voor de biographie van Adriaen Willaert. BORREN 205–215
743a —— Lowinsky, Edward E. Problems in Adrian Willaert's Iconography. REESE/65TH 576–594
743b [Wüst] Quellmalz, Alfred. Der Spielmann, Komponist und Schulmeister Paul Wüst (um 1470–1540). Beiträge zu seiner Lebensgeschichte. MÜLLER-BLATTAU/70TH 221–231
744 ♪ Zacharias da Teramo, Antonio. *Patrem omnipotentem*. JEPPESEN 86–95
745 ♪ Zacharie, Nicolaus. *Et in terra*. KROHN 154–157

BAROQUE ERA: GENERAL

See also nos. 80, 97, 387a, 405, 409a, 411a, 412, 431, 435, 443, 532d, 545, 550, 559a, 562, 575, 575b, 661, 1312, 1514, 1799, 2198, 2558, 2569, 2621b, 2695a

746 Aldrich, Putnam. The Authentic Performance of Baroque Music. DAVISON 161–171
747 Alewyn, Richard. Feste des Barock. JBMV 101–111
747a Apfel, Ernst. Bemerkungen zum geschichtlichen Zusammenhang zwischen dem barocken und mittelalterlichen modalen Rhythmus. MÜLLER-BLATTAU/70TH 34–45
748 Barblan, Guglielmo. Il Termine *barocco* e la musica. ANGLÉS I, 93–108
749 Blankenburg, Walter. Der Harmonie-Begriff in der lutherisch-barocken Musikanschauung. GURLITT 44–56
750 Blume, Friedrich. Begriff und Grenzen des Barock in der Musik. MOBERG 77–87, & BLUME/S 209–217; also in *Manierismo, barocco, rococò* (Rome 1962)
751 ——. Die Musik des Barock. BLUME/S 67–123; orig. in *MGG* I, col. 1275
752 Boyden, David. Dynamics in Seventeenth- and Eighteenth-Century Music. DAVISON 185–193
753 Corte, Andrea della. Il Barocco e la musica. LAURENCIE 165–176
754 Eggebrecht, Hans H. Barock als musikgeschichtliche Epoche. JBMV 168–191; MÜNNICH/80THM 3–30
755 ——. Zum Figur-Begriff der musica poetica. GURLITT 57–69
756 Fellerer, Karl Gustav. Gregorianischer Choral und Orgelspiel im 18. Jahrhundert. WAESBERGHE 31–37
757 ——. Vom *stylo theatrali* in der Musiktheorie des 18. Jahrhunderts. NIESSEN 55–61
758 ——. Zum Wort-Ton-Problem in der Kirchenmusik des 16./17. Jahrhunderts. SCHENK 183–192
759 Haas, Robert. Geschichtliche Opernbeziehungen, ein Überblick. KRETZSCHMAR 43–45
760 Hammerschlag, János. A zenei díszítések világából. [From the World of Musical Ornamentation] KODÁLY/70TH 199–200

760a Holschneider, Andreas. Musik in Arkadien. GERSTENBERG/60TH 59–67

761 Jammers, Ewald. Die Barockmusik und ihre Stellung in der Entwicklungsgeschichte des Rhythmus. BOLLERT 255–278

762 Landshoff, Ludwig. Über das vielstimmige Accompagnement und andere Fragen des Generalbasspiels. SANDBERGER 189–208

763 LaRue, Jan. Bifocal Tonality, an Explanation for Ambiguous Baroque Cadences. DAVISON 173–184

763a Meyer, Ernst Hermann. Zur Frage der Aufführung alter Musik, eine Plauderei für meinen alten Studienkollegen Walter Wiora. WIORA/60TH 57–61

764 Moser, Hans Joachim. Der Maler Caravaggio und die Musik. FELLERER/60TH 350–353

765 Niessen, Carl. Das Maschinenwunder der barocken Oper. CU 243–249.

766 Pontius, Josef. Zur Datierung einer anonymen Tabulatur aus der Bipontina. MÜLLER-BLATTAU 75–82

767 Riemann, Hugo. Basso ostinato und basso quasi ostinato; eine Anregung. LILIENCRON 193–202

768 Schenk, Erich. Musikalische Irrgärten. SCHERING 194–206

768a Schrade, Leo. Über die Natur des Barockrhythmus. SCHRADE/D 360–384; orig. (in Italian) in *Rivista Musicale Italiana* 61 (1954) 3–27

769 Sutherland, Gordon. Notes on the Significance of Seventeenth- and Eighteenth-Century Music Criticism. DAVISON 195–203

770 Westrup, Jack A. The Cadence in Baroque Recitative. JEPPESEN 243–252

770a Wolff, Hellmuth Christian. Das Opernpublikum der Barockzeit. ENGEL 442–452

BAROQUE ERA: ITALY

See also no. 567a

771 Barblan, Guglielmo. Venezia e Roma sono le uniche scuole del barocco musicale italiano? BESSELER 285–289

771a Boyer, Ferdinand. Les Orsini et les musiciens d'Italie au debut du XVIIe siècle. HAUVETTE 301–310

772 Dent, Edward J. A Jesuit at the Opera in 1680. RIEMANN 381–393

773 Fellerer, Karl Gustav. Zur italienischen Chorallehre im 17./18. Jahrhundert. OSTHOFF 129–137

773a Ghisi, Federico. Antiche canzoni popolari nella "Corona di sacre laudi" di Matteo Coferati (1689). BORREN/90TH 69–81

774 Grout, Donald J. The Chorus in Early Opera. BLUME/F 151–161

774a Günther, Renate. Zum Problem der Affektdarstellung in der italienischen Frühmonodie. MÜNNICH/80THM 81–95

775 Hucke, Helmut. Die Besetzung von Sopran und Alt in der Sixtinischen Kapelle. ANGLÉS I, 379–396

776 ——. Verfassung und Entwicklung der alten neapolitanischen Konservatorien. OSTHOFF 139–154

777 Junker, Hermann. Zwei *Griselda* Opern. SANDBERGER 51–64

778 Lang, Paul H. The Formation of the Lyric Stage at the Confluence of Renaissance and Baroque. ENGEL 143–154

779 Ortiz, Ramiro. Radici e propaggini francesi, rumene e spagnuole della *Liberta* di P. Metastasio. BALDENSPERGER II, 151–161

780 Osthoff, Helmuth. Gedichte von Tomaso Stigliani auf Giulio Caccini, Claudio Monteverdi, Santino Garsi da Parma und Claudio Merulo. ANGLÉS II, 615–621

781 Palisca, Claude V. The First Performance of Euridice. QC 1–24

782 Paumgartner, Berhard. Codices aus der Frühzeit der Monodie. MÜLLER VON ASOW [153–154]

783 Pirro, André. La Musique des Italiens d'après les remarques triennales de Jean-Baptiste Duval (1607–1609). LEMONNIER 175–185

784 Prunières, Henry. Les Musiciens du Cardinal Antonio Barberini. LAURENCIE 119–122

784a Racek, Jan. Die italienische begleitete Monodie und das Problem der Entwicklung der italienischen Solokantate. BORREN/90TH 166–191

784b Roncaglia, Gino. Un capitolo di antica storia musicale Modenese ed Estense (con notizie e documenti inediti). BARBLAN/60TH 256–270

785 ——. L. A. Muratori, la musica e il maggior compositore modenese del suo tempo. MURATORI/M 277–318

785a Sartori, Claudio. Un catalogo di Giuseppe Sala del 1715. FÉDEROV 112–116

786 Schering, Arnold. Zur Geschichte der Solosonate in der ersten Hälfte des 17. Jahrhunderts. RIEMANN 309–325

786a Szabolcsi, Bence. Osteuropäische

Züge in der italienischen Monodie des 17. Jahrhunderts. RACEK/60TH 319–324
787 Vetter, Walther. Zur Stilproblematik der italienischen Oper des 17. und 18. Jahrhunderts. SCHENK 561–573
788 Wagner, Peter. Die konzertierende Messe in Bologna. KRETZSCHMAR 163–168

BAROQUE ERA: GERMANY & AUSTRIA

See also nos. 502a, 510a

789 Blankenburg, Walter. Die Aufführungen von Passionen und Passionskantaten in der Schlosskirche auf dem Friedenstein zu Gotha zwischen 1699 und 1770. BLUME/F 50–59
790 Blume, Friedrich. Die Handschrift *T 131* der New York Public Library. FELLERER/60TH 51–66
791 ——. Die Musik des Barock in Deutschland. BLUME/S 187–209; orig. in *MGG* 3, col. 303
791a Clemen, Otto. Das Programm zu einem Musikfest in Nürnberg im Mai 1643. GLAUNING I, 18–24
791b Engelbrecht, Christiane. Die Hofkapelle des Landgrafen Carl von Hessen-Kassel. GUTBIER 141–173
792 Federhofer, Helmut. Alte Liederdrucke in der Universitätsbibliothek Graz. ZODER 39–45
793 ——. Zur Musikpflege im Benediktinerstift Michaelbeuern (Salzburg). FELLERER/60TH 106–127
793a Geiringer, Karl. *Ed ist genug, so nimm Herr meinen Geist;* 300 Years in the History of a Protestant Funeral Song. SACHS/C 283–292
793b Goslich, Siegfried. Persönlichkeiten der Bremer Musikgeschichte. MÜNNICH/80THM 59–80
794 Gotzen, Joseph. Über die Trutz-Nachtigall von Friedrich von Spee und die Verbreitung ihrer Melodien. KAHL 60–85
795 Haas, Robert. Dreifache Orchesterteilung im Wiener Sepolchro. KOCZIRZ 8–10
796 Hamel, Fred, & Albert Rodemann. Unbekannte Musikalien im Braunschweiger Landestheater. ALBERT 72–79
797 Klaus, Gregor. Zur Orgel- und Musikgeschichte der [Weingarten] Abtei. WK 230–253
798 Löffler, Hans. Thüringer Musiker um Joh. Seb. Bach. ATL 105–122
799 Moser, Hans Joachim. Die andere Kaffeekantate. SCHNEIDER/80TH 173–176
800 ——. Eine augsburger Liederschule im Mittelbarock. Aus einer Geschichte des mehrstimmigen Liedes im 17. Jahrhundert. KROYER 144–148
801 ——. Brauchtümliches im Thüringer Chorlied des Frühbarock. STEIN 48–56
802 ——. Eine pariser Quelle zur wiener Triosonate des ausgehenden 17. Jahrhunderts: der Codex Rost. FISCHER/W 75–81
803 ——. Zur älteren Musikgeschichte des Burgenlandes. RAABE 114–118
804 ——. Zwischen Schütz und Bach. MOSER/70TH 106–118; orig. in *Wissenschaftliche Zeitschrift der Karl-Marx-Univ., Leipzig, Gesellschafts- und Sprachwissenschaftliche Reihe* 5 (1954/1955)
805 Müller von Asow, Erich H. Die alte Orgel in der evangelischen Pfarrkirche zu Hermannstadt. BIEHLE 31–35
805a Nettl, Paul. Etwas über das erste Wiener Liederbuch. ENGLE 250–259
806 ——. Eine wiener Tänzehandschrift um 1650. KOCZIRZ 23–25
807 Paulke, Karl. Die Kantorei-Gesellschaft zu Finsterwalde. SCHEURLEER 241–249
808 Pietzsch, Gerhard. Dresdener Hoffeste vom 16.–18. Jahrhundert. SEIFFERT 83–86
809 Pirro, André. Remarques de quelques voyageurs sur la musique en Allemagne et dans les pays du nord de 1634 à 1700. REIMANN 325–340
810 Pisk, Paul A. Die melodische Struktur der unstilisierten Tanzsätze in der Klaviermusik des deutschen Spätbarock. SCHENK 397–405
810a Riedel, Friedrich W. Die Kaiserkrönung Karls VI. (1711) als musikgeschichtliches Ereignis. GOTTRON 34–40
811 Schenk, Erich. Österreichisches im Klavierbuch der Regina Clara Imhoff. ZODER 162–167
812 Schmidt, Gustav F. Die älteste deutsche Oper in Leipzig am Ende des 17. und Anfang des 18. Jahrhunderts. SANDBERGER 209–257
813 Schmitz, Arnold. Arbeiten zur mittelrheinischen Musikgeschichte. SCHIEDERMAIR/80TH 118–123
814 Schneider, Max. Ein braunschweiger Freudenspiel aus dem Jahre 1648. SEIFFERT 87–94

814a Schramm, Willi. Beiträg zur Musikgeschichte der Stadt Glashütte. SEIFFERT/70THA 29–64
815 Seiffert, Max. Die Orgel der Stadtkirche zu Delitzsch. KRETZSCHMAR 149–151
816 Süss, C. Die Manuskripte protestantischer Kirchenmusik zu Frankfurt am Main. LILIENCRON 350–357
817 Ursprung, Otto. Die Chorordnung von 1616 am Dom zu Augsburg; ein Beitrag zur Frage der Aufführungspraxis. ADLER 137–142
817a Weiler, Klaus. Musiker am kurkölnischen Hofe des 17. Jahrhunderts. FELLERER/60THS 285–307
817b Wohnhaas, Theodor. Nürnberger Gesangbuchdrucker und -verleger im 17. Jahrhundert. STÄBLEIN/70TH 301–315
818 Wolffheim, Werner. Mitteilungen zur Geschichte der Hofmusik in Celle (1635–1706), und über Arnold M. Brunckhorst. LILIENCRON 421–439

BAROQUE ERA: LOW COUNTRIES, FRANCE, IBERIAN COUNTRIES, & LATIN AMERICA

See also nos. 82a, 485a, 565, 575, 1116a

819 Barwick, Steven. Puebla's Requiem Choirbook. DAVISON 121–127
819a Castellà i Raich, Gabriel. Notícia d'uns mestres orgueners. PUIG I CADAFALCH I, 95–100
819b Cohen, Albert. Survivals of Renaissance Thought in French Theory 1610–1670: a Bibliographical Study. REESE/65TH 82–95
819c Enschedé, J. W. Het oude groote orgel in de Sint Bavokerk te Haarlem. BREDIUS 25–36
819d Federhofer, Hellmut. Eine Angelica- und Gitarrentabulatur aus der zweiten Hälfte des 17. Jahrhunderts. WIORA/60TH 313–316
820 Gérold, Théodore. Das Liederalbum einer französischen Provinzdame um 1620. ADN 92–129
821 Kastner, Santiago. Harfe und Harfner in der iberischen Musik des 17. Jahrhunderts. JEPPESEN 165–172
821a ——. La música en la Catedral de Badajoz (años 1654–1764). SUBIRÁ/80TH 223–238
822 Keyzer, Berten de. Bijdrage tot de geschiedenis van het muziekleven in onze kerken. Instrumentisten in de St.-Baafs-Kathedraal te Gent (XVIIe en XVIIIe eeuw). MUEREN 75–83
823 Lancaster, H. Carrington. Comedy versus Opera in France, 1683–1700. BROWN 257–263
823a Launay, Denise. À propos de deux manuscrits musicaux aux armes de Louis XIII. FÉDEROV 63–67
823b Linden, Albert van der. Inventaire de la musique de l'église Saint-Michel à Gand au XVIIIe siècle. BORREN/90TH 206–218
824 Madurell Marimon, Josep M. Tres fundacions liturgiques Montserratines. ANGLÉS II, 499–515
825 Pincherle, Marc. La Musique dans l'éducation des enfants au XVIIIe siècle. MASSON II, 115–121
825a Querol, Miguel. El *cancionero musical* de Olot. SUBIRÁ/80TH 57–65
825a[1] Quitin, José. Les Le Radde musiciens liégeois du XVIIe siècle en service à la Cour de Bonn. FELLERER/60THS 190–198
825b Raugel, Félix. Les Silbermann facteurs d'orgues alsaciens et les organistes et organiers français de leur temps. BORREN/90TH 192–195
825c Reisser, Jan. Jak vzikla opera ve Francii [How Opera Originated in France] NEJEDLÝ/50TH 161–181
825d Romeu Figueras, José. Las poesías catalanas del manuscrito musical de Olot. SUBIRÁ/80TH 45–55
826 Subirá, José. El "Cuatro" escénico español, sus antecedentes, evoluciones y desintegración. ANGLÉS II, 895–921
827 Titcomb, Caldwell. Carrousel Music at the Court of Louis XIV. DAVISON 205–213
827a Veldhuyzen, Marie. Eine Amsterdamer Melodien-Handschrift aus dem 18. Jahrhundert. WIORA/60TH 357–360
827b Vente, Maarten Albert. Thomas Houben, orgelmaker te Ratingen (omstreeks 1730). FELLERER/60THS 260–284

BAROQUE ERA: ENGLAND & SCANDINAVIA

See also nos. 550a, 790

827c Cutts, John P. Seventeenth-Century Lyrics. Oxford, Bodleian, Ms. Mus. b.1. HANDSCHIN/M 142–209

827d ♪ English dances in an Austrian lute tabulature (Ms. Kremsmünster, *Stifte L. 81*). RACEK 254–257

828 Hennerberg, C. F. Une Collection d'oeuvres pour viola, basso et violone du XVII:me siècle. KROHN 50–54

829 Jacquot, Jean. Echos anglais des controverses sur la musique française et italienne (1700–1750). MASSON II, 55–63

829a Kent, H. S. K. Puritan Attitudes to Music: a Study in History and Ideas. BISHOP 191–224

830 Moberg, Carl Allan. Essais d'opéras en Suède sous Charles XII. LAURENCIE 123–132

831 ——. Olof Rudbeck d. ä. och musiken. RUDBECK 176–210

832 Rolland, Romain. La Vie musicale en Angleterre au temps de la restauration des Stuarts d'après le journal de Samuel Pepys. RIEMANN 294–309

832a Schenk, Erich. Englische Schauspielmusik in Österreichischer Tabulatur-Überlieferung. RACEK/60TH 253–261

833 Schiørring, Nils. Nogle håndskrevne dansk-norske koralbøger fra det 18. århundredes første halvdel. JEPPESEN 253–266

833a Spink, Ian. Sources of English Song, 1620–1660: a Survey. BISHOP 117–136

834 Sundström, Einar. Notiser om drottning Kristinas italienska musiker. MOBERG 297–309

835 Vretblad. Åke. Något om parodiekniken i *Sions sånger* (1743–45). MOBERG 397–401

836 Westrup, Jack A. Cathedral Music in Seventeenth Century England. BLUME/F 375–380

BAROQUE ERA: HUNGARY & SLAVIC COUNTRIES

See also nos. 786a, 1149a

837 Barna, István. *Ungarischer Simplicissimus*, adalékok a XVII. század magyar zenei művelődéstörténetéhez [*Ungarischer Simplicissimus*, Contributions to the Cultural History of Hungarian Music in the 17th Century] KODÁLY/70TH 495–514

838 Bónis, Ferenc. A Vietórisz-kódex szvit-táncai [The Dance Suites of the Vietorisz Codex] KODÁLY/75TH 265–336, German summary 755–756

838a Csomasz-Tóth, Kálmán. Az Eperjesi graduál. II: Kórusok és népénekdallamok [The Gradual of Eperjes. II: Choruses and Folk Melodies] KODÁLY/75TH 199–264, German summary 755

838b Cvetko, Dragotin. Contribution à la question sur l'année de la fondation de l'Academia Philharmonicorum Labacensis. WIORA/60TH 342–347

838c Fukač, Jiří. Archaische Tendenzen in der Prager Barockmusik um das Jahr 1700. RACEK/60TH 93–105

839 ♪ Hungarian Christmas music. KODÁLY/75TH 464–498

839a Keldysh, Ivriy. K voprosu ob ictokakh russkogo partesnogo peniya [Concerning the Sources of Russian Polyphonic Singing] FEICHT 269–283

839b Papp, Géza. Przyczynki do związków muzyki polskiej z węgierską w XVII wieku [Notes on the Connection between Polish and Hungarian Music in the 17th Century] FEICHT 235–251

840 Piotrowski, Wacław. Wpływy polskie w muzyce królewieckiej XVII-go i pierwszej połowy XVIII-go wieku [Polish Influences on Music in Königsberg in the 17th and First Half of the 18th Centuries.] CHYBIŃSKI/50TH 57–65

840a Racek, Jan. Zum Problem der Periodisierung des tschechischen Musikbarocks im 17. und 18. Jahrhundert. ŠTĚDROŇ/60TH 71–87, summary in Czech at end of article

840b Rybarič, Richard. Slovenská hudba 17. až 18. storočia ve svetle novoobjavených pramenov [Slovakian Music of the 17th and 18th Centuries in the Light of Newly Discovered Sources] RACEK/60TH 227–244, summary in German

840c Schoenbaum, Camillo. *Threnodia huius temporis*. RACEK/60TH 273–278

841 Schram, Ferenc. Adalékok Betlehemes-játékaink dallamainak eredetéhez [Contributions to the Origin of the Melodies of our Nativity Plays] KODÁLY/75TH 461–501, German summary 758–759

842 Szweykoski, Zygmunt M. Wenecki koncert rondowy w polskiej praktyce kompozytorskiej okresu baroku [The Venetian concert rondo and the Polish Practice of Composition in the Baroque Period] FEICHT 220–226

843 ♪ Vietorisz codex. Dance suites, 17th century. KODÁLY/75TH 290–336

BAROQUE ERA: JOHANN SEBASTIAN BACH

See also nos. 699, 1080, 1087a, 1100

844 Abert, Hermann. Bach und die moderne Liturgie. SCHEURLEER 33–38
845 [Art of the Fugue] Steglich, Rudolf. Der erste Contrapunctus der *Kunst der Fuge* J. S. Bachs. SCHNEIDER/80TH 157–166
846 Besch, Hans. Eine Auktionsquittung J. S. Bachs. SMEND 74–79
847 Blume, Friedrich. Johann Sebastian Bach. BLUME/S 363–412; orig. in *MGG* 1, col. 962
848 ——. Johann Sebastian Bach im Wandel der Geschichte. BLUME/S 412–447; orig. in *Musikwissenschaftliche Arbeiten* 1 (Kassel 1947) & *Two Centuries of Bach* (London 1950)
849 ——. Neue Bachforschung. BLUME/S 448–466; orig. in *Svensk tidskrift för musikforskning* 37 (1955)
850 ——. Umrisse eines neuen Bach-Bildes. BLUME/S 466–479; orig. in *Musica* 16 (1962)
851 Boell, Heinrich. Die Bach-Interpretation im Wandel der Anschauungen. RAABE 164–170
852 [Brandenburg Concertos] Wackernagel, Peter. Beobachtungen am Autograph von Bachs Brandenburgischen Konzerten. SCHNEIDER/80TH 129–138
853 —— Krey, Johannes. Zur Entstehungsgeschichte des ersten Brandenburgischen Konzerts. BESSELER 337–342
854 Braun, Werner. Die Brüder Nagel und das Collegium musicum J. S. Bachs. SCHNEIDER/80TH 167–171
855 [Canons] Wolffheim, Werner. Ein unbekannter Canon J. S. Bachs. WOLF 217–221
855a [Cantatas] Dürr, Alfred. Bach's Chorale Cantatas. BUSZIN 111–120
856 —— ——. Der Eingangssatz zu Bachs Himmelfahrts-Oratorium und seine Vorlage. ALBRECHT 121–126
857 —— Gudewill, Kurt. Über Formen und Texte der Kirchenkantaten Johann Sebastian Bachs. BLUME/F 162–175
858 ——Wolffheim, Werner. Das Autograph der J. S. Bachschen Hochzeitskantate *Vergnügte Pleissen-Stadt.* KRETZSCHMAR 180–184
859 [Chorale Preludes] Tangeman, Robert S. The Ritornello Forms in Bach's Catechism Chorale Preludes. DAVISON 235–241
860 [Chromatic Fantasy] Fano, Fabio. La vera lezione della *Fantasia cromatica e fuga* di Bach. EINSTEIN/C 157–164
861 [Concertos] Besseler, Heinrich. Zur Chronologie der Konzerte Joh. Seb. Bachs. SCHNEIDER/80TH 115–128
862 —— Boettcher, Hans. Bachs Kunst der Bearbeitung dargestellt am Tripelkonzert a-moll. RAABE 95–113
863 —— Keller, Hermann. Johann Sebastian Bachs Violinkonzerte. GEWANDHAUS 40–63
863a —— Kolneder, Walter. Besetzung und Satzstil. Zu Johann Sebastian Bachs Violinkonzerten. WIORA/60TH 329–334
864 Dadelsen, Georg von. Originale Daten auf den Handschriften J. S. Bachs. ALBRECHT 116–120
865 Elvers, Rudolf. Verzeichnis der von Felix Mendelssohn Bartholdy herausgegebenen Werke Johann Sebastian Bachs. SÖHNGEN 145–149
866 Federhofer, Helmut. Bemerkungen zum Verhältnis von Harmonik und Stimmführung bei Johann Sebastian Bach. BESSELER 343–350
866a ——. Johann Nepomuk Davids Analysen von Werken Johann Sebastian Bachs. SCHMITZ 147–159
866b Friedrich, Wilfried. Die Funktion des tönenden Namens BACH in den Werken Bachs. MÜNNICH/80THM 34–57
867 [Fugues] Abert, Hermann. Tonart und Thema in Bachs Instrumentalfugen. WAGNER 1–10
868 —— Gárdonyi, Zoltán. Zur Fugentechnik Johann Seb. Bachs. KODÁLY/80TH 117–126
869 —— Kilian, Dietrich. Studie über Bachs Fantasie und Fuge c-moll (BWV 562). ALBRECHT 127–135
869a Geck, Martin. Bachs künstlerischer Endzweck. WIORA/60TH 319–328
869b Geering, Arnold & Armand Hiebner. Ein Führer zu Bach. Aus Adolf Hamms Einführungen in seine Konzertprogramme. HAMM 109–154
870 [Goldberg Variations] Müller-Blattau, Joseph. Bachs Goldberg-Variationen. GURLITT 207–219
871 Goldschmidt, Hugo. Die Mehrsinnigkeit der charakterisierenden Themen in S. Bachs Kirchenmusik. KRETZSCHMAR 37–42
872 [Inventions] Lorenz, Alfred. Das

Relativitätsprinzip in den musikalischen Formen. ADLER 179–186
873 —— Reuter, Fritz. Einführung in die zweistimmigen Inventionen Bachs. SCHNEIDER/80TH 153–155
874 Janetzky, Kurt. Zum Erscheinen der Bach-Studien für Waldhorn. HOFMEISTER 48–57
875 [Little Organ Book] Dadelsen, Georg von. Zur Entstehung des Bachschen Orgelbüchleins. BLUME/F 74–79
875a [Lute Music] Radke, Hans. War Johann Sebastian Bach Lautenspieler? ENGEL 281–289
876 Mahrenholz, Christhard. Johann Sebastian Bach und der Gottesdienst seiner Zeit. MAHRENHOLZ 205–220; orig. in *Musik und Kirche* 20 (1950)
877 Moser, Hans Joachim. Sebastian Bachs Stellung zur Kirchenliedrhythmik der Lutherzeit. MOSER/70TH 144–158; orig. in *Bach Jahrbuch* (1917)
878 ——. Zur Ausführung der Ornamente bei Bach. MOSER/70TH 159–172; orig. in *Bach Jahrbuch* (1916) combined here with: Bemerkungen zu Bachs vokaler Ornamentik, in *Neue Musikzeitung* 45 (1924)
879 [Masses] Dadelsen, Georg von. Eine unbekannte Messen-Bearbeitung Bachs. FELLERER/60TH 88–94
880 —— David, Hans T. Die Gesamtanlage von Bachs h-moll Messe. WOLF 13–23
881 —— Keller, Hermann. Gibt es eine h-moll Messe von Bach? MERSMANN 69–75
882 —— Rosenthal, Wolfgang. Gemeinsamer Dienst an Johann Sebastian Bachs hoher Messe. MAUERSBERGER 135–137
882a —— Wolff, Christoph. Zur musikalischen Vorgeschichte aus Johann Sebastian Bachs Mess in h-moll. STÄBLEIN/70TH 316–326
883 [Musical Offering] Orel, Alfred. J. S. Bachs *Musikalisches Opfer*. OREL 33–53; orig. in *Die Musik* (Nov./Dec. 1937)
884 Nettl, Paul. Volks- und volkstümliche Musik bei Bach. SCHENK 391–396
885 Neumann, Werner. Welche Handschriften J. S. Bachscher Werke besass die Berliner Singakademie? ALBRECHT 136–142
885a Nowak, Leopold. Ein Bach-Fund. FÉDEROV 95–98
886 [Passions] Fellerer, Karl Gustav. Bachs Johannes-Passion in der lateinischen Fassung Fortunato Santinis. SCHNEIDER/80TH 139–145
887 —— Fischer, Wilhelm. *Barrabam*. SCHEURLEER 115–118
888 —— Mendel, Arthur. Traces of the Pre-History of Bach's St. John and St. Matthew Passions. DEUTSCH/80TH 31–48
889 —— Moser, Hans Joachim. Zum Bau von Bachs Johannes-Passion. MOSER/70TH 172–174; orig. in *Bach Jahrbuch* (1932)
890 —— Pears, Peter, Some Notes on the Translation of Bach's Passions. BRITTEN 84–91
891 —— Smend, Friedrich. Zur Kenntnis des Musikers Fortunato Santini. BÖMER 90–98
—— See also no. 1080
892 Platen, Emil. Zur Frage der Kürzungen in den Dacapoformen J. S. Bachs. SCHMIDT-GÖRG 224–234
893 Preuss, Hans. Bachs Bibliothek. ZAHN 105–129
894 Ramin, Günther. Johann Sebastian Bach als Ende und Anfang und seine Bedeutung für die geistige Entwicklung der Jugend. SCHWEITZER/80TH 184–192
895 Rassow, Peter. Bach in den Zeiten. STRAUBE 352–361
896 [Recitatives] Drux, Herbert. *Zwölftonordnungen* in Rezitativen Johann Sebastian Bachs. FELLERER/60TH 95–105
897 Reichert, Georg. Harmoniemodelle in Johann Sebastian Bachs Musik. BLUME/F 281–289
898 Riedel, Friedrich W. Musikgeschichtliche Beziehungen zwischen Johann Joseph Fux und Johann Sebastian Bach. BLUME/F 290–304
899 Rubardt, Paul. Zwei originale Orgeldispositionen J. S. Bachs. BESSELER 495–503
900 Ruhnke, Martin. Moritz Hauptmann und die Wiederbelebung der Musik J. S. Bachs. BLUME/F 305–319
900a Schrade, Leo. Bach: the Conflict Between the Sacred and the Secular. SCHRADE/D 424–470; orig. New York: Merlin (1954)
901 Schünemann, Georg. Neue *Attestate* Seb. Bachs. LILIENCRON 290–296
901a Siegele, Ulrich. Von Bachschen Modellen und Zeitarten. GERSTENBERG/60TH 162–165

902 [Sinfonias] Tiersot, Julien. Sur les origines de la symphonie; une "sinfonia" de Jean-Sébastian Bach. LAURENCIE 177–184
902a Steglich, Rudolf. Johann Sebastian Bach über sich selbst und im Urteil der Mit- und Nachwelt. ENGEL 393–405
903 [Suites] Floros, Constantin. Die Thematik in Johann Sebastian Bachs Orchestersuiten. SCHENK 193–204
904 —— Oberst, Günther. J. S. Bachs französische und englische Suiten. ABERT 116–124
905 Vetter, Walther. Der Festschrift zum Geleit. SCHNEIDER/80TH 5–10
906 [Well-Tempered Clavier] Erpf, Hermann. Über Bach-Analysen am Beispiel einer Fuge aus dem *Wohltemperierten Klavier*. GURLITT 70–76
907 —— Frączkiewicz, Aleksander. Odpowiedź tonalna modulująca w fugach J. S. Bacha z "Das wohltemperierte Klavier" [Modulating Tonal Answers in the Fugues of J. S. Bach in "The Well-tempered Clavier"] FEICHT 298–306
907a —— Heinitz, Wilhelm. Taktprobleme in J. S. Bachs *Wohltemperierten Klavier*. SCHNEIDER/80TH 147–151
907b —— Hermelink, Siegfried. Bemerkungen zum ersten Präludium aus Bachs Wohltemperiertem Klavier. MÜLLER-BLATTAU/70TH 111–121
908 Wiora, Walter. Goethes Wort über Bach. ALBRECHT 179–191
909 Wolff, Christoph. Die Rastrierungen in den Originalhandschriften Joh. Seb. Bachs und ihre Bedeutung für die diplomatische Quellenkritik. SMEND 80–92
910 Wolff, Hellmuth Christian. Zur Melodiebildung J. S. Bachs. SCHENK 609–622

BAROQUE ERA: GEORGE FRIDERIC HANDEL

See also no. 1000

910a [Agrippina] Redlich, Hans F. Handel's *Agrippina* (1709): Problems of a Practical Edition. HIRSCH 15–23
910b Ameln, Konrad. Brief vom Dolmetschen. Über die Notwendigkeit neuer deutscher Textfassungen zu den Oratorien Händels. MÜLLER-BLATTAU/70TH 28–33
911 Barclay Squire, William. Handel in 1745. RIEMANN 423–433
912 Coopersmith, Jacob M. Four Unpublished Letters of Georg Friedrich Handel. ENGEL 60–66
913 Cudworth, Charles. Two Handelian Anecdotes. DEUTSCH/80TH 49–50
914 ♪ *Ein hoher Geist muss immer höher denken.* LILIENCRON 300–303
915 Federhofer, Helmut. Unbekannte Kopien von Werken Georg Friedrich Händels und anderer Meister seiner Zeit. DEUTSCH/80TH 51–65
916 Lang, Paul H. Handel, Churchman or Dramatist? BLUME/F 214–220
916a Mann, Alfred. Zum Concertistenprinzip bei Händel. EHMANN/60TH 77–82
917 Moser, Hans Joachim. Händels zeitstilistische Entwicklung. MOSER/70TH 174–189; orig. in *Wege zu Händel*, hrsg. vom Händel-Festkomitee der Stadt Halle (1953)
918 [*Samson*] Ameln, Konrad. Vom Werdegang eines Händel-Rezitativs. MÜLLER-BLATTAU 3–9
918a Schrade, Leo. Georg Friedrich Händels Lebensform. SCHRADE/D 471–489; orig. in *Zeitschrift für Deutsche Bildung* 10 (1934) 529–541
919 Seiffert, Max. Händels deutsche Gesäng. LILIENCRON 297–314
920 Serauky, Walter. Johann Adam Hiller als Erwecker der Händel-Tradition im 18. Jahrhundert. GEWANDHAUS 36–40
920a Smith, William C. Do You Know What You Are About? (A Rare Handelian Pamphlet). OLDMAN 114–119
921 ♪ *Süsse Stille, sanfte Quelle.* LILIENCRON 310–314
922 Zimmerman, Franklin B. Handel's Purcellian Borrowings in his Later Operas and Oratorios. DEUTSCH/80TH 20–30

BAROQUE ERA: OTHER INDIVIDUAL COMPOSERS, PERFORMERS, ETC.

923 [Albrici] Moberg, Carl Allan. Vincenzo Albrici (1631–1696), eine biographische Skizze mit besonderer Berücksichtigung seiner schwedischen Zeit. BLUME/F 235–246
924 —— ——. Vincenzo Albrici und das Kirchenkonzert. JEPPESEN 199–216
925 [Barcotto] Lunelli, Renato. Un Trattatello di Antonio Barcotto colma le lacune dell'*Arte organica*. EINSTEIN/C 135–155
926 [Baroni] Sartori, Claudio. Quin-

dici lettere di Leonora Baroni musicista analfabeta. SCHENK 446–452
927 [Baumgarten] Schmitz, Eugen. C. G. v. Baumgartens *Andromeda.* KRETZSCHMAR 136–137
928 ♪ Bekwark (Backfark), Valentinus. *Non dite mai ch'io habia il forte,* lute. CHYBIŃSKI/70TH 198–217
929 [Bianciardi] Haas, Robert. Das Generalbassflugblatt Francesco Bianciardis. WOLF 48–56
930 [Blondet] Fellerer, Karl Gustav. N. Sorets *La Céciliade* mit Musik von Abraham Blondet (1606); ein Beitrag zur Geschichte der französischen Oper. BIEHLE 47–58
930a [Blow] Shaw, Watkins. The Autographs of John Blow (1649–1708). OLDMAN 85–95
931 [Bokemeyer] Wolffheim, Werner. Eine Kolleg-Ankündigung des Kantors Heinrich Bokemeyer. SCHEURLEER 393–396
931a [Bonomi] Cvetko, Dragotin. *Il Tamerlano* de Giuseppe Clemente Bonomi. WELLESZ/80TH 108–113
932 ♪ Bononcini, Giovanni. *La Maddalena a' piedi di Christo. Piangi ma il pianto.* MURATORI/M 318[b–d]
933 [Bononcini, Giovanni] Valabrega, Cesare. Il *Bononcini* di Schenk. SCHENK 558–560
934 [Bontempi] Engländer, Richard. Die erste italienische Oper in Dresden, Bontempis *Il Paride in musica* (1662). MOBERG 119–134
935 [Boxberg] Sørensen, Søren. Über einen Kantatenjahrgang des Görlitzer Komponisten Christian Boxberg. JEPPESEN 217–242
935a [Božan] Schoenbaum, Camillo. Jan Joseph Božans "Slavíček rájský (Paradíesnachtigall 1719)" und die tschechischen katholischen Gesangbücher des XVII. Jahrhunderts. FEICHT 252–267
[Butler, E.] See no. 984b
936 [Brescianello] Damerini, Adelmo. *Sei concerti a tre* sconosciuti di G. A. Brescianello. SCHENK 96–104
937 ——. *I concerti a tre* di G. Antonio Brescianello. EINSTEIN/C 165–170
938 [Buffardin] Kollpacher-Hass, Ingrid. Pierre-Gabriel Buffardin, sein Leben und Werk. SCHENK 298–306
939 [Buxtehude] Blume, Friedrich. Dietrich Buxtehude. BLUME/S 302–319; orig. in *MGG* 1, col. 548
940 ——. Dietrich Buxtehude in Geschichte und Gegenwart. BLUME/S 351–363
941 ——. Das Kantatenwerk Dietrich Buxtehudes. BLUME/S 320–351; orig. in *Peters Jahrbuch* 47 (1940)
942 [Casparini] Flade, Ernst. Eugen Casparini und seine Tätigkeit zu S. Giustina in Padua. BIEHLE 18–26
943 [Cassini] Fabbri, Mario. Giovanni Maria Cassini, *Musico dell'umana espressione;* Contributo su documenti originali. SCHENK 135–159
944 ♪ Cavalli, Francesco. *La Didone. Non fu natural.* JEPPESEN 190–191
945 ♪ ——. *La Doriclea. Udite amanti.* JEPPESEN 195–198
946 ♪ ——. *La Virtu degli strali d'amore. Non ha seno colei.* JEPPESEN 193.
947 [Cavalli] Hjelmberg, Bjørn. Aspects of the Aria in the Early Operas of Francesco Cavalli. JEPPESEN 173–198
947a [Cernohorský] Safařík, Jiří. Černohorskýs Zweifache Textvertonung der Offertoriums für den XII. Sonntag nach Pfingsten. ŠTĚDROŇ/60TH 97–105, summary in Czech at end of article
948 ♪ Cesti, Antonio. *L'Orontea.* Selections. MARINUZZI 153–181
949 [Cesti] Pirrotta, Nino. Le prime opere di Antonio Cesti. MARINUZZI 153–181
950 [Charpentier] Gastoué, Amédée. Notes sur les manuscrits et sur quelques oeuvres de M.-A. Charpentier. LAURENCIE 153–164
950a —— Kolneder, Walter. Die "Regles de Composition" von Marc-Antione Charpentier. MÜLLER-BLATTAU/70TH 152–159
950b —— Massenkeil, Günther. Marc-Antione Charpentier als Messenkomponist. SCHMIDT-GÖRG/70TH 228–238
951 —— Raugel, Félix. Marc-Antoine Charpentier. FELLERER/60TH 417–420
952 [Clementi, O.] Koczirz, Adolf. Eine Gitarrentabulatur des kaiserlichen Theorbisten Orazio Clementi. LAURENCIE 107–115
952a Settari, Olga. [Comenius] Über das Gesangbuch des Johann Amos Comenius. ŠTĚDROŇ/60TH 89–96, summary in Czech at end of article
953 ♪ Conti, Francesco B. *Il Trionfo dell'amicizia e dell'amore. Perdono mia bella.* SCHRADE 138–143

954 [Conti] Arlt, Wulf. Zur Deutung der Barockoper *Il Trionfo dell'amicizia e dell'amore* (Wien 1711). SCHRADE 96–145
955 [Dassoucy] Prunières, Henry. Le Page de Dassoucy; Contribution à l'histoire des moeurs musicales au XVIIe siècle. ADLER 153–160
956 [Davies] Clarke, Henry L. Moll Davies, First Lady of English Opera. DAVISON 215–224
957 [Destouches] Masson, Renée P.-M. André Destouches à Siam. MASSON II, 95–102
958 [Düben] Norlind, Tobias. Die Familie Düben. KRETZSCHMAR 110–112
959 [Du Mage] Raugel, Félix. L'Organiste Pierre Du Mage. (v. 1676–1751). MASSON II, 125–132
959a [Durón] Siemens Hernańdez, Lothar G. Nuevas aportaciones para la biografía de Sebastián Durón. SUBIRÁ/80TH 137–159
960 [Fabricius] Wolf, Johannes. Das Stammbuch des Georg Fabricius. LAURENCIE 133–151
961 [Faille] Borren, Charles van den. Le Livre de clavier de Vincentius de la Faille (1625). LAURENCIE 85–96
961a ♪ Falconieri, Andrea. *Dov' io credea* (*Il Quinto Libro delle Musiche,* 1619). BORREN/90TH 184–185
961b [Feckler] Gottron, Adam. Joseph Paris Feckler, Kurmainzer Hofkappellmeister 1728–1735. SCHMITZ 186–193
962 [Franck] Gudewill, Kurt. Die *Laudes Dei vespertinae* von Melchior Franck. ALBRECHT 88–100
963 —— Moser, Hans Joachim. Melchior Franck (um 1580–1639) als Förderer musikalischer Volkskunde. MOSER/70TH 58–62; orig. in *Zeitschrift Germanien* (1939)
964 [Frescobaldi] Apel, Willi. Die handschriftliche Überlieferung der Klavierwerke Frescobaldis. FELLERER/60TH 40–45
965 ♪ Froberger, Johann Jacob. Allemande & double in D. ADLER 151
966 [Froberger] Tessier, André. Une Pièce inédite de Froberger. ADLER 147–152
967 [Fux] Federhofer, Helmut. Johann Joseph Fux als Musiktheoretiker. ALBRECHT 109–115
—— See also no. 911
968 [Gabrieli, G.] Woodworth, G. Wallace. Texture versus Mass in the Music of Giovanni Gabrieli. DAVISON 129–138
969 [Gallicano, Prince of] Squire, William Barclay. An Opera under Innocent X. SCHEURLEER 65–71
970 [Gaultier] Tessier, André. Ennemond Gaultier, sieur de Nève (env. 1575–17 décembre 1651). LAURENCIE 97–106
971 [Geyer family] Prüfer, Arthur. Aus Eislebens kirchenmusikalischer Vergangenheit. KRETZSCHMAR 119–121
971a ♪ Giamberti, Giuseppe. *O belle lagrimette* (*Raccolta d'arie spirituali,* 1640). BORREN/90TH 186–187
971b [Gorczycki] Węcowski, Jan. Grzegorz Gerwazy Gorczycki w świetle najnowszych odkryć i badań [Grzegorz Gerwazy Gorczycki in the Light of the Newest Discoveries and Investigations] FEICHT 227–234
972 [Gramelow] Thierfelder, Albert. *Ich weiss, dass mein Erlöser lebt* von Martin Gramelow. KRETZSCHMAR 161–162
972a [Graupner] McCredie, Andrew D. Christoph Graupner as Opera Composer. BISHOP 74–116
973 [Grimm] Riemer, Otto. Heinrich Grimm, ein mitteldeutscher Musiker. SCHERING 180–193
[Hasse, Johann Adolph] See no. 1101
974 [Hassler] Blume, Friedrich. Die Familie Hassler. BLUME/S 217–229; orig. in *MGG* 5, col. 1798
975 [Hidalgo] Moll, Jaime. Nuevos datos para la biografía de Juan Hidalgo, arpista y compositor. ANGLÉS II, 585–589
976 —— Ursprung, Otto. *Celos* usw., Text von Calderón, Musik von Hidalgo, die älteste erhaltene spanische Oper. SCHERING 223–240
977 ♪ Hoffer, Johann Josef. Five Ballets, strings. VNB 557–574
978 [Huygens] Zeeman, P. Christiaan Huygens en de muzikale echo. MENGELBERG 151–153
979 ♪ d'India, Sigismondo. *Fresch'erbette novelle.* EINSTEIN/C 130
980 ♪ ——. *O dolcezze amarissime.* EINSTEIN/C 123
981 ♪ ——. *Pianget'occhi miei lassi.* EINSTEIN/C 124
982 ♪ ——. *Là tra le selve.* EINSTEIN/C 122
983 [d'India] Mompellio, Federico. Sigismondo d'India e il primo libro

di *Musiche da cantar solo*. EINSTEIN/C 113–134

984 [Iversen] Elling, Christian. Koncertmester Iversens portraet. ANDERSON/75TH 36–40

984a [Jarzębski] Tomkiewicz, Władyslaw. Adam Jarzębski jako serwitor krolewski (przycznkí biograficzne) [Adam Jarzębski as a Royal Servant (a Biographical Note)] FEICHT 210–219

984b [Jovenardi] Subirá, José. Dos músicos del Rey Felipe IV: B. Jovenardi y E. Butler. BALDELLÓ 201–223

985 [Käfer] Bolte, Johannes. Zum *Schloss in Österreich*, MEIER/60TH 34–35

986 —— Schiedermair, Ludwig. Briefe Johann Philipp Käfers. SANDBERGER 121–128

987 [Keiser] Krogh, Torben. Reinhard Keiser in Kopenhagen. WOLF 79–87

988 —— Kümmerling, Harald. Fünf unbekannte Kantaten in Reinhard Keisers Autograph. SCHNEIDER/80TH 177–181

988a [Kerll] Tagliavini, Luigi Ferdinando. Un' importante fonte per la musica cembalo-organistica di Johann Kaspar Kerll. Il Ms. DD/53 della Biblioteca Musicale "G. B. Martini" di Bologna. BARBLAN/60TH 283–293

989 [Keyrleber] Willert, Paul. Ein Kanonblatt des 17. Jahrhunderts und sein Verfasser Johann Georg Keyrleber. BESSELER 317–322

990 [Konink] Noske, Frits. Une Partition hollandaise d'*Athalie*. (1697). MASSON II, 105–111

990a [Krebs] Tittle, Karl. Die Choralbearbeitungen für Orgel von Johann Ludwig Krebs. ENGEL 406–427

990b ♪ Krieger, Adam. Songs, Selections. WIORA/60TH 307–312

990c [Krieger] Schiørring, Nils. Wiedergefundene Melodien aus der verschollen Adam-Krieger-Ariensammlung 1675. WIORA/60TH 304–312

991 [Kühnhausen] Adrio. Adam. Die Matthäus-Passion von J. G. Kühnhausen (Celle um 1700). SCHERING 24–35

992 [Lauze, F. de] Ecorcheville, Jules. Un Livre inconnu sur la danse. RIEMANN 288–293

993 ♪ Le Camus, Sébastien. *Ous ferez les témoins*. BORREN/80TH 129

994 [Le Camus] Lesure, François. Histoire d'une édition posthume: Les *Airs* de Sébastien Le Camus (1678). BORREN/80TH 126–129

995 [Le Cocq] Wessely, Othmar. Ein Musiklexikon von François Le Cocq. ALBRECHT 101–108

996 [Leopold I] Nettl, Paul. Kaiser Leopold als deutscher Liedkomponist. ADLER 161–163

997 —— Wessely, Othmar. Kaiser Leopolds I *Vermeinte Bruder-und Schwesterliebe;* ein Beitrag zur Geschichte des Wiener Hoftheaters in Linz. SCHENK 586–608

998 [Loeillet] Vermeire-Roos, R. De Loeillets, een voornaam geslacht van musici te Gent in de XVIIe en XVIIIe eeuw. MUEREN 209–215

999 [Lorentz] Lundgren, Bo. Nikolajorganisten Johan Lorentz i Kopenhamn, ett försök till en biografi. MOBERG 249–263

1000 [Lotti] Spitz, Charlotte. Die Opern *Ottone* von G. F. Händel (London 1722) und *Teofane* von A. Lotti (Dresden 1719), ein Stilvergleich. SANDBERGER 265–271

1001 [Lully] Noack, Friedrich. Die Musik zu der Molièrschen Komödie *Monsieur de Pourceaugnac* von Jean Baptiste de Lully. WOLF 139–147

1002 —— Pincherle, Marc. L'Interpretazione orchestrale di Lulli. MARINUZZI 139–152

1003 —— Torrefranca, Fausto. La prima opera francese in Italia? (L'*Armida* di Lulli, Roma 1690). WOLF 191–197

1004 ♪ Mace, Thomas. *Tattle de moys* for lute. [Suite no. 1, lesson 8, & suite no. 2, lesson 6] ENGEL 141–142

1005 [Mace] Kinkeldey, Otto. Thomas Mace and his *Tattle de moy*. ENGEL 128–142

1005a [Maffei, S.] Sterzi, M. Attorno ad un'operetta del March. Scipione Maffei messa all'indice. CIAN 141–165

1006 [Mangeant] Verchaly, André. A propos des chansonniers de Jacques Mangeant (1608–1615). MASSON II, 169–177

1007 [Mareschall] Linden, Albert van der. La Légende d'un psautier perdu de Samuel Mareschall. BORREN 308–317

1008 ♪ Marini, Biagio. Sonata per l'organo e violino ò cornetto, op. 8 (1626). RIEMANN 320–325

1008a [Matthaei] Forchert, Arno. Ein

Traktat über die Modi Musici vom Jahre 1652. STÄBLEIN/70TH 57–63

1009 [Mauriz] Tschulik, Norbert. Mauriz von Menzingen; eine Studie zur Geschichte des deutschen Sololiedes im Barock. SCHENK 551–557

1009a [Mazzocchi] Gallico, Claudio. La "Querimonia" di Maddalena di D. Mazzocchi e l'interpretazione di L. Vittori. BARBLAN/60TH 133–147

1010 —— Osthoff, Helmuth. Domenico Mazzochis Vergil-Kompositionen. FELLERER/60TH 407–416

1010a [Melosio] Pirrotta, Nino. Il caval zoppo e il vetturino. Cronache di Parneso 1642. BARBLAN/60TH 215–226

1011 [Mercker] Seiffert, Max. Matthias Mercker, ein ausgewanderter holländischer Musiker. SCHEURLEER 291–301

1011a [Mezler] Haacke, Walter. Das *Odaeum litteratae iuventutis* von Thomas Mezler. Übersetzung des Widmungsbriefes nebst einigen Anmerkungen über ein Schulliederbuch des 17. Jahrhunderts. MÜNNICH/80THM 96–106

1012 [Michael] Adrio, Adam. Tobias Michaels *Musicalische Seelenlust* (1634–1637); über einige Fragen der musikalischen Aufführungs- und Editionspraxis im frühen 17. Jahrhundert. OSTHOFF 115–128

1013 [Michna] Bužga, Jaroslav. Der tschechische Barockkomponist Adam Michna z Otradovic (um 1600–1676). BESSELER 305–315

1013a —— Trolda, Emil. Neznámé skladby Adama Michny (Příspěvek k dějinám české cirkevní hudby XVII. stol.) [Unknown Compositions of Adam Michna (Contributions to the History of Czech Church Music in the 17th Century)] NEJEDLÝ/50TH 69–101

1014 [Mielczewski] Feicht, Hieronim. Marcin Mielczewski—*Missa super O gloriosa Domina.* CHYBIŃSKI/70TH 218–232

1014a [Miguel de Irízar] López-Calo, José. Corresponsales de Miguel de Irízar. SUBIRÁ/80TH 197–222

1015 ♪ Monteverdi, Claudio. *Combattimento di Tancredi e Clorinda* (Schütz MS?). OSTHOFF 215–227

1015a [Monteverdi] Damerini, Adelmo. Il senso religioso nelle musiche sacre di Claudio Monteverdi. BARBLAN/60TH 48–60

1016 —— Ghisi, Federico. L'Orchestra in Monteverdi. FELLERER/60TH 187–192

1017 —— Heuss, Alfred. Ein Beitrag zu dem Thema: Monteverdi als Charakteristiker in seinen Madrigalen. LILIENCRON 93–109

1018 —— Osthoff, Wolfgang. Monteverdis *Combattimento* in deutscher Sprache und Heinrich Schütz. OSTHOFF 195–227

1019 —— Redlich, Hans F. Monteverdi e l'orchestra. MARINUZZI 183–199

1019a —— Rosenthal, Albi. A Hitherto Unpublished Letter of Claudio Monteverdi. WELLESZ/80TH 103–107

1019b —— Schrade, Leo. Claudio Monteverdi, ein Revolutionär der Musikgeschichte. SCHRADE/D 385–395; orig. in *Neue Zeitschrift für Musik* 123 (1962) 153–157

1020 —— Schwartz, Rudolf. Zu den Texten der ersten fünf Bücher der Madrigale Monteverdis. KRETZSCHMAR 147–148

1020a [Motley] Dart, Thurston. Richard Motley, Dancing-master. OLDMAN 96–99

1021 [Moulinié] Launay, Denise. Notes sur Etienne Moulinié, maître de la musique de Gaston d'Orléans. MASSON II, 67–78

1022 [Nathusius] Schering, Arnold. Aus der Selbstbiographie eines deutschen Kantors: Elias Nathusius, 1676. SCHNEIDER/60TH 84–91

1023 [Nivers] Garros, Madeleine. L'Art d'accompagner sur la basse-continue d'après Guillaume-Gabriel Nivers. MASSON II, 45–51

1024 [Noordt] Fischer, Pieter. Rond en thema van Anthoni van Noordt. WAESBERGHE 39–44

1025 ♪ Orologio, Alexander. *Intradae quinque et sex vocibus*, no. 3. SCHEURLEER 223–225

1026 [Orologio] Nef, Karl. Die Intraden von Alexander Orologio. SCHEURLEER 219–225

1027 [Pachelbel] Woodward, Henry. Musical Symbolism in the Vocal Works of Johann Pachelbel. DAVISON 225–234

1028 [Padbrué] Noske, Frits. Padbrué en Vondel. WAESBERGHE 123–136

1029 ♪ Pękiel, Barthołomiej. *Tres canones simul cantantur.* WOLF 187–189

1030 [Pękiel] Simon, Alicja. Ein Kanon aus Marco Scacchis *Cribrum musicum ad triticum siferticum.* WOLF 184–189

1030a [Pergolesi] Degrada, Francesco. Uno sconosciuto intermezzo di Giovanni Battista Pergolesi. BARBLAN/60TH 80–91
1031 ♪ Pfleger, Augustin, *Ach, dass ich Wassers genug hätte.* SCHNEIDER/60TH 136
1032 [Pfleger] Blume, Friedrich. Augustin Pfleges Kieler Universitäts-Oden. BLUME/S 275–302; orig. in *Arch. f. Musikf.* 8 (1943)
1033 —— Stein, Fritz. Ein unbekannter Evangelienjahrgang von Augustin Pfleger. SCHNEIDER/60TH 126–136
1033a [Poglietti] Riedel, Friedrich W. Alessandro Pogliettis Oper *Endimione.* ENGEL 298–313
1034 [Polonais] Opieński, Henri. Jacob Polonais et Jacobus Reys. RIEMANN 349–353
1035 [Praetorius] Blume, Friedrich. Schlussbericht zur Gesamtausgabe der musikalischen Werke von Michael Praetorius. BLUME/S 265–274; orig. in the *Gesamtausgabe* 22, xlv–lii
1036a —— Samuel, Harold E. Michael Praetorius. BLUME/S 229–264; orig. in *Z. f. Musikw.* 17 (1935)
1036a ——. Samuel, Harold E. Michael Praetorius on Concertato Style. BUSZIN 95–109
1037 [Prinner] Federhofer, Helmut. Eine Musiklehre von Johann Jacob Prinner. OREL/70TH 47–57
1038 [Profe] Adrio, Adam. Ambrosius Profe (1589–1661) als Herausgeber italienischer Musik seiner Zeit. FELLERER/60TH 20–27
1039 ♪ Purcell, Henry. Four Short Fantasies for 3 Viols. STRAVINSKY/75TH 62–65
1039a [Purcell] Fortune, Nigel. A New Purcell Source. OLDMAN 109–113
1039b —— Lewis, Anthony. Notes and Reflections on a New Edition of Purcell's "The Fairy Queen." OLDMAN 104–108
1040 —— Ravenzwaai, G. van. Henry Purcells muzikale synthese in Engelands Restauratie-periode. MUEREN 201–207
1041 —— Wailes, Marylin. Four Short Fantasies by Henry Purcell. STRAVINSKY/75TH 59–65
1042 —— Westrup, Jack A. Purcell's Music for *Timon of Athens.* FELLERER/60TH 573–578
1042a —— ——. Purcell's Parentage. OLDMAN 100–103
—— See also no. 922
1043 [Puteanus] Hüschen, Heinrich. Der Polyhistor Erycius Puteanus (1574–1646) und sein Musiktraktat. MIES 1–25
1043a [Quagliati] Corte, Andrea della. Il valore artistico del "Carro di Fedeltà d'Amore." RACEK/60TH 55–58
1044 [Quiel] Feldmann, Fritz. Evangelische Kirchenmusik in schlesischer Landstadt; von der Persönlichkeit und dem Wirken J. Heinr. Quiels. SCHNEIDER/60TH 10–25
1045 [Rameau] Lebeau, Elisabeth. J. J. M. Decroix et sa collection Rameau. MASSON II, 81–91
1046 —— Masson, Paul-Marie. Une Lettre inédite de Rameau. LAURENCIE 201–207
1047 —— Pischner, Hans. Zur Vorgeschichte einiger im theoretischen Werk Jean Philippe Rameaus behandelter Probleme der Harmonik. MÜNNICH 9–39
1048 —— Schaeffner, André. L'Orgue de barbarie de Rameau. MASSON II, 135–150
1049 [Rasi] Einstein, Alfred. Ein Emissär der Monodie in Deutschland, Francesco Rasi. WOLF 31–34
1050 ♪ Rathgeber, Valentin. *Ach höchster Gott und Herr* (*Ohrenvergnügendes . . . Tafel-Confect* II, 5). WAESBERGHE 153–154
1051 ♪ ——. *Der hat vergeben* (*Ohrenvergnügendes . . . Tafel-Confect* I, 10). WAESBERGHE 151–152
1052 [Rathgeber] Schmidt-Görg, Joseph. Neues zum augsburger Tafel-Konfekt. WAESBERGHE 149–155
1053 [Reincken] Pirro, André. Notes pour servir, éventuellement, à la biographie de Reincken. SCHEURLEER 251–264
1054 [Reussner] Koletschka, Karl. Esaias Reussner Vater und Sohn, und ihre Choralbearbeitung für die Laute; eine Parallele. KOCZIRZ 14–17
1055 —— Münnich, Richard. Ein Brief Esaias Reussners. LILIENCRON 173–175
[Reys, Jacob] See no. 1034
1056 [Riccioni] Sartori, Claudio. Barbara Riccioni: Profilo di una cantante della fine del secolo XVII. FELLERER/60TH 454–460
1057 [Rist] Krabbe, Wilhelm. Zur Frage der Parodien in Rists *Galathea.* KRETZSCHMAR 58–61
1058 ♪ Ritter, Christian. *Brautmesse*

(1669). *Stehe auf.* RIEMANN insert after p. 380: 1–3

1059 ♪ ——. *Diese sind's die da kommen sind. Stürmt der Wind und Wetter gleich.* RIEMANN insert after p. 380: 6–8

1060 ♪ ——. *Salve me puerule. O magnum et admirabile mysterium.* RIEMANN insert after p. 380: 4–5

1061 ♪ ——. Sonatina, organ. RIEMANN insert after p. 380: 9–16

1062 [Ritter] Buchmayer, Richard. Christian Ritter, ein vergessener deutscher Meister des 17. Jahrhunderts. RIEMANN 354–380

1063 [Ruckers] Stellfeld, J.-A. Johannes Ruckers de jongere en de Koninklijke Kapel te Brussel. BORREN 283–291

1064 [Ruetz] Stahl, Wilhelm. Kaspar Ruetz, ein lübeckischer Zeit-und Amtsgenosse J. S. Bachs. SCHEURLEER 327–338

1065 [Salmenius] Andersson, Otto. Johannes Salmenius och musiken i Åbo Katedralskola under 1600-talet. KROHN 6–24, German summary iii; ANDERSSON, O./85TH 32–42

1066 [Salzinger] Gottron, Adam. Was versteht Ivo Salzinger unter lullistischer Musik? ANGLÉS I, 361–368

1066a [Scacchi] Federhofer, Hellmut. Marco Scacchis "Cribrum Musicum" (1643) und die Kompositionslehre von Christoph Berhard. ENGEL 76–90

1066b [Scarlatti, A.] Dent, Edward J. A Pastoral Opera by Alessandro Scarlatti. HIRSCH 7–14

1067 [Scarlatti, D.] Kirkpatrick, Ralph. Domenico Scarlatti's Choral Music. DAVISON 243–246

1067a —— Pestelli, Giorgio. Contributo per un ordinamento cronologico delle sonate di Domenico Scarlatti. BARBLAN/60TH 195–200

[Scheibe, Johann Adolf] See no. 1355

1068 [Scheidt] Mahrenholz, Christhard. Die Bearbeitung geistlicher und weltlicher Melodien in Samuel Scheidts *Tabulatura nova* 1624. MAHRENHOLZ 103–114

1069 —— ——. Der 3. Band von Samuel Scheidts *Tabulatura nova* 1624 und die Gottesdienstordnung der Stadt Halle. MAHRENHOLZ 114–122; orig. in Z. *f. Musikf.* 109 (1948)

1070 —— ——. Samuel Scheidt und die Orgel. MAHRENHOLZ 122–135; orig. in *Musik und Kirche* 25 (1955)

1071 [Schein] Gurlitt, Wilibald. Ein Autorenprivileg für Johann Hermann Schein von 1628. FELLERER/60TH 200–204

1072 —— Prüfer, Arthur. J. H. Scheins *Cymbalum Sionium.* LILIENCRON 176–192

1073 [Schildt] Werner, Theodor W. Archivalische Nachrichten und Dokumente zur Kenntnis der Familie Schildt. KROYER 130–139

1074 [Scholze] Seiffert, Max. Die Sperontes-Lieder: *Ich bin nun wie ich bin—Ihr Schönen, höret an* und Seb. Bach. STEIN 66–70

1075 [Schop] Moser, Andreas. Johann Schop als Violinkomponist. KRETZSCHMAR 92–95

1076 [Schütz] Benesch, Otto. Schütz und Rembrandt. DEUTSCH/80TH 12–19

1077 —— Ehmann, Wilhelm. Die *Geistliche Chormusik* von Heinrich Schütz in ihrer musikalischen Darstellung. WLH 75–83

1078 —— Gerber, Rudolf. Wort und Ton in den *Cantiones sacrae* von Heinrich Schütz. ABERT 57–71

1079 —— Gümmer, Paul. Der Gesangstil in den *Kleinen geistlichen Konzerten* von Heinrich Schütz. WLH 84–85

1080 ——Hoffmann, Hans. Die Gestaltung der Evangelisten-Worte bei H. Schütz und J. S. Bach. SCHNEIDER/60TH 49–58

1081 —— Kraft, Günther. Schütz; Gedenkstätten in Thüringen. MAUERSBERGER 84–92

1082 —— Lütge, Karl. Heinrich Schütz, *Kläglicher Abschied.* KRETZSCHMAR 85–87

1083 —— Mahrenholz, Christhard. Heinrich Schütz und das erste Reformationsjubiläum 1617. MAHRENHOLZ 196–204; orig. in *Musik und Kirche* 3 (1931)

1083a —— Mittring, Gerhard. *Totendienst und Christuspredigt.* Zum Text der *Musikalischen Exequien* von Heinrich Schütz. EHMANN/60TH 43–63

1084 —— Moser, Hans Joachim. Heinrich Schütz als Lehrer, Prediger und Prophet. MOSER/70TH 93–106; orig. in *Bekenntnis zu Heinrich Schütz* (Kassel 1954)

1085 —— ——. Schütz und das evangelische Kirchenlied. MOSER/70TH 75–93; orig. in *Jahrbuch der Staatlichen Akad. f. Kirchen- und Schulmusik* 3 (1929/1930)

1086 ——Schering, Arnold. Zur Metrik der *Psalmen Davids* von Heinrich Schütz. WAGNER 176–180

1087 —— Schneider, Max. Zum Weihnachtsoratorium von Heinrich Schütz. KROYER 140–143

1087a —— Schrade, Leo. Heinrich Schütz and Johann Sebastian Bach in the Protestant Liturgy. SCHRADE/D 396–423; orig. in *The Musical Heritage of the Church*, 4. Valparaiso. Indiana (1954) 31–42

—— See also no. 1018

1088 ♪ Schuyt, Cornelis. *Bewaert Heer Hollandt*. BORREN/80TH 102

1089 [Schuyt] Smijers, Albert. Een canon van Cornelis Schuyt. BORREN/80TH 100–105

1090 [Selle] Arnheim, Amalie. Thomas Selle als Schulkantor in Itzehoe und Hamburg. LILIENCRON 35–50

1091 —— Moser, Hans Joachim. Aus der Frühgeschichte der deutschen Generalbasspassion. MOSER/70TH 63–74; orig. in *Peters Jahrbuch* 27 (1920)

1092 [Silbermann] Mahrenholz, Christhard. Grundsätze der Dispositionsgestaltung des Orgelbauers Gottfried Silbermann. GURLITT 174–186, & MAHRENHOLZ 75–87

1093 [Speer] Moser, Hans Joachim. Daniel Speer als Dichter und Musiker. MOSER/70TH 119–144; orig. in *Euphorion* 34/3 (1933) & *Acta M.* 9 (1937)

1093a [Spiess] Federl, Ekkehard. Der *Tractatus Musicus* des Pater Meinrad Spiess (1683–1761). STÄBLEIN/70TH 39–46

1094 [Spongia] Einstein, Alfred. Ein Concerto grosso von 1619. KRETZSCHMAR 26–28

1095 ♪ Staden, Siegmund Theophil. *Seelewig. Von der Welt Eitelkeit*. LILIENCRON 265–275

1096 [Staden] Schmitz, Eugen. Zur musikgeschichtlichen Bedeutung der Harsdörfferschen *Frauenzimmergesprächspiele*. LILIENCRON 254–277

1096a [Stainer, J.] Heckmann, Harald. Ein später Brief von Jakob Stainer. WIORA/60TH 317–318

1097 [Steffani] Croll, Gerhard. Zur Chronologie der düsseldorfer Opern Agostino Steffanis. FELLERER/60TH 82–87

1097a —— Werner, Theodor Wilhelm. Agostino Steffanis Operntheater in Hannover SEIFFERT/70TH 65–79

1098 [Stobaeus] Haase, Hans. Eine wichtige Quelle für Johannes Stobaeus Grudentinus, 6 Sammelbände aus Königsberger Beständen in Göttingen. BLUME/F 176–188

1099 [Stradella] Einstein, Alfred. Ein Bericht über den turiner Mordanfall auf Alessandro Stradella. SANDBERGER 135–137

1099a [Telemann] Maertens, Willi. Georg Philipp Telemanns Hamburger "Kapitänsmusiken." WIORA/60TH 335–341

1100 —— Ruhnke, Martin. Telemann im Schatten von Bach? ALBRECHT 141–152

1101 —— Stein, Fritz, Eine komische Schulmeister-Kantate von Georg Philipp Telemann und Johann Adolf Hasse. SCHNEIDER/80TH 183–190

1102 [Tessarini] Dunning, Albert. Some Rules on the Biography of Carlo Tessarini and his Musical Grammar. SCHENK 115–122

1103 ♪ Theile, Johann. *Harmonischer Baum*. SEIFFERT 97–99

1104 [Theile] Schenk, Erich. Johann Theiles *Harmonischer Baum*. SEIFFERT 95–100

1105 [Uttini] Tegen, Martin. Uttinis tryckt triosonater op. 1. MOBERG 311–320

1106 [Visconti] Monterosso, Raffaello. Gasparo Visconti, violinista cremonese del secolo XVIII. SCHENK 378–388

1106a [Vivaldi] Andrews, Herbert Kennedy. The Red Priest. OGG 232–247

1107 —— Eller, Rudolf. Die Entstehung der Themenzweiheit in der Frühgeschichte des Instrumentalkonzerts. BESSELER 323–335

1107a —— Rinaldi, Mario. Alla scoperta di Vivaldi operista. BARBLAN/60TH 240–253

1108 ♪ Vivarino, Ignatio. *Il primo libro di motetti*. Sonata no. 7 RIEMANN 319–320

1109 [Vondel] Denis, Valentin. De muziek bij Vondel. CLOSSON 88–109 (see also no. 1029)

1109a [Vossius, G. J.] Hüschen, Heinrich. Der Polyhistor Gerhard Johann Vossius (1577–1649) als Musikschriftsteller. WIORA/60TH 182–190

1110 [Vossius, I.] Serauky, Walter. Die Affekten-Metrik des Isaac Vossius in ihrem Einfluss auf Joh. Kuhnau und Joh. Seb Bach. SCHNEIDER/80TH 105–113

1111 [Vulpius] Eggebrecht, Hans H. Das Leben des Melchior Vulpius. SCHNEIDER/80TH 87–104

1112 [Walliser] Bähre, A. Christoph Thomas Walliser. SPG I, 355–384
1113 [Weiss] Prusik, Karl. Die Sarabande in den Solopartien des Lautenisten Sylvius Leopold Weiss (1686–1750) nach den Tabulaturen der Wiener Nationalbibliothek. KOCZIRZ 36–37
1114 [Werckmeister] Serauky, Walter. Andreas Werkmeister als Musiktheoretiker. SCHNEIDER/60TH 118–125
1115 [Wiedeman] Becker, Adolf. Michel Wiedeman, der unbesorgte Musicante. KRETZSCHMAR 15–17
1115a ♪ Zamponi, Giuseppe. *Quel guardo ch'ardea* (*Raccolta d'arie spirituali*, 1640). BORREN/90TH 188–191
1116 [Zellbell] Morin, Gösta. Ferdinand Zellbell d. ä., liv och verk. MOBERG 265–271

See also nos. 74, 82, 198, 443, 507, 559a, 752, 787, 793a, 797, 813, 821a, 826, 827a, 1415a, 2562

CLASSICAL ERA: GENERAL

1116a Aaronson, Brenda C. & Barbara Krader. A Partial Survey of Late 18th Century Publications of Czech Music in Western Europe. RACEK/60TH 12–21
1116b Alvarez Solar-Quintes, Nicolás. La imprenta musical en Madrid en el siglo XVIII. SUBIRÁ/80TH 161–195
1116c Andersson, Otto. Musikliterarische Fäden zwischen Holland und Finnland am Ende des 18. Jahrhunderts. SCHEURLEER 43–48
1117 Bakker, Mynko Geerink. Kerkelijke koraalspel volgens een catechismus uit 1787. BERNET KEMPERS 38–40
1118 Blume, Friedrich. Die Musik der Klassik. BLUME/S 123–186; orig. in *MGG* 7, col. 1027
1119 Biehle, Herbert. Kastratenkunst und Gesangspädagogik. MÜLLER VON ASOW [5–8]
1120 Borrel, Eugène. L'Orchestre du Concert Spirituel et celui de l'opéra de Paris, de 1751 à 1800, d'après les spectacles de Paris. MASSON II, 9–15
1121 ——. Un Paradoxe musical au XVIIIe siècle. LAURENCIE 217–221
1122 ——. La Strumentazione della sinfonia francese del sec. XVIII. MARINUZZI 7–22
1122a Braubach, Max. Die Mitglieder der Hofmusik unter den vier letzten Kurfürsten von Köln. SCHMIDT-GÖRG/70TH 26–63
1123 Engelke, Bernhard. Neues zur Geschichte der Berliner Liederschule. RIEMANN 456–472
1124 Falvy, Zoltán. A Linus-féle XVIII. századi táncgyüjtemény [The Linus Dance Collection of the 18th Century] KODÁLY/75TH 407–443, German summary, 756–757
1125 Fédorov, Vladimir. Lettres de quelques voyageurs russes du XVIIIe siècle. BLUME/F 112–123
1126 Feicht, Hieronym. Musikalische Beziehungen zwischen Wien und Warschau zur Zeit der wiener Klassiker. SCHENK 174–182
1127 Fellerer, Karl Gustav. Thematisches Verzeichnis der fürstbischöflichen freisingischen Hofmusik von 1796. DEUTSCH/80TH 296–302
1128 ——. Zur Melodielehre im 18. Jahrhundert. KODÁLY/80TH 109–115
1128a ——. Zur musikalischen Akustik im 18. Jahrhundert. MÜLLER-BLATTAU/70TH 80–88
1129 Frotscher, Gotthold. Ein danziger Musikantenspiegel vom Ende des 18. Jahrhunderts. SCHERING 68–75
1130 Gálos, Rezö. Erdélyi hangversenyek a XVIII. században [Transylvanian Concerts in the 18th Century] BARTÓK/E 489–499, summary 556
1131 Gérold, Théodore. Le Réveil en France au XVIIIe siècle de l'intérêt pour la musique profane du moyen âge. LAURENCIE 223–234
1132 Glasenapp, Franz von. Eine Gruppe von Symphonien und Ouvertüren für Blasinstrumente von 1793–1795 in Frankreich. SCHNEIDER/80TH 197–207
1133 Gottron, Adam. Musik in sechs mittelrheinischen Männerklöstern im 18. Jahrhundert. SCHENK 214–230
1134 Haas, Robert. Über das wiener Dilettanten-Konzert 1782. OREL/70TH 77–80
1135 ——. Von dem wienerischen Geschmack in der Musik. BIEHLE 59–65
1136 Heyer, Hermann. Vermächtnis und Verpflichtung. KONWITSCHNY 9–21
1137 Hoffmann-Erbrecht, Lothar. Der galante Stil in der Musik des 18. Jahrhunderts; zur Problematik des Begriffs. SCHENK 252–260
1138 Johansson, Cari. Studier kring

Patrik Alströmers musiksamling. MOBERG 195–207
1139 Klein, Herbert. Nachrichten zum Musikleben Salzburgs in den Jahren 1764–1766. OREL/70TH 93–101
1140 LaRue, Jan. Major and Minor Mysteries of Identification in the 18th-Century Symphony. KINKELDEY/80TH 181–196
1141 Lesure, François. Le Manuscrit Lavergne et le répertoire des maîtrises du Sud-Ouest de la France vers 1750. FELLERER/60TH 315–320
1142 Lindfors, Per. Musik för en *Barmhärtighetsinrättning* [Music for a Charitable Institution] MOBERG 239–248
1143 ♪ Linus dance book. KODÁLY/75TH 420–431
1143a Matthäus, Wolfgang. Ein unbekannter Mainzer Musikalienhändler aus der Zeit des ausgehenden Kurstaates. GOTTRON 51–53
1144 Murányi, Róbert Árpád. Két XVIII. századi iskoladráma dallamai [The Songs of Two 18th-Century School Dramas] BARTÓK/E 501–507, summary 557
1145 Nowak, Leopold. Ein Druck mit Melodien für Theophilanthropen. STUMMVOLL 61
1145a Plavec, Josef. K otázce repatriace hudebních Bohemik [On the Question of the Repatriation of Czech Music] RACEK/60TH 195–205, summary in German
1145b Pöhlmann, Egert. Eine fränkische Dorforgel des Biedermeier. STÄBLEIN/70TH 187–190
1145c Racek, Jan. Die tschechische Musik des 18. Jahrhunderts und ihre Stellung in der europäischen Musikkultur. SCHMIDT-GÖRG/70TH 296–308
1146 Rodriguez-Moñino, A. Instrumentos músicos para el Infante Don Gabriel (Doce documentos inéditos de 1777–1784). ANGLÉS II, 723–724
1147 Schering, Arnold. Das öffentliche Musikbildungswesen in Deutschland bis zur Gründung des leipziger Konservatoriums. KML 61–80
1148 Schoenbaum, Camillo. Die böhmischen Musiker in der Musikgeschichte Wiens vom Barock zur Romantik. SCHENK 475–495
1148a ——. Harmonia pastoralis bohemica. WIORA/60TH 348–356
1149 Schünemann, Georg. Ein Sing- und Spielbuch des 18. Jahrhunderts. WOLF 179–183
1149a Straková, Theodora. Das Musikalieninventar von Pirnitz (Brtnice). Ein Beitrag zur Geschichte der Musik in Mahren um Mitte des 18. Jh. RACEK/60TH 279–287
1150 Subirá, José. Conciertos espirituales españoles en el siglo XVIII. FELLERER/60TH 519–529
1151 Szabolcsi, Bence. Kleine Beiträge zur Melodiegeschichte des 18. Jahrhunderts. SCHENK 532–538
1151a Terrayová-Dokulilová, Maria Jana. Ein Dokument zur Geschichte der Orgelmusik in der zweiten Hälfte des 18. Jahrhunderts (Sammelhandschrift A XII/220—Ms Martin). ŠTĚDROŇ/60TH 107–128, summary in Czech at end of article
1151b Unverricht, Hubert. Musik in Mainz im Spiegel der Sächsisch-Thüringischen allgemeinen Zeitschriften aus dem letzten Viertel des 18. Jahrhunderts. GOTTRON 41–50
1151c Walter, Rudolf. Der Orgelbau für die Fürstabtei St. Blasien 1772/75. FELLERER/60THM 259–319
1152 Wieder, Joachim. Bickham's *Musical Entertainer* in der englischen Buchkunst des 18. Jahrhunderts. JUCHHOFF 147–158
1153 Wolf, Werner. Die Gewandhauskonzerte im Spiegel der Kritik. KONWITSCHNY 72–86

CLASSICAL ERA: OPERA

1154 Andorfer, Eduard. Das alte Opernhaus am Tummelplatz in Graz. SCHÜTZ 470–485
1155 Bédarida, Henri. L'Opéra italien jugé par un amateur français en 1756. LAURENCIE 185–200
1155a Brockett, Oscar G. The Fair Theatres of Paris in the Eighteenth Century: the Undermining of the Classical Ideal. KITTO 251–270
1156 Engelke, Bernhard. Aus den entscheidenden Entwicklungsjahren der opéra-comique. SCHERING 51–60
1157 Engländer, Richard. Zur Psychologie des Gustavianischen Opernrepertoires. JEPPESEN 267–283
1158 Goldschmidt, Hugo. Das Cembalo im Orchester der italienischen Oper der zweiten Hälfte des 18. Jahrhunderts. LILIENCRON 87–92
1159 Grout, Donald J. The *Opéra comique* and the *Théâtre italien* 1715 to 1762. ANGLÉS I, 369–377
1160 Guiet, René. La Question de la langue française dans les querelles

musicales au XVIIIème siècle. NIELSON 91–102
1161 Haraszti, Emile. Mátyás Király az énekes szinpadon [King Matthias on the Lyric Stage] MATTHIAS II, 491–522
1162 Horányi, Mátyás. Az Esterházy-opera; adalékok Eszterháza és Kismarton zene- és színháztörténetéhez [The Esterházy Opera; a Contribution to the Musical and Theatrical History of Eszterháza and Kismarton] KODÁLY/75TH 729–744, German summary 762
1163 Jourda, Pierre. Note sur l'histoire du théâtre à Montpellier au XVIIIe siècle. MORNET 133–140
1164 Linden, Albert van der. Quelques aspects de la querelle des bouffons à Bruxelles. MASSON II, 161–166
1164a Nowak-Romanowicz, Alina. Niektóre problemy opery polskiej między oświeceniem a romantyzmem [Several Problems Concerning the Polish Opera between the Time of the Enlightenment and the Romantic Era] FEICHT 328–336
1165 Refardt, Edgar. Die Schweiz im musikalischen Bühnenwerk. REFARDT 83–91; orig. in *Schweizerische Musikz.* 75 (1935)
1165a Riedel, Friedrich W. Die Libretto-Sammlung im Benediktinerstift Göttweig. FÉDEROV 105–111
1166 Schmidt-Görg, Joseph. Wiener Opernaufführungen im Winter 1815/1816 nach den Tagebuchaufzeichnungen eines jungen Geigers. SCHENK 453–462
1167 Schneider, Günter. Stilelemente der Sprache des deutschen bürgerlichen Singspiels im 18. Jahrhundert. FELLERER 52–57
1168 Springer, Hermann. Neue Materialien zur italienschen Operngeschichte des achtzehnten Jahrhunderts. HARNACK 226–231
1169 Subirá, José. Les Influences françaises dans la tonadilla madrilène du XVIIIe siècle. LAURENCIE 209–216
1170 ——. Opéras français chantés en langue espagnole. MASSON II, 153–157
1170a Vetter, Walther. Tschechische Opernkomponisten: ein Stilkundlicher Versuch. RACEK/60TH 353–363
1171 Wichmann, Heinz. Das Wesen der Naturbewegung und ihr Einfluss auf die französische Oper. ABERT 177–189

CLASSICAL ERA: MANNHEIM SCHOOL

1172 Altmann, Wilhelm. Nachträge zu Hugo Riemanns Verzeichnis der Druckausgaben und thematischen Katalog der mannheimer Kammermusik des XVIII. Jahrhunderts. RIEMANN/70TH 620–628
1173 Bedbur, Magda. Das Finale in den Symphonien Matthias Georg Monns. FELLERER 47–51
1174 Heuss, Alfred. Über die Dynamik der Mannheimer Schule. RIEMANN 433–455
1175 Korte, Werner. Darstellung eines Satzes von Johann Stamitz (Zur Musikgeschichte als Kunstwissenschaft). FELLERER/60TH 283–292
1176 Larsen, Jens Peter. Zur Bedeutung der Mannheimer Schule. FELLERER/60TH 303–309
1177 Mathias, F. X. Thematischer Katalog der im strassburger Münsterarchiv aufbewahrten kirchenmusikalischen Werke Fr. X. Richters (1769–1789). RIEMANN 394–422
1178 Sandberger, Adolf. Aus der Korrespondenz des pfalzbayerischen Kurfürsten Karl Theodor mit seinem römischen Ministerresidenten. KRETZSCHMAR 128–131
1179 Schering, Arnold. Fünf Briefe von Karl Stamitz; Bruchstücke einer Selbstbiographie. STEIN 57–65

CLASSICAL ERA: JOSEPH HAYDN

1180 ♪ [Baryton music] Baryton trio no. 53. KODÁLY/75TH 688[b–g]
1181 ♪—— Baryton trio no. 109. KODÁLY/75TH 688[h–l]
1182 —— Csuka, Béla. Haydn és a baryton. KODÁLY/75TH 669–728, German summary 761–762
1183 Blume, Friedrich. Haydn als Briefschreiber. BLUME/S 564–570; orig. in *Neue Zürcher Zeitung* (Mar. 13, 1960)
1184 ——. Haydn, der Klassiker. BLUME/S 552–558; orig. in *Hausmusik* 23 (1959)
1185 ——. Haydn und Mozart. BLUME/S 570–582
1186 ——. Der Meister der klassischen Musik. BLUME/S 558–564; orig. in *Neue Zürcher Zeitung* (May 31, 1959)

1187 [Canons] Larsen, Jens Peter. En Haydnsk gådekanon. MOBERG 215–226
1188 [*Creation*] Schnürl, Karl. Haydns *Schöpfung* als Messe. SCHENK 463–476
1189 ♪ *Du sollst an einen Gott glauben.* MOBERG 218, 224
1189a Feder, Georg. Gedanken über den Kritischen Apparat aus der Sicht der Haydn-Gesamtausgabe. SCHMIDT-GÖRG/70TH 73–81
1190 ——. Zur Datierung Haydnscher Werke. HOBOKEN 50–54
1191 Fellerer, Karl Gustav. Zum Joseph-Haydn-Bild im frühen 19. Jahrhundert. HOBOKEN 73–86
1192 Geiringer, Karl. Eigenhändige Bemerkungen Haydns in seinen Musikhandschriften. HOBOKEN 87–92
1193 [*L'Infedeltà delusa*] Vécsey, Jenö. *L'Infedeltà delusa* (Haydn operájanak felújitásja). KODÁLY/70TH 423–438
1194 Larsen, Jens Peter. Zu Haydns künstlerischer Entwicklung. FISCHER/W 123–129
1195 Luithlen, Victor. Haydn-Erinnerungen in der Sammlung alter Musikinstrumente des Kunsthistorischen Museums zu Wien. HOBOKEN 110–114
1196 [Operas] Bartha, Dénes. Haydn als Opernkapellmeister. BESSELER 361–365 (See also no. 1193)
1196a —— Scott, Marion M. The Opera Concerts of 1795. HIRSCH 24–28
1197 Orel, Alfred. Joseph Haydn. OREL 54–74
1198 [Piano music] Feder, Georg. Probleme einer Neuordnung der Klaviersonaten Haydns. BLUME/F 92–103
1199 —— Larsen, Jens Peter. Eine bisher unbeachtete Quelle zu Haydns frühen Klavierwerken. SCHMIDT-GÖRG 188–195
1200 Reindl, Johannes. Zur Entstehung des Refrains der Kaiserhymne Joseph Haydns. SCHENK 417–433
1201 Sandberger, Adolf. Notenbild und Werktreue. STEIN 183–187
1202 Schmid, Ernst F. Josef Haydns Jugendliebe. FISCHER/W 109–122
1202a Schrade Leo. Joseph Haydn als Schöpfer der klassischen Musik. SCHRADE/D 506–518; orig. in *Universitas* 17 (1962) 767–778
1203 [String quartets] Blume, Friedrich. Joseph Haydns künstlerische Persönlichkeit in seinen Streichquartetten. BLUME/S 526–551; orig. in *Peters Jahrbuch* 38 (1931)
1203a [Symphonies] Bartha, Dénes. Volkstanz-Stilisierung in Joseph Haydns Finale-Themen. WIORA/60TH 375–384
1204 —— Grasberger, Franz. Form und Ekstase; über eine Beziehung Haydn-Schubert-Bruckner in der Symphonie. HOBOKEN 93–100
1204a —— Idaszak, Danuta. Rękopisy symfonii Józefa Haydna w zbiorach Archiwum Gnieźnieńskiego [Manuscript of a Symphony of Joseph Haydn in the Gniezno archives] FIECHT 307–313
1205 —— Larsen, Jens Peter. Probleme der chronologischen Ordnung von Haydns Sinfonien. DEUTSCH/80TH 90–104
1205a —— Unverricht, Hubert. Die Simrock-Drucke von Haydns Londoner Sinfonien. Simrocks Verbindungen mit Haydn. FELLERER/60THS 235–259
1205b [*Te Deum*] Becker-Glauch, Imgard. Joseph Haydns *Te Deum* für die Kaiserin: eine Quellenstudie. SCHMIDT-GÖRG/70TH 1–10
1206 ["*Toy Symphony*"] Halm, Hans. Eine unbekannte Handschrift der *Kinder-Symphonie*. HOBOKEN 101–102
1207 Valkó, Arisztid. Haydn magyarországi működése a levéltári akták tükrében [Haydn's Activities in Hungary as Revealed in the Archives] KODÁLY/75TH 627–667, German summary 760

CLASSICAL ERA: WOLFGANG AMADEUS MOZART

See also no. 1185

1208 Bauer, Wilhelm A. Amadeus? DEUTSCH/80TH 105–109
1208a Belza, Igor'. Ob odnoy publikatsii professora Yana Ratska [Concerning a Publication of Professor Yana Ratska] RACEK/60TH 23–28
1209 Bernet Kempers, Karel P. Hemiolenrhythmik bei Mozart. OSTHOFF 155–161
1210 Blume, Friedrich. Wolfgang Amadeus Mozart. BLUME/S 583–669; orig. in *MGG* 9, col. 699
1211 ——. Wolfgang Amadeus Mozart, Geltung und Wirkung. BLUME/S 670–686; orig. in *The Mozart Companion* (London 1956)
1212 Breazul, G. Die ersten Mozart-Aufführungen in Rumänien. MÜLLER VON ASOW [9–23]

1213 Broder, Nathan. Van Swieten or Constanze? ENGEL 48–52

1214 [Concertos] Bartha, Dénes. Zur Identifikation des "Strassburger Konzerts" bei Mozart. BLUME/F 30–33

1215 —— Blume, Friedrich. Mozarts Konzerte und ihre Überlieferung. BLUME/S 686–714; orig. in *The Mozart Companion* (London 1956)

1216 [*Così fan tutte*] Mitchell, Donald. The Truth about *Così*. BRITTEN 95–99

1217 Deutsch, Otto Erich. Das Mozartbildnis von Barbara Krafft. FISCHER/W 9–13

1217a ——. Spurious Mozart Letters. OLDMAN 120–123

1217b [*Don Giovanni*] Cartford, Gerhard M. Kiergekaard and Mozart, a study. BUSZIN 121–140

1218 —— Macchia, Giovanni. Di alcuni precedenti del *Don Giovanni* di Mozart e da Ponte. SILVA 169–194

1219 —— Refardt, Edgar. Der Konzertschluss der *Don Juan*-Ouverture. REFARDT 92–94; orig. in *Basler Nachrichten*, Sonntagsblatt 19 (1930)

1220 Engel, Hans. Richard Wagners Stellung zu Mozart. FISCHER/W 39–48

1221 [*Die Entführung*] Deutsch, Otto Erich. Ein neuer Brief Leopold Mozarts an seine Tochter. PAUMGARTNER 57–58

1222 [*Galimathias*] Malherbe, Charles. Le *Galimathias musicum* de W. A. Mozart. RIEMANN 472–478

1223 Gerstenberg, Walter. Über den langsamen Einleitungssatz in Mozarts Instrumentalmusik. FISCHER/W 25–32

1224 Gregor, Joseph. Das wiener Theater in Mozarts Zeit. MÜLLER VON ASOW [55–63]

1225 Haas, Robert. Ein unbekanntes Mozartbildnis. FISCHER/W 15–20

1226 Handschin, Jacques. Mozart und unsere Zeit. HANDSCHIN 199–207; orig. in *Neue Schweizer Rhundshau* 22 (1929)

1227 Hederer, Edgar. Mozart. BURCKHARDT 163–173

1228 Hollenfeltz, Jean-Louis. Trois documents inédits pour servir à l'histoire de la biographie de Mozart par Nissen. BORREN 197–204

1229 Hummel, Walter. Das Mozart-Album der Internationalen Mozartstiftung. DEUTSCH/80TH 110–119

1230 [Idomeneo] Böhm, Karl. Aufführungspraxis der Opera seria am Beispiel des *Idomeneo*. PAUMGARTNER 17–21

1230a King, A. Hyatt. Mozart and Peter Anton Kreusser. OLDMAN 124–126

1231 Laaff, Ernst. Mozarts geistliche Werke; zwischen Katholizismus und Freimaurerei. MERSMANN 76–82

1232 Lang, Paul Henry. Mozart after 200 Years. KINKELDEY/80TH 197–205

1233 Mies, Paul. Notation und Herausgabe bei einigen Werken von W. A. Mozart, Franz Schubert und Johannes Brahms. SCHMIDT-GÖRG 213–223

1234 Nadler, Joseph. Das literarisch-geistige Bild Wiens zur Zeit Mozarts. MÜLLER VON ASOW [143–152]

1235 Nettl, Paul. Mozart and the Czechs. EINSTEIN 329–342

1236 Oepen, Heinz. Mozarts Opern auf der kölner Bühne um die Wende des 18./19. Jahrhunderts. FELLERER 58–62

1237 Oldman, Cecil B. Thomas Attwood's Studies with Mozart. SCHEURLEER 227–240

1237a Paumgartner, Bernhard. Mozart im zwanzigsten Jahrhunderts. DAMDK 30–32

1238 [Piano Music] Fischer, Kurt von. Mozarts Klaviervariationen. ALBRECHT 168–173

1239 ——Gerstenberg, Walter. Über Mozarts Klaviersatz. GURLITT 108–116

1240 —— Kaul, Oskar. Über Mozarts vierhändige Klaviermusik. MÜLLER VON ASOW [100–107]

1240a —— King, A. Hyatt. An Unrecorded English Edition of Mozart's Duet-Sonata K.19d. HIRSCH 29–34

1241 —— Merian, Wilhelm. Mozarts Klaviersonaten und die Sonatenform. NEF 174–201

1242 —— Oldman, Cecil B. Cipriani Potter's Edition of Mozart's Pianoforte Works. DEUTSCH/80TH 120–127

1243 —— Schellong, Dieter. Mozarts Bedeutung für die Klaviermusik. BARTH 688–699

1243a Plath, Wolfgang. Bemerkungen zu einem missdeuteten Skizzenblatt Mozarts. GERSTENBERG/60TH 143–150

1244 ——. Miscellanea Mozartiana I. DEUTSCH/80TH 135–140

1245 Raeburn, Christopher. Mosel und Zinzendorf über Mozart. DEUTSCH/80TH 155–158

1246 Rech, Géza. Aus dem Briefarchiv der Internationalen Stiftung Mozarteum. DEUTSCH/80TH 159–167

1246a ——. "Mozart auf dem Theater" in der theaterwissenschaftlichen

Abteilung der Internationalen Stiftung Mozarteum, Salzburg. BORREN/90TH 196–201
1247 Rehm, Wolfgang. Miscellanea Mozartiana II. DEUTSCH/80TH 141–154
1248 Reichert, Ernst. Über den Mozart-Gesang. PAUMGARTNER 108–118
1249 [Requiem] Blume, Friedrich. Requiem und keine Ende. BLUME/S 714–734; orig., Engl., in MQ 47 (1961)
1250 —— Mörner, C. G. Stellan. F. S. Silverstolpes im Jahre 1800 (oder 1801) in Wien niedergeschriebene Bemerkungen zu Mozarts Requiem. OREL/70TH 113–119
1251 Roth, Ernst. Auf den Spuren Mozarts Anno 1829. PAUMGARTNER 59–69
1252 St. Foix, Georges de. Les Editions françaises de Mozart, 1765–1801. LAURENCIE 247–258
1252a ——. Le problème de la Fantaisie en ut mineur de Mozart (Koechel 396). BORREN/75TH 219–221
1252b Schrade, Leo. Mozart und die Romantiker. SCHRADE/D 519–536; orig. in *Bericht über die musikwissenschaftliche Tagung der Internat. Stiftung Mozarteum vom 2. bis 5. August 1931.* Leipzig (1932) 22–38
1253 Senn, Walter. Mozartiana aus Tirol. FISCHER/W 49–59
1254 [Songs] Friedlaender, Max. Mozarts Lieder. LILIENCRON 81–86
1254a Stockhausen, Karlheinz. Kadenzrhythmik bei Mozart. STEINECKE 38–72
1255 [String quartets] Chailley, Jacques. Sur la signification du quatuor de Mozart K. 465 dit "Les Dissonances" et du 7ème quatuor de Beethoven. JEPPESEN 283–292
1255a —— Cuyler, Louise E. Mozart's Six Quartets Dedicated to Haydn. SACHS/C 293–299
1256 —— St.-Foix, Georges de. Le dernier quatuor de Mozart. ADLER 168–173
1256a [Symphonies] Abert, Anna Amalia. Stilistischer Befund und Quellenlage zu Mozarts Lambacher Sinfonie KV Anh. 221 = 45a. ENGEL 43–56
1257 —— Grüss, Hans. Zur Analyse der Sinfonien g-moll (KV 550) und C-dur (KV 551) von Wolfgang Amadeus Mozart. BESSELER 367–375
1258 —— Westrup, Jack A. Cherubino and the G minor Symphony. NEWMAN 181–191
1259 Tenschert, Roland. Zwischen den Formen: Einthematik—Dualität; Rondo—Sonate. FISCHER/W 33–37
1260 Turrini, Giuseppe. Il Mozart e l'Accademia Filarmonica di Verona. MÜLLER VON ASOW [186–201]
1261 Valentin, Erich. Die goldene Spur; Mozart in der Dichtung Hermann Hesses. OREL/70TH 197–206
1262 ——. Mozarts *Weinwirt Albert;* Skizzen zu einem Porträt. FELLERER/60TH 549–557
1263 ——. Zu Mozarts Fénelon-Lektüre. FISCHER/W 21–24
1264 [Violin music] Müller, Theodor. Grundsätzliches zur Interpretation der Violinwerke W. A. Mozarts. PAUMGARTNER 119–127
1265 Wiora, Walter. Über den Volkston bei Mozart. ZODER 185–193
1266 [*Zaide*] Senn, Walter. Mozarts *Zaide* und der Verfasser der vermutlichen Textvorlage. OREL/70TH 173–186
1267 [*Zauberflöte*] Engländer, Richard. The Sketches for *The Magic Flute* at Upsala. EINSTEIN 343–355
1267a —— Feil, Arnold, Mozarts Duett "Bei Männern, welche Liebe fühlen." Periodisch-metrische Fragen. GERSTENBERG/60TH 45–54
1267b —— Gröger, Sibylle. Max Slevogt und die "Zauberflöte" von W. A. Mozart. KURTH 69–77
1268 —— Heuss, Alfred. Wie verhält es sich mit den Taktstrichen in dem *Zauberflöten*-Duett *Bei Männern, welche Liebe fühlen.* ADLER 174–178
1269 —— Paumgartner, Bernhard. Eine Text-Bearbeitung der *Zauberflöte* von 1795. DEUTSCH/80TH 128–134
1270 —— Prüfer, Arthur. Goethe und die *Zauberflöte.* MÜLLER VON ASOW [155–157]
1270a —— Schenk, Erich. Die "Zauberflöte" in Dreivierteltakt. FEICHT 314–327
1271 ——Schmitz, Eugen. Formgesetze in Mozarts *Zauberflöte.* SCHNEIDER/80TH 209–214
1272 —— Schuh, Willi. *Il Flauto magico.* BLUME/F 327–339
1273 —— ——. *Die Zauberflöte* im Mannheimer Nationaltheater 1794. DEUTSCH/80TH 168–182
1274 —— Wellesz, Egon. An Ancestor of Papageno. DEUTSCH/80TH 183–186
1275 —— Zallinger, Meinhard von. Tradition und Schlamperei;

Bemerkungen zur Ausgabe der *Zauberflöte*. PAUMGARTNER 102–107
1276 Zimmermann, Ewald. Das Mozart-Preisausschreiben der Gesellschaft für Musikforschung. SCHMIDT-GÖRG 400–408

CLASSICAL ERA: LUDWIG VAN BEETHOVEN

See also no. 1255

1277 Anderson, Emily. Charles Neate, a Beethoven Friendship. DEUTSCH/80TH 196–202
1278 ——. Two Letters from Beethoven to Prince Nikolas Galitzin. SCHMIDT-GÖRG 1–9
1278a Beck, Hermann. Die Proportion der Beethovenschen Tempi. GERSTENBERG/60TH 6–16
1279 Birtner, Herbert. Zur deutschen Beethovenauffassung seit R. Wagner. SCHIEDERMAIR/60TH 1–40
1280 Boyer, Jean. Les Titres d'ouvrages notés par Beethoven dans les *Cahiers de conversation* (1819–1824). LICHTENBERGER 123–132
1281 Bücken, Ernst. Das Wort-Ton-Problem bei Beethoven. SCHIEDERMAIR/60TH 162–176
1282 [Canons] Schünemann, Georg. Neue Kanons von Beethoven. SCHERING 207–212
1283 [Concerti] Goldschmidt, Harry. Motivvariation und Gestaltmetamorphose. BESSELER 389–409
1284 —— Moser, Hans Joachim. Die Form von Beethovens Violinkonzert. MOSER/70TH 198–205; orig. in *Neues Beethoven Jahrbuch* 9 (1939)
1285 [Not used]
1286 [Dona nobis pacem] Orel, Alfred. Ein *Dona nobis pacem* von der Hand Ludwig van Beethovens. FELLERER/60TH 402–406
1287 Duncan, Barbara. Falling leaves. KINKELDEY 118–121
1288 [Fantasy, op. 80] Vetter, Walther. Die musikalischen Wesensbestandteile in der Kunst Moritz von Schwinds. SEIFFERT 113–124
1288a [*Fidelio*] Hess, Willy. Eine unbekannte Frühfassung zweier Nummern der Oper *Leonore*. SCHMIDT-GÖRG/70TH 118–131
1289 Glück, Franz. Prolegomena zu einer neuen Beethoven-Ikonographie. DEUTSCH/80TH 203–212
1290 [Grosse Fuge] Bauer, Harold. From the Correspondence of Harold Bauer and O. G. Sonneck. ENGEL 39–47
1290a Grundmann, Herbert. Per il clavicembalo o piano-forte. SCHMIDT-GÖRG/70TH 100–117
1290b Jäger-Sunstenau, Hanns. Beethoven als Bürger der Stadt Wien. SCHMIDT-GÖRG/70TH 132–145
1291 Jonas, Oswald. Musikalische Meisterhandschriften. HOBOKEN 103–109
1292 Kahl, Willi. Zu Beethovens Naturauffassung. SCHIEDERMAIR/60TH 220–265
1293 Kinsky, Georg. Beethovens Brief an Baron de Trémont. LAURENCIE 269–273
1293a Köhler, Karl-Heinz. Beethovens Gespräche: einige Gedanken zur Veröffentlichung der Konversationshefte des Meisters. ENGEL 192–199
1293b Kropfinger, Klaus. Zur thematischen Funktion der langsamen Einleitung bei Beethoven. SCHMIDT-GÖRG/70TH 197–216
1294 [Marches] Steglich, Rudolf. Über Beethovens Märsche. OREL/70TH 187–195
1294a Mies, Paul. . . . quasi una fantasia. SCHMIDT-GÖRG/70TH 239–249
1295 [Missa Solemnis] Mahling, Friedrich. Beethovens *Missa solemnis* im Erlebnis eines deutschen Malers der Gegenwart. STEIN 33–47
1296 —— Schmidt-Görg, Joseph. Zur melodischen Einheit im Beethovens *Missa solemnis*. HOBOKEN 146–152
1297 —— Schmitz, Arnold. Zum Verständnis des Gloria in Beethovens *Missa solemnis*. BLUME/F 320–326
1297a Moser, Hans Joachim. Beethovengesichter vor und nach Beethoven. DESDERI/70TH 101–103
1298 Müller-Blattau, Joseph. Beethoven im Spätwerk. SCHNEIDER/80TH 215–225
1299 Ney, Elly. Bekenntnis zu Ludwig van Beethoven. RAABE 59–68
1300 Orel, Alfred. Beethoven und Grillparzer. OREL 85–94; orig. in *Euphorion* 28/2 (1927)
1301 ——. Ein Verlegerbrief über eine Beethoven-Gesamtausgabe. KOCZIRZ 29–35
1301a Pečman, Rudolf. Ästhetisch-theoretische Ausgangspunkte und stilistische Verwandtschaft im Schlaffen von Jírí Benda und Ludwig van

Beethoven. ŠTĚDROŇ/60TH 43–52, summary in Czech at end of article

1302 [Piano sonatas] Becking, Gustav. *Hören* und *Analysieren;* zu Hugo Riemanns Analyse von Beethovens Klaviersonaten. RIEMANN/70TH 587–603

1302a —— Finscher, Ludwig. Beethovens Klaviersonate opus 31, 3. Versuch einer Interpretation. WIORA/60TH 385–396

1303 —— Souchay, Marc-André. Zur Sonate Beethovens. ABERT 133–153

1304 —— Steglich, Rudolf. Dokumentarisches zur Lebensgeschichte eines Beethovenschen Sonatensatzes. DEUTSCH/80TH 213–225

1305 —— ——. Zum Adagio der Eleonorensonate Beethovens. SCHMIDT-GÖRG 309–314

1306 Prod'homme, Jacques-Gabriel. Beethoven et Pleyel. ADLER 190–194

1307 Racek, Jan. Beethoven und Goethe in Bad Teplitz, 1812. SCHENK 406–416

1307a Radcliffe, Philip F. Beethoven in 1950. HIRSCH 52–55

1308 Refardt, Edgar. Beethovens Anfänge in der Schweiz. REFARDT 95–98; orig. in *Basler Nachrichten* 137 (1937)

1309 [*Ruinen von Athen*] Batka, Richard. Zur Griepenkerl'schen Bearbeitung von Beethovens *Ruinen von Athen* für den Konzertsaal. RIEMANN 479–483

1309a Sakka, Keisei. Beethovens Klaviere: der Klavierbau und Beethovens künstlerische Reaktion. SCHMIDT-GÖRG/70TH 327–337

1310 Sandberger, Adolf. Zu Beethovens Briefen. LILIENCRON 247–249

1311 Schenk, Erich. Barock bei Beethoven. SCHIEDERMAIR/60TH 177–220

1312 ——. Beethovens Reisebekanntschaft von 1787, Nanette von Schaden. FELLERER/60TH 461–473

1313 Schiedermair, Ludwig. Zu Beethovens Schicksalsidee. RAABE 69–77

1313a Schmidt, Hans. Die gegenwärtige Quellenlage zu Beethovens Chorfantasie. SCHMIDT-GÖRG/70TH 355–371

1314 Schmidt-Görg, Joseph. Das gregorianische *Pange-lingua* bei Beethoven, ein neuer Fund. JOHNER 109–111

1315 ——. Stand und Aufgaben der Beethoven-Genealogie. SCHIEDERMAIR/60TH 114–161

1316 Schmitz, Arnold. Die Beethoven-Apotheose als Beispiel eines Säkularisierungsvorgangs. WAGNER 181–189

1317 ——. Zur Frage nach Beethovens Weltanschauung und ihrem musikalischen Ausdruck. SCHIEDERMAIR/60TH 266–293

1317a Schmoll, Adolf. Zur Geschichte des Beethoven-Denkmals. Das Künstler-Denkmal. MÜLLER-BLATTAU/70TH 242–277

1318 Schrade, Leo. Das französische Beethovenbild der Gegenwart. SCHIEDERMAIR/60TH 41–113

1319 [Songs] Moser, Hans Joachim. Kleine Beiträge zu Beethovens Liedern. MOSER/70TH 189–198; orig. in *Neues Beethoven Jahrbuch* 2 (1925)

1320 —— Müller-Blattau, Joseph. *Sehnsucht* von Goethe viermal komponiert von Beethoven. ANGLÉS II, 603–608

1320a —— Schmidt-Görg, Joseph. Zur Entstehungszeit von Beethovens Gellert-Liedern. DESDERI/70TH 157–161

1321 —— Schmitz, Eugen. *In questa tomba oscura.* SANDBERGER 258–264

1321a Stich, Norbert. Satzgattungen in Beethovens Instrumental Werken. SCHMIDT-GÖRG/70TH 379–385

1321b [String quartets] Draeger, Hans Heinz. A Quantitative Analysis of Music as Exemplified by Beethoven's Sketches for His Opus 131. WIORA/60TH 79–85

1321c —— Mies, Paul. Bemerkungen zu Beethovens Notation mit Beispielen aus den späten Streichquartetten. RACEK/60TH 161–165

1321d —— Orel, Alfred. Das Autograph des Scherzos aus Beethovens Streichquartett op. 127. ENGEL 274–280

1321e [String trios] Platen, Emil. Beethovens Streichtrio D-dur, opus 9, Nr. 2. Zum Problem der thematischen Einheit mehrsätziger Formen. SCHMIDT-GÖRG/70TH 260–282

1321f —— Salmen, Walter. Zur Gestaltung der "Thèmes russes" in Beethovens op. 59. WIORA/60TH 397–404

1322 [Symphonies] Hess, Willy. Zur Frage der Teilwiederholung in Beethovens Symphoniesätzen. SCHMIDT-GÖRG 142–155

1323 —— Hoffmann, Hans. Beethovens formale Gestaltung als Grundlage der Interpretation; dargestellt an der

Durchführung des I. Satzes der VI. Symphonie. STEIN 137–152

1323a —— Laaff, Ernst. Der musikalische Humor in Beethovens achter Symphonie. SCHMITZ 213–229

1323b —— Riezler, Walter. Das Chorfinale. CURTIUS, L./60TH 9–14

1324 —— Steglich, Rudolf. Motivischer Dualismus und thematische Einheit in Beethovens Neunter Sinfonie. BESSELER 411–424

1325 —— ——. "Zwei Prinzipe" in Beethovens fünfter Symphonie. FISCHER/W 131–141

1326 [*Todt! stöhnt es*] Forbes, Elliot. A Neglected Work in Beethoven's Choral Music, the Funeral Cantata. DAVISON 253–261

1326a Tyson, Alan. Moscheles and His "Complete Edition" of Beethoven. OLDMAN 136–141

1327 Unger, Max. Aus unbekannten Beethovenbriefen. MÜLLER VON ASOW [202–207]

1327a [Variations] Geiringer, Karl. Bemerkungen zum Bau von Beethovens "Diabelli Variationen." ENGEL 117–124

1327b —— Kolneder, Walter. Evolutionismus und Schaffenschronologie zu Beethovens Righini-Variationen. FELLERER/60THS 119–132

1327c —— Müller-Blattau, Joseph. Diabelli-Variationen im *Vaterländischen Künstlerverein* (1824). OREL/70TH 127–132

1327d —— Oldman, Cecil B. Beethoven's *Variations on National Themes:* Their Composition and First Publication. HIRSCH 45–51

1328 Vetter, Walther. Eine politische Beethoven-Betrachtung. SCHERING 241–249

1328a Virneisel, Wilhelm. Aus Beethovens Skizzenbüchern. SCHMIDT-GÖRG/70TH 428–440

1329 ——. Kleine Beethoveniana. SCHMIDT-GÖRG 361–376

1330 ——. Zu Beethovens Skizzen und Entwürfen. SCHIEDERMAIR/80TH 150–155

1331 Weise, Dagmar. Beethovens Jugendtagebuch. SCHENK 68–88

CLASSICAL ERA: OTHER INDIVIDUAL COMPOSERS, PERFORMERS, ETC.

1332 [Albrechtsberger] Koczirz, Adolf. Albrechtsbergers Konzerte für Maultrommel und Mandora. KRETZSCHMAR 55–57

1333 [Andrez] Dreses, P. Opzoekingen naar de uitgaven van de XVIIIe eeuwse Luikse muziekdrukker Benoît Andrez. MUEREN 93–97

1333a [Anthoin] Fellerer, Karl Gustav. Ferdinand d'Anthoins Ästhetik der Kirchenmusik 1784. SCHMIDT-GÖRG/70TH 82–92

1334 [Bach, C. P. E.] Müller, Werner. Die Artikulation im Klavierwerk C. Ph. E. Bachs. MÜLLER-BLATTAU 51–63 (see also nos. 1138, 1980a)

1335 [Bach, J. C. F.] Geiringer, Karl. Unbeachtete Kompositionen des Bückeburger Bachs. FISCHER/W 99–107

1336 [Bach, J. S. (1748–1778)] Schnapp, Friedrich. Nur ein Brief. SMEND 93–94

1337 —— Stechow, Wolfgang. Johann Sebastian Bach the Younger. PANOFSKY I, 427–436

1338 [Bach, W. F.] Meisner, Heinrich. Porträts aus dem Kreise Philipp Emanuel und Wilhelm Friedemann Bachs. SEIFFERT 101–112

1339 —— Müller-Blattau, Joseph. Bindung und Freiheit; zu W. Fr. Bachs Fugen und Polonaisen. FISCHER/W 83–98

1340 —— Weston, George B. Some Works Falsely Ascribed to Friedemann Bach. DAVISON 247–251

1341 [Barthélémon] Pincherle, Marc. Sur François Barthélémon. LAURENCIE 235–245

Benda, G. See no. 1301a

1342 [Bouvink] Corbet, August. De anonieme *Verhandeling over de muziek* uitgegeven door J. A. Bouvink te 's-Gravenhage in 1772. MUEREN 67–74

1343 [Breitkopf] Deininger, Hans F. Briefe Johann Gottlob Immanuel Breitkopfs an den Augsburger Bibliophilen und Bibliographen Georg Wilhelm Zapf während der Jahre 1779–87. MÜLLER VON ASOW [24–54]

1343a —— Schmieder, Wolfgang. Johann Gottlob Immanuel Breitkopfs Privatbibliothek, Werden und Vergehen. GLAUNING II, 73–87

1343b [Burney] Corbet, August. Dr. Charles Burney's *Reis doorheen de Oostenrijkse Nederlanden* (1772); II [Dutch translation of Burney's text]. BORREN/75TH 222–230

1343c —— Hutchings, Arthur. The Unwritten Burney. OLDMAN 127–135

1344 [Conrad. J. G.] Werner, Arno. Ein sächsischer Landschulmeister und seine Musikbücherei. SCHERING 250–258

1344a [Corrette] Lesure, François & G. Thibault. La méthode de mandoline de Michel Corrette (1772). FÉDEROV 72–76
1345 [Diderot] Voxler, Felix. Diderot and the *Leçons de clavecin.* TODD II, 231–249
1346 [Dittersdorf] Altmann, Wilhelm. Die Streichquintette Dittersdorfs. ADLER 187–189
1347 —— LaRue, Jan. Dittersdorf Negotiates a Price. ALBRECHT 156–159
1347a [Druschetzky] Weinmann, Alexander. Ein vergessener österreichischer Musiker. SCHMIDT-GÖRG/70TH 450–461
1348 [Eberlin] Pauly, Reinhard G. Johann Ernst Eberlin's Concerted Liturgical Music. SCHRADE 146–177
1349 [Eckard] Reeser, Eduard. De natalschap van Johann Gottfried Eckard. HOBOKEN 122–130
1350 [Floquet] Briquet, Marie. L'*Alceste* de E. J. Floquet. MASSON II, 19–29
1350a [Fredenheim] Johansson, Cari. Carl Friedrich Fredenheim and His Collection of Eighteenth-century Music. FÉDEROV 46–49
1351 [Fuchs, I. J.] Schenk, Erich. Eine wiener Musiksammlung der Beethoven-Zeit. BESSELER 377–388
1352 ♪ Gluck, Christoph Willibald. *Rendi mi alle ritorte.* MÜLLER VON ASOW [133–136]
1353 [Gluck] Droescher, Georg. Christof Willibald Gluck; ein Vortrag gehalten zur Vorfeier seines 200. Geburtstages im Kgl. Schauspielhause zu Berlin am 3. Mai 1914. GEIGER 47–64
1353a —— Finscher, Ludwig. *Che farò senza Euridice?* Ein Beitrag zur Gluck-Interpretation. ENGEL 96–110
1354 —— Geiringer, Karl. Gluck und Haydn. DEUTSCH/80TH 75–81
1355 —— Hammerich, Angul. Gluck und Scheibe in Kopenhagen. KRETZSCHMAR 46–48
1356 —— Helfert, Vladimír. Die Jesuiten-Kollegien der böhmischen Provinz zur Zeit des jungen Gluck. WOLF 57–64
1357 —— Mies, Paul. Aus einer alten Schlossbibliothek. MÜLLER VON ASOW [132–142]
1358 —— Müller-Blattau, Joseph. Ritter Gluck in Zweibrücken. ZWEIBRÜCKEN 165–169
1359 —— Orel, Alfred. Einige Bemerkungen zu Tanzdramen Christoph Willibald Glucks. DEUTSCH/80TH 82–89
1360 ——Rühlmann, Franz. Zur Wiederbelebung Glucks. STEIN 161–182
1361 —— Schenk, Erich. Zur Aufführungspraxis des Tremolo bei Gluck. HOBOKEN 137–145
1361a —— Sternfeld, Frederick W. Expression and Revision in Gluck's *Orfeo* and *Alceste.* WELLESZ/80TH 114–129
1362 [Godecharles] Clercx, Suzanne. Les Godecharles, musiciens bruxellois au XVIIIe siècle. CLOSSON 69–80
1362a [Goethe] Müller-Blattau, Joseph. Goethes Kantate zur Jubelfeier der Reformation (1817), ein Beitrag zur Religiosität des späten Goethe. WIORA/60TH 405–412
1363 [Goldoni] Wirth, Helmut. Carlo Goldoni und die deutsche Oper. ALBRECHT 160–167
1364 [Graumann] Federhofer, Hellmut. Ein thematischer Katalog der Dorothea Graumann (Freiin von Ertmann). SCHMIDT-GÖRG 100–110
1364a [Grétry] Mooser, R.-Aloys. Grétry sur les scènes Russes du XVIIIe siècle. BORREN/90TH 114–125
1365 —— Sonneck, Oscar G. Footnote to the Bibliographical History of Grétry's Operas. SCHEURLEER 321–326
1365a [Grossman] Mrowiec, Karol. Duety na dwoje skrzpiec Z. S. Grossmanna [Z. S. Grossmann's Duos for Two Violins] FEICHT 337–349
1366 [Grund] Klier, Karl M. Andachts- und Liederbücher der wiener Buchbinder- und Druckerfamilie Grund, 1742–1858. GUGITZ 139–152
1367 [Hamal] Bragard, Roger. *Li voyedje di Tchaufontainne.* CLOSSON 48–59
1367a [Herder] Dobbek, Wilhelm. Johann Gottfried Herder: Kallichoe, der Quell der Schönheit. WIORA/60TH 105–111
1367b —— Schrade, Leo. Herder's Conception of Church Music. SCHRADE/D 490–505; orig. in *The Musical Heritage of the Church,* 2. Valparaiso, Indiana (1946)
1367c [Hermes, J. T.] Langen, August. Zur Liedparodie im deutschen Roman des 18. Jahrhunderts. WIORA/60TH 362–374
1368 [Herschel] Duckles, Vincent.

William F. Herschel's Concertos for Oboe, Viola and Violin. DEUTSCH/80TH 66–74
1368a [Hertel] Schenk, Erich. Johann Wilhelm Hertel und das Haus Breitkopf. ENGEL 314–325
1368b [Holzmann] Federhofer, Hellmut. Eine Salzburger Generalbasslehre (1803). STÄBLEIN/70TH 33–38
1368c [Imbault] Guiomar, Paule. J. J. Imbault. FÉDEROV 43–46
1368d [Kirnberger] Vogel, Martin. Die Kirnberger-Stimmung vor und nach Kirnberger. SCHMIDT-GÖRG/70TH 441–449
1368e [Klein, B.] Mies, Paul. Ein Sinfonie-Fragment von Bernhard Klein. FELLERER/60THS 144–154
1368f [Krommer] Padrta, Karel. Die Menuett-Typen in Werke des Komponisten Kramář-Krommer. ŠTĚDROŇ/60TH 31–42, summary in Czech at end of article
1368g [Lang, J. G.] Schmidt-Görg, Joseph. Ein Wappenbrief für den kurfürstlich-trierschen Konzertmeister Johann Georg Lang. ENGEL 326–330
1368h [Mach] Miazga, Tadeusz. Alan Mach, skryptor i kompozytor choralny XVIII wieku [Alan Mach, scribe and choral composer of the 18th Century] FEICHT 284–297
1369 [Martini] Allorto, Riccardo. Il Canto ambrosiano nelle lettere di G. B. Martini e di Charles Burney. SCHENK 1–4
1370 [Mendelssohn, M.] Hirschberg, Leopold. Moses Mendelssohns Psalmen in der klassischen Musik. MENDELSSOHN 115–128
1371 [Mocarte] Trapier, Elizabeth Du Gué. Goya's Portrait of Pedro Mocarte, Choir Singer in Toledo Cathedral. SUIDA 368–373
1371a [Momigny] Palm, Albert. Ein Beitrag zum Solfege aus den Anfängen der Schulmusik in Frankreich. GERSTENBERG/60TH 107–121
1372 [Mortiz] Werner, Theodor W. Der Roman *Anton Reiser* als musikgeschichtliche Quelle. ADLER 207–215
1373 [Mozart, L.] Tagliavini, Luigi F. Un Oratorio sconosciuto di Leopold Mozart. DEUTSCH/80TH 187–195
1374 [Müthel] Salmen, Walter. Johann Gottfried Müthel, der letzte Schüler Bachs. BESSELER 351–359
1374a [Mysliveček] Pečman, Rudolf. De Gamerrovo libreto k poslední opeře Josefa Myslivečka [De Gamerra's Libretto for the Last Opera of Josef Mysliveček] RACEK/60TH 183–194, summary in German
1375 [Nardini] Altmann, Wilhelm. Nardinis angebliches Violinkonzert in E. KRETZSCHMAR 9–11
1376 ♪ Ossowsky, Stanislaus. *12 Langaus-Deutsche*, solo violin. KODÁLY/80TH 314–316
1377 [Ossowsky] Schenk, Erich. Der Langaus. KODÁLY/80TH 301–316
1377a ♪ Paisiello, Giovanni. *Viva la pace. Viva Arianna.* CORTESE 178–183
1377b ——. Speziale, G. C. Musiche nuzialí inedite di Giovanni Paisiello. CORTESE 169–183
1378 [Paolucci] Fellerer, Karl Gustav. Giuseppe Paoluccis *Arte prattica di contrappunto.* CU 251–260
1379 [Parent] Fellerer, Karl Gustav. F. N. Parents Revolutionsgesänge (1799). ALBRECHT 174–178
1380 [Pepusch] Bronson, Bertrand H. *The Beggar's Opera.* CASE 14–49; orig. in *Univ. of Cal. Publ. in English* 8 (1941)
1380a [Pleyel] Benton, Rita. Ignace Pleyel, Disputant. FÉDEROV 21–24
1381 —— Klingenbeck, Josef. Ignaz Pleyel, sein Streichquartett im Rahmen der wiener Klassik. SCHENK 276–297
1382 [Pollio] Wangermée, Robert. Le Traité du chant sur le livre de P. L. Pollio, maître de musique à la Collégiale Saint-Vincent à Soignies dans le seconde moitié du XVIIIe siècle. BORREN 336–350
1383 [Reichardt] Salmen, Walter. J. F. Reichardt und die europäische Volksmusik. MÜLLER-BLATTAU 83–94
1384 —— Schünemann, Georg. Reichardts Briefwechsel mit Herder. SCHNEIDER/60TH 110–117
1384a [Richard, Viscount Fitzwilliam] Cudworth, Charles. Richard, Viscount Fitzwilliam, and the French Baroque Music in the Fitzwilliam Museum, Cambridge. FÉDEROV 27–31
1384b [Righini] Federhofer, Hellmut. Vincenzo Righini's Oper *Alcide al Bivio.* WELLESZ/80TH 130–144
1384c [Ritter] Fuhrmann, Roderich. Die Klavier-Kammermusik Peter Ritters. ENGEL 111–116
1385 ♪ Sailer, Sebastian. *Von Kain und Abel.* ABERT Beilage 1–32.
1386 [Sailer] Boettcher, Hans. Neues zu Sebastian Sailer. ABERT 31–43

1387 [Salieri] Haas, Robert. Antonio Salieris vergessene Familie. SCHNEIDER/80TH 191–196
1387a —— Schenk, Erich. Salieris "Landsturm" Kantate von 1799 in ihren Beziehung zu Beethovens "Fidelio." SCHMIDT-GÖRG/70TH 338–354
—— See also no. 1208a
1388 [Sammartini] Barblan, Guglielmo. Contributo alla biografia di G. B. Sammartini alla luce dei documenti. SCHENK 15–27
1389 —— Sartori, Claudio. Sammartini post-mortem. ALBRECHT 153–155
1390 [Scheidler] Zuth, Josef. Über Christian Gottlieb Scheidler. KOCZIRZ 50–56
1391 [Schmittbaur] Niemöller, Klaus W. Joseph Aloys Schmittbaurs Werke und ihre Würdigung im 18. Jahrhundert. FELLERER/60TH 377–390
1392 ♪ Seedo. *The Lottery,* 2 airs. ANGLÉS II, 805 & 807
1393 ♪ ——. *The Dumb Lady Cured. O Cursed Power of Gold.* ANGLÉS II, 806
1394 ♪ ——. *The Devil to Pay. Ye Gods! You Gave Me a Wife.* ANGLÉS II, 808–809
1395 [Seedo] Rubsamen, Walter H. Mr. Seedo, Ballad Opera, and the *Singspiel.* ANGLÉS II, 775–809
1395a [Siebigk] Feldman, Fritz. Breslaus Musikleben zur Zeit Beethovens aus der Sicht L. A. L. Siebigks. SCHMITZ 160–171
1395b [Smrčzka] Ginzburg, Lev. Sonaty Yozefa Kristiana Smrchki [Sonatas of Josef Christian Smrčzka] RACEK/60TH 107–114
1395c [Sperger] Federhofer, Hellmut. Musiktheoretische Schriften aus Johannes Matthias Spergers Besitz. RACEK/60TH 71–77
1396 ♪ Székely, László. Music book. KODÁLY/75TH 361–406
1397 [Székely] Benkő, András. Székely László kótáskönyve [László Székely's Music Book] KODÁLY/75TH 345–406, English summary 756
1397a [Tulinberg] Andersson, Otto. Erik Tulinberg, en finländsk musikamatör från det gustavianska tidevarvet. ANDERSSON, O./85TH 43–63; orig. in *Finsk Tidskrift* (Feb. 1930) 122–151
1398 [Vitzthumb] Bremt, F. van den. Een verloren gewaand werk *Céphalide ou les mariages Samnites* van I. Vitzthumb, op tekst van Prins Karel-Jozef de Ligne. MUEREN 183–191
1399 [Wagenseil] Vetter, Walther. Der deutsche Charakter der italienischen Oper Georg Christoph Wagenseils. FELLERER/60TH 558–572
1400 —— ——. Italienische Opernkomponisten um Georg Christoph Wagenseil; ein stilkundlicher Versuch. BLUME/F 363–374
1401 —— ——. Der Opernkomponist Georg Christoph Wagenseil und sein Verhältnis zu Mozart und Gluck. ABERT 165–176
1402 [Weiss] Tappolet, Willy. Johann Kaspar Weiss, ein Beitrag zur Musikgeschichte Genfs im 18. Jahrhundert. FELLERER/60TH 530–534
1402a [Zach] Senn, Walter. Johann Zach: Reisen und Aufenthalte in Tirol. RACEK/60TH 245–251
1402b [Zannetti] Unverricht, Hubert. Francesco Zannettis Streichtrios. SCHMIDT-GÖRG/70TH 410–427

ROMANTIC ERA: GENERAL

See also nos. 82, 143, 557, 559a, 793a, 805, 908, 1136, 1147, 1148, 1153, 1161, 1164a, 1166, 1220, 1233, 1252b, 1384c, 2685b, 2694a, 2708b

1403 Adams, Nicholson B. French Influence on the Madrid Theatre in 1837. MENÉNDEZ PIDAL/E VII, 134–151
1404 Altmann, Wilhelm. Über einige mit Unrecht vergessene Streichquartette KROHN 1–5
1404a Andersson, Otto. Musikuppfattningen i Åbo vid 1800-talents ingang. Tal vid musikaliska sällskapets i Åbo 140-årfest den 24 januari 1930. ANDERSSON, O./85TH 131–138; orig. in *Åbo Underrättelser* (Jan. 25, 1930)
1404b Arlt, Wulf. Die Neuordnung der kölner Dommusik in den Jahren 1825/1826. FELLERER/60THS 1–30
1405 ♪ *Baron Steuben's American March.* STEUBEN 165
1405a Belza, Igor'. Muzykal'nye polonica XIX veka v Sovetskom Soyueye [Polish Music of the 19th Century in the Soviet Union.] FEICHT 370–377
1405b Bernet Kempers, Karel P. Die Dichter und die romantische Musik. ENGEL 57–69
1406 ——. Isometrische Begriffe und die Musik des 19. Jahrhunderts. BLUME/F 34–49

1406a ——. Die Komponisten und die Dichtkunst. WIORA/60TH 95–104
1407 Böckmann, Paul. Klang und Bild in der Stimmungslyrik der Romantik. BENZ 103–125
1408 Bónis, Ferenc. Magyar táncgyüjtemény az 1820-as évekből [A Hungarian Dance Collection from the 1820s] KODÁLY/70TH 697–732
1409 Branscombe, Peter. Some Viennese *Hamlet* Parodies and a Hitherto Unknown Musical Score for One of Them. DEUTSCH/80TH 337–344
1410 Broeckx, Jan L. Muziekhistorische feiten als kultuurhistorische symptomen. Muzikale stijl als spiegel van de levenshouding in de XIXe eeuw. MUEREN 53–62
1411 Bücken, Ernst. Romantik und Realismus; zur Periodisierung der romantischen Epoche. SCHERING 46–50
1412 Chávarri, Eduardo L. El Nacionalismo en la música española. PEDRELL 199–200
1413 Dannemann, Erna. Musikpflege und Musikerziehung in einer englischen Provinz. BESSELER 505–508
1414 Ehinger, Hans. Die Rolle der Schweiz in der *Allgemeinen musikalischen Zeitung*, 1798–1848. NEF 19–47
1414a Ewerhart, Rudolf. Zur Orgelpraxis am Dom zu Münster in der zweiten Hälfte des 19. Jahrhunderts. FELLERER/60THM 247–257
1414b Federhofer, Hellmut. Zwei Mainzer Sammlungen von Musikerbriefen des 19. Jahrhunderts. GOTTRON 1–33
1414c Fellerer, Karl Gustav. Die kölner Dommusik und die kirchenmusikalische Reform im 19. Jahrhundert. CCZ 324–340
1415 Fournol, Etinenne. De l'entrée des slaves dans l'histoire de la musique. BOYER 75–82
1415a Gottron, Adam. "Capella Fuldensis" und die fuldaer Dommusik im 19. Jahrhundert. FELLERER/60THM 139–145
1416 Gurvin, Olav. *Ja, vi elsker dette landet;* et essay om utførelsen [*Ja, vi elsker* . . . ; An Essay on Interpretation] MOBERG 163–170
1417 Hafner, Johannes. München als Ausgangspunkt der regensburger kirchenmusikalischen Restauration. SCHREMS 153–156
1418 Handschin, Jacques. Die europäische Rolle der russischen Musik. HANDSCHIN 275–286; orig. in *Neue Zürcher Zeitung* 2501, 2509, & 2513 (1930)
1419 ——. Das russische Lied. HANDSCHIN 287–290; orig, in *Neue Zürcher Zeitung* 220 (1927)
1420 Hill, Richard S. The Melody of *The Star-Spangled Banner* in the United States before 1820. WROTH 151–193 (also issued separately Wash., D.C.: Lib. of Congress, 1951)
1421 Kahl, Willi. Musik als Erbe; von der Aufklärung zur Romantik. MERSMANN 64–68
1422 ——. Zur musikalischen Renaissancebewegung in Frankreich während der ersten Hälfte des 19. Jahrhunderts. SCHMIDT-GÖRG 156–174
1422a Keller, Wilhelm. Das verurteilte Lied. BOSSE/50TH 80–89
1422b Kirchmeyer, Helmut. Aus der religiös-konfessionellen Polemik in der Musikspekulation des 19. Jahrhunderts. FELLERER/60THM 67–87
1422c Kunz, Lucas. Zwei beuroner Kantoren, Skizzen und Hinweise. FELLERER/60THM 91–109
1422d Lippman, Edward A. The Tonal Idea of Romanticism. WIORA/60TH 419–426
1423 Loth, Peter. Ein Jahrhundert Chorschaffen in Zweibrücken. ZWEIBRÜCKEN 288–291
1424 Malen, Aarne. Eräs yritys suomalaisaiheisen laulunäytelmän tekemiseksi v. 1829 [An Essay concerning an Operetta with Finnish Motives from the Year 1829] KROHN 108–111, German summary v
1425 Mersmann, Hans. Sonatenformen in der romantischen Kammermusik. WOLF 112–117
1426 Niemann, Walter. Charakterköpfe norddeutscher Schumannier in der Klaviermusik. [Ernst Haberbier, Friedrich Wilhelm Markull, Heinrich Steil, Karl Lührs. Hugo Ulrich, Albert Dietrich, Louis Ehlert, Robert Radecke, Constantin Bürgel] SEIDL/AR 199–222
1426a Niemöller, Klaus Wolfgang. Das Fugato als Ausdrucksmittel im 19. Jahrhundert. WIORA/60TH 413–418
1427 Norlind, Tobias. Adatok a keringő és a polka történetéhez/Zur Geschichte des Walzers und der Polka. KODÁLY/60TH 189–194
1428 Nowak, Leopold. Ländler,

Walzer und Wienerlieder im Klavierbuche einer preussischen Prinzessin. ZODER 133–148

1428a Overath, Johannes. Albert Gereon Stein (1809–1881), ein Wegbereiter der liturgisch-kirchenmusikalischen Erneuerung in Köln. FELLERER/60THM 111–123

1429 Prahács, Margit. Zene a régi óvodákban (1828–1860) [Music in the Old Nursery Schools (1828–1860)] KODÁLY/70TH 515–566

1430 Rebling, Oskar. Kleine Beiträge zur Musikgeschichte der Stadt Halle. SCHNEIDER/80TH 271–276

1431 Refardt, Edgar. Männerchöre und Männerchorkomponisten in der Schweiz. REFARDT 75–78; orig. in *Neue Zürcher Zeitung* 1588 (1926)

1432 ——. Die Musik in den *Alpenrosen.* NEF 202–209

1433 ——. Eine musikalische Schweizerreise im Jahre 1838. REFARDT 64–67; orig. in *Schweizerische Musikz.* 71 (1931)

1434 ——. Vom Oratoriengesang in der Schweiz. REFARDT 68–74; orig. in *Schweizerische Musikz.* 87 (1947)

1435 ——. Von der Schweizerfamilie zum Winkelried. REFARDT 79–82; orig. in *Schweizerische Musikz.* 74 (1934)

1435a Reuter, Clemens. Rheinischer Orgelbau um 1850. Die Orgel zu Vernich, Kreis Euskirchen. FELLERER/60THS 199–218

1435b Scharnagl, August. Die regensburger Tradition, ein Beitrag zur Geschichte der katholischen Kirchenmusik im 19. Jahrhundert. FELLERER/60THM 9–16

1435c Schwermer, Johannes. Aspekte zur cäcilianischen Ästhetik. FELLERER/60THM 219–232

1435d Sidler, Hubert. Die cäcilianische Erneuerung in der Schweiz. FELLERER/60THM 209–218

1436 Sommerfeldt, W. P. Musiklivet i Christiania de Ole blev født, en dagbog fra 1875. SANDVIK 223–246

1437 Stephenson, Kurt. Bonner Burschenlieder 1819; das erste Studentenliederbuch an der rheinischen Friedrich-Wilhelms-Universität. SCHIEDERMAIR/80TH 140–149

1438 ——. Die deutschen Lieder von 1843. SCHMIDT-GÖRG 315–360

1438a Sýkora, Václav Jan. Pražská konzervatoř za ředitelů Webera a Kittla [The Prague Conservatory under the Direction of Weber and Kittl] PLAVEC/60TH 127–145, summaries in German & Russian

1439 Taut, Kurt. Aus einem Musikerstammbuch des 19. Jahrhunderts. SEIFFERT 125–135

1439a Thürmer, Helmut. Zur Deklamationsproblem im deutschen Sololied. SCHMIDT-GÖRG/70TH 386–393

1440 Toye, Francis. The New Interest in Italian Nineteenth-Century Opera. NEWMAN 157–172

1441 Valentin, Caroline. *Ach, wie ist's möglich dann* von H. von Chézy und seine erste Melodie. LILIENCRON 358–386

1441a Valentin, Erich. Über den Umgang mit Handbüchern, ein Erfahrungsbericht. BOSSE/50TH 139–141

1441b Wallon, Simone. L'alliance franco-russe dans la chanson française de 1890 à 1901. FÉDEROV 126–136

1442 Waltershausen, Hermann W. v. Der stilistische Dualismus in der Musik des 19. Jahrhunderts. ADLER 202–206

1443 Wangermée, R. L'Improvisation pianistique au début du XIXe siècle. MUEREN 227–253

1444 ——. Les premiers concerts historiques à Paris. CLOSSON 185–193

1445 Wiora, Walter. Über die sogenannten nationalen Schulen der osteuropäischen Musik. AUBIN 301–322

ROMANTIC ERA: FRANZ SCHUBERT

See also no. 1233

1446 Bernet Kempers, Karel P. Ganztonreihen bei Schubert. WAESBERGHE 7–10

1446a Brown, Maurice J. E. An Introduction to Schubert's Sonatas of 1817. HIRSCH 35–44

1447 ——. Schubert: Three Dance-Music Manuscripts. DEUTSCH/80TH 226–231

1448 Handschin, Jacques. Schuberts Kirchenmusik. HANDSCHIN 208–212; orig. in *Neue Zürcher Zeitung* 2110 (1928)

1449 ♪ [Ländler] Ländler, piano, D. 366, no. 7. RIEMANN 484

1450 Mantuani, Josef. Ein Kapitel über die Musikpflege Laibachs zur Zeit Schuberts. ADLER 195–201

1451 Molnár, Antal. Schubert emlékezete [In Memory of Schubert] BARTOK/E 535–542, summary 558

1452 Orel, Alfred. Schuberts Künstlergestalt. OREL 94–112

1453 [Piano Music] Deutsch, Otto Erich. Schuberts *Ungarische Melodie* (D. 817) KODÁLY/80TH 89–93

1454 —— Friedlaender, Max. Ein Albumblatt Franz Schuberts [auf die Rückseite der Gesangszene *Der Liedler* geschrieben] WAHLE 11–12

1455 —— ——. Eine bisher ungedruckte Komposition Schuberts. RIEMANN 484

1456 —— Krohn, Ilmari. Franz Schuberts *Moments musicaux* Prinzessin Dornröschen. MÜLLER VON ASOW [119–127]

1457 [Songs] Blume, Friedrich. Goethes Mondlied in Schuberts Kompositionen. BLUME/S 813–833; orig. in *Jahrbuch der Bär* (1928)

1458 —— Friedlaender, Max. Ein unbekanntes Duett-Fragment Franz Schuberts. WOLF 36–37

1459 —— Gerstenberg, Walter. Schubertiade; Anmerkungen zu einigen Liedern. DEUTSCH/80TH 232–239

1460 —— Georgiades, Thrasybulos. *Das Wirtshaus* von Schubert und das Kyrie aus dem gregorianischen Requiem. BENZ 126–135

1461 —— Holschneider, Andreas. Zu Schuberts *Frühlingsglaube*. DEUTSCH/80TH 240–244

1462 —— Levi, Vito. Le Arie e ariette di Schubert su testo italiano. SCHENK 307–314

1463 —— Orel, Alfred. Die *Forelle*. OREL 113–125; orig. in *Arch F. Musikf.* 2 (1937)

1464 —— ——. Der ursprüngliche Text zu Schuberts *Liebeslauschen*. BIEHLE 71–81

1465 [String quintets] Abert, Anna Amalie. Rhythmus und Klang in Schuberts Streichquintett. FELLERER/60TH 1–11

1466 [Symphonies] Laaff, Ernst. Schuberts grosse c-dur Symphonie; erkennbare Grundlagen ihrer Einheitlichkeit. BLUME/F 204–213

1467 —— ——. Schuberts h-moll Symphonie; motivische Analyse zum Nachweis von erkennbaren Grundlagen ihrer Einheitlichkeit. ABERT 93–115

1468 ♪ [Waltzes] Waltz in G, piano. WAHLE 11–12

1469 Werner, Theodor W. Schuberts Tod; Versuch einer Deutung. WOLF 214–216

ROMANTIC ERA: RICHARD WAGNER

See also nos. 1220, 1521

1470 Abraham, Gerald. Wagner's Second Thoughts. NEWMAN 9–28

1471 Burch, Gladys. The Literary Taste of Richard and Cosima Wagner. ENGEL 53–59

1471a Cogni, Giulio. Wagner poeta. BARBLAN/60TH 35–45

1472 Ferran, André. Baudelaire et la musique. HUGUET 387–393

1473 Krech, Hans. Richard Wagner als Sänger und Sprecher. SCHNEIDER/80TH 255–264

1474 [Liebesverbot] Engel, Hans. Über Richard Wagners Oper *Das Liebesverbot*. BLUME/F 80–91

1474a Papírník, Atnon. "O.π." příspěvek k bojům o Wagnera u nás ["O.π.", a Contribution to the Struggle for Wagner in Our Land] HOSTINSKÝ/60TH 103–110

1475 [Parsifal] Valentin, Erich. Wagners *Parsifal* in Braunschweig 1882, mitgeteilt nach dem Briefwechsel Ludwig Schemanns und Hans Sommers. MÜLLER VON ASOW [208–221]

1476 Prod'homme, Jacques-Gabriel. Trois lettres inédites de Cosima Wagner. LAURENCIE 282–286

1477 Prüfer, Arthur. Richard Wagner und Jakob Grimm. SEIDL/AR 234–259

1477a Redlich, Hans F. Wagnerian Elements in Pre-Wagnerian Opera. WELLESZ/80TH 145–156

1478 Riesenfeld, Paul. Die Auswanderung vom heiligen Gralsberge, Variationen zu dem Thema: Ergo vivamus. SEIDL/AR 152–179

1479 [Siegfried] Stephani, Hermann. Der Wanderer im *Siegfried*. SEIDL/AR 269–273

1480 Stephani, Hermann. Felix Draesekes Aufenthalt bei Richard Wagner in Luzern 1859 nach Draesekes noch unveröffenlichten *Lebenserinnerungen*. MÜLLER VON ASOW [171–175]

1481 Sternfeld, Richard. Die zwei Reiche in Wagners Dramen. SEIDL/AR 260–268

1482 [*Tannhäuser*] Ferran, André. *Tannhäuser* à l'opéra de Paris en 1861, caricatures et parodies. MORNET 189–197

1483 —— Sandberger, Adolf. Zu den literarischen Quellen von Richard Wagners *Tannhäuser*. SCHEURLEER 267–269

1484 —— Tonnelat, E. Richard Wagner et Wolfram von Eschenbach. LICHTENBERGER 257–266

1484a Vacková, Jiřina. Ohlasy tvůrčích principů Richarda Wagnera v díle Antonína Dvořáka [Echos of the Creative Principles of Richard Wagner in the Works of Antonín Dvořák.] PLAVEC/60TH 181–187, summaries in German & Russian

1485 Vermeil, Edmond, Le Génie constructif de Richard Wagner. LICHTENBERGER 267–293

1486 Viotta, H. A. Richard Wagners verhouding tot de muziekgeschiedenis. SCHEURLEER 359–365

1487 Wagner, Cosima. [Letters to Anton Seidl]. SEIDL/AN 199–202

1488 Wagner, Richard. [Letters to Anton Seidl]. SEIDL/AN 187–198

ROMANTIC ERA: OTHER INDIVIDUAL COMPOSERS, PERFORMERS, ETC.

1489 [Albéniz] Jankélévitch, Vladimir. Albéniz et l'état de verve. MASSON II, 197–209

1490 [Arnold] Refardt, Edgar. Gustav Arnold. REFARDT 33–46; orig. in *Schweizerische Musikz.* 90 (1950)

1491 [Augundson] Bjørndal, Arne. Myllarguten på det Norske Teater i Bergen 1850 [Møllarguten (i.e., Augundson) at the Norwegian Theatre in Bergen] BJØRNDAL 175–182

1492 [Becker] Tappolet, Willy. Georges Becker, 24 Juli 1834 bis 18. Juli 1928. SCHENK 539–544

1493 ♪ Becker, Reinhold. *Albumblatt.* SEEBACH 26

1494 [Berlioz] Handschin, Jacques. Hector Berlioz. HANDSCHIN 213–222; orig. in *Vereinsblatt der Basler Liedertafel* 10 (1931/1932)

1494a —— Meyerstein, E. H. W. Thoughts on *Les Troyens.* HIRSCH 60–63

1495 [Berwald] Brandel, Åke. Släkten Berwald, dess tidigare historia och dess verksamhet i Ryssland. [The Berwald Family, its Early History and its Activity in Russia] MOBERG 89–97

1496 ♪ Bezeredj, Amalia. *Flori könyve.* KODÁLY/70TH 528–542

1497 [Bizet] Dean, Winton. Bizet's *Ivan IV.* NEWMAN 58–85

1497a —— Westrup, Jack. Bizet's *La Jolie Fille de Perth.* WELLESZ/80TH 157–170

1498 [Borodin] Handschin, Jacques. Borodin und sein *Fürst Igor.* HANDSCHIN 238–241; orig. in *Die Tribüne,* hrsg. v.d. Bühnen der Stadt Köln, 22 (1952/1953)

1499 [Bosret] Montellier, Ernest. *Li bia bouquet* et son auteur, Nicolas Bosret. CLOSSON 145–152

1500 [Brahms] Bernet Kempers, Karel P. Die "Emanzipation des Fleisches" in den Liedern von Johannes Brahms. SCHENK 28–30

1500a —— Czesla, Werner. Motivische Mutationen im Schaffen von Johannes Brahms. SCHMIDT-GÖRG/70TH 64–72

1500b —— Fellinger, Imogen. Zur Entstehung der "Regenlieder" von Brahms. GERSTENBERG/60TH 55–58

1500c —— Komma, Karl Michael. Das "Scherzo" der 2. Symphonie von Johannes Brahms, eine melodisch-rhythmische Analyse. WIORA/60TH 448–457

1501 —— Kross, Siegfried. Brahms und der Kanon. SCHMIDT-GÖRG 175–187

1502 ——Moser, Hans Joachim. Zur Sinndeutung der c-moll Symphonie von Johannes Brahms. MOSER/70TH 220–223; orig. in *Österreichische Musikz.* 8 (1953)

1503 —— Orel, Alfred. Johannes Brahms; das Leben im Werk. OREL 126–135

1504 ——Refardt, Edgar. Brahms in der Schweiz. REFARDT 103–114; orig. in *Schweizerische Musikz.* 73 (1933)

1505 ——Siegmund-Schultze, Walther. Brahms' vierte Symphonie. SCHNEIDER/80TH 241–254

1506 ——Stephenson, Kurt. Johannes Brahms und Georg Dietrich Otten. FELLERER/60TH 503–518

1507 —— ——. Der junge Brahms und Reményis *Ungarische Lieder.* SCHENK 520–531

—— See also no. 1233

1508 [Bruch] Fellerer, Karl Gustav. Aus Max Bruchs Briefwechsel mit Emil Kamphausen. SCHIEDERMAIR/80TH 17–28

1508a —— ——. Max Bruch und der Urheberschutz. BOSSE/50TH 11–24

1508b —— ——. Max Bruchs Breslauer Dirigententätigkeit. SCHMIDT 172–179

1509 —— ——. Max Bruchs Messensätze. SCHMIDT-GÖRG 111–116

1509a —— ——. Zu Max Bruchs "Siechentrost"-Liedern op. 54. ENGEL 91–95

1510 —— Kahl, Willi. Zur Entstehung

und bonner Uraufführung von Max Bruchs *Achilleus,* 1885, nach grösstenteils unveröffentlichten Briefen. MIES 26–54

1510a —— Kross, Siegfried. Max Bruch als Student in Bonn. FELLERER/60THS 133–136

1511 [Bruckner] Bauer, Moritz. Zur Form in den sinfonischen Werken Anton Bruckners. KRETZSCHMAR 12–14

1512 —— Blume, Friedrich. Anton Bruckner. BLUME/S 844–871; orig. in *MGG* 2, col. 342

1512a —— Boetticher, Wolfgang. Zur Kompositionstechnik des späten Bruckner. NOWAK/60TH 11–19

1513 —— Dehnert, Max. Bruckner und die Gewandhauskapellmeister. KONWITSCHNY 57–63

1513a —— Fellerer, Karl Gustav. Bruckners Persönlichkeit. NOWAK/60TH 21–26

1513b —— Geiringer, Karl. Anton Bruckners Vorbilder. NOWAK/60TH 27–31

1513c —— Grasberger, Franz. Anton Bruckners Arbeitsweise. NOWAK/60TH 33–37

1514 —— Gross, Werner. Anton Bruckner das Barock; Versuch einer vergleichenden Künstebetrachtung. BADT 260–291

1515 ——Hausegger, Siegmund von. Die Zeitmassbestimmungen der beiden Fassungen von Bruckners I. Symphonie. RAABE 160–164

1515a —— Hess, Willy. Die Gesamtausgabe der Werke Anton Bruckners. NOWAK/60TH 39–44

1515b —— Jancik, Hans. Anton Bruckner in seiner Kammermusik. NOWAK/60TH 45–51

1515c —— Jochum, Eugen. Zur Interpretation der fünften Symphonie von Anton Bruckner, ein Rechenschaftsbericht. NOWAK/60TH 53–59

1515d —— Kellner, Altman. Der Organist Anton Bruckner. NOWAK/60TH 61–65

1515e —— Kosch, Franz. "Der Beter Anton Bruckner." Nach seinen persönlichen Aufzeichnungen. NOWAK/60TH 67–73

1515f —— Kronsteiner, Hermann. Bruckners Kirchenmusik und die Liturgie. NOWAK/60TH 75–78

1515g —— Kronsteiner, Joseph. Erste Brucknermesse in Rom. NOWAK/60TH 79–82

1516 —— Nowak, Leopold. Anton Bruckner, Künstler zwischen Welt und Gott. HILBER 67–69

1517 —— ——. Anton Bruckners Formwille dargestellt am Finale seiner V. Symphonie. ANGLÉS II, 609–613

1518 —— ——. Das Finale von Bruckners VII. Symphonie, eine Formstudie. FISCHER/W 143–148

1518a —— ——. Form und Rhythmus im ersten Satz des Streichquintetts von Anton Bruckner. ENGEL 260–273

1519 —— ——. Probleme bei der Veröffentlichung von Skizzen dargestellt an einem Beispiel aus Anton Bruckners *Te Deum.* HOBOKEN 115–121

1520 —— ——. Symphonischer und kirchlicher Stil bei Anton Bruckner. FELLERER/60TH 391–401

1521 —— Orel, Alfred. Bruckner und Wagner. OREL 158–167

1522 —— ——. Bruckner und Wien. ALBRECHT 225–231

1523 —— ——. Zum Probleme der Bewegung in den Symphonien Anton Bruckners. OREL 136–157; orig. in *In memoriam Anton Bruckner* (Wien: 1924)

1523a —— Racek, Fritz. Ein neuer Text zu Bruckners "Vaterländischem Weinlied?" NOWAK/60TH 83–86

1523b —— Redlich, Hans F. Das programmatische Element bei Bruckner. NOWAK/60TH 87–97

1523c ——Sittner, Hans. Anton Bruckner und die Gegenwart. NOWAK/60TH 99–104

1523d —— Tittel, Ernst. Bruckners musikalischer Ausbildungsgang. NOWAK/60TH 105–111

1523e —— Waldstein, Wilhelm. Bruckner als Lehrer. NOWAK/60TH 113–120

1523f —— Weinmann, Alexander. Anton Bruckner und seine Verleger. NOWAK/60TH 121–138

1524 [Bull] Bjørndal, Arne. Ole Bull og Valestrand. BJØRNDAL 239–284; orig. in *Fra Fjon til Fusa* (1950)

1525 [Burgmein] Compositionen von J. Burgmein. RICORDI 165–168

1525a [Cavaillé-Coll] Alexis, Georges L. J. Aristide Cavillé-Coll et ses amis belges (Lettres inédites de J. Lemmens et du Chevalier X. van Elewyck) CLOSSON 30–45

1525b [Čelakovský] Závodský, Artur. Fr. L. Čelakovský v proudu společenského zpěvu let třicátých. PLAVEC/60TH 93–103, summaries in German & Russian

1526 [Charoton] Rosset, G. A. Les Charoton de Mont-la-Ville. ANSERMET 75–81

1527 ♪ Chopin, Frédéric. Fugue in A minor, piano. CHYBIŃSKI/70TH 248

1528 [Chopin] Bronarski, Ludwik. Kilka uwag o obiegniku w utworach Chopina. [Some Remarks Concerning Turns in the Works of Chopin] CHYBIŃSKI/70TH 233–241

1529 ——. Rękopisy muzyczne Chopina w Genewie [Chopin Musical Autographs in Geneva] CHYBIŃSKI/50TH 93–105

1530 —— Chomiński, Józef M. Die Entwicklungsprobleme des Chopinschen Stils. BESSELER 437–446

1530a —— Kobylańska, Krystyna. Fryderyk Chopin i Oskar Kolberg nieznane przyczynki [Frédéric Chopin and Oscar Kolberg. Some new contributions] FEICHT 378–390

1530b —— Lissa, Zofia. Inspiracje chopinowskie w twórczości Maxa Regera [The Influence of Chopin on the Works of Max Reger] FEICHT 393–424

1531 —— Miketta, Janusz. Fuga a-moll Fryderyka Chopina. CHYBIŃSKI/70TH 242–257

1532 —— Querido, I. Chopin's derde klaviersonate en Dirk Schäfer. SCHÄFER 11–17; orig. in *Van den Akker* (Amsterdam 1911)

1533 —— Windakiewiczowa, Helena. Tematy obce w muzyce Chopina, notatki badawcze [Foreign Themes in Chopin's Music, Some Questions] CHYBIŃSKI/70TH 258–262

1534 —— Wójcik-Keuprulian, Bronisława. O trioli W mazurkach Chopina [Triplets in Chopin's Mazurkas] CHYBIŃSKI/50TH 107–114

—— See also no. 1290

1535 ♪ Costa, P. Mario. *Carulì, cu st'uocchie doce.* NEUMANN 15–21

1536 ♪ ——. *La Luna nova.* NEUMANN 23–27

1536a [Crusell] Andersson, Otto. Bernhard Henrik Crusell. ANDERSSON, O./85TH 64–77; orig. in *Finsk Tidskrift* 61 (1926) 28–46

1536b [Cui] Anglés, Higinio. Relations épistolaires entre César Cui et Philippe Pedrell. FÉDEROV 15–21

1537 [Czerny] Textor, K. A. Een vergeten Werk: Carl Czerny, *Systematische Anleitung zum fantasieren auf dem Pianoforte*, op. 200. SCHEURLEER 339–345

1537a [David] Schwarz, Werner. Eine Musikerfreundschaft des 19. Jahrhunderts. Unveröffentlichte Briefe von Ferdinand David an Robert Schumann. MÜLLER-BLATTAU/70TH 282–303

1538 [Donizetti] Dent, Edward. Donizetti, an Italian Romantic. NEWMAN 86–107

1539 Dukas, Paul. *Ariane et Barbe-Bleue;* moralité à la façon des contes de Perrault. DUKAS 4–7

1540 ——. Le nouveau lyrisme. DUKAS 8–17; orig. in *Minerva* (15 février 1903)

1540a [Dvořák] Branberger, Jan. Anton Dvořák und die Musik der Gegenwart. DAMDK 25–30

—— See also no. 1484a

1541 —— Šourek, Otakar. Antonin Dvořák und Hans Richter. MÜLLER VON ASOW [162–170]

1542 [Eichendorff] Moser, Hans Joachim. Eichendorff und die Musik. MOSER/70TH 205–220; orig. in *Aurora; Eichendorff Jahrbuch* (1943)

1543 ♪ Engel, Carl. *The Days of Men are but as Grass.* ENGEL 191–192

1544 ♪ ——. *I Will Lift Up Mine Eyes.* ENGEL 192–193

1545 ♪ ——. *No Man had E'er the Skill.* ENGEL 194–195

1546 [Engel] Reese, Gustave. More about the Namesake. ENGEL 181–195

1547 [Engel, J. C.] Sachs, Curt. J. C. Engel and the Kroll Opera. ENGEL 196–199

1548 [Erkel] Barna, István. Erkel Ferenc első operái az egykorú sajtó tükrében [Comments on Erkel's Early Operas in the Contemporary Press] BARTÓK/E 175–218, English summary 552

1549 —— Cosma, V., & I. Lakatos. Erkel Ferenc élete és munkássága, mint öszekötő kapocs a magyar és román zenekultúra között [Erkel's Life and Work as a Link between Hungarian and Rumanian Musical Art] BARTÓK/E 17–24, summary 549

1550 —— Martóthy, János. Erkel Ferenc opera-dramaturgiája és az opera fejlődésének néhány kérdése [Erkel's Opera Dramaturgy and Some Problems concerning the Development of the Opera] BARTÓK/E 25–174, summary 549–551

1551 —— Mosonyi, Mihály. Erkel Ferenc, *Bánk Bán*-ja. BARTÓK/E 9–16, summary 549
1552 —— Ujfalussy, József. A *Hunyadi László és* irodalmi előzményei [*László Hunyadi* and its Antecedents in Literature] BARTÓK/E 219–230, summary 552–553
1553 [Evenepoel] Denis, Valentin. Guillaume Lekeu (1870–1894) et Henri Evenepoel (1872–1891). BORREN 163–174
1554 ♪ Franz, Emil. *Hast du ein Herz gefunden.* LGR 7–8
1555 [Fröhlich] Refardt, Edgar. Schweizer Psalmen. REFARDT 28–30; orig. in *Eidgenössisches Sängerblatt* (1941)
1556 ♪ Gambardella, S. *Oi petteno, che piettene.* NEUMANN 65–66
1557 [Generali] Schiedermair, Ludwig. Eine Autobiographie Pietro Generalis. LILIENCRON 250–253
1558 [Glinka] Fédorov, Vladimir. Mihail Ivanovič Glinka en Espagne. ANGLÉS I, 223–237
1559 [Goethe] Blume, Friedrich. Goethe und die Musik. BLUME/S 757–813; orig. publ. as monograph (Kassel: 1948)
1560 —— ——. Johann Wolfgang von Goethe. BLUME/S 735–757; orig. in *MGG* 5, col. 432
1561 —— Moser, Hans Joachim Goethe und die musikalische Akustik. LILIENCRON 145–172
1562 —— Sauerlander, Annemarie. Goethe's Relation to Music. HEWITT 39–55
1562a ♪ Gounod, Charles. *Spiritus Dei.* COLOMBO 135
1563 [Gounod] Hopkinson, Cecil. Notes on the Earliest Editions of Gounod's *Faust.* DEUTSCH/80TH 245–249
1563a ♪ Granier, Désiré. *I Latin d'America.* COLOMBO 134
1564 Grieg, Edvard. Med Bjørnson i gamle dag. BJØRNSON 4–8
1565 [Grieg] Bjørndal, Arne. Edvard Grieg og folkemusikken. BJØRNDAL 285–316; orig. in *Fra Fjon til Fusa* (1951)
1566 —— Fellerer, Karl Gustav. Halfdan Cleve und Edvard Grieg. BLUME/F 124–136
1567 —— Sandvik, Ole M. Edvard Grieg und die norwegische Volksmusik. SCHEURLEER 271–275
1568 [Grillparzer] Lach, Robert. Grillparzers Novelle *Der arme Spielmann* und die Musikwissenschaft. SCHLOSSER 35–45
1568a [Gustdorff] Oberborbeck, Felix. Ein Document musischer Erziehung im bergischen Lande aus der Beginn des 19. Jahrhunderts. FELLERER/60THS 155–165
1568b [Hagen] Valentin, Erich. Ein Vergessener: Theodor Hagen. Zur Musikgeschichte des 19. Jahrhunderts. ENGEL 428–432
1569 [Hanslick] Blume, Friedrich. Eduard Hanslick. BLUME/S 833–843; orig. in *MGG* 5, col. 1482
1570 ♪ Hauptmann, Moritz. Canon a 4. SEIFFERT 131–132
1571 [Hauptmann] Krehl, Stephan. Moritz Hauptmann, ein Dank- und Gedenkwort. KML 49–60
—— See also no. 913
1572 [Hebel] Refardt, Edgar. Die Vertonungen der Gedichte Hebels. REFARDT 120–126; orig. in *Basler Nachrichten*, Sonntagsblatt 19 (1938)
1573 [Hegar] Refardt, Edgar. Friedrich Hegar. REFARDT 47–50; orig. in *Basler Nachrichten* 278 (1941)
1573a [Hegel] Lissa, Zofia. Hegel und das Problem der Formintegration in der Musik. WIORA/60TH 112–119
1574 [Heimsoeth] Kahl, Willi. Heimsoeth und Thibaut, ein vergleichender Beitrag zur Geschichte der musikalischen Renaissance bewegung des 19. Jahrhunderts. OREL/70TH 81–91
1575 [Heise] Behrend, William. Peter Heise ein dänischer Liederkomponist. RIEMANN 496–503
1576 ♪ Hettersdorf, Joseph E. von. *Eginhart und Emma. Ach wie wärs möglich sein.* LILIENCRON 374–386
1577 [Hoffmann, E. T. A.] Lichtenhahn, Ernst. Über einen Ausspruch Hoffmanns und über das Romantische in der Musik. SCHRADE 178–198
1578 —— Schmitz, Eugen. Musikhistorisches zu Hoffmanns *Kater Murr.* WALZEL 209–211
[d'Indy] See no. 1965a
1579 [Jahn] Kahl, Willi. Otto Jahn und das Rheinland. FELLERER/60TH 264–282
1579a [Jenista] Ginzburg, Lev. Josef Jenista (1795–1853). K historii rusko-českých hudebních vztahů. PLAVEC/60TH 119–125, summary in Czech
1580 [Kandler] Schiedermair, Ludwig. Venezianer Briefe F. S. Kandlers aus

den Jahren 1818–20. RIEMANN 485–495
1580a [Karłowicz] Dzięgbowska, Elżbieta. Mieczyslaw Karłowicz jako krytyk muzyczny [Mieczyslaw Karłowicz as Music Critic] FEICHT 425–438
1580b ♪ Katschthaler, Johann B. *Papsthymne* and *Sarkanerlied*. FELLERER/60THM 208
1580c [Katschthaler] Tittel, Ernst. Kardinal Katschthaler, ein Cäcilianer auf dem Salzburger Fürstenthron. FELLERER/60THM 197–208
1580d [Kątski] Śledziński, Stefan. Na marginesie symfonii a-moll Antoniego Kątskiego [Notes on the Symphony in A Minor of Anton Kątski] FEICHT 362–369
1580e [Köchel] Deutsch, Otto Erich. Aus Köchels Jugendtagen. ENGEL 70–75
1581 [Law] Lowens, Irving. Andrew Law and the Pirates. KINKELDEY/80TH 206–223
[Lekeu, Guillaume] See no. 1553
1582 [Lesueur] Nef, Karl. Die Passionsoratorien Jean-François Lesueurs. LAURENCIE 259–268
1583 [Leuthold] Refardt, Edgar. Die frühesten Vertonungen der Gedichte Leutholds, Kellers und C. F. Meyers. REFARDT 115–119; orig. in *Schweizerische Musikz.* 77 (1937)
1584 ♪ Leva, Enrico de. *Nu iuorno me*. NEUMANN 31–35
1585 ♪ Liszt, Franz. *Búcsúzóra* [Farewell]; piano (Raabe 251). BARTÓK/L 264–265
1586 ♪ ——. *Csárdás macabre*, piano (Raabe 224). BARTÓK/L 248–263
1587 ♪ ——. *Magyar arcképek* [Hungarian Portraits]; *László Teleky*, piano (Raabe 205). BARTÓK/L 245–247
1588 [Liszt] Bárdos, Lajos. Modális harmóniák Liszt műveiben [Modal Harmonies in the Works of Liszt] BARTÓK/L 55–89, English & German summaries 550–551
1589 —— Bartók, Béla. Liszt problémák. BARTÓK/L 17–25, English, French, & German summaries 548–549
1590 —— ——. Liszt zenéje és a mai közönség [Liszt's Music and the Audiences of Today] BARTÓK/L 13–15, English, French, & German summaries 547
1591 —— Felix, Werner. Die Reformideen Franz Liszts. MÜNNICH 104–115
1592 —— Gárdonyi, Zoltán. Distanciaelvü jelenségek Liszt zenéjében [Manifestations of the Distance Principle in Liszt's Music] BARTÓK/L 91–100, English & German summaries 551
1593 —— Kecskeméti. I. Unbekannte Eigenschrift der XVIII. Rhapsodie von Franz Liszt. KODÁLY/80TH 173–179
1594 —— Kraft, Günther. Franz Liszt und die nationalen Schulen in Europa. MÜNNICH 85–103
1595 —— Lakatos, István. Kolozsvári Liszt emlékek [Memories of Liszt from Kolozsvár] BARTÓK/L 101–108
1596 —— Prahács, Margit. Kiadatlan és ismeretlen Liszt-levelek a Zenemüvészeti Főiskola levéltárában [Unpublished and Unknown Letters by Liszt in the Possession of the Franz Liszt Academy of Music, Budapest] BARTÓK/L 109–210, English & German summaries 552–553
1597 —— Refardt, Edgar. Die basler Männerchöre von Franz Liszt. REFARDT 99–102; orig. in *Schweizerische Musikz.* 82 (1942)
1598 —— Révész, Imre. Liszt és Lamennais. KODÁLY/70TH 115–124
1599 —— Schnapp, Friedrich. Verschollene Kompositionen Franz Liszts. RAABE 119–153
1600 —— Szabolcsi, Bence. Liszt Ferenc estéje [Franz Liszt's Late Years] BARTÓK/L 211–265, English & German summaries 553–554
1601 —— Tóth, Aladár. Liszt Ferenc a magyar zene útján. Liszt magyarsága és a magyar Liszt kultusz [Franz Liszt on the Road of Hungarian Music. Liszt's Hungarianism and the Hungarian Liszt Cult] BARTÓK/L 27–54, English & German summaries 549–550
1602 [Loeffler] From the Correspondence of Charles Martin Loeffler. ENGEL 155–160
1603 [Loewe] Serauky, Walter. Zu Carl Loewes Biographie und musikalischem Schaffen. SCHERING 213–222
1603a [Malibran] Pardini, Enrico. Maria Felicita Malibran nella leggenda Lucchese. DESDERI/70TH 105–109
1604 [Marx] Fellerer, Karl Gustav. Adolf Bernhard Marx und Gottfried Fink. OREL/70TH 59–65
1605 ♪ Mátray, Gábor. *Cserni György*. BARTÓK/E 296–319
1606 [Mátray] Várnai, Péter. Egy magyar muzsikus a reformkorban;

Mátray Gábor élete és munkássága a szabadsúgharcig [A Hungarian Musician in the Reform Age: Gábor Mátray's Life and Activity to 1848] BARTÓK/E 231–321, summary 553–555

1606a [Měchura] Očadlík, Mirko. Opery L. E. Měchury. NEJEDLÝ/50TH 129–160

1607 [Mendelssohn] Elvers, Rudolf. Ein Jugendbrief von Felix Mendelssohn. SMEND 95–97

1608 —— Engel, Hans. Die Grenzen der romantischen Epoche und der Fall Mendelssohn. DEUTSCH/80TH 259–272

1609 —— Geck, Martin. Sentiment und Sentimentalität im volkstümlichen Liede Felix Mendelssohn-Bartholdys. ALBRECHT 200–206

1610 —— Kippenberg, Anton. Gruss und Angebinde. STRAUBE 114–130

1611 —— Schmieder, Wolfgang. Ein unveröffentlichter Brief von Felix Mendelssohn-Bartholdy. KAHL 92–95

1612 —— Seidl, Arthur. Felix Mendelssohn-Bartholdy zu Ehren. KML 41–48

1613 —— Sietz, Reinhold. Die Verhandlungen um Johann Nepomuk Hummels Nachfolge in Weimar; mit einem unveröffentlichten Brief Mendelssohns. KAHL 86–91

1614 —— Vetter, Walther. Die geistige Welt Mendelssohns. KONWITSCHNY 38–52

—— See also nos. 865, 1674

1615 [Meyer] Refardt, Edgar. Conrad Ferdinand Meyer-Vertonungen. REFARDT 127–133; orig. in *Schweizerische Musikz.* 84 (1944)

1616 [Meyerbeer] Cooper, Martin. Giacomo Meyerbeer. NEWMAN 38–57

1616a —— Klein, John W. Giacomo Meyerbeer (1791–1864). OLDMAN 142–148

1617 [Mioduszewski] Feicht, Hieronim. X Michał Marcin Mioduszewski C. M. (1787–1868). CHYBIŃSKI/50TH 67–91

1618 [Mosafinn] Bjørndal, Arne. Ola Mosafinn, 1828–1912. BJØRNDAL 138–145; orig. in *Spelemannsbladet* 9 (1949)

1618a [Moscheles] Heussner, Ingeborg. Formale Gestaltungsprinzipe bei Ignaz Moscheles. ENGEL 155–165

1619 [Mussorgsky] Handschin, Jacques. Mussorgski und sein *Boris Godunow*. HANDSCHIN 234–237; orig. in *Die Tribüne*, hrsg. von den Bühnen der Stadt Köln, 23 (1953/1954)

1620 —— ——. Zum 40. Todestag Mussorgskis. HANDSCHIN 229–233; orig. in *Neue Zürcher Zeitung* 467 (1921), & *National-Zeitung* 144 (Basel 1921)

1620a —— Hoffmann-Erbrecht, Lothar. Die russischen Volkslieder in Mussorgskis "Boris Godunow." WIORA/60TH 458–465

1621 [Neukomm] Schanzlin, Hans Peter. Briefe des Haydn-Schülers Neukomm an den schweizer Komponisten Schnyder von Wartensee. HOBOKEN 131–136

1622 [Nicolai, Otto] Rieger, Erwin. Zwei Briefe Otto Nicolais an Raphael Georg Kiesewetter. SCHENK 434–439

1623 —— Virneisel, Wilhelm. Otto Nicolai als Musiksammler. SCHNEIDER/80TH 227–240

—— See also no. 1671

1624 ♪ Nicolai, W. F. G. *Feestmarsch naar egyptische motieven.* LEEMANS XV–XX

1625 [Niedermeyer] Fauré, Gabriel. Souvenirs. FAURÉ 3–9

1626 ♪ Nordraak, Rikard. *Ja, vi elsker.* MOBERG 165, 167

1626a [Ostrčil] Vanicky, Jaroslav. Ostrčil a Fibich. PLAVEC/60TH 169–180, summaries in German & Russian

1627 [Paganini] Pellizzari, Achille. Un Viaggio strano. MARIOTTI 187–212

1627a [Palla] Patzaková, A. J. Hynek Palla: jeho mládí a první skladby. Z chystané monographie [Hynek Palla: His Youth and First Compositions. From a Monograph in Preparation] NEJEDLÝ/50TH 102–128

1628 [Pedrell] Bellaigue, Camille. Una Opéra national espagnol, *Los Pirineos.* PEDRELL 49–62

1629 —— ——. Un *Tristan* espagnol, *La Celestina* de Felipe Pedrell. PEDRELL 175–186

1630 —— Besora, Enrique S. Pedrell y Tortosa. PEDRELL 307–314

1631 —— Bonaventura, Arnaldo. *La Celestina*, tragicomedia lirica de Calisto y Melibea, música del maestro Felipe Pedrell. PEDRELL 149–152

1632 Curzon, Henri de. Une nouvelle oeuvre de Felipe Pedrell, *La Célestine.* PEDRELL 127–136

1633 —— Dagnino, Ed. L'Opera di Pedrell nel movimento musicale moderno. PEDRELL 327–332

1634 —— Gibert, Vincents Ma. de. La *Glosa.* PEDRELL 273–278

1635 —— Millet, Lluís. *La Celestina* del mestre Felip Pedrell. PEDRELL 103–125
1636 —— Mitjana, Rafael. Felipe Pedrell et *Les Pyrénées.* PEDRELL 153–159
1637 —— ——. *Los Pirineos.* PEDRELL 63–94
1638 —— Oliva y Milà, Joan. *Ramón Lull.* PEDRELL 320–322
1639 —— Tebaldini, Giovanni. Filippo Pedrell ed il dramma lirico spagnuolo. PEDRELL 3–32
—— See also no. 1536b
1639a [Piel] Mies, Paul. Eine ungedruckte Messe von Peter Piel. FELLERER/60THM 243–247
1639b [Proksch] Karabec, Stanislav. K vlivu českých hudebních tradic na učitele Bedřicha Smetany Josefa Proksche. [Concerning the Influence of Czech Music Traditions on Bedrich Smetana's Teacher, Josef Proksch] PLAVEC/60TH 147–153, summaries in German & Russian
1640 [Regondi] Zuth, Josef. Eine Handschrift von Giulio Regondi. GRÜNWALD 17–19
1640a [Rietz] Sietz, Reinhold. Das Stammbuch von Julius Rietz. FELLERER/60THS 219–234
1641 [Rimsky-Korsakov] Abraham, Gerald. Rimsky-Korsakov as Self-Critic. BLUME/F 16–21
1641a [Ritter, J. W.] Salmen, Walter. Fragmente zur romantischen Musikanschauung von J. W. Ritter. MÜLLER-BLATTAU/70TH 235–241
1642 [Rochlitz] Müller-Blattau, Joseph. Friedrich Rochlitz und die Musikgeschichte. ALBRECHT 192–199
1643 [Rossini] Schroeder, A. E. Henri Vandamme, een belgische Rossinivereerder uit de 19de eeuw. MUEREN. 151–156
1644 [Ruzitska] Ruzitska, Lajos. A Kolozsvári zenekonzervatórium és Ruzitska György; képek Kolozsvár zenei eletéből a XIX. században [The Kolozsvar Music Conservatory and György Ruzitska; Musical Life in Kolozsvar in the 19th Century] KODÁLY/70TH 601–610
1645 [Sabon] Refardt, Edgar. Ein genfer Musiker in den Napoleonskriegen. REFARDT 31–32; orig. in *Schweizerische Musikz.* 71 (1931)
1645a [Saint-Saëns] Andriessen, Willem. De oude Camille Saint-Saëns en de jonge dichter. ANDRIESSEN, W. 106–108
1646 [Santini] Fédorov, Vladimir. A propos de quelques lettres de Santini à Bottée de Toulmon. FELLERER/60TH 128–136
1647 —— ——. V. V. Stasov chez l'abb. F. Santini à Rome. HOBOKEN 55–62
1647a [Schindler] Schmidt-Görg, Joseph. Anton Schindlers musikalischer Nachlass im Beethoven-Archiv zu Bonn. RACEK/60TH 263–272
1648 —— Sietz, Reinhold. Anton Schindler und Ferdinand Hiller in ihren persönlichen Beziehungen; mit zwei ungedruckten Briefen Schindlers. SCHIEDERMAIR/80TH 133–139
1649 [Schumann] Boetticher, Wolfgang. Neue Materialien zu Robert Schumanns wiener Bekanntenkreis. SCHENK 39–55
1650 —— Carner, Mosco. La Riorchestrazione di Mahler delle sinfonie di Schumann. MARINUZZI 23–46
1651 —— Heyer, Hermann. Robert Schumann als Musikkritiker. GEWANDHAUS 73–89
1652 —— Hohenemser, Richard. Formale Eigentümlichkeiten in Robert Schumanns Klaviermusik. SANDBERGER 21–50
1652a —— Maniates, Maria Rika. The D Minor Symphony of Robert Schumann. WIORA/60TH 441–447
1653 —— Schenk, Erich. Robert Schumann und Peter Lindpaintner in Wien. SCHMIDT-GÖRG 267–282
1654 —— Strich, Fritz. Byrons *Manfred* in Schumanns Vertonung; einleitender Vortrag zu seiner musikalischen Aufführung in Bern. SINGER 167–181
1655 —— Weise, Dagmar. Ein bisher verschollenes Manuskript zu Schumanns *Album für die Jugend.* SCHMIDT-GÖRG 383–399
—— See also no. 1537a
1656 [Seidl] Anton Seidl's Literary Work. SEIDL/AN 205–240
1656a [Serov] Abraham, Gerald. The Operas of Serov. WELLESZ/80TH 171–183
1657 [Silcher] Refardt, Edgar. *Zu Strassburg auf der Schanz.* REFARDT 147–149; orig. in *Eidgenössisches Sängerblatt* (1938)
1657a [Smetana] Bartoš, František. Smetanovský pracovník [Smetana Studies] PLAVEC/60TH 356–358
1657b —— Goll, Jaroslav. Smetana a

Hostinský. HOSTINSKÝ/60TH 93–98; orig. in *Wiener Abendpost* 28 (1901)
1657c —— Pečírka, Jaromír. Bedřich Smetana a Josef Mánes. NEJEDLÝ/50TH 24–29
1657d —— Střelcová, Věra. Několik poznámek k interpretaci *Čertovy Stěny* Bedřicha Smetany [Some Remarks on the Interpretation of *The Devil's Wall* by Bedřich Smetana] RACEK/60TH 289–301, summary in German
1657e —— Vrba, Přemysl. K prvnímu zahraničnímu provedení Smetanovy *Prodané Nevěsty* v Petrohradě roku 1871 [Concerning the First Foreign Performance of Smetana's *Bartered Bride* in Petrograd in the year 1871] PLAVEC/60TH 155–167, summaries in German & Russian
1657f [Śmietański] Mrygoń, Adam. Emil Władyslaw Śmietański pianista, pedagog, kompozytor. FEICHT 350–361
1657g [Spohr] Heussner, Horst. Der Kofkapellmeister Ludwig Spohr, ein sozialgeschichtliches Porträt. ENGEL 134–154
1658 —— Istel, Edgar. Fünf Briefe Spohrs an Marschner. LILIENCRON 110–115
—— See also no. 1670a
1659 [Spontini] Barchiesi, Raffaele. Un Musicista marchigiano a Parigi durante l'impero di Napoleone. FALLETTI 507–514
1660 —— Bouvet, Charles. Un Opéra allemand de Spontini, *Agnes von Hohenstaufen*. LAURENCIE 275–281
1660a —— Fellerer, Karl G. Gasparo Spontini und die Kirchenmusikreform. WIORA/60TH 427–434
1660b [Stendhal] Bartoš, Josef. Stendhal hudebník. První skizza k větší práci o Stendhalovi [Stendhal the Musician. Preliminary Sketches to a Larger Work on Stendhal] NEJEDLÝ/50TH 30–68
1661 [Stenhammar] Wallner, Bo. Wilhelm Stenhammars stråkkvartett-skisser. MOBERG 355–373
1662 [Strauss, J.] Pfannhauser, Karl. Eine menschlich-künstlerische Strauss-Memoire. OREL/70TH 139–150
1663 [Tchaikovsky] Abraham, Gerald. Tchaikovsky's First Opera. FELLERER/60TH 12–19
1664 —— Handschin, Jacques. Tschaikowski. HANDSCHIN 223–228; orig. in *Neue Zürcher Zeitung* 2087 & 2096 (1927)
1665 —— Rizhkin, I. J. Asaf'evskii analiz *Pikovoi damy* i *Evgeniia Onegina* Chaikovskogo. ASAF'EV 55–67
—— See also no. 1861d
1665a [Thibaut] Savelsberg, Ernst. Anton Friedrich Justus Thibaut und der Heidelberger Singkreis. FELLERER/60THM 17–39
—— See also no. 1571
1666 [Thielemans] Auda, Antoine. Pierre-Léon-Benoît Thielemans, organiste et compositeur, 1825–1898. BORREN 54–71
1667 [Tieck] Bolte, Johannes. Aus einer Anekdotensammlung Ludwig Tiecks. KRETZSCHMAR 22–25
1668 [Tinel] Tinel, Paul. Les Discours et rapports d'Edgar Tinel aux assemblées générales de la Société de Saint-Grégoire. Closson 153–165
1669 [Tveit] Bjørndal, Arne. Felemakaren Johannes Bårdsen Tveit, 1786–1847. BJØRNDAL 154–174; orig. in *Folkekunst* (1949)
1669a [Verdi] Mompellio, Federico. Critiche di Verdi ai critici. DESDERI/70TH 97–100
1669b —— Schueller, Herbert M. *Othello* Transformed: Verdi's Interpretation of Shakespeare. WILCOX 129–155
1670 [Vieuxtemps] Müller von Asow, Erich H. Ein ungedruckter Brief von Henri Vieuxtemps an W. A. Mozart Sohn. SCHENK 389–390
1670a [Weber] Abert, Anna Amalie. Webers "Euryanthe" und Spohrs "Jessonda" als grosse Opern. WIORA/60TH 435–440
1671 —— Köhler, Karl-Heinz. Carl Maria von Webers Beziehungen zu Berlin. BESSELER 425–435
1671a —— Laux, Karl. Carl Maria von Webers Münchner Beitrag zur deutschen Oper. ENGEL 221–230
1672 —— Schnoor, Hans. Stufen des 19. Jahrhunderts. STRAUBE 233–260
1673 —— Schünemann, Georg. Carl Maria von Weber in Berlin; sein erster Besuch im Jahre 1812. RAABE 78–94
1674 —— Wirth, Helmut. Natur und Märchen in Webers *Oberon*, Mendelssohns *Ein Sommernachtstraum* und Nicolais *Die lustigen Weiber von Windsor*. BLUME/F 389–397
1675 [Widmann] Refardt, Edgar. Die Musiktexte J. V. Widmanns. REFARDT 134–139; orig. in *Der Bund* 447 (1938)
1676 [Widor] Handschin, Jacques.

Charles-Marie Widor. HANDSCHIN 242–245; orig. in *Neue Basler Zeitung* 18 (Mar. 1937)
1676a [Witt] Stein, Franz A. Franz Xavier Witt und seine *Missa in Honorem S. Raphaelis Archangeli Quinque Vocum* Op. 33. FELLERER/60THM 233–242
1676b [Zöller] Haase, Rudolf. Ein Notenheft aus dem Jahre 1850. FELLERER/60THS 86–94

POST-ROMANTIC AND MODERN ERA: GENERAL

See also nos. 793a, 1136, 1153, 1165, 1413, 1414a, 1423, 1431, 2386a

1677 Abeele, G. van den. Bij de herleving van oude muziek. MUEREN 167–176
1677a Adorno, Thoedor W. Über einige Schwierigkeiten des Komponierens heute. MÜLLER-BLATTAU/70TH 15–27
1677b ——. Vers une musique informelle. STEINECKE 73–102
1678 Altmann, Wilhelm. Die Ur- und Erstaufführungen von Opernwerken auf deutschen Bühnen in den letzten 25 Spielzeiten. UNIVERSAL 247–275
1678a Andersson, Otto. Finlandssvensk musikodling. Tal vid jubileumsfesten i Ekenäs den 5–7 juli 1946. ANDERSSON, O./85TH 139–144; orig. in *Västra Nyland* (July 6, 1946)
1678b Bäcker, Ursula. Eine bergische Stadt lernt Singen. Aus der Vorgeschichte des Lenneper Chorlebens zu Beginn des 19. Jahrhunderts. FELLERER/60THS 31–38
1679 Bartók, Béla. The Influence of Peasant Music on Modern Music. BARTÓK/T 71–76
1680 Baur, Jürg. Das kurze Klavierstück und seine Stellung in der modernen Musik. FELLERER 63–66
1681 Berg, Alban. Verbindliche Antwort auf eine unverbindliche Rundfrage. UNIVERSAL 220–225
1682 Berten, Walter. Musikpolitik-Musiksoziologie-Musikdramaturgie, Begriffsbestimmungen und Zielsetzungen. RAABE 52–58
1683 Bie, Oskar. Der Tanz. UNIVERSAL 125–129
1684 Biehle, Herbert. Das Institut [Biehle] BIEHLE 101–103
1685 Binder, Julius. Der Staat der Musik. VECCHIO 31–37
1685a Blume, Friedrich. Das musikalische Kunstwerk in der Geschichte. STÄBLEIN/70TH 9–27
1685b Boulez, Pierre. Discipline et communication. STEINECKE 25–37
1685c Brelet, Gisèle. Musicalisation de l'espace dans la musique contemporaine. WIORA/60TH 495–500
1685d Casella, Alfredo. Neoklassizismus in Italien. DAMDK 23–25
1686 Cogni, Giulio. Il Problema dell'interiorità nella musica contemporanea. SCHENK 89–95
1687 Collaer, Paul. La Composition musicale, de 1939 à 1945. CLOSSON 81–87
1688 ——. Poésie et musique dans la mélodie française contemporaine. BORREN 149–162
1689 Cross, Joan. The Bad Old Days. BRITTEN 175–184
1690 Daisne, Johan. Zur Geschichte von Lili Marleen. LIEP 68–71
1691 Egk, Werner. Musik als Ausdruck ihrer Zeit. RAABE 23–28
1691a Ehmann, Wilhelm. Changes in Choral Singing in Europe Today. BUSZIN 193–199
1692 Engel, Hans. Der Musiker, Beruf und Lebensformen. RAABE 187–211
1693 Engelbrecht, Christiane. Die Psalmvertonung im 20. Jahrhundert. SÖHNGEN 153–161
1694 Fellerer, Karl Gustav. Alte Musik im Musikleben der Gegenwart. MERSMANN 44–50
1695 ——. Europäisches Musikschaffen. HILBER 60–66
1696 50 Komponisten: Porträts, Lebensdaten, Werke in der Universal-Edition. UNIVERSAL 285–332
1697 Gruenberg, Louis. Vom Jazz und anderen Dingen; Rückblick und Ausblick. UNIVERSAL 229–236
1698 Handschin, Jacques. Die alte Musik als Gegenwartsproblem. HANDSCHIN 338–341; orig. in *Neue Zürcher Zeitung* 786 (1927)
1699 ——. Musikalisches aus Russland. HANDSCHIN 263–274; orig. in *Basler Nachrichten* 332 & 333 (1920)
1700 ——. La Naissance d'une musique russe d'orgue vers 1914. MASSON II, 189–193
1701 ——. Das Problem der modernen Oper. HANDSCHIN 342–347; orig. in *Neue Zürcher Zeitung* 1074 & 1081 (1928)
1702 ——. Die Stellung der Musik im Rahmen der Gesamtkultur. HANDSCHIN

355–358; orig. in *Schaffhauser Nachrichten* (Oct. 17, 1947)
1703 Haase, Karl. Grundlagen einer bodenständigen Musikpflege. STEIN 104–111
1704 Hauer, Josef M. Wende der Musik? UNIVERSAL 237–240
1705 Hausegger, Siegmund von. Kunst und Öffentlichkeit. SEIDL/AR 56–57
1706 Hope-Wallace, Philip. Meditation. NEWMAN 124–129
1707 Hürlimann, Martin. Was ist Wahrheit? Bemerkungen eines Liebhabers zur heutigen Situation der Musikkritik. PAUMGARTNER 70–80
1708 Jenkner, Hans. Wir brauchen die Oper der Zeit. BOTE 51–56
1708a Jurrès André. Les compositeurs néerlandais et l'Orchestre du Concertgebouw. FÉDEROV 49–53
1709 Kaminski, Heinrich. Evolution oder Revolution. UNIVERSAL 60–62
1709a Karkoschka, Erhard. Zur Problematik einer temperierten Notation. GERSTENBERG/60TH 78–87
1709b Kestenberg, Leo. Wandlungen des deutschen Musiklebens. DAMDK 19–22
1709c Křenek, Ernst. Komponieren als Beruf. DAMDK 32–37
1710 ——. Musik in der Gegenwart. UNIVERSAL 43–60
1711 Lamm, Albert. Erziehung zur Kunst. SEIDL/AR 79–96
1712 Lemacher, Heinrich & Paul Mies. Die Gesellschaft für neue Musik in *Köln*. SCHIEDERMAIR/80TH 69–76
1712a Lemacher, Heinrich. Dei Gesellschaft für Neue Musik in Köln 1925–1933. FELLERER/60THS 137–143
1713 ——. Der Kölner Gürzenichchor, 1946–1952. KAHL 113–120
1714 Lissa, Zofia. Formprobleme der Filmmusik. FELLERER/60TH 321–335
1715 Litt, Theodor. Musik und Menschenbildung. STRAUBE 96–112
1716 Loth, Peter, Zweibrücken und das Pfalzorchester. ZWIEBRÜCKEN 292–293
1717 Lothar, Ernst. Salzburg als geistiger Raum. PAUMGARTNER 22–28
1718 Malipiero, Gian Francesco. Ein Brief. UNIVERSAL 241–246
1719 Mersmann, Hans. Die Musik des 20. Jahrhunderts. UNIVERSAL 31–42
1720 Mies, Paul. Der Glockenklang als Problem des Impressionismus. BIEHLE 66–70
1721 Mjöen, Reidar. Strömungen in der neunorwegischen Tonkunst. SCHEURLEER 213–217
1721a Moser, Hans Joachim. Zuständigkeitsgrenzen der Musiksoziologie. ENGEL 245–249
1722 Neher, Caspar. Salzburger Schauplätze. PAUMGARTNER 38–40
1723 Oberborbeck, Felix. Neue Musikerberufe. RAABE 222–228
1724 Oehlmann, Werner. Gottesvorstellung und Gottesgegenwart in der modernen Musik. SÖHNGEN 194–196
1724a Petyrek, Felix. Musikalische Eindrücke aus Griechenland. DAMDK 47–50
1724b Pincherle, Marc. Le malentendu des concerts. BORREN/90TH 135–143
1725 Pisk, Paul A. Musikalische Volksbildung. UNIVERSAL 155–168
1725a Pujman, Ferdinand. Nová vina [New wave] NEJEDLÝ/50TH 9–18
1726 Reich, Willi. Zur Geschichte der Zwölftonmusik. OREL/70TH 151–157
1727 Reinold, Helmut. Zur Bedeutung musiksoziologischen Denkens für die Musikgeschichte. FELLERER 67–72
1728 Sapp, Norma B. Music via Television. DAVISON 303–311
1729 Scharnagl, August. Zur Geschichte des Regensburger Domchors. SCHREMS 125–152
1730 Schmidt, Harold C. Problems of Choral Texture in the Twentieth Century. DAVISON 279–291
1730a Schmidt-Joos, Siegfried. Der dritte Strom. Versuche einer Synthese van Jazz und Neuer Musik. BOSSE/50TH 121–132
1730b Schnebel, Dieter. Bericht von neuer Orgelmusik. GERSTENBERG/60TH 151–160
1731 Schön, Ernst. Musik und Technik. UNIVERSAL 192–197
1731a Schrade, Leo. Altes im Neuen Werk. SCHRADE/D 570–591; based on art. in *Neue Zürcher Zeitung* 602 (19 Feb, 1961)
1731b ——. "Herkules am Scheideweg"; zur neuen Musik der Nachkriegsjahre. SCHRADE/D 592–608
1732 Silbermann, Alfons. Musiksoziologisches Akrostichon. MERSMANN 135–142
1733 Stefan, Paul. Vor fünfundzwanzig Jahren; Musik um die Jahrhundertwende. UNIVERSAL 212–219
1734 Stein, Fritz. Berufsfreudiger Orchesternachwuchs. RAABE 212–221
1734a Steinecke, Wolfgang. Kranich-

stein: Geschichte, Idee, Ergebnisse. STEINECKE 9–24

1734b Steinhard, Erich. Deutsche Komponisten der Tschechoslawakei. DAMDK 16–18

1734c Stockhausen, Karlheinz. Die Einheit der musikalischen Zeit. ADORNO/60TH 365–377

1735 Storck, Karl. Tempel der Kunst. SEIDL/AR 58–78

1736 Stuckenschmidt, Hans H. Deutung der Gegenwart. GURLITT 246–254

1736a Teichmüller, Robert. Meine Schüler aus Böhmen. DAMDK 50–52

1737 Tittel, Ernst. Der Einfluss des gregorianischen Chorals auf die zeitgenössische Musik in Österreich. JOHNER 111–114

1738 ——. Zur Problematik der modernen Musik. HILBER 76–86

1739 Uszkoreit, Hans-Georg. Orchester auf Konzertreisen. KONWITSCHNY 64–71

1740 Weidemann, Alfred. Schallplatte und Musikkultur. BOTE 71–74

1741 Weigand, Wilhelm. Kultur und Mittler. SEIDL/AR 50–55

1742 Weill, Kurt. Bekenntnis zur Oper. UNIVERSAL 226–228

1743 Weissmann, Adolf. Rasse und Nation in der Musik. UNIVERSAL 86–105

1744 Wellek, Albert. Problematik der modernen Musik. ROTHACKER 335–344

1745 Wellesz, Egon. Die Oper und diese Zeit. UNIVERSAL 106–113

1746 Winter, Carl. Musik-Kult-Kultur. SCHREMS 44–62

1747 Wiora, Walter. Komponist und Mitwelt; ein Beitrag zur soziologischen Musikgeschichte. MERSMANN 171–196

1748 Wolff, Hellmuth Christian. Schönheit und Ausdruck; ein Beitrag zur Klärung der Gegensätze in der modernen Musik. OSTHOFF 181–194

1749 Wouters, Jos. De nieuwe muziek in historisch perspectief. BERNET KEMPERS 60–61

1750 Zimmermann, Heinz W. Was ist neue Musik? Zur Kritik der Kriterien. SÖHNGEN 197–212

1751 Zingel, Hans J. Die Harfe in der Musik unserer Zeit. SCHNEIDER/80TH 285–293

POST-ROMANTIC AND MODERN ERA: HOUSE AND YOUTH MUSIC

1751a Amtmann, Paul. Musik im Spiel. MIRBT/70TH 148–152

1752 Berten, Walter M. Musik im Leben. LEMACHER 22–26

1753 Fett, Armin. Trossingen, Ende oder Zukunft? JÖDE 163–172

1754 Fischer, Erich. Die musikalischen Hauskomödien in der Öffentlichkeit. BOTE 57–60

1755 Handschin, Jacques. Die Musik in der deutschen Jugendbewegung. HANDSCHIN 348–354; orig. in *Annalen* 2 (1928)

1756 Hermann, Hugo. Wege nach Trossingen. JÖDE 161–163

1757 Oberborbeck, Felix. Die Jugendoper der Geganwart. MIRBT 68–70

1757a ——. Zur Sociologie der Jugendmusik. MÜNNICH/80THM 127–140

1758 Preussner, Eberhard. Hausmusik. RAABE 29–37

1759 Roeseling, Kaspar. Heinrich Lemacher und die geistliche Hausmusik. LEMACHER 38–44

1760 Rohwer, Jens. Das organische Kunstwerk. JÖDE 199–210

1761 Sachse, Wolfgang. Jugend und Musik. BOTE 65–70

1762 Scheidler, Bernhard. Im Hohenecker Kreis. JÖDE 74–89

1763 Scheuber, Josef K. Musik und Familie. HILBER 90–93

1764 Warner, Theodor. Das Jugendsingspiel. MIRBT 61–67

1764a Wismeyer, Ludwig. "Wenn alle Brünnlein fliessen" und das Lied der Grossstadt 1963. BOSSE/50TH 142–148

1765 Wölki, Konrad. Zupfmusik zwischen 1919 und 1956. JÖDE 157–160

POST-ROMANTIC AND MODERN ERA: INDIVIDUAL COMPOSERS, PERFORMERS, ETC.

1766 [Abert] Blume, Friedrich. Hermann Abert und die Musikwissenschaft. BLUME/S 1–10, & ABERT 18–30

1767 [Adler] Engel, Carl. Guido Adler in Retrospect (1855–1941). EINSTEIN 391–400

1767a [Adorno] Křenek, Ernst. Briefe an Theodor W. Adorno. ADORNO/60TH 361–364

1767b —— Leibowitz, René. Der Komponist Theodor W. Adorno. ADORNO/60TH 355–359

1767c —— Steuermann, Eduard. Briefe an Theodor W. Adorno. ADORNO/60TH 360

1768 ♪ d'Albert, Eugen. [Piano Piece]. SEEBACH 7

1768a Albrecht, Hans. Litterae. BORREN/90TH 5
1769 ♪ Ambrosius, H. *Schlaf nur ein.* MÜLLER VON ASOW [232]
1770 ♪ Ansermet, Ernest. *Chanson des dragons.* RAMUZ 132–133
1771 ♪ Ansorge, Conrad. *Verleuchtender Tag.* op. 26, no. 3. SEIDL/AR 45–49
1772 ♪ Aubert, Louis. *Sept pièces de piano sur le nom de Fauré,* no. 3. FAURÉ suppl. 14–17
1773 ♪ Aubin, Tony. *Le Sommeil d'Iskender.* DUKAS suppl. 25–30
1774 ♪ Averkamp, Anton. *Albumblad voor Dr. D. F. Scheurleer.* SCHEURLEER 63–64
1774a ♪ Axman, Emil. *Pozdrav Josefu Bohuslavu Foerstrovi.* FOERSTER/90TH 13
1775 ♪ Bachner, G. *Frühlingslied.* MÜLLER VON ASOW [233–234]
1776 ♪ Bammer, J. *Ausfahrtsegen.* MÜLLER VON ASOW [235–236]
1777 ♪ Barber, Samuel. *Ad bibinem cum me rogaret ad cenam.* ENGEL 35–38
1778 ♪ Barraine, Elsa. *Hommage à Paul Dukas.* DUKAS suppl. 31–32
1779 ♪ Bartók, Béla. *Tombeau de Claude Debussy.* DEBUSSY suppl. 12–13
1780 [Bartók] Doflein, Erich. Über Bartóks letzte Lebensjahre; Emigration und Charakter—Schicksal und Spätwerk. MERSMANN 30–43
1781 —— Ferand, Ernest. Begegnung mit Béla Bartók. BRODY 87–123
1781a Járdányi, Pál. Die Volksmusik in Bartóks Kunst. WIORA/60TH 466–470
1782 —— Lendvai, Ernő. Bevezetés a Bartók-művek elemzésébe [Introduction to an Analysis of Bartók's Music] BARTÓK/L 461–503, English & German summaries, 557–558
1783 —— Siegmund-Schultze, W. Tradition und Neuerertum in Bartóks Streichquartetten. KODÁLY/80TH 317–328
1784 —— Szabolcsi, Bence. A csodálatos Mandarin [The Miraculous Mandarin] BARTÓK/L 519–533, English & French summaries 559
1785 —— Twittenhoff, Wilhelm. Zur Struktur und Thematik des Violinkonzerts von Béla Bartók. MERSMANN 143–157
1786 —— Wellesz, Egon. Die Streichquartette von Béla Bartók, BARTÓK/40TH 98–100
1787 ♪ Beck, Conrad. *Fox-trot [Hommage à Albert Roussel],* piano. ROUSSEL supp. 23–26
1787a ♪ Bender, Jan. *The Peace of God* (A Four-part Canon). BUSZIN 143
1788 [Berg] Redlich, Hans F. Unveröffentlichte Briefe Alban Bergs an Arnold Schönberg. BLUME/F 272–280
1789 ♪ Bernet Kempers, Karl P. *Koninklijke Nederlandsche Toonkunstenaars Vereeniging.* BERNET KEMPERS 20
1789a ♪ Bialas, Günther. *Jede Blüte will zur Frücht.* MÜNNICH/70TH [36–38]
1789b ♪ ——. *Welkes Blatt.* MÜNNICH/80THM 141
1790 ♪ Biebl, Franz. *Rumpeldipum.* Selections. HAAS 21–25
1791 ♪ Bittner, Julius. *Des Abends,* Lied für Altstimme. SEEBACH 28
1791a ♪ Böhme, Fritz. *Frühling. Sommer. Herbst* (3 songs). MÜNNICH/70TH [14–25]
1791b ♪ Bořkovec, Pavel. *Mistru J. B. Foerstrovi. Na slova H. B.* FOERSTER/90TH 14
1792 ♪ Borris, Siegfried. *Alle gute Gabe.* SÖHNGEN 184
1793 ♪ ——. *Kein Tierlein ist auf Erden.* SÖHNGEN 182–183
1794 ♪ Bresgen, Cesar. *Bauer, in deinen Händen.* HAAS 26–27
1795 ♪ ——. *Lob der Arbeit.* HAAS 28–29
1796 [Britten] Piper, Myfanwy. Some Thoughts on the Libretto of *The Turn of the Screw.* BRITTEN 78–83
1797 [Burkhard] Otto, Hans. Der a cappella-Burkhard. MAUERSBERGER 60–66
1797a —— Sievers, Gerd. Das *Ezzolied* in der Vertonung von Willy Burkhard und Johann Nepomuk David Ein Vergleich. ENGEL 335–363
1798 [Busoni] Bekker, Paul. Busoni. UNIVERSAL 79–85
1798a —— Kindermann, Jürgen. Zur Kontroverse Busoni-Pfitzner. Futuristengefahr—Missverständnis einer Kritik? WIORA/60TH 471–477
1799 —— Presser, Diether. Busonis *Sonatina brevis* als Bearbeitung eines barocken Instrumentalstückes. KAHL 96–102
1799a ♪ Caggiano, Roberto. *Kirie.* DESDERI/70TH 25–27
1799b Closson, Ernest. Litterae. BORREN/90TH 32–34
[David, J. N.] See no. 1797a
1799c ♪ Davies, Peter Maxwell. *In nomine II.* TIPPETT/60TH 83
1799d ——. Peart, Donald. Peter Maxwell Davies: *The Shepherd's Calendar.* BISHOP 249–255
1800 [Debussy] Brailoiu, Constantin.

Pentatonismes chez Debussy. BARTÓK 385–426
1801 —— Correspondance inédite entre Saint-Saëns et Maurice Emmanuel à propos de Claude Debussy. EMMANUEL 30–34
1802 —— Dille, D. Inleiding tot het vormbegrip bij Debussy. BORREN 175–196
1803 —— Lesure, François. L'Affaire Debussy-Ravel; lettres inédites. BLUME/F 231–234
1804 —— ——. Debussy et le XVIe siècle. ALBRECHT 242–245
1805 —— Linden, A. van der. Le premier concert Debussy en Belgique (1894). MUEREN 193–200
1806 —— Mies, Paul. Widmungsstücke mit Buchstaben-Motto bei Debussy und Ravel. SCHENK 363–368
1807 ♪ Deis, Carl. *Tributum ad angelum*, A Fugal Fantasia. ENGEL 79–87
1808 ♪ Delage, M. *A Roussel*, voice, flute & piano. ROUSSEL suppl. 1–8
1808a Dent, Edward J. Litterae. BORREN/90TH 48
1809 ♪ Denyn, Jef. Preludium in B voor beiáard. DENYN 31–34
1810 [Denyn] Lannoy, Maurice. Jef Denyn et les carillons de France. DENYN 175–184
1810a [Diaghilev] Hopkinson, Cecil. Diaghilev, Chaliapine, and Their Contracts. OLDMAN 149–153
1811 [Distler] Schmolzi, Herbert. Das Verhältnis von Wort und Ton in Hugo Distlers *Choralpassion*, op. 7. KAHL 103–112
1812 —— Schwinger, Wolfram. *Wachet auf, ruft uns die Stimme.* Hugo Distler; ein kurzes aber lebendiges Kapitel deutscher Musikgeschichte. MAUERSBERGER 42–52
1812a ♪ Dobiáš, Václav. *Pozdrav zemi. Na Slova K. H. Máchy.* FOERSTER/90TH 15
1812b Doppelbauer, Josef Friedrich. *Missa psalmodica.* MARX, K./70TH 94–97
1813 ♪ Drdla, F. *Duo concertante*, violin, violoncello & piano. MÜLLER VON ASOW [237–238]
1814 ♪ Dukas, Paul. *Tombeau de Claude Debussy. La Plainte, au loin, du faune . . .* DEBUSSY suppl. 1–5
1815 [Dukas] Favre, Georges. Quelques lettres inédites de Paul Dukas. MASSON II, 181–185
1815a Einstein, Alfred. Litterae. BORREN/90TH 57–59
1816 ♪ Eisler, Hanns. *Rezitativ und Fuge.* BECHER 126–127
1817 [Eisler] Vetter, Walther. Das Wissen um die soziale Rolle der Musik; Streiflichter auf das Wirken Eislers. BESSELER 457–464
1818 ♪ Enesco, Georges. *Sept pièces de piano sur le nom de Fauré*, no. 2. FAURÉ suppl. 11–13
1818a [Enesco] Vancea, Zeno. K Enescovu postavení v Rumunské a světove hudbě [Enesco's Position in Rumanian and in World Music] RACEK/60TH 347–351, summary in German
1819 ♪ Erpf, Hermann. *Drei feste Brücken.* JÖDE 212
1820 ♪ Falla, Manuel de. *Pour le tombeau de Paul Dukas.* DUKAS suppl. 7–9
1821 ♪ ——. *Tombeau de Claude Debussy, Homenaja*, guitar. DEBUSSY suppl. 30–31
1822 [Fauré] Fortassier, Pierre. Rythme verbal et rythme musical à propos de la prosodie de Gabriel Fauré. MASSON I, 29–37
1823 ♪ Fiebach, Otto. *Die Eine.* SEEBACH 58
1823a [Foerster] Beneš, K. J. Příspěvek k otázce Foersterových operních textů [Contributions to the Question of Foerster's Opera Texts] NEJEDLÝ/50TH 182–191
1823b —— Krejči, Iša. J. B. Foerstera mužské sbory [J. B. Foerster's Music for Male Choruses] NEJEDLÝ/50TH 192–198
1824 ♪ Franckenstein, Cl. *Vöglein Schwermut.* MÜLLER VON ASOW [239–241]
1824a ♪ Friedrich, Wilfried. *Die Lustigen von Weimar.* MÜNNICH/80THM 142
1825 [Fürnberg] Mayer, Hans. Nachwort zur Mozart-Novelle. FÜRNBERG 143–147
1826 —— Rebling, Eberhard. Louis Fürnberg, der Musiker. FÜRNBERG 151–154
1827 ♪ Fuleihan, Anis. Extract from *Views and Reviews.* ENGEL 103–105
1828 ♪ Gansser, Hans. *Ein Führer, Volk und Reich.* HAAS 30–31
1829 [Gatti] Cassella, Alfredo. Lettera a Guido M. Gatti. CASELLA 200–201
1830 ♪ Gebhard, Hans. *Fantasy*, piano. HAAS 32–39
1831 ♪ Gebhard, Ludwig. *Burleske*, brass quintet, tympani & piano. HAAS 40–44

1832 ♪ Gebhard, Max. *Rondino über H-A-A-S.* HAAS 45–48
1833 [Gershwin] Keller, Hans. Rhythm; Gershwin and Stravinsky. STRAVINSKY/75TH 19–31
1833a [Ghedini] Salvetti, Guido. La lirica da camera di Giorgio Federico Ghedini. BARBLAN/60TH 271–282
1834 [Gilbert] Downes, Olin. Henry Gilbert, Nonconformist. ENGEL 88–94
1835 [Godowsky] Philipp, Isidor. Recollections of Leopold Godowsky. ENGEL 179–180
1835a ♪ Goehr, Alexander. *The Sword Sung on the Barren Heath* (Canon a 4). TIPPETT/60TH 70
1836 ♪ Goossens, Eugene. *Tombeau de Claude Debussy.* DEBUSSY suppl. 10–11
1836a ♪ Gostuški, Dragutin. *Polychronion [1961]* (based on a Byzantine melody for Manuel II Palaeologus and his wife). OSTROGORSKY 149–161
1837 ♪ Graener, P. *Gebet.* MÜLLER VON ASOW [242]
1838 [Gregor] Strauss, Richard. Parerga für Joseph Gregor; aus dem Anlasse seiner *Weltgeschichte des Theaters.* GREGOR 237–239
1838a Gümbel, Martin. Zu meinem Divertimento für Streicher (1960, Bärenreiter Verlag). MARX, K./70TH 98–101
1838b Gurlitt, Wilibald. Litterae. BORREN/90TH 82–83
1839 [Haas] Mies, Paul. Gregorianik als Grundlage in *Lieder der Sehnsucht* von Joseph Haas. JOHNER 114–117
1839a ♪ Hába, Karel. *Lístek do památníku J. B. Foerstrovi.* FOERSTER/90TH 16
1839b [Hába] Vysloužil, Jiří. Alois Hába als Kompositionslehrer. RACEK/60TH 379–387
1840 ♪ Hådell, Norlén, Olrog, Pim-Pim, & Sundblad. *Passagerarnas vals.* SALÉN 96–103
1841 ♪ Hafstetter, Ernst. *Turmmusik, Volk auf dem Wege.* HAAS 49–52
1841a Handschin, Jacques. Litterae. BORREN/90TH 84
1842 ♪ Hausegger, S. *Säerspruch.* MÜLLER VON ASOW [243–244]
1843 [Held] Ott, Alfons. Musikalisches Porträt. HELD 28–30
1843a ♪ Henze, Hans Werner. *Sarabande.* TIPPETT/60TH 46
1844 ♪ Hindemith, Paul. *Dolorum solacium.* ANSERMET 17
1845 [Hindemith] Austin, William. Hindemith's *Frau Musica:* The Versions of 1928 and 1943 Compared. DAVISON 265–271
1846 —— Kleemann, Hans. Das Kompositionsprinzip Paul Hindemiths und sein Verhältnis zur Atonalität ABERT 80–92
1846a —— Stephani, Martin. Hindemiths Apotheose der Gesetzmässigkeit als Wagnis des Glaubens an "Die Harmonie der Welt." EHMANN/60TH 83–89
—— See also nos. 1996, 2502
1847 Höckner, Hilmar. Jahre der Freundschaft. JÖDE 38–46
1848 ♪ Höller, Karl. Largo appassionato, violin & piano. HAAS 53–60
1849 ♪ Hoerée, Arthur. *Fanfare, Hommage à Albert Roussel.* ROUSSEL suppl. 27–30
1850 [Hofmannsthal] Beau, Albin E. Hofmannsthals Wendung zur Oper. TIEMANN 318–324
1851 —— Schuh, Willi. Hofmannsthal und die Oper. KORRODI 168–180
1852 Holzmeister, Clemens. Über meine Arbeiten für das Festspielhaus. PAUMGARTNER 29–37
1853 ♪ Honegger, Arthur. *Sur le nom d'Albert Roussel.* ROUSSEL suppl. 9–12
1854 [Honegger] Refardt, Edgar. Die Musik Arthur Honeggers in den Basler Konzerten. REFARDT 59–63; orig. in *Basler Nachrichten,* Sonntagsblatt 10 (1952)
1854a —— Schrade, Leo. Vom Sinn der Musik in Honeggers Werk. SCHRADE/D 556–569
1855 [Hornbostel] Handschin, Jacques. Erich M. von Hornbostel. HANDSCHIN 385–388; orig. in *Neue Zürcher Zeitung* 2209 (1935)
1856 [Huber] Refardt, Edgar. Hans Huber. REFARDT 51–54; orig. in *Basler Nachrichten* 269 (1952)
1857 —— ——. Die verloren geglaubte Murten-Kantate Hans Hubers. REFARDT 55–58; orig. in *Eidgenössisches Sängerblatt* (1939)
1858 ♪ Ibert, Jacques. *Toccata sur le nom de Roussel,* piano. ROUSSEL suppl. 20–22
1859 [Jahnn] Maack, Rudolf. Hans Henny Jahnn und die Orgel. JAHNN 50–53
1860 —— Ramin, Günther.

Wiedererwecker alter Musik. JAHNN 53–54
1861 —— Italiaander, Rolf. Leben, Bücher, Orgeln. JAHNN 3–9
1861a [Janáček] Blažek, Zdeněk. Spojavací formy v teorii Leoše Janáčka. RACEK/60TH 29–37, summary in German
1861b —— Brod, Max. Bemerkungen zur letzten Oper Janáčeks. RACEK/60TH 39–44
1861c —— Flothius, Marius. Über die Notwendigkeit einer kritischen Gesamtausgabe der Werke Leoš Janáčeks. RACEK/60TH 87–91
1861d —— Stědroň, Bohumír. Janáček a Čajkovskij. NEJEDLÝ/75TH 201–217, summaries in English & Russian
1861e —— ——. Ke zrodu opery Leoše Janáčka *Její Pastorkyňa* [The Genesis of Leoš Janáček's Opera *Jenufa*] RACEK/60TH 325–345, summary in German
1861f —— ——. K Janáčkovým nápěvkům mluvy [Concerning Janáček's Speech Melodies] PLAVEC/60TH 197–235, summaries in German & Russian
1861g —— Stuckenschmidt, Hans Heinz. Leoš Janáčeks Ästhetik und seine Stellung in der Weltmusik. RACEK/60TH 303–307
1861h —— Tučapský, Antonin. Interpretace Janáčkových sborů [The Interpretation of Janáček's Men's Choruses] PLAVEC/60TH 69–77
1861i —— Tvrdoň, Jozef. Leoš Janáček a súčasni slovenskí skladatelia [Leoš Janáček and Contemporary Slovakian Composers] PLAVEC/60TH 189–195, summaries in German & Russian
1861j —— Vetterl, Karel. Lidová píseň v Janáčkových sborech do roku 1885 [Folk Song in Janáček's Men's Choruses to 1885] RACEK/60TH 365–378, summary in German
1861k —— Wolff, Hellmuth Christian. Janáčeks festliche Messe und der religiöse Stilwandel der Neuzeit. RACEK/60TH 397–402
1861l [Jean-Aubry] Davies, John Howard. Entente-cordiale G. Jean-Aubry and a Generation of Anglo-French Musical Journalism in *The Chesterian*. FÉDEROV 31–33
1862 ♪ Jensen, L. I. *Die Debatte, eine Fabel*. SCHEURLEER 177–180
1863 [Jeppesen] Mathiassen, Finn. Jeppesens *Passacaglia*. JEPPESEN 293–308
1864 ♪ Jerger, W. Sonata, violin & piano. 2d. movement. MÜLLER VON ASOW [245–246]
1864a ♪ Jirák, K. B. Lék. *Na verše Otakara Fischera "Hořící Keř." Mistru J. B. Foerstrovi k 86. narozeninám.* FOERSTER/90TH 17–18
1865 ♪ Jobst, Max. *Sprichwörtliches*. HAAS 61–63
1866 ♪ ——. *Verkannte Kunst*. HAAS 64–66
1867 ♪ Jochum, Otto. *Musik*. HAAS 67–69
1868 [Jöde] [Letter to Fritz Wartenweiler on his 70th Birthday] WARTENWEILER 231–239
1869 ♪ Jora, M. *Kleine Suite*, violin & piano. MÜLLER VON ASOW [247–249]
1870 ♪ Junk, V. *An die Nacht*. MÜLLER VON ASOW [250–251]
1871 ♪ Kaiser, Alfred. *Wär's dunkel*. SEEBACH 94
1871a Karkoschka, Erhard. Vier Stufen für Orchester 1966. MARX, K./70TH 102–105
1872 Kempff, Wilhelm. Mein erstes Frontkonzert (1916). RAABE 235–236
1873 [Kernstock] Schnerich, Alfred. Ein Brief Ottokar Kernstocks über Kunst an A. Schnerich. MÜLLER VON ASOW [158–161]
1874 ♪ Klussmann, Ernst G. *Variationen über das Volkslied Lieblich ergrünen so Auen als Felder*. HAAS 70–77
1875 ♪ Kodály, Zoltán. *Intermezzo*, string trio. KODÁLY/75TH insert iii–xii
1876 ♪ ——. Sonata, violoncello & piano, op. 4. KODÁLY/75TH insert xv–xxxv
1877 [Kodály] Eösze, László. Kodály Zoltán gyermekkarai [Children's Choruses of Zoltán Kodály] KODÁLY/75TH 105–132, English summary 749–750
1878 —— Lakatos, István. Kodály müvészetének útja Erdélyben/Die Musik von Zoltán Kodály in Siebenbürgen. KODÁLY/60TH 143–153
1879 —— Ujfalussy, József. A *Psalmus Hungaricus*. KODÁLY/75TH 21–25, German summary 747
1880 —— ——. Zoltán Kodály et la naissance du *Psalmus Hungaricus*. KODÁLY/80TH 357–366
1881 —— Weissmann, János. Kodály concerto-ja és *Páva*-variációi [Kodály's Concerto and the Peacock Variations]

KODÁLY/75TH 27–41, German summary 747–748
1882 ♪ Koechlin, Charles. *Sept pièces de piano sur le nom de Fauré*, no. 5. FAURÉ suppl. 26–27
1883 ♪ Könnecke, Eduard. *Improvisation*. SEEBACH 110.
1884 [Konwitschny] Krause, Ernst. Der Operndirigent Franz Konwitschny. KONWITSCHNY 27–35
1885 ♪ Kornauth, E. *Durcheinander*. MÜLLER VON ASOW [252–253]
1885a ♪ Krauss, Albrecht. *Nacht*. MÜNNICH/70TH [32–35]
1886 ♪ Krein, Julien. *Pièce à la mémoire de Paul Dukas*. DUKAS suppl. 20–22
1886a ♪ Krejčí, Iša. "*Scherzino*" *J. B. F.* FOERSTER/90TH 19–22
1886b ♪ Krejčí, Miroslav. *Madrigal*. FOERSTER/90TH 23
1887 [Kremplsetzer] Refardt, Edgar. Ein Operettentext von Wilhelm Busch. REFARDT 150–154; orig. in *Basler Nachrichten* 176 (1949)
1887a ♪ Křička, Jaroslav. *Entrata akademica na motiv J. B. F.* FOERSTER/90TH 28
1887b ♪ Krombholc, Jaroslav. *Hrdlo písně. Na slova Karla Jílka*. FOERSTER/90TH 24–27
1887c ♪ Kvapil, Jaroslav. *Pozdravné fanfary pro žestové nástroje, tympany a malý buben v příležitosti 85. narozenin Mistra J. B. Foerstra*. FOERSTER/90TH 29
1888 ♪ Lach, R. *Am See*. MÜLLER VON ASOW [254–255]
1889 ♪ Ladmirault, Paul. *Sept pièces de piano sur le nom de Fauré*, no. 6. FAURÉ *suppl*. 28–32
1890 [Lambrino] Keussler. Gerhard von. Zur Erinnerung an Télémaque Lambrino. MÜLLER VON ASOW [108–118]
1891 ♪ Lang, Hans. *Nun will ich aufflammen*. HAAS 80–81
1892 ♪ ——. *O mein Land*. HAAS 78–79
1892a Laurencie, Lionel de la. Litterae. BORREN/90TH 105
1893 [Leip] Elsner, Wilhelm. Verneigung vor der Musik. LEIP 17–27
1894 ♪ Lenaerts, Willy. *Fantasia voor beiaard*. DENYN 91–96
1895 [Lipatti] Sacher, Paul. Dinu Lipatti. BRITTEN 165–170
1895a Liuzzi, Fernando. Litterae. BORREN/90TH 113
1896 [Lowell] Wager, Willis. Amy Lowell and Music. ENGEL 209–213
1897 [Ludwig] Handschin, Jacques. Friedrich Ludwig. HANDSCHIN 389–390; orig. in *Neue Zürcher Zeitung* 1941 (1930)
1898 [Lutosławski] Brennecke, Wilfried. Die *Trauermusik* von Witold Lutosławski. BLUME/F 60–73; also FEICHT 457–471
1899 ♪ Maasalo, Armas. *Störst är kärleken*. BÉEN 197
1899a [Mahler] Dorfmüller, Kurt. Gustav-Mahler-Documente in München. FÉDEROV 33–39
1900 —— Klemm, Eberhardt. Notizen zu Mahler. BESSELER 447–455
1901 —— Redlich, Hans F. Gustav Mahler's Last Symphonic Trilogy. ALBRECHT 246–250
1902 —— ——. Mahler's Enigmatic "Sixth." DEUTSCH/80TH 250–256
1903 —— Reich, Willi. Ein heiteres Dokument aus der wiener Mahler-Zeit. DEUTSCH/80TH 257–258
1904 —— Schönberg, Arnold. Aus der Rede Schönbergs über Gustav Mahler (1913). SCHÖNBERG/60TH 66–70
1905 —— ——. Gustav Mahler. SCHÖNBERG/75TH 60–82; orig. in his *Style and Idea* (New York 1950)
1906 —— Stein, Erwin. Mahler, Reger, Strauss und Schönberg. UNIVERSAL 63–78; Eng. transl. in his *Orpheus in New Guises* (London 1953)
—— See also no. 1650
1907 ♪ Maler, Wilhelm. Sonatine, 2 violins & viola. HAAS 82–86
1908 ♪ Malipiero, Gian-Francesco. *Tombeau de Claude Debussy, Hommage*. DEBUSSY suppl. 8–9
1909 ♪ Manén, Joan. [Piano piece] SEEBACH 124
1910 [Mariani] Barblan, Guglielmo. Angelo Mariani e la sua *scala esatonale*. EINSTEIN/C 171–174
1911 ♪ Markevitch, Igor. *Pour Ramuz*, voice & piano. RAMUZ 134–137
1912 ♪ Martinez, Praxedes. *Himno a la paz de Honduras*. CARÍAS 212–213
1912a [Marx, K.] Karkoschka, Erhard. Neue Methoden der musikalischen Analyse und einige Anwendungen auf spätere Instrumentalwerke von Karl Marx. MARX, K./70TH 57–67
1913 ♪ Marz, J. *Auftrag*. MÜLLER VON ASOW [256–258]
1914 ♪ Mayr, Hanns. Sonata, violin & piano. HAAS 87–88
1915 [Medtner] Ilyin, Ivan. Sonata

Form in Medtner. MEDTNER 180–188
1916 ♪ Mengelberg, Rudolf. *Dis al.* SCHEURLEER 207–210
1917 Menuhin, Yehudi. A Chivalrous Tradition. BRITTEN 74–77
1918 ♪ Messiaen, Olivier. *Pièce pour le tombeau de Paul Dukas.* DUKAS suppl. 23–24
1919 ♪ Metzl, Vladimir. *Premierenfieber, Quinten-Humoreske.* SEEBACH 124
1920 ♪ Michielson, L. P. J. *Improvisatie voor Dr. D. F. Scheurleer.* SCHEURLEER 211–212
1921 ♪ Milhaud, Darius. *Quatrain, hommage à Albert Roussel,* voice & piano. ROUSSEL suppl. 31–32
1922 ♪ Mohler, Philip. *Fantasiestück,* flute & piano. HAAS 89–98
1923 ♪ Mojsisovics, Roderich von. *Steirischer Künstler-Huldigungszug.* KIENZL 6–11
1924 [Moldenhauer] Nettl, Paul. Hans Moldenhauer, Pionier der Musikwissenschaft. OREL/70TH 133–137
1924a [Moniuszko] Rudziński, Witold. Pieśni Moniuszki we Francji [The Songs of Moniuszko in France] FEICHT 391–392
1925 ♪ Mraczek, J. G. *Fromm.* MÜLLER VON ASOW [259]
1926 ♪ Nees, Staf. *Klacht en troost over Jef Denyn.* DENYN 50–51
1927 [Nef] Handschin, Jacques. Karl Nef. HANDSCHIN 391–394
1928 [Nielsen] Winding-Sørensen, Dag. Carl Nielsen. SANDVIK 201–222
1929 ♪ Niemann, W. *Bilder aus dem Orient; Sultan.* MÜLLER VON ASOW [260–261]
1930 ♪ Olsen, Sparre. *Bondesong.* ØRJASAETER 150
1931 [Ørjasaeter] Olsen, Sparre. Tore Ørjasaeter som musikkritiker. ØRJASAETER 149–150
1932 ♪ Pepping, Ernst. *Glückwunsch.* SÖHNGEN 213–217
1933 [Pepping] Manicke, Dietrich. Gesetz und Freiheit; Gedanken zum Schaffen Ernst Peppings. MAUERSBERGER 53–59
1933a ♪ Perrachio, Luigi. *Danza.* DESDERI/70TH 111–114
1934 [Pfitzner] Schwarz, Werner. Die Bedeutung des Religiösen im musikdramatischen Schaffen Hans Pfitzners. MÜLLER-BLATTAU 95–111
——— See also no. 1798a
1935 [Philipp] Rahner, Hugo E. [Das Werk von Franz Philipp] PHILIPP 124–144
1936 ♪ Pierné, Gabriel. *Prélude sur le nom de Paul Dukas.* DUKAS suppl. 10–11
1936a Pirro, André. Litterae. BORREN/90TH 144
1936b ♪ Plavec, Josef. *Josefu B. Foerstrovi, Na slova F. X. Šaldy.* FOERSTER/90TH 30–34
1936c [Plavec] Hradil, F. M. Zamyšlení nad sborovým uměním Josefa Plavec. [Design in the Choral Works of Josef Plavec] PLAVEC/60TH 263–280
1936d —— Mikoda, Bořivoj. Instrumentální skladby Josefa Plavec. PLAVEC/60TH 307–324
1936e —— Mrázek, Miroslav. Plavcova kantáta *My, národ český a slovenský.* PLAVEC/60TH 281–293
1936f —— Mrkos, Zbyněk. O přátelství Josefa B. Foerstra a Josefa Plavec [Concerning the Friendship of Josef B. Foerster and Josef Plavec] PLAVEC/60TH 359–365
1936g —— Pražák, Přemysl. Propagátor a vykladač B. Smetany [Propagator and expounder of B. Smetana] PLAVEC/60TH 349–355
1936h —— Siebr, Rudolf. Plavcova kantáta *Nesmrtelná ves* (na pamět' obce Ležáky a jejich obyvatel) [Plavec's Cantata *Nesmrtelná ves* (in Memory of Ležáky and Its Inhabitants] PLAVEC/60TH 295–307
1936i —— Vrchotová-Pátová, Jarmila. Písňová tvorba [Plavec's Songs] PLAVEC/60TH 251–262
1937 ♪ Poulenc, Francis. *Pièce brève sur le nom d'Albert Roussel.* ROUSSEL suppl. 13–16
1937a Prunières, Henri. Litterae. BORREN/90TH 165
1938 [Puccini] Krohn, Ilmari. Puccini: *Butterfly.* SCHEURLEER 181–190
1939 ♪ Rauch, Joseph. *Abendgang.* HAAS 101–102
1940 ♪ ——. *Das Schicksal sprach.* HAAS 99–100
1941 ♪ Ravel, Maurice. *Sept pièces de piano sur le nom de Fauré,* no. 1: *Berceuse,* violin & piano. FAURÉ suppl. 7–10
1942 ♪ ——. *Tombeau de Claude Debussy,* duo, violin & violoncello. DEBUSSY suppl. 24–29
1943 ♪ ——. *Tripatos.* RAVEL suppl. 1–4
1944 [Ravel] Ackere, J. van. Aspecten

van het melos bij Ravel. MUEREN 157–165

1945 —— Sannemüller, Gerd. Ravels Stellung in der französischen Musik. ALBRECHT 251–256

—— See also nos. 1804, 1806

1945a [Reger] Andriessen, Willem. Max Reger. ANDRIESSEN, W. 109–111

1945b —— Barker, John Wesley. The Organ Works of Max Reger. BISHOP 56–73

1946 —— Denecke, Heinz Ludwig. Max Regers Sonatenform in ihrer Entwicklung. STEIN 26–32

1947 —— Friemann, Witold. Moje wspomnienia o Dr. Maksie Regerze [My Reminiscences of Dr. Max Reger] CHYBIŃSKI/50TH 183–187

1948 —— Güntzel, Ottomar. Das Max-Reger-Archiv in Meiningen, seine Geschichte und Bedeutung. REGER 85–90

1949 —— Joachim, Heinz. Max Reger. BOTE 44–50

1949a —— Lissa, Zofia. Max Regers Metamorphosen der "Berceuse" op. 83 von Frédéric Chopin. FÉDEROV 79–84

1949b —— Range, Heinz. Einige Urteile Max Regers über Komponisten seiner Generation aus unveröffentlichten Briefen der Münchener Jahre 1902–1905. ENGEL 290–297

1950 —— Stein, Fritz. Eine Max Reger-Erinnerung. SÖHNGEN 150–152

1951 —— ——. Max Reger und Karl Straube. STRAUBE 42–79

1952 —— Therstappen, Hans J. Über die Grundlagen der Form bei Max Reger. STEIN 71–80

1953 —— Wirth, Helmut. Max Reger et son oeuvre. MASSON II, 213–220

—— See also nos. 1530b, 1905

1954 ♪ Richter, P. *Errinnerung.* MÜLLER VON ASOW [262–263]

1955 [Riemann] Kahl, Willi. Der obscure Riemann; ein Brief F. Chrysanders. SCHIEDERMAIR/80TH 54–56

1956 —— Wolff, Hellmuth Christian. Hugo Riemann, der Begründer der systematischen Musikbetrachtung. SCHNEIDER/80TH 265–270

1957 ♪ Rodrigo, Joaquin. *Hommage à Paul Dukas.* DUKAS suppl. 15–19

1958 ♪ Röhrling, A. *Hymne.* MÜLLER VON ASOW [264–265]

1959 ♪ Roger-Ducasse, Jean J. *Sept pièces de piano sur le nom de Fauré,* no. 7. FAURÉ suppl. 33–47

1959a [Rogowski] Bristiger, Michał. L. M. Rogoskiego skale i idee muzyczne [The Scales and Musical Ideas of L. M. Rogowski] FEICHT 446–456

1960 [Romagnoli] Grande, Carlo del. Ettore Romagnoli, studioso di musica greca e compositore. ROMAGNOLI 79–82

1961 ♪ Ropartz, Joseph G. *A la mémoire de Paul Dukas.* DUKAS suppl. 12–14

1962 ♪ Rosenberg, Hilding. *Funderingar över en doktorsavhandling och synnerligen sekvens nr. 40* [*Meditations on a Doctoral Dissertation, Especially Sequence No. 40*] MOBERG 13–15

1963 ♪ Rottiers, Jef. *Preludium in F voor beiaard.* DENYN 86–87

1964 ♪ Roussel, Albert. *Tombeau de Claude Debussy. L'accueil des muses.* DEBUSSY suppl. 6–7

1965 ♪ ——. *Trio d'anches inachevé,* andante. ROUSSEL suppl. 1–4

1965a [Roussel] Linden, Albert van der. Deux interviews de compositeurs en 1908 (Albert Roussel & Vincent d'Indy). BORREN/75TH 242–244

1965b Sandberger, Adolf. Litterae. BORREN/90TH 203

1966 ♪ Satie, Erik. *Tombeau de Claude Debussy. Que me font ces vallons.* DEBUSSY suppl. 32

1967 ♪ Schaik, J. A. S. *Fons vitae eruditio possidentis.* SCHEURLEER 277–278

1968 ♪ Schaller, Paul. *Abend-Trunk.* HAAS 105–106

1969 ♪ ——. *Nacht am Flusse.* HAAS 103–104

1970 [Schenker] Federhofer, Helmut. Heinrich Schenker. HOBOKEN 63–72

1970a ♪ Schilling, Hans Ludwig. *Ricercare: Veni creator spiritus.* DESDERI/70TH 155–156

1971 ♪ Schillings, Max. *Albumblatt.* SEEBACH 138

1972 ♪ Schiske, Karl. *Allegro energico,* op. 32, no. 1. FISCHER/W 159–160

1973 [Schiske] Orel, Alfred. Zur Formbildung in der neuen Musik; das *Allegro energico,* op. 32, nr. 1, von Karl Schiske. FISCHER/W 149–160

1974 ♪ Schmalz, Oskar F. *Ehüejerbuebelied.* SCHMALZ 40–41

1975 ♪ ——. *Mis Schwyzerland.* SCHMALZ 62–63

1975a [Schmidt, F.] Wickes, Lewis. Franz Schmidt's Oratorio "The Book with Seven Seals." BISHOP 37–55

1976 ♪ Schmitt, Florent. *Sept pièces de piano sur le nom de Fauré,* no. 4. FAURÉ suppl. 17–25

1977 ♪——. *Tombeau de Claude Debussy. Et Pan, au fond des blés lunaires, s'accouda.* DEBUSSY suppl. 14–21
1978 ♪——. *Tombeau de Paul Dukas.* DUKAS suppl. 1–6
1979 ♪Schönberg, Arnold. Birthday Canons for 3 Voices. ENGEL 200–205
1980 ——. Gesinnung oder Erkenntnis? UNIVERSAL 21–30
1980a [Schönberg] Kirchmeyer, Helmut. Die zeitgeschichtliche Symbolik des Pierrot Lunaire. BOSSE/50TH 90–112
1980b —— Newlin, Dika. C. P. E. Bach and Arnold Schoenberg; a Comparison. SACHS/C 300–306
1980c —— Perle, George. Pierrot Lunaire. SACHS/C 307–312
1981 —— Pfannkuch, Wilhelm. Zu Thematik und Form in Schönbergs Streichsextett. BLUME/F 258–271
—— See also nos. 1788, 1903, 1905, 2021
1982 ♪Schubert, Heinz, *Tadiw-upanishad/Alles ist vergangen.* HAAS 107–120
1983 ♪Schuman, William. *Three-Score Set*, piano. ENGEL 206–208
1984 [Schweitzer] Davison, Archibald T. The Transcendentalism of Albert Schweitzer. SCHWEITZER/70TH 199–211
1984a —— Morel, Fritz. Albert Schweitzer als Musiker. SCHWEITZER/85TH 77–90
1985 ——Schrade, Leo. Schweitzer's Aesthetics, an Interpretation of Bach. SCHWEITZER/70TH 173–195
1986 —— Weinrich, Carl. Albert Schweitzer's Contribution to Organ Building. SCHWEITZER/70TH 215–225
1986a [Shaw, G. B.] Dent, Edward J. Corno di Bassetto. SHAW 122–130
1986b [Sibelius] Andersson, Otto. Sibelius och Kajanus. ANDERSSON, O./85TH 78–86; orig. in *Hufvudstadsbladet* (Dec. 8, 1956 & Jan. 3, 1957)
1986c —— ——. Jean Sibelius och Svenska teatern. ANDERSSON, O./85TH 87–100; orig. in *Hufvudstadsbladet* (Dec. 9, 1955)
1986d —— ——. Dring Sibelius' fjärde symfoni. ANDERSSON, O./85TH 101–110; orig. in *Tidning för Musik* (1910/1911) 171–173
1987 ♪Skorzeny, F. *Im Volkston.* MÜLLER VON ASOW [266–267]
1988 ♪Söhner, Leo. *Sängerspruch.* HAAS 121–123
1989 [Sonneck] Engel, Carl. O. G. Sonneck, ein Charakterbild. ADLER 216–220
1990 [Spitteler] Refardt, Edgar. Musik zu Spitteler. REFARDT 140–142; orig. in *Der kleine Bund* 18 (1938)
1991 ♪Steccanella, Manlio. *Inno a gorizia.* BATTISTI 28–29
1992 [Stein] Harewood, The Earl of. In Memoriam. Erwin Stein 1885–1958. BRITTEN 160–164
1993 [Straube] Hasse, Karl. Karl Straube als Orgelkünstler. STRAUBE 153–194
—— See also no. 1951
1993a Strauss, Richard. Mein geliebter Bubi. STRAUSS, F. 7–10
1994 ♪——. *Tüchtigen stellt das schnelle Glück.* SEEBACH 160
1995 [Strauss, R.] Abert, Anna Amalie. Stefan Zweigs Bedeutung für das Alterswerk von Richard Strauss. BLUME/F 7–15
1995a —— Bella, Ján Levoslav. Korrespondence [with Ludevít Procházka and Richard Strauss] BELLA/80TH 118–154
1996 —— Brennecke, Wilfried. Die Metamorphosen-Werke von Richard Strauss und Paul Hindemith. ALBRECHT 268–284
1997 —— Ehlers, Paul, Vom dramatischen Strauss. SEIDL/AR 180–198
1997a —— Kergl, Max. Richard Strauss am Dirigentenpult. STRAUSS, F. 45–46
1997b —— Melichar, Alois. Einige Bemerkungen über den Dirigenten Richard Strauss. STRAUSS, F. 55–63
1998 —— Mennicke, Carl. Über Richard Strauss' *Elektra.* RIEMANN 503–524
1999 —— Müller von Asow, Erich H. Joseph Gregor in seinen Beziehungen zu Richard Strauss. GREGOR 228–232
1999a —— Ott, Alfons. Couperin als Quelle für Richard Strauss. FÉDEROV 99–103
1999b —— ——. Documenta musicae domesticae Straussiana. STRAUSS, F. 67–81
1999c —— Razumovsky, Andreas. Über den Text des *Rosenkavalier.* ADORNO/60TH 225–240
1999d —— Roth, Ernst. Das Königliche in der Musik von Richard Strauss. STRAUSS, F. 91–94
2000 —— Schmieder, Wolfgang. 57 unveröffentlichte Briefe und Karten von Richard Strauss in der Stadt- und Uni-

versitätsbibliothek, Frankfurt/Main. OSTHOFF 163–179

2000a —— Schuh, Willi. Der Sohn im Wort und in der Musik des Vaters. STRAUSS, F. 103–114

2000b —— Trenkler, Ernst. Das Erlebnis Richard Strauss. STRAUSS, F. 127–133

2000c —— Trenner, Franz. Richard Strauss und seine Vaterstadt. STRAUSS, F. 137–149

2000d —— Wilhelm, Kurt. Sinfonia domestica. STRAUSS, F. 153–158

—— See also nos. 1838, 1850, 1905

2001 ♪ Stravinsky, Igor. *Petit Ramusianum harmonique.* RAMUZ 13–15

2002 [Stravinsky] Engel, Hans. Der Komponist als Ästhetiker: Strawinsky. ALBRECHT 257–267

2003 —— Handschin, Jacques. Was Stravinsky kann und was er nicht kann. HANDSCHIN 246–248; orig. in *Theater-Zeitung des Stadttheaters Basel* 36/10 (1951/1952)

2003a —— Martinotti, Sergio. Presenza dell'ultimo Stravinski. BARBLAN/60TH 166–178

2004 —— Mellers, Wilfred. Stravinsky's *Oedipus* as 20th-Century Hero. STRAVINSKY/80TH 300–312

2005 —— Morton, Lawrence. Stravinsky and Tchaikovsky: *Le Baiser de la fée.* STRAVINSKY/80TH 313–326

2006 —— Nelson, Robert U. Stravinsky's Concept of Variations. STRAVINSKY/80TH 327–339

—— See also no. 1833

2007 ♪ Strom, Kurt. *Rondo scherzando,* viola & piano. HASS 124–129

2008 ♪ Stuten, Jan. *Faust; Prolog im Himmel.* STUTEN 17–19

2008a [Suchoně] Sokolová, Véra. Ke zrodu slovenské národní opery. PLAVEC/60TH 237–248

2009 [Szymanowski] Golachowski, Stanislaw. Niedokończony koncert fortepianowy Karola Szymanowskiego [An Unfinished Piano Concerto of Karol Szymanowski] CHYBIŃSKI/70TH 263–274

2009a —— Helman, Zofia. Nieznana pieśń Karola Szymanowskiego [Unknown Songs of Karol Szymanowski] FEICHT 439–445

2010 —— Lissa, Zofia. Szymanowski und die Romantik. KODÁLY/80TH 223–242

2011 ♪ Tansman, Alexander. *Hommage à Albert Roussel. Berceuse.* ROUSSEL suppl. 17–19

2011a Tessier, André. Litterae. BORREN/90TH 204

2011b ♪ Thyrestam, Gunnar. *Larghetto.* DESDERI/70TH 181–182

2012 ♪ Unger, H. *Kukuks Tod.* MÜLLER VON ASOW [268–269]

2013 ♪ ——. *Menuett.* HASS 130–131

2013a ♪ Vomáčka, Boleslav. *Zdravice. Na slova Josefa Chaloupky.* FOERSTER/90TH 35

2013b ♪ Vycpálek, Ladislav. *Mistru J. B. Foerstrovi.* FOERSTER/90TH 36

2014 ♪ Wagenaar, Johan. *Het vinnich stralen van de son.* SCHEURLEER 367–368

2015 [Wagner, P.] Handschin, Jacques. Peter Wagner. HANDSCHIN 395–397; orig. in *Neue Zürcher Zeitung* 2021 (1931)

2015a [Webern] Deppert, Heinrich. Rhythmische Reihentechnik in Weberns *Orchestervariationen* opus 30. MARX, K./70TH 84–93

2016 —— Eimert, Herbert. Interval Proportions. WEBERN/R 93–99

2017 —— Jone, Hildegard. A Cantata. WEBERN/R 7–8

2018 —— Klammer, Armin. Webern's Piano Variations, op. 27, 3rd movement. WEBERN/R 81–92

2019 —— Kolneder, Walter. Klangtechnik und Motivbildung bei Webern. MÜLLER-BLATTAU 27–50

2020 —— Metzger, Heinz-Klaus. Analysis of the Sacred Song, op. 15, no. 4. WEBERN/R 75–80

2021 —— ——. Webern and Schönberg. WEBERN/R 42–45

2022 —— Pousseur, Henri. Webern's Organic Chromaticism. WEBERN/R 51–60

2023 —— Spinner, Leopold. Analysis of a Period. WEBERN/R 46–50

2024 —— Stockhausen, Karlheinz. Structure and Experiential Time. WEBERN/R 64–74

2025 ♪ Wenzel, Eberhard. *Vespera iam venit.* SÖHNGEN 133–136

2025a ♪ Werner, Fritz. *Drei kleine Spruchmotteten.* MÜNNICH/70TH [26–31]

2025b ♪ ——. *Musikalische Haus- und Lebensregelns.* MÜNNICH/80THM 143–149

2025c ♪ ——. *Sieh nicht was andre tun.* MÜNNICH/80THM 150–152

2026 ♪ Wolpert, F. A. *Lied eines theokritischen Ziegenhirten.* MÜLLER VON ASOW [270–272]

2026a [Zich] Burjanek, Josef. Estetika a kritika moderní opery v článcích

Otakara Zicha ve vlčkově *Osvětě* 1912–1916 [Aesthetics and the Criticism of Modern Opera in the Articles of Otakar Zich which Appeared in *Osvěta*, 1912–1916] RACEK/60TH 45–53, summary in German

2027 ♪Zöllner, Heinrich. *Strophenliedlein.* SEEBACH 172

ETHNOMUSICOLOGY: GENERAL

See also nos. 83a, 101, 566, 571, 827a, 1679, 2474, 2491, 2496–2498, 2547, 2570, 2590, 2598, 2599, 2602, 2604

2027a Andersson, Otto. Upprepning och parallellism [revised] ANDERSSON, O./85TH 170–202; orig. in *Budklaven* 20 (1941) 113–150

2027b Arnberg, Matts. Inspelningar i folkmusikforskningens tjänst. SALÉN/70TH 29–45

2028 Belaiev, Victor M. A népi harmóniarendszer [The System of Folk Harmony] KODÁLY/70TH 75–86

2029 Bimberg, Siegfried. Über die Bedeutung der Volksmusik für die Entwicklung der Musikkultur. HOFMEISTER 58–61

2030 Brailoiu, Constantin. Un Problème de tonalité: la métabole pentatonique. MASSON I, 63–75

2031 Chailley, Jacques. Incidences pédagogiques des recherches d'ethnologie musicale. KODÁLY/80TH 65–71

2031a Collaer, Paul. Esprit et formes des cultures musicales archaïques. BORREN/90TH 35–47

2032 Danckert, Werner. A félhangnélküli pentatónia eredete/ Der Ursprung der halbtonlosen Pentatonik. KODÁLY/60TH 9–18

2033 Graf, Walter. Neue Möglichkeiten, neue Aufgaben der vergleichenden Musikwissenschaft. SCHENK 231–245

2034 Groven, Eivind. Det natursvarande i musikk-kjensla vår. [The Natural Variety in our Musical Sensibility] SANDVIK 32–38

2034a Hegele, Günter. Kritik an Schlagern? BOSSE/50TH 34–43

2034b Karpeles, Maud. The International Folk Music Council. ALMEIDA 293–297

2035 Kertész, Gyula. A népdal gépi felvétele. [The Recording of Folksong] KODÁLY/70TH 659–662

2036 Keyser, P. de. Enkele losse beschouwingen over volksliedkunde. MUEREN 85–92

2036a Klusen, Ernst. Über gregorianisches Melodiengut im rheinischen Volkslied. FELLERER/60THS 103–118

2037 Kodály, Zoltán. Eine Vorbedingung der vergleichenden Liedforschung. BARTÓK/S 7–8

2038 Krohn, Ilmari. Psalmengesang in der Volkssprache. WAGNER 118–123

2039 Kunst, Jaap. Fragment of an Essay on *Music and Sociology*. BARTÓK/S 143–145

2039a ——. Fragments from Diaries Written During a Lecture Tour in the New World (October 4, 1955–March 3, 1956) and a Trip to Australia (May 15–August 28, 1959). SACHS/C 328–342

2040 Lach, Robert. Vergleichende Sprach- und Musikwissenschaft. KRETSCHMAR 128–139

2041 Molnár, Antal. A népzenekutatás kérdéseiből [On the Problems of Folkmusic Research] KODÁLY/70TH 331–338

2042 Meyers, Charles S. The Ethnological Study of Music. TYLOR 235–253

2043 Nef, Karl. Zur Geschichte des Volksliedinteresses. KRETZSCHMAR 105–109

2043a Nygard, Holger Olof. Ballad, Folkevise, Chanson Populaire. HUDSON 39–65

2044 Rajeczky, Benjámin. Népdaltörténet és gregorián-kutatás/Storia del canto gregoriano e le ricerche sul canto popolare. KODÁLY/60TH 308–312

2045 Riemann, Ludwig. Die Beziehungen der heutigen Volksmusik zur Kunstmusik. LILIENCRON 203–214

2046 Schaeffner, André. Primitív, exotikus zene és modern nyugateurópai muzsika/Musique primitive ou exotique et musique moderne d'Occident. KODÁLY/60TH 213–218

2047 Schneider, Marius. Pitágoras en la herreria. ORTIZ III, 1371–1373

2048 ——. Pythagoras in der Schmiede. KAHL 126–129 (same as no. 2047)

2049 Schurter, Hans. Volk und klassische Musik. WARTENWEILER 119–120

2049a Seeger, Charles. The Folkness of the Non-folk vs. the Non-folkness of the Folk. BOTKIN/65TH 1–9

2049b Stockmann, Doris. Hörbild und Schallbild als Mittel musikethnologischer Dokumentation. WIORA/60TH 503–511

2050 Szabolcsi, Bence. A primitív dallamosság; a hanglejtéstől az ötfokúságig/ Primitive Melodik; vom Tonfall zur Pentatonie. KODÁLY/60TH 19–31
2051 Vavrinecz, Béla. Aszimmetrikus ritmusok. KODÁLY/70TH 567–592
2052 Wiora, Walter. Musikgeschichte und Urgeschichte. MOBERG 375–396
2053 ——. Zwischen Einstimmigkeit und Mehrstimmigkeit. SCHNEIDER/80TH 319–334

ETHNOMUSICOLOGY: AFRICA

See also nos. 2598, 2604

2053a Brandel, Rose. Polyphony in African Music. SACHS/C 26–41
2054 Dahle, P. Blessing. Eine Siegeshymne der Ama-Zulu; Entstehung, Text und Töne des Sandlwana Liedes. MEINHOF 174–195
2055 Günther, Robert. Die Gutuwu der Mbarakwengo-Buschmänner. FELLERER/60TH 193–199
2056 Gutmann, Bruno. Grusslieder der Wadschagga. MEINHOF 228–232
2057 Heinitz, Wilhelm. Analyse eines abessinischen Harfendliedes. MEINHOF 263–274
2058 Kappe, Gustav. Tanz und Trommel der Neger. SCHAUINSLAND 64–67
2059 Laman, K. E. The Musical Tone of the Teke Language. MEINHOF 118–124
2060 Nuez Caballero, Sebastián de la. Instrumentos musicales populares en las Islas Canarias. ORTIZ II, 1145–1162
2061 Olbrechts, Frans M. De studie van de inheemse muziek van Belgisch-Congo. MUEREN 147–150
2062 Pepper, H. Notes sur une sanza d'Afrique Equatoriale ORTIZ II, 1191–1201
2063 Schneider, Marius. Egyiptomi parasztdalok; dallamtipológiai tanulmány/Lieder ägyptischer Bauern; eine melodietypologische Untersuchung. KODÁLY/60TH 154–183
2064 Tiling, Maria v. Frauen- und Kinderlieder der Suaheli. MEINHOF 288–300
2064a Wachsmann, Klaus P. Pen-equidistance and Accurate Pitch: a Problem from the Source of the Nile. WIORA/60TH 583–592

ETHNOMUSICOLOGY: AMERICA, NORTH & SOUTH

See also nos. 2570, 2590, 2602, 2604

2065 Abraham, O., & Erich M. von Hornbostel. Phonographierte Indianermelodien aus British Columbia. BOAS 447–474
2066 Barbeau, Marius. *Trois beaux canards*, 92 versions canadiennes. BARBEAU 97–138
2067 Brassard, François. Recordeurs de chansons. BARBEAU 191–202
2067a Bronson, Bertrand H. Folk Song in the United States, 1910–1960. Reflections from a Student's Corner. SEEMAN/75TH 1–11
2068 Ceballos Novelo, Roque C. Los Instrumentos musicales su origen legendario. GAMIO 317–320
2069 Collaer, Paul. Musique caraïbe et maya. BARTÓK/S 125–142
2069a Corrêa de Azevedo, Luis-Heitor. As modinhas de Joachim Manuel. ALMEIDA 609–621
2070 Courlander, Harold. Musical Instruments of Haiti. EINSTEIN 371–383
2071 Densmore, Frances. Music in its Relation to the Religious Thought of the Teton Sioux. HOLMES 67–79
2072 Dumézil, Georges. De l'opérette au mythe; le père et la mère Aigles et le cheminement de l'eau. LEVY 123–134
2072a Fowke, Edith. A Sampling of Bawdy Ballads from Ontario. BOTKIN/65TH 45–61
2072b Goldstein, Kenneth S. The Ballad Scholar and the Longplaying Record. BOTKIN/65TH 35–44
2073 Hand, Wayland D. Wo sind *Die Strassen von Laredo?* Die Entwicklungsgeschichte einer amerikanischen Cowboy Ballade. PEUCKERT 144–161
2073a Haywood, Charles. Negro Minstrelsy and Shakespearean Burlesque. BOTKIN/65TH 77–92
2073b Kennedy, Philip Houston. Present Status of Ballad Collecting and Geographical Ballad Distributions in North Carolina. HUDSON 66–82
2074 Lach, Robert. Die musikalischen Konstruktionsprinzipien der altmexikanischen Tempelgesänge. WOLF 88–96
2074a Leach, MacEdward. John Henry. BOTKIN/65TH 93–106
2074b McCulloh, Judith. Some Child

Ballads on Hillbilly Records. BOTKIN/65TH 107–129
2075 Mendoza, Vicente T. Algo del folklore negro en Mexico. ORTIZ II, 1095–1111
2076 ——. La Canción de aliento entrecortado en México y en América es de origen hispano. ANGLÉS II, 517–535
2076a Nettl, Bruno. Blackfoot Music in Browning, 1965, Functions and Attitudes. WIORA/60TH 593–598
2077 Ortiz Oderigo, Néstor R. El *Calypso,* expressión musical de los negros de Trinidad. ORTIZ II, 1165–1172
2077a Patterson, Daniel W. Inspiration and Authority in the Development of the Shaker Spiritual. HUDSON 111–120
2077b Periera Salas, Eugenio. Danzas y cantos populares de la *Patria Vieja.* LENZ 58–76
2077c Rhodes, Willard. Folk Music, Old and New. BOTKIN 11–19
2077d Ribiera, Maria de Lourdes Borges. O baile dos congos. ALMEIDA 639–692
2077e Rosemberg, Tobias. Música del Aconquija. ALMEIDA 91–96
2077f Stekert, Ellen. Cents and Nonsense in the Urban Folksong Movement, 1930–1966. BOTKIN/65TH 153–168

ETHNOMUSICOLOGY: ASIA & OCEANIA

See also no. 2499

2078 Arsunar, Ferruh. Kisázsiai török pentaton dallamok/Des mélodies pentatones des Turcs d'Asie Mineure. KODÁLY/60TH 322–328
2079 Bake, Arnold. A Javanese Musical Puzzle. SAMUEL 24–26
2080 Bhaduri, M. B. Hindu Influence on Munda Songs. ROY 256–260
2080a Bose, Fritz. Rabindranath Tagore und die moderne indische Musik. WIORA/60TH 565–570
2080b Christensen, Dieter. Zur Mehrstimmigkeit in kurdischen Wechselgesängen. WIORA/60TH 571–577
2081 Collaer, Paul. La Musique des Protomalais. KODÁLY/80TH 71–88
2081a Correia Afonso, Francisco. A origem e evolução do "Mandó." LEITE I, 446–457
2081b Daniélou, Alain. Problèmes de terminologie dans l'interprétation des textes sanskrits sur la musique. WIORA/60TH 561–564
2082 Eckardt, Hans. Zur Frage und Bedeutung der Rangô. BESSELER 35–42
2082a Ellis, Catherine J. Aboriginal Songs of South Australia. BISHOP 137–190
2082a1 Emsheimer, Ernst. Ein giljakisches Schallgerät. WIORA/60TH 599–608
2082b ——. Maultrommeln in Sibirien und Zentralasien. EMSHEIMER/60TH 13–27; orig. in *Ethnos* 6 (1941) 109–127
2082c ——. Mongolische Musik. EMSHEIMER/60TH 93–99; orig. in *MGG* 9 (1961) 460–466
2082d ——. Schamanentrommel und Trommelbaum. EMSHEIMER/60TH 50–61; orig. in *Ethnos* 11 (1946) 166–181
2082e ——. Eine sibirische Parallele zur lappischen Zaubertrommel? EMSHEIMER/60TH 68–75; orig. in *Ethnos* 13 (1948) 17–26
2082f ——. Singing Contests in Central Asia. EMSHEIMER/60TH 86–93; orig. in *IFMC Journal* 8 (1956) 26–29
2083 Farmer, Henry G. Zenei kölcsönhatások Kelet- és Kozépázsia között/Wechselwirkungen mittel- und ostasiatischer Musik. KODÁLY/60TH 32–42
2084 Fujii, Seishin. A buddhizmus és a zene/Der Buddhismus und die Musik. KODÁLY/60TH 139–142
2084a Fukushima, Kazuo. No-Theater und japanische Musik. STEINECKE 103–111
2085 Gerson-Kiwi, Edith. Musiker des Orients, ihr Wesen und Werdegang. KODÁLY/80TH 125–132
2085a ——. Women's Songs from the Yemen; Their Tonal Structure and Form. SACHS/C 97–103
2086 Graf, Walter. Zur Ausführung der lamaistischen Gesangsnotation. KODÁLY/80TH 133–147
2086a ——. Zur gesanglichen Stimmgebung der Ainu. WIORA/60TH 529–535
2087 Handschin, Jacques. Indische Musik. HANDSCHIN 306–309; orig. in *Neue Zürcher Zeitung* 2040 (1932)
2088 Holst, Imogen. Indian Music. BRITTEN 104–110
2089 Hurgronje, C. S. Een arabisch minnelied met luitbegleiding. MENGELBERG 141–143
2089a Kaufmann, Walter. Folksongs of the Gond and Baiga. EINSTEIN 280–288
2090 Kishibe, Shigeo. A Chinese

Painting of the T'ang Court Women's Orchestra. SACHS/C 104–117
2090a Kuttner, Fritz A. Zur Entwicklung des Musikbegriffes in Chinas Frühgeschichte. WIORA/60TH 536–544
2091 Lach, Robert. Orientalistik und vergleichende Musikwissenschaft. KARABACEK 155–193
2092 Land, J. P. N. Essais de notation musicale chez les Arabes et les Persans. LEEMANS 315–316
2092a Mabuchi, Usaburo. Ein japanisches Kinderlied. WIORA/60TH 552–560
2093 Marçais, Georges. Les Figures d'hommes et de bêtes dans les bois sculptés d'époque fâtimite conservés au Musée Arabe du Caire; Etude d'iconographie musulmane. MASPERO III, 241–257
2094 Müller, F. W. K. *Ikkaku sennin*, eine mittelalterliche japanische Oper, transkribiert und übersetzt . . . nebst einem Exkurs zur Einhornsage. BASTIAN 515–537
2095 Meyers, Charles S. The Beginnings of Music. RIDGEWAY 560–582
2095a Picken, Lawrence. Central Asian Tunes in the Gagaku Tradition. WIORA/60TH 545–551
2096 ——. Twelve Ritual Melodies of the T'ang Dynasty. BARTÓK/S 147–173
2096a Purohit-Roy, Trina. Zur Improvisation indischer Ragas. SCHMIDT-GÖRG/70TH 283–295
2097 Ránki, György. Indokínái dallamok [Indochinese Melodies] KODÁLY/70TH 413–422
2098 Roy, Trina. Outlines of Tagore's Music. SCHMIDT-GÖRG 235–266
2099 Schermann, L. Musizierende Genien in der religiösen Kunst des birmanischen Buddhismus. HIRTH 345–353
2099a Schneider, Marius. Ein anamitisches Wiegenlied. Ein Beitrag zum Verhältnis von Musik und Sprache. MÜLLER-BLATTAU/70TH 278–281
2100 Tegethoff, Wilhelm. *Lili Rabaulenses*. FELLERER 73–104
2101 Twitchett, D. C. & A. H. Christie. A Medieval Burmese Orchestra. WALEY 176–195
2102 Wang, Kwang-Chi. Musikalische Beziehungen zwischen China und dem Westen im Laufe der Jahrtausende. KAHLE 217–224
2103 Wellesz, Egon. Die orientalische Musik im Rahmen der musikgeschichtlichen Forschung. KRETZSCHMAR 172–174
2104 Wolff, Hellmuth Christian. Rabindranath Tagore und die Musik. FELLERER/60TH 590–593
2105 Yuen Ren Chao. Tone, Intonation, Singsong, Chanting, Recitative, Tonal Composition and Atonal Composition in Chinese. JAKOBSON 52–59

ETHNOMUSICOLOGY: EUROPE (GENERAL)

See also nos. 460, 464, 884, 1383, 2548d

2105a Anderluh, Anton. Volkslied und Volksmusik in der Gegenwart. MAIER/75TH 39–49
2105a[1] Andersson, Otto. Några särdrag i rimamelodierna. ANDERSSON, O./85TH 283–290; orig. in STRÖMBACK 130–138
2105a[2] ——. Västsibirisk ringsang och nordisk sångdans. ANDERSSON, O./85TH 147–169; orig. in *Budklaven* 16 (1937) 37–64
2105a[3] Bachmann, Werner. Die Verbreitung des Quintierens im europäischen Volksgesang des späten Mittelalters. SCHNEIDER/80TH 25–29
2105b Bartók, Béla. Népdalkutatás keleteurópában. KODÁLY/70TH 73–74
2105b[1] Brednich, Rolf Wilhelm. Die Legende vom Elternmörder in Volkserzählung und Volksballade. SEEMAN/75TH 116–143
2105b[2] Hoerburger, Felix. Gleichbleibende Zeilenschlüsse als formbildendes Prinzip in der instrumentalen Volksmusik. STÄBLEIN/70TH 101–108
2105c Maróthy, János. Az európai nepdal születése. KODÁLY/75TH 503–626
2105d Ortutay, Gyula. Az "europai" ballada kérdéséhez. KODÁLY/70TH 125–132
2105d[1] Seeman, Erich. Ein Balladenmotiv auf Wanderung. Studie zur Technik der europäischen Volksballade. MÜLLER-BLATTAU/70TH 304–311
2105d[2] Stęszewski, Jan. Die Apokope, eine Eigentümlichkeit im Volksliedvortrag. WIORA/60TH 641–647
2105d[3] Suppan, Wolfgang. Die Beachtung von "Original" und "Singmanier" im deutschsprachigen Volkslied. SEEMAN/75TH 12–30
2105e ——. Bi- bis tetrachordische

Tonreihen im Volkslied deutscher Sprachinseln Süd—und Osteuropas. KODÁLY/80TH 329–356
2105e[1] Vargyas, Lajos. Totenklage und Vorgeschichte der Ungarn. WIORA/60TH 623–627

ETHNOMUSICOLOGY: EUROPE (INDIVIDUAL COUNTRIES)

See also nos. 460, 464, 884, 1383

2105e[2] [Austria] Anderluh, Anton. Das Tanzlied und die Tanzmelodie im Volkslied, mit besonderer Berücksichtigung des Kärntnerliedes. MAIER/75TH 79–90
2106 —— Commenda, Hans. Aus dem Notenbüchl vom Urähnl; Volksmusik aus Bad Ischl. ZODER 8–15
2107 —— Holaubek-Lawatsch, Gundl, & Ernst L. Uray. Hochzeitslieder aus der Weststeiermark. ZODER 54–60
2107a —— Horak, Karl. Die Mazurka als österreichischer Volkstanz. MAIER/75TH 95–115
2108 —— ——. Volkstänze aus Unken im Lande Salzburg. ZODER 61–72
2109 —— Kirnbauer, Franz. Bergmannsbrauchtum und Bergmannslied in Kärnten. ANDERLUH 93–100
2110 — Klier, Karl M. Altösterreichische Brauchtumslieder. ANDERLUH 67–92
2111 —— ——. Eine Volksliedlehrstunde in Eisenstadt. ZODER 73–78
2112 —— Koschier, Franz. Die gailtaler Burschenschaft und ihr Lindentanz. ZODER 79–87
2113 —— ——. Das heiligenbluter Sternsingen. ANDERLUH 113–125
2113a —— ——. Kärntner Hochzeitstänze. MAIER/75TH 116–136
2114 —— Kotek, Georg. Das bäuerliche Volksliedsingen der Ravag in Payerbach 1935. ZODER 88–101
2115 —— ——. Ein Volksliedfund aus Oberkärnten. ANDERLUH 49–53
2116 —— Kretzenbacher, Leopold. Zur *Rabenmutter*-Ballade bei Deutschen und Slowenen in Innerösterreich. ZODER 102–112
2116a —— Kumer, Zmaga. Das gottscheer Volkslied vom warnenden Vogel und seine slovenische Vorlage. SEEMAN/75TH 52–62
2117 ——Maier, Roman. Drei Kärntnerlieder. ANDERLUH 34–37
2118 —— Maierbrugger, Matthias. Kirchtag in Kaning. ANDERLUH 101–106
2118a —— Mittergradnegger, Günther. Die kärntner Lehrer-Quintette und ihre Lieder. MAIER/75TH 50–58
2119 —— Moser, Oskar. Das gailtaler Dreikönigsingen. ZODER 113–132
2120 —— ——. Die kärntner Sternsingbräuche; Beiträge zur Erforschung ihrer Vergangenheit und Gegenwart. ANDERLUH 126–164
2120a —— ——. Von Tanzburschen und Tanzschaffen. Einige Beiträge zur Geschichte der Tanzsitten und des Volkstanzes in Kärnten. MAIER/75TH 137–172
2120b —— Petrie, Bertl. Vazierende Musikanten. MAIER/75TH 59–69
2121 —— Robitsch, Hans. Neues von den brücker Almpfeiferln. ZODER 149–153
2121a —— Schmidt, Leopold. Einige Welser Flugblattlieder. SEEMAN/75TH 95–103
2122 —— ——. Das Elkorn-Singen in Lichtenfels; ein angebliches Zeugnis für das mittelalterliche Brauchtumslied in Niederösterreich. ZODER 168–174
2123 —— Schmiedl, Hausa. Heiligenbluter Sternsingerlieder. ANDERLUH 107–112
2124 —— Seemann, Erich. Entführung unterm Tanze, eine unveröffentlichte Gottscheer Ballade. ZODER 175–184
2125 —— Wolfram, Richard. Vom Singen in der Gottschee. ZODER 194–203
2125a —— Zenker-Starzacher. Volkstanz Ballade-Märchen. MAIER/75TH 33–38
2125b —— Zoder, Raimund. Alte Volkstanzmelodien aus Kärnten. MAIER/75TH 91–94
2126 —— ——. Eine unbekannte Kärntnerlieder-Sammlung aus dem Jahre 1871. ANDERLUH 38–48
2127 [Bulgaria] Katzarova-Koukoudova, Raïna. Bulgarische Tänze und Tanzrhythmen. MÜLLER VON ASOW 78–99
2128 —— ——. Három bolgár nemzedék népdalénekesnői/Trois générations de chanteuses bulgares. KODÁLY/60TH 235–244
2129 —— ——. Phénomènes polyphoniques dans la musique populaire bulgare. KODÁLY/80TH 161–172
2130 —— ——. Verbreitung und Varianten eines bulgarischen Volkstanzes. BARTÓK/S 69–87

2130a [Czechoslovakia] Mátl, Josef. Skrifácká hudba na Horácku jako pozustatek hudby gotické. [Bowed music from the Horácko region as surviving Gothic music] PLAVEC/60TH 105–118
2130b —— Vetterl, Karel. Zur Klassifikation und Systematisierung der Volksweisen im westlichen Karpatenraum. WIORA/60TH 633–640
2130c —— Vysloužil, Jiří. Zu den Ethnomusikologischen Aspekten beim Studium der tschechischen Musikgeschichte. ŠTĚDROŇ/60TH 137–150, summary in Czech at end of article
2130d [Denmark] Andersson, Otto. Upprepningsstrofen [revised] ANDERSSON, O./85TH 203–260; orig. in *Budklaven* 29 (1950)
2130e —— Dal, Erik. Ahasverus in Dänemark. Volksbuch, Volkslieder und Verwandtes. SEEMAN/75TH 144–170
2131 —— Nielsen, H. Grüner. Nogle samsøske folkemelodier. KRISTENSEN 140–146
2132 [England] Bayard, Samuel P. A Miscellany of Tune Notes. THOMPSON 151–176
2133 —— Karpeles, Maud. Cecil Sharp, Collector of English Folk Music. BARTÓK/S 445–452
2133a [Finland] Adolfsson, Alfhild. En nyländsk rövarhövding i folkminne och folkdikt. NIKANDER 165–181
2133b —— Andersson, Otto. "Du gamla, du fria" i Finland. ANDERSSON, O./85TH 311–325; orig. in SALÉN 70TH 9–28
2133c —— ——. Framförandet av Kalevalarunorna [revised] ANDERSSON, O./85TH 361–372; orig. in *Budklaven* 15 (1936) 65–80
2133d —— ——. Kalevalameter-fornyrdislag. ANDERSSON, O./85TH 347–360; orig. in *Budklaven* 16 (1937) 84–100
2133e —— Bose, Fritz. Typen der Volksmusik in Karelian. Ein Reisebericht. SEIFFERT/70THA 96–118
2134 ——Danckert, Werner. Melodiestile der finnisch-ugrischen Hirtenvölker. BARTÓK/S 175–183
2134a —— Krohn, Ilmari. Melodien der Permier. WICHMANN 89–95
2134b —— Krohn, Kaarle. Zaubermacht des Gesanges, statistisch-geographische Untersuchung. WICHMANN 96–108
2135 —— Kuusisto, Taneli. Kansansävelmätoisintojen osoittaminen säkeittäisen vertailun avulla [Determining Folksong Variants by a Comparison of Individual Verses] KROHN 91–107, German summary v
—— See also nos. 2584, 2585
2136 [France] Vargyas, Lajos. Les Analogies hongroises avec les chants *Guillanneu.* KODÁLY/80TH 367–378
2137 —— Wallon, Simone. La Chanson *Sur le pont d'Avignon* au XVIe et au XVIIe siècle. MASSON I, 185–192
2138 [Germany] Bachmann, Werner. Der *Zupfgeigenhansl;* zur Entstehung eines musikalischen Volksbuches. HOFMEISTER 68–74
2139 —— Becker, Albert. Bänkelsang in der Pfalz am Rhein. MEIER/70TH 16–24
2140 —— Böhm, Max. Volksmusikalische Erinnerungen an ein oberfränkisches Dorf im Fichtelgebirge. ZODER 1–7
2140a —— Bolte, Johannes. Eine portugiesischer Melodie in Deutschland. LEITE I, 187–191
2141 —— Erdmann, Hans. Erzgebirgische Bergmusikanten in Mecklenburg. SCHENK 123–134
2142 —— Friedlaender, Max. Das Grossvaterlied und Grossvatertanz. KRETZSCHMAR 29–36
2142a —— Heiske, Wilhelm. Deutsche Volkslieder in jiddischen Sprachgewand. Ein Betrachtung zu "Verklingenden Weisen." SEEMAN/75TH 31–44
2142b —— Hoerburger, Felix. Die handschriftlichen Notenbücher der bayerischen Bauernmusikanten. MÜLLER-BLATTAU/70TH 122–128
2142c —— Jonsson, Bengt R. Ältere deutsche Lieder in schwedischer Überlieferung. Einige Beobachtungen. SEEMAN/75TH 45–51
2143 —— Klusen, Ernst. Die rheinischen Fassungen des Liedes von den 12 heiligen Zahlen im Zusammenhang der europäischen Überlieferung. SCHIEDERMAIR/80TH 57–68
2143a —— ——. Über landschaftliche Volksmusikforschung. Grundsätze und Demonstrationen. MÜLLER-BLATTAU/70TH 129–151
2143b —— Klusen, Ernst. Zur Typologie des gegenwärtigen Jugendliedes. WIORA/60TH 485–494
2144 —— Koschinsky, Fritz. *Der*

Bauernhimmel, Volkslied aus Schlesien. SCHNEIDER/60TH app. 2–7
2145 —— Meier, John. Alter Rechtsbrauch im bremischen Kinderspiel. BREMEN 229–244
2146 —— Moser, Hans J., & Fred Quellenmalz. Volkslieder des 15. Jahrhunderts aus St. Blasien. MEIER/70TH 146–156
2147 —— Müller-Battau, Joseph. Kontrafakturen im älteren geistlichen Volkslied. FELLERER/60TH 354–367
2147a ———. Lothringische und pfälzische Volkslieder. Ein Abschlussbericht. SEEMAN/75TH 80–94
2148 —— Polheim, Karl. Zum Problem des Zersingens. ANDERLUH 54–66
2149 —— Rietsch, Heinrich. Kurze Betrachtungen zum deutschen Volkslied. LILIENCRON 215–227
2150 —— Salmen, Walter. Volksinstrumente in Westfalen. KODÁLY/80TH 271–279
2151 —— Schrammek, Winfried. Birkenblattblasen. BESSELER 7–14
2152 —— Schünemann, Georg. Freiberger Bergmusiker. KRETZSCHMAR 141–146
2153 ———. Volksfeste und Volksmusik im alten Nürnberg. SEIFFERT 53–60
2154 —— Schwaen, Kurt. Das Instrumentarium unserer Volksmusik. HOFMEISTER 75–80
2155 —— Stroh, Fritz. Bänkellieder im Volksmund. WOSSIDLO 180–188
2155a —— Vargyas, Lajos. Zur Verbreitung deutscher Balladen und Erzähllieder in Ungarn. SEEMAN/75TH 63–79
2155b —— Wittrock, Wolfgang. Zum melismatischen Singen der Wolgadeutschen. WIORA/60TH 648–650
2156 —— Zoder, Raimund. Der Warschauer. MEIER/70TH 300–306
—— See also no. 526a
2157 [Greece] Baud-Bovy, Samuel. La Strophe de distiques-rimés dans la chanson grecque. BARTÓK/S 365–383
2158 ———. Sur la strophe de la chanson *cleftique*. GRÉGOIRE II, 53–78
2159 [Holland] Mincoff-Marriage, Elisabeth. Einige niederländische Lieder mit fremdländischen Beziehungen. MEIER/70TH 138–140
2160 ——Veldhuyzen, Marie. Liederen bij gezelschapsspelen. BERNET KEMPERS 58–59
——See also no. 18b
2161 [Hungary] Bartha, Dénes. Grundfragen der Musikkultur in Ungarn. SCHERING 36–45
2162 ———. Horváth Ádám népdalfeljedgyzéseinek ritmusáról [Adam Horvath's Notation of Rhythm in Folksongs] KODÁLY/70TH 267–278
2163 —— Bartók, Béla. A régi magyar népzenéröl/Über die alte ungarische Bauernmusik. KODÁLY/60TH 5–8
2164 —— Bartók, János. Az ötfokúság formái népzenénkben [The Pentatonic Scale Forms in our Folk Music] KODÁLY/70TH 733–742
2165 —— Csenki, Imre, & Sándor Csenki. Népdalgyüjtés a magyarországi cigányok között/A Collection of Folk Music among the Gypsies in Hungary. KODÁLY/60TH 343–362
2166 —— Csomosz Tóth, Kálmán. Halottas énekeskönyveink dallamai [The Melodies of our Books of Dirges] KODÁLY/70TH 287–330
2167 —— Dincsér, Oszkár. A változat a magyar négzenei kutatásban/Die Varianten in der ungarischen Volksmusikforschung. KODÁLY/60TH 128–138
2168 —— Domokos, Pál Péter. A Népművészeti Intézet újabb gyüjtéseiből [The Folk Art Institute's More Recent Collections] KODÁLY/70TH 339–372
2169 —— Gárdonyi, Zoltán. Népzenénk és a zenei forma elemei [Our Folk Music and the Basic Elements of Musical Form] KODÁLY/70TH 405–413
2170 —— Jagamas, János. Beiträge zur Dialektfrage der ungarischen Volksmusik in Rumänien. BARTÓK/S 469–501
2171 —— Járdányi, Pál. The Determining of Scales and Solmization in Hungarian Musical Folklore. BARTÓK/S 301–306
2172 ———. Hangnem-típusok a magyar népzenében [Key Types in Hungarian Folk Musik] KODÁLY/70TH 255–266
2173 ———. A magyar népdalgyüjtés új feladatai/Von der neuen Aufgabe des ungarischen Volksliedsammelns. KODÁLY/60TH 111–113
2174 —— Kerényi, György. Egy 19. századi dallam életrajza/L'Histoire d'une mélodie du XIXe siècle. KODÁLY/60TH 275–282
2175 ———. *Megy a kosár.*

KODÁLY/75TH 445–461, English summary 757–758
2176 ——. The Melody Core of Ushering in Summer in Transdanubia, Hungary. KODÁLY/80TH 181–214
2177 ——. A regős-ének magja [Origins of the Minstrel Songs] KODÁLY/70TH 241–254
2178 ——. The System of Publishing the Collection of Hungarian Folksongs, *Corpus musicae popularis Hungaricae.* BARTÓK/S 453–468
2179 —— Kiss, Lajos. A Lengyel László-játék [The László Lengyel Play] KODÁLY/70TH 373–398
2180 ——. Szlavóniai magyar népdalok/Ungarische Volkslieder aus Slavonien. KODÁLY/60TH 317–321
2181 ——. Les Traits caractéristiques de l'exécution vocale et instrumentale à propos d'une ballade populaire hongroise. KODÁLY/80TH 215–222
2182 —— Krohn, Ilmari. Módszertani kérdések az összehasonlító népdalkutatásban/Zur Methode der vergleichenden Volksmelodienforschung. KODÁLY/60TH 97–110
2183 Lajtha, László. Egy "hamis" zenekar [An "Out-of-Tune" Orchestra] KODÁLY/70TH 169–198
2184 ——. Ujra magtalált magyar népdaltípus/Découverte d'un ancien type de chanson populaire. KODÁLY/60TH 219–234
2185 —— Major, Ervin. Népdal és verbunkos [Folksong and Recruiting Songs] KODÁLY/70TH 221–240
2186 —— Petró, Sándor. Egy karácsonyi ének élete/Varianten eines Weihnachtsliedes. KODÁLY/60TH 184–188
2186a —— Rajeczky, Benjámin. Ost und West in den ungarischen Klageliedern. WIORA/60TH 628–632
2187 ——. Parallelen spätgregorianischer Verzierungen im ungarischen Volkslied. BARTÓK/S 337–348
2188 —— Székely, András. *Szent Györgyi István daloskönyve* [*The István Szent Györgyi Song Book*] KODÁLY/70TH 675–696
2189 —— Szentjóbi, Miklós. Szöveg és dallam kapcsolata a magyar népdalban/Text und Melodie im ungarischen Volkslied. KODÁLY/60TH 329–336
2190 —— Vargyas, Lajos. Kétféle végződés egy dallam változataiban/Two Different Endings in the Variants of a Melody. KODÁLY/60TH 297–299
2191 ——. Ugor réteg a magyar népzenében [The Ugric Stratum of Hungarian Folk Music] KODÁLY/70TH 611–658
2192 ——. Die Wirkung des Dudelsacks auf die ungarische Volkstanzmusik. BARTÓK/S 503–540
2193 —— Várnai, Péter. A makói árvíz nótája [The Song of the Makó Flood] KODÁLY/60TH 593–600
2194 —— Vikár, Béla. Erdélyi út a fonográffal/Mit dem Phonograph in Siebenbürgen. KODÁLY/60TH 88–96
2195 —— Vörös, Károly. A Rákócziznóta dallamának egy ismeretlen változata [An Unknown Variant of the Rákóczi Song] KODÁLY/75TH 337–343, English summary 756
2196 —— Wiora, Walter. Mittelalterliche Parallelen zu altungarischer Melodik. KODÁLY/80TH 379–389
—— See also nos. 181b, 1781a, 2499
2196a [Iceland] Andersson, Otto. Framsades eller sjöngos de isländska rimorna? ANDERSSON, O./85TH 275–282; orig. in PIPPING, R. 13–20
2196b ——. Några särdrag i rimamelodierna. STRÖMBÄCK 130–138
2197 [Italy] Ghisi, Federico. Un Canto narrativo popolare su Francesco I re di Francia nella tradizione bilingue del Piemonte. BLUME/F 146–150
2198 ——. Una Canzone popolare del teschio parlante appartenente alla tradizione narrativa barocca. ANGLÉS I, 331–333
2198a ——. Contributo alla canzone popolare nelle valli Valdesi del Piemonte. BARBLAN/60TH 153–163
2199 —— Heiske, Wilhelm. Zur *Donna Lombarda.* MEIER/85TH 59–80
2200 —— Nataletti, Giorgio. Az olasz népzenei hagyomány tanulmányozsása az elmult húsz évben/Forschungen der musikalischen Volksüberlieferungen in Italien während der letzten zwanzig Jahre. KODÁLY/60TH 283–296
2201 —— Springer, Hermann. Sizilianische Volksmusik in Settecentoüberlieferung. KRETZSCHMAR 152–154
2202 ——. Vilota und Nio; zur Entwicklungsgeschichte der italienischen Volksmusik. LILIENCRON 315–328
—— See also no. 773a

2202a [Lapland] Emsheimer, Ernst. A Lapp Musical Instrument. EMSHEIMER/60TH 62–67; orig. in *Ethnos* 12 (1947) 86–92

2202b ——. Lappische Musik. EMSHEIMER/60TH 81–85; orig. in *MGG* 8 (1960) 213–216

2202c ——. Lappischer Kultgesang. EMSHEIMER/60TH 76–80; orig. in *Kongressbericht Lüneberg*, 1950, 153–157

2202d ——. Zur Ideologie der lappischen Zaubertrommel. EMSHEIMER/60TH 28–49; orig. in *Ethnos* 9 (1944) 141–169

2202e —— Lagercrantz, Eliel. Eine lappische Melodie aus Varanger. WICHMANN 109–118

2202f — Strömbäck, Dag. The Realm of the Dead on the Lappish Magic Drums. CAMPBELL, A. 216–220

2203 [Norway] Bjørndal, Arne. Bygdebøkene og bygdemusikken [Country Books and Country Music] BJØRNDAL 146–163; orig. in *Heimen* (1948)

2204 ——. Då ein høyrde underjordisk musikk på Kyrkje-Byrkjeland i Fana [When I Heard Underground Music, i.e., Troll Songs, at the Byrkjeland Church in Fana] BJØRNDAL 93–116; orig. in *Bergens Museums Årbok* (1945) Hist. antikv.-rekke 7

2205 ——. Eldeste norske folkeviseprentet [The Oldest Printed Norwegian Folksongs] BJØRNDAL 117–122; orig. in *Syn og Segn* (1947)

2206 ——. Dei gamle spelemennene [The Old Fiddlers] BJØRNDAL 123–129; orig. in *Fra Fjon til Fusa* (1948)

2207 ——. I Vesterweg [In the West] BJØRNDAL 317–335

2208 ——. Norsk folkemusikk; litt um dei eldeste fråsegnene og kjeldone [Norwegian Folk Music; Concerning the Earliest Sources] BJØRNDAL 16–32; orig. in *Heidersskrift til Gustav Indregø* (1939)

2209 ——. Soga om springaren *Nordfjorden* [The Tales about the Springar Dance *Nordfjorden*] BJØRNDAL 203–238

2210 ——. Sognemusikken [Music from Sogne] BJØRNDAL 183–202; orig. in *Norske Bygder* 4

2211 ——. Springaren *Heldalen*. BJØRNDAL 135–137; orig. in *Fra Fjon til Fusa* (1949)

2212 — Eggen, Erik. Folkemusik og kunstmusik. BRUUN 83–93

2213 ——. Skalaen i sinklarmarsjen. SANDVIK 24–31

2214 — Grüner-Nielsen, H. Degnesang, *Kingotoner*, i herningegnen i 1860erne. HANSEN 239–249

2215 — Gurvin, Olav. Norsk programmatisk folkemusikk. SANDVIK 39–51

2216 — Sandvik, Ole Mörk. Melismer og rytmiske eiendommelegheter i norsk folksmusik [Melismas and Rhythmic Characteristics in Norwegian Folk Music] KROHN 112–116

2217 ——. Original eller variant? MOBERG 283–286

2217a [Poland] Bielawski, Ludwik. Wartość rytmiczna a tempo w zapisach melodii ludowych [The Value of the Rhythm and Tempo in the Notation of Folk Melodies] FEICHT 64–76

2217b — Poźniak, Włodzimierz. Ogólna charakterystyka skal na terenie Wielkopolski i Małopolski. Z badán nad podstawami tonalnymi polskiej pieśni ludowej [General Characteristics of the Scales of the Area of Great Poland and Little Poland. An Inquiry into the Tonal Basis of Polish Folk Songs] FEICHT 37–54

2218 — Prosnak, Jan. Z zagadnień polskiego folkloru muzycznego [Concerning Polish Musical Folklore] CHYBIŃSKI/70TH 320–338

2219 — Sobiescy, Marian, & Jadwiga Wielkopolskie wiwaty [Great Polish Wiwats] CHYBIŃSKI/70TH 275–319

2219a — Sobiescy, Marian. Z sagadnień polskiego ludowego instrumentarium muzycznego (mazanki, serby, skrzypce) [Problems of the Polish Folk Instruments (Mazanki, Serby, Fiddle). FEICHT 24–36

2219b — Stęszewski, Jan. Z zagadnień wariabilności muzyki ludowej [The Problems of the Variability of Folk Music] FEICHT 55–63

2220 — Turczynowiczowa, Maria. Schematy *Wielkiego Księstwa Poznańskiego*. [Kolberg, O., comp.] CHYBIŃSKI/70TH 339–346

2221 — Windakiewiczowa, Helena. Ze studjów nad formą muzyczną pieśni ludowych; okres kolisty [From the Studies of the Musical Form of Folk

Songs; the Circular Period] CHYBIŃSKI/50TH 115–123

2222 —— Zawadski, Marian. Lengyel zeneszerzők és lengyel népi muzsika/ Compositeurs polonais et musique populaire polonaise. KODÁLY/60TH 313–316

—— See also no. 2130b

2222a [Portugal] d'Aurora, Conde. Romarias de Ribeira Lima. ALMEIDA 335–343

2223 —— Pires de Lima, J. A., & F. C. Pires de Lima. Os fieis de Deus. HOYOS SÁINZ 257–264

2224 [Rumania] Alexandru, Tiberiu. Tilinca ein uraltes rumänisches Volksinstrument. BARTÓK/S 107–121

2225 —— Brailoiu, Constantin. A román népzene/Die rumänische Volksmusik. KODÁLY/60TH 300–307

2226 —— Comişel, Emilia. La Ballade populaire roumaine. BARTÓK/S 27–50

2227 —— Drăgoi, Sabin V. Musical Folklore Research in Rumania and Béla Bartók's Contribution to it. BARTÓK/S 9–25

2228 —— Ligeti, György. Egy aradmegyei román együttes [A Rumanian Ensemble from the County of Arad] KODÁLY/70TH 399–404

2228a [Russia] Väisänen, A. O. Das Zupfinstrument Gusli bei den Wolgavölkern. WICHMANN 303–330

—— See also no. 1620a

2228b [Scandinavia] Norlind, Tobias. Melodiken i den skandinaviska folkviseballaden. EK 51–57

2229 [Scotland] Palmgren, Carl. On the Music of Robert Burns' Songs. ERDMANN 224–230

2230 —— Shaw, Margaret Fay. Gaelic Folksongs from South Uist. BARTÓK/S 427–443

2231 [Slovakia] Kresánek, Jozef. Bartóks Sammlung slowakischer Volkslieder. BARTÓK/S 51–68

2232 —— Manga, János. Zoborvidéki lakodalmas énekek/Canti nuziali della zona di Zobor (Zoborvidék) KODÁLY/60TH 195–212

2233 [Spain] Collet, Henri. Musique espagnole et musique russe. MARTINENCHE 15–22

2234 —— Garcia Matos, M. Veijas canciones y melodías en la música instrumental popular de laz danzas procesionales practicadas aún en España. ANGLÉS I, 283–305

2235 —— Gelats, Joan Amades. Ritos primitivos de Siembra. ORTIZ I, 65–80

2236 —— Gil, Bonifacio. La Canción vaquera en la tradición hispánica. ANGLÉS I, 335–359

2236a ——. Panorama de la canción popular burgalesa. SUBIRÁ/80TH 85–102

2237 —— Mendoza, Vicente T. *La Cachucha.* HOYOS SÁINZ 223–233

2238 —— Sanchis Guarner, M. Folklore geogràfic de la Comarca d'Alcoi. FABRA 380–400

2238a —— Schneider, Marius. Vier Klagelieder aus dem cancionero de la casa Medinaceli. STÄBLEIN/70TH 226–233

2238b —— Tomás i Parés, Juan. Canciones populares de trabajo. BALDELLÓ 225–239

2239 ——. *L'Hereu Mill,* arxiu vivent de cançons populars catalanes. ANGLÉS II, 923–940

2240 —— Torner, Eduardo M. Ensayo de clasificación de las melodías de romance. MENÉNDEZ PIDAL II, 391–402

—— See also no. 223b

2240a [Sweden] Andersson, Otto. Adolf Iwar Arwidsson och Svenska fornsånger. ANDERSSON, O./85TH 326–346; orig. in *Saga och Sed, Kungl. Gustav Adolfs Akademiens Årsbok* (1936) 39–61

2241 —— Andersson, Otto. Bröllopsmusik på säckpipa [Wedding Music on the Bagpipe] MOBERG 17–36; ANDERSSON, O./85TH 291–310

2241a ——. Sjöngo varjagerna svenska folkvisor? ANDERSSON, O./85TH 261–274; orig. in EK 1–8

2241b —— Dencker, Nils. "Till österland vill jag fara." EK 58–71

2241c —— Forsén, Olof. Fiskardansen. EK 211–215

2242 —— Jonsson, Nils. En gammal sjömansvisa [An Old Sailors' Song] SALÉN 87

2242a ——Moberg, Carl-Allen. Bröllopsmusiken på Runö. SALÉN/70TH 96–111

2243 ——. Kuhreihen, Lobetanz und Galder. HANDSCHIN/I 27–38

2244 —— Schiørring, Nils. C. B. Rutström och Rasmus Nyerup; et bidrag till den svensk-danske folkevises melodihistoire. MOBERG 287–296

2245 —— Walin, Stig. Kungl. Musikaliska Akademien och den svenska folksmusiken; en materialsamling ur protokollen från 1840-talets början till 1870-talets slut [The Royal

Music Academy and Swedish Folk Music; Documents from 1840 to 1870] MOBERG 321–337
2246 [Switzerland] Refardt, Edgar. *Wie ein stolzer Adler*. REFARDT 143–146; orig. in *Schweizer Volkskunde* 28 (1938)
2247 —— Wiora, Walter. Alpenländische Liedweisen der Frühzeit und des Mittelalters im Lichte vergleichender Forschung. MEIER/85TH 169–198
2248 [Turkey] Bartók, Béla. On Collecting Folksongs in Turkey. BARTÓK/T 19–23
2248a —— Reinhard, Kurt. Die Quellensituation der türkischen Kunstmusik. WIORA/60TH 578–582
2249 —— ——. Zur Variantenbildung im türkischen Volkslied, dargestellt an einer Hirtenweise. BESSELER 21–34
2249a [Yiddish] Rubin, Ruth. Slavic Influences in Yiddish Folksong. BOTKIN/65TH 131–152
2249b [Yugoslavia] Hoerburger, Felix. Auf dem Weg zur Grossform. Beobachtungen zur instrumentalen Volksmusik der südlichen Balkanvolker. WIORA/60TH 615–622
2250 —— Lord, Albert B. The Role of Sound Patterns in Serbo-Croatian Epic. JAKOBSON 301–305
2251 —— Širola, Božidar. Horvát népi hangszerek/Kroatische Volksmusikinstrumente. KODÁLY/60TH 114–127
2252 —— ——. Die Volksmusik der Kroaten. BARTÓK/S 89–106
2253 —— Žganec, Vinko. Die Elemente der jugoslawischen Folklore-Tonleitern im serbischen liturgischen Gesange. BARTÓK/S 349–363

BIBLIOGRAPHY

See also nos. 823a, 995, 1143a, 1151b, 1350a, 1384a, 1414b, 1861a

2254 Adler, Guido. Ein Musikkatalog aus unserer Zeit. SCHUERLEER 39–41
2255 Autographen ausgestellt in der Internationalen Musik- und Theater-Ausstellung in Wien, 1892. RICORDI 159–162
2256 Autographen von Opern, Operetten, Oratorien, Cantaten, u.s.w., Eigenthum der Firma G. Ricordi & Co. RICORDI 145–155
2257 Bach, Ursula. Bemerkungen zur Fachbibliographie der Musikwissenschaft. VORSTIUS 17–19
2258 Badura-Skoda, Eva. Eine private Briefsammlung. DEUTSCH/80TH 280–290
2259 Bush, Helen E., & David J. Haykin. Music Subject Headings. KINKELDEY 39–45
2260 Ciceri, Angelo. L'Archivio della Veneranda Fabbrica del Duomo di Milano. MERCATI 165–183
2261 Clasen, Theo. Die musikalischen Autographen der Universitäts-Bibliothek Bonn. SCHMIDT-GÖRG 26–65
2262 Dagnino, Eduardo. L'Archivio musicale di Montecassino. MONTE CASSINO I, 273–296
2262a Deutsch, Otto Erich. Theme and Variations. HIRSCH 68–71
2263 Dreimüller, Karl. Musikerbriefe an einen rheinischen Musikliebhaber aus der Sammlung Ludwig Bisschopinck in München-Gladbach. HOBOKEN 29–49
2264 Engel, Carl. Concert, A.D. 2025, in the Library of Congress. PUTNAM 140–145
2264a Fukač, Jiří. Zur inneren Systematik musikalischer Verzeichnisgattungen. ŠTĚDROŇ/60TH 21–30, summary in Czech at end of article
2264b Gerboth, Walter. Index of Festschriften and Some Similar Publications. REESE/65TH 183–307
2265 Goff, Frederick R. Early Music Books in the Rare Books Division of the Library of Congress. KINKELDEY 58–74
2265a Gottron, Adam. Die Musikbibliothek des Frh. Karl Anton von Hoheneck zu Mainz († 1771). MÜLLER-BLATTAU/70TH 89–96
2266 Grasberger, Franz. Katalogisierungsprobleme einer Musikbibliothek. VORSTIUS 172–181
2266a Hirsch, Paul. Musik-Bibliophilie. Aus den Erfahrungen eines Musik-Sammlers. ZOBELTITZ 247–254
2267 Hofmann, Gustav. Musikpflege und wissenschaftliche Universitätsbibliothek. STUMMVOLL 41–43
2268 Kahl, Willi. Musikhandschriften aus dem Nachlass Ernst Bückens in der Kölner Universitäts- und Stadtbibliothek. JUCHOFF 159–171
2269 King, A. Hyatt. The History and Growth of the Catalogues in the Music Room of the British Museum. DEUTSCH/80TH 303–308
2269a La Rue, Jan. Classification of Watermarks for Musicological Purposes. FÉDEROV 59–63
2270 Lach, Robert. Aus dem Hand-

schriftenschatze der Musikaliensammlung der Wiener Nationalbibliothek. WN 553–574

2270a Lebaeu, Elisabeth. Les catalogues de vente de tableaux et d'objets d'art, source de documentation musicale. FÉDEROV 67–72

2270b Lindberg, Folke. Broadcasting Libraries and Archives as Music Research Centres. FÉDEROV 76–79

2271 ——. Sveriges Radios musikbibliotek; en undersökning om dess tillkomst och förste år [The Swedish Radio Music Library; An Examination of its Early Years] MOBERG 227–237

2272 Lunelli, Renato. Di alcuni inventari delle musiche già possedute dal coro della parrocchiale di Merano. SCHENK 347–362

2273 Luther, Wilhelm M. Der Komponist und seine Eigenschrift. JUCHHOFF 172–186

2274 Mertens, C. Proeve eener documentatie over onze belgische toonkunstenaars, musicologen en instrumentenbouwers. BORREN 216–239

2275 Meyer-Baer, Kathi. Classifications in American Music Libraries. HIRSCH 76–82

2275a ——. Über Musikbibliographie. WOLF 118–122

2276 Mies, Paul, & Klaus W. Niemöller. Bibliographie zur Musikgeschichte der Stadt Köln. MIES 55–80

2277 Mörner, C. G. Stellan. Rariteter ur en akatalogiserod notsamling i Kungl. Biblioteket i Stockholm [Curiosities from an Uncataloged Collection in the Royal Library, Stockholm] MOBERG 273–281

2278 Moser, Hans Joachim. Im Zeitalter des Schallbandarchivs. MOSER/70TH 247–252 (orig. 3 separate studies: *Im Zeitalter des Schallbandarchivs; Gefährdung des Lebendigen durch die Technik;* & *Wider den Missbrauch der Perfektion*)

2278a Nowak, Leopold. Die Musikhandschriften aus Fuggerschem Besitz in der Österreichischen Nationalbibliothek. BICK 505–515

2278b ——. Die Musiksammlung [der Österreichischen Nationalbibliothek] BICK 119–138

2278c Olrog, Ulf Peder. Svenskt Visarkiv, 1951–1960. Nagot om dess tillkomst, arbetsresultat och framtida uppgifter. SALÉN/70TH 112–132

2279 Pérez Gómez, Antonio. Grabaciones en discos microsurco de música y canciones españolas hasta fines del siglo XVI. ANGLÉS II, 623–645

2279a Querol, Miguel. Lista de los catálogos musicales publicados en España. FÉDEROV 103–105

2280 [Ricordi] Brief-fac-simili. RICORDI 69–141

2281 Riedel, Friedrich W. Die Bibliothek des Aloys Fuchs. ALBRECHT 207–224

2281a Schenk, Erich. Die österreichische Musiküberlieferung der Züricher Zentralbibliothek. BICK 576–581

2281b Schmidt-Phiseldeck, Kay. Notes sur les buts du catalogage des livres et de la musique. FÉDEROV 117–121

2282 Schmieder, Wolfgang. Aphorismen zur Musik-Dokumentation. ALBRECHT 285–288

2283 ——. "Menschliches Allzumenschliches" oder einige unparteiische Gedanken über Thematische Verzeichnisse. DEUTSCH/80TH 309–318

2283a ——. Werkstatt-Erfahrungen beim Katalogisieren von Musikhandschriften. FÉDEROV 121–125

2284 Schneider, Max. *Denkmäler der Tonkunst* vor hundert Jahren. LILIENCRON 278–289

2285 Schulz, Gottfried. Musikbibliographie und Musikbibliotheken. SANDBERGER 129–134

2286 Versyp, J. Die muziekbibliotheek van de St-Salvatorskerk te Gent in 1754. MUEREN 217–225

2287 Verzeichnis der grösstentheils von Sigismund Streit dem grauen Kloster geschenkten Musikalien. BGGK 5–18

2287a Vlasto, Jill. The Rowe Music Library, King's College, Cambridge. HIRSCH 72–75

2288 Wackernagel, Peter, Aus glücklichen Zeiten der Preussischen Staatsbibliothek. SMEND 61–65

2288a Weinhold, Liesbeth. Musiktitel und Datierung. FÉDEROV 136–140

2289 Weinmann, Alexander. Die Wiener Zeitung als Quelle für die Musikbibliographie. HOBOKEN 153–160

2290 Weinmann, Karl. Die Proskesche Musikbibliothek in Regensburg. LILIENCRON 387–403

2291 Zehnter, Hans. Die handschriftlichen Nachlässe von schweizer Komponisten in der Universitätsbiblio-

thek Basel. SCHWARBER 297–315
2291a ——. Musikerbriefe in der Universitätsbibliothek Basel. FÉDEROV 140–149
2292 Die zeitgenössischen Komponisten der Salzburger Festspiele in Faksimile-Wiedergaben ihrer Opern. PAUMGARTNER 41–55

MUSICOLOGY AS A DISCIPLINE

See also nos. 98, 2033, 2040–2042, 2049a, 2052, 2475a

2293 Bartha, Dénes. Bemerkungen zum New-Yorker Kongress der I.G.M.W., 1961. KODÁLY/80TH 53–64
2294 Blume, Friedrich. Musikforschung und Musikpraxis. STEIN 13–25
2295 Dehnert, Max. Wert und Unwert des Anekdotischen; ein Beitrag zur biographischen Methodik. SCHNEIDER/80TH 357–364
2296 Demuth, Norman. A propos des voyages de Ch. Burney. MASSON II, 33–42
2296a Donà, Mariangela. Le musicologia in Italia. BARBLAN/60TH 94–101
2297 Felber, Erwin. Die Musikwissenschaft. UNIVERSAL 139–154
2297a Fellerer, Karl Gustav. Musik und Musikwissenschaft. DESDERI/70TH 61–69
2298 Goslich, Siegfried. Gedanken zur geisteswissenschaftlichen Musikbetrachtung. SCHERING 90–95
2299 Grainger, Percy A. The Specialist and the All-Round Man. ENGEL 115–119
2300 Handschin, Jacques. Der Arbeitsbereich der Musikwissenschaft. HANDSCHIN 23–28; orig. in *Basler Nachrichten,* Sonntagsblatt 26 (July 6, 1952)
2301 ——. Belange der Wissenschaft. HANDSCHIN 60–69; orig. in *Schweizer Annalen* (1936)
2302 ——. Gedanken über moderne Wissenschaft. HANDSCHIN 51–59; orig. in *Annalen* 2 (1928)
2303 ——. Humanistische Besinnung. HANDSCHIN 376–384; orig. in *Neue Zürcher Zeitung* 797 & 813 (1932)
2304 ——. Über das Studium der Musikwissenschaft. HANDSCHIN 38–50; orig. in *Mitteilungen der Schweizerischen Musikforschenden Gesellschaft* 3 (1956)
2305 ——. Vom Sinn der Musikwissenschaft. HANDSCHIN 29–37; orig. in *Neue Zürcher Zeitung* 903 & 919 (1929)
2305a Hughes, Anselm. Ninety Years of English Musicology. BORREN/90TH 93–97
2306 Lenaerts, René. Wegen en doelstellingen der muziekwetenschap. CLOSSON 139–144
2307 Linden, Albert van der. Gloses sur l'étymologie du mot *musique.* GESSLER 735–741
2308 Lissa, Zofia. Uwagi o metodzie marksistowskiej w muzykologii [Notes on the Marxist Method Applied to Musicology] CHYBIŃSKI/70TH 50–119
2309 Meyer, Ernst. H. Künstlerisches und wissenschaftliches Denken. SCHNEIDER/80TH 303–310
2310 Moberg, Carl-Allan. Musikforskningen och den praktiske musikodlingen. SANDVIK 165–173
2311 Mörner, C. G. Stellan. Musikwissenschaft und Langspielplatte. DEUTSCH/80TH 327–336
2312 Moser, Hans Joachim. Der Musikforscher zwischen Tonkunst und Wissenschaft, der Tonkünstler zwischen Musik und Forschung. PAUMGARTNER 144–150
2313 ——. Das schöne Abenteuer der Musikforschung. MOSER/70TH 1–7
2314 ——. Über den Sinn der Musikforschung. MOSER 158–170
2314a ——. Über die Zukunft der Musikwissenschaft. BOSSE/50TH 113–116
2315 Mueren, Floris van der. Wat de musicologie niet vergeten mag. BORREN 318–326
2316 Nettl, Paul. Musikwissenschaft in Amerika. FISCHER/W 171–177
2317 Reinhold, Helmut. Musik, Wissen und Musikwissenschaft. KAHL 130–139
2318 Sonneck, Oscar G. The Future of Musicology in America. PUTNAM 423–428
2319 Vetter, Walther. Voraussetzung und Zweck in der Musikwissenschaft. OREL/70TH 207–212
2320 Wolf, Johannes. Musik und Musikwissenschaft. RAABE 38–44
2321 ——. Musikwissenschaft und musikwissenschaftlicher Unterricht. KRETZSCHMAR 175–179
2321a Wolff, Hellmuth Christian. Grenzen der Musikwissenschaft. WIORA/60TH 66–72

ACOUSTICS

See also nos. 1368d, 1562, 2368, 2480, 2553, 2575, 2593

2322 Chailley, Jacques. La Monocorde et la théorie musicale. WAESBERGHE 11–20

2323 Darmois, Eugène. Les Sons de combinaison. MASSON I, 23–26

2324 Enkel, Fritz. Über die Darstellung der räumlichen Struktur ausgedehnter Klangkörper bei der einkanaligen Rundfunkübertragung. SCHMIDT-GÖRG 81–99

2325 Fickénscher, Arthur. The *Polytone* and the Potentialities of a Purer Intonation. EINSTEIN 356–370

2326 Fricke, Jobst P. Die Innenstimmung der Naturtonreihe und der Klänge. FELLERER/60TH 161–177

2327 Handschin, Jacques. Akustisches aus Russland. HANDSCHIN 249–262, & SCHEURLEER 143–157

2328 Husson, Raoul. Le Contenu de la sensation musicale et son étude expérimentale. MASSON I, 41–50

2329 Kelletat, Herbert. Zur Tonordnung (Wohltemperierung) im Werke Johann Sebastian Bachs. MÜLLER-BLATTAU 19–26

2330 Laker, Karl. Die 80,000 Quinte. KIENZL 35–38

2331 Lissa, Zofia. Znaczenie akustyki dla teorji harmonji [The Importance of Acoustics for the Theory of Harmony] CHYBIŃSKI/50TH 149–182

2332 Meyer-Eppler, W. Die dreifache Tonhöhenqualität. SCHMIDT-GÖRG 202–212

2333 Reinecke, Hans-Peter. Hugo Riemanns Beobachtungen von Divisionstönen und die neueren Anschauungen zur Tonhöhenwahrnehmung. ALBRECHT 232–241

2334 Schischkoff, Georgi. Beiträge zur analytischen Vokalforschung. HUBER 87–97

2335 Souriau, Etienne. Le Problème de la notation mathématique de la musique. MASSON I, 53–60

2335a Ungeheuer, Gerold. Periodizität und Tonhöhe. SCHMIDT-GÖRG/70TH 394–409

PHILOSOPHY & PSYCHOLOGY

See also nos. 67, 84, 100, 103, 366b, 366c, 424, 1367a, 1421, 1422b, 1478, 1573a, 1711, 1750, 2298, 2328

2335b Aber, Adolf. "Kapellmeistermusik?" HIRSCH 64–67

2336 Adolfs, Eug. Musikale spraakverwarring. BERNET KEMPERS 33–34

2337 Amorós, José. El Problema de las relaciones subjetivas entre colores y sonidos. ANGLÉS I, 29–60

2337a Andersson, Otto. Att njuta av musik och att förstå musik. ANDERSSON, O./85TH 125–130; orig. in *Hufvudstadsbladet* (May 20, 1947)

2337b ——. Om musikhörandet. Installationsföredrag den 27 november 1926. ANDERSSON, O./85TH 111–124; orig. in *Åbo Akademis Årsskrift* (1926/28) 235–254

2338 Baird, John W. Memory for Absolute Pitch. TITCHENER 43–74

2339 Bergelt, Robert. Några engelska musikestetiker under 1700-talet. HERRLIN 244–260

2340 Blume, Friedrich. Musik, Anschauung und Sinnbild. SEIFFERT 143–150

2341 ——. Was ist Musik? BLUME/S 872–886; orig. in *Musikalische Zeitfragen* 5 (1959)

2341a [Bouché] Moulaert, Pierre. Le Docteur Bouché et la musique. BOUCHÉ 118–124

2341b Boulez, Pierre. Nécessité d'une orientation esthétique. ADORNO/60TH 332–354

2342 Brenn, Franz. Zur Möglichkeit und Aufgabe der Musikpsychologie. HANDSCHIN/I 191–200

2342a Chailley, Jacques. Niveaux psychologiques dans l'assimilation du langage musical. WIORA/60TH 41–47

2343 [Cohen] Moos, Paul. Hermann Cohen als Musikästhetiker. KRETZSCHMAR 88–91

2343a Dadelsen, Georg von. Über das Wechselspiel von Musik und Notation. GERSTENBERG/60TH 17–25

2344 Della Corte, Andrea. La Comicità e la musica; saggio bibliografico e critico. SCHENK 105–114

2345 Dickinson, George S. Analogical Relations in Musical Pattern. KINKELDEY/80TH 262–269

2345a Fano, Fabio. Problemi ed

orientamenti critici del nostro tempo. BARBLAN/60TH 125–132
2346 Flath, Walter, Einfühlung der Entstellung? GRÜNWALD 12–17
2346a Fónagy, Ivan & Klara Magdics. Emotional Patterns in Intonation and Music. ESSEN 293–313
2347 Franceschi, Alfredo. Reflexiones sobre el contenido de la música. SARMIENTO 257–278
2347a Furtwängler, Wilhelm. Eine zeitgemässe Betrachtung. CURTIUS, L./60TH 4–8
2348 Guttmann, Alfred. Musik-Psychologie und Musik-Pädagogik. AALL 207–220
2349 Handschin, Jacques. Die Lehre von der Sphärenharmonie. HANDSCHIN 359–364; orig. in *Neue Zürcher Zeitung* 1372 (1926)
2350 ——. Das Männliche und das Unmännliche in der Musik. HANDSCHIN 370–373; orig. in *Basler Nachrichten*, Sonntagsblatt 41 (Oct. 11, 1953)
2351 ——. Mennyiség és minőség a zenében/Quantité et qualité dans la musique. KODÁLY/60TH 55–71; French summary HANDSCHIN 374–375
2352 ——. Die Sphärenharmonie in der Geistesgeschichte. HANDSCHIN 365–369; orig. in *Neue Zürcher Zeitung* 2435 (1929)
2353 [Hegel] Wiora, Walter. Einsichten Hegels in das Wesen der Musik. BESSELER 509–515
2354 [Heinse] Goldschmidt, Hugo. Wilhelm Heinse als Musikästhetiker. RIEMANN 10–19
2354a Herrgott, Fritz. Musische Erdarbeit. BOSSE/50TH 44–50
2355 Hornbostel, Erich M. von. Gestaltpsychologisches zur Stilkritik. ADLER 12–16
2356 ——. Tonart und Ethos. WOLF 73–78
2357 [Huber] Riezler, Walter. Zwei Vorlesungen. HUBER 65–74
2357a Kolinski, Mieczyslaw. Gestalt Hearing of Intervals. SACHS/C 368–374
2358 Lach, Robert. Das Inhaltsproblem in der Musikästhetik; ein Beitrag zur Grundlegung der musikalischen Hermeneutik. KRETZSCHMAR 74–79
2359 Lauterburg, Otto. Vom Dienst der Musik. WARTENWEILER 68–82
2359a Lissa, Zofia. O wielowarstwowości kultury muzycznej [Concerning the Multi-faceted Nature of Musical Culture] RACEK/60TH 124–143, summaries in German & Czech
2360 ——. Zur historischen Veränderlichkeit der musikalischen Apperzeption. BESSELER 475–488
2361 Łobaczewska, Stefanja. O ekspresjoniźmie muzycznym [Concerning Expressionism in Music] CHYBIŃSKI/50TH 125–147
2362 Mahling, Friedrich. Etwas über Stimmung. BIEHLE 13–17
2362a Manacorda, Guido. Del mirabile "numero." DESDERI/70TH 91–96
2363 Marschner, Franz. Der Wertbegriff als Grundlage der Musikwissenschaft. RIEMANN 20–40
2363a Matějček, Antonín. Výtvarné umění a hudba [The Fine Arts and Music]. NEJEDLÝ/50TH 19–23
2364 Mayer, Ernst. Gedanken eines Laien über Wesen und Sinn der Musik. PAUMGARTNER 81–86
2365 Medtner, Nikolai K. From *The Music and the Fashion.* MEDTNER 222–226
2366 ——. Inspiration. MEDTNER 221; orig. in *The Chesterian* 10 (1929)
2367 Michel, Paul. Musikalisches Hören, Musikalität und menschliches Grosshirn. MÜNNICH 116–127
2368 Monfort, Franz. L'Ethos des tonalités. BORREN 240–259
2369 Moser, Hans Joachim. Fortschritt oder Stilwandel? MOSER/70TH 243–244; orig. in *Düsseldorfer Nachrichten* (1921)
2370 ——. Musik zwischen Seele und Kosmos. MOSER/70TH 255–259; orig. in *Universitas* 6 (1951)
2371 ——. Musikalischer Erbgang und seelische Mutation. MOSER/70TH 260–261; orig. in *Gesellschaft für Musikforschung, Kongressbericht* (Lüneburg 1950)
2372 ——. Das Vielerlei der Zeitbegriffe und die Musik. ANGLÉS II, 599–602
2373 Müller, Alfred Dedo. Der göttliche Ursprung der Musik. MAUERSBERGER 97–106
2374 ——. Musik und Trinität. SÖHNGEN 172–180
2375 Norton, Edwin L. The Intellectual Element in Music. GARMAN 167–201
2376 Nuten, P. Over muziekesthetiek in Duitsland von 1700 tot ± 1760. MUEREN 133–145
2377 Oboussier, Robert. Anliegen und Gegenstand der Musik. JASPERS 420–427

2378 [Pauler] Tóth, Dionys. Pauler und die Musik. PAULER 201–207
2379 Pielke, W. Atmen und Singen. KRETZSCHMAR 113–118
2380 Preetorius, Emil. Tonkunst und Bildkunst, ihr Wesen, ihre Wirkung. RAABE 49–51
2380a Rahe, Heinrich. Gottes Spuren, Symbole und Gleichnisse in der Musik-Stellungnahme zu P. Peter Singers Metaphysischen Blicken in die Tonwelt. FELLERER/60THM 41–66
2380b Reinecke, Hans-Peter. Über Allgemein-Vorstellungen von der Musik. Eine experimentelle Untersuchung musikalischer Stereotype mit der Methode des Polaritäts-Profils. WIORA/60TH 31–40
2381 [St. Augustine] Vogel, Heinrich. Ein Lied und seine Zeit; eine Frage im Anschluss an eine Stelle aus den *Confessiones Augustini.* SMEND 42–45
2382 Seeger, Charles. On the Moods of a Music-Logic. KINKELDEY/80TH 224–261
2383 Siebeck, Hermann. Sprechmelodie und Tonmelodie in ihrem ästhetischen Verhältnis. RIEMANN 3–9
2384 Steglich, Rudolf. Zweierlei Wissenschaft im Spiegel der Musik. SCHENK 516–519
2385 Stephani, Hermann. Das ästhetische Allgemeingesetz. SEIDL/AR 128–136
2386 Stumpf, Carl. Konsonanz und Konkordanz. LILIENCRON 329–349
2386a Terenzio, Vincenzo. La musica a la crisi dell'estetica. BARBLAN/60TH 295–306
2387 Uhde, Jürgen. Zeit und Musik. BARTH 753–763
2388 Ursprung, Otto. Stilvollendung; ein Beitrag zur Musikästhetik. KROYER 149–163
2389 [Volkelt] Moos, Paul. Volkelts ästhetische Normen. LILIENCRON 138–144
2390 ——. Volkelts Einfühlungslehre. RIEMANN 40–48
2390a Waltershausen, H. W. v. Die universelle Bildung des Musikers. DAMDK 38–40
2391 Weischedel, Wilhelm. Fragment über die Musik. MERSMANN 158–163
2391a Wellek, Albert. Grösse in der Musik. SCHMITZ 265–280
2391b ——. Musik als Bekenntniskunst und die Überwindung des programmatischen Denkens. RACEK/60TH 389–396
2392 Westphal, Kurt. Historische und absolute Bedeutung in der Musik. SCHNEIDER/80TH 311–318
2393 Wetzel, Hermann. Zur psychologischen Begründung des Rhythmus und die aus ihr fliessende Bestimmung der Begriffe Takt und Motiv. RIEMANN 100–121
2394 Wiora, Walter. Musica poetica und musikalisches Kunstwerk. FELLERER/60TH 579–589
2395 ——. Zwischen absoluter und Programmusik. BLUME/F 381–388
2396 Zingerle, Hans. Zum Problem einer Stilgeschichte der ästhetischen Qualitäten. FISCHER/W 161–170

PEDAGOGY

See also nos. 33, 407, 409, 412, 435, 685, 776, 825, 1112, 1119, 1147, 1413, 1568a, 1727, 2301, 2348, 2478, 2481, 2487, 2507

2397 Andries, M. Beantwoordt de inrichting van paedagogische leergangen aan de hogere muziekscholen aan een behoefte? MUEREN 47–51
2398 Bachmann, Fritz. Musikalische Volkskunstarbeit und JALE-Tonsilben. MÜNNICH 81–84
2399 Beninger, Eduard. Die Intervall-Leitern von Howard und ihre historische Bedingtheit für die Klavierdidaktik. HOWARD 13–16
2399a Beránek, Vratislav. Hudební výchova ve školském rozhlase [Music Education in (Czech) Educational Broadcasting] PLAVEC/60TH 79–90
2400 Berger, Gregor. Vor dreissig Jahren; Erinnerungen eins rheinischen Schulmusikers. SCHIEDERMAIR/80TH 9–13
2401 Bieder, Eugen. Zur einheitlichen Ausbildung des Musikerziehers. STEIN 83–95
2402 Bimberg, Siegfried. Das JALE-Silbensystem Richard Münnichs als Grundlage der Erziehung zum Melodiebewusstsein. MÜNNICH 66–76
2403 Braunfels, Walter. Von den Aufgaben der Schule. UNIVERSAL 133–138
2403a Corte, Andrea della. L'istituzione dei conservatorii. DESDERI/70TH 41–47
2403b Fanti, Napoleone. Su un programma razionale degli studi pianistici. DESDERI/70TH 49–59; extract of an article which appeared in *Muzyka Polska*, Zeszy 5, 21, (1938), 3–69

2404 Fortner, Wolfgang. Komposition als Unterricht. GURLITT 100–107
2405 Freistedt, Heinrich. Die Bedeutung des wandernden Do-Schlüssels für die Erziehung des Chorsängers zum Blatt-Singen. JOHNER 118–120
2405a Freyhan, Hans Walter. Zur gegenwärtigen Lage der englischen Schulmusik. WIORA/60TH 478–484
2406 Friedrich, Wilfried. Musikpädagogische Revolution. JÖDE 187–198
2406a ——. Stillstand ist Rückschritt. Betrachtung zur Lage in der Schulgesangsmethodik. MÜNNICH/70TH [62–72]
2407 Fuchs, Johannes. Schweizerische Kirchenmusikschule; ein Blick ins Jahr 1965. HILBER 94–96
2407a Gieseking, Walter. Moderne Anschlagsprobleme. DAMDK 44–46
2407b Gregor, Vladimír. Výchovný význam hudebně dramatických děl pro děti [Educational Significance of Music Dramas for Children] PLAVEC/60TH 45–56, summaries in German & Russian
2407c Gümmer, Paul. Stimmerziehung und Chorausbildung in einer Kirchenmusikschule. EHMANN/60TH 103–107
2408 Haerten, Heinz. Studienstiftung. MERSMANN 51–54
2408a Handerer, Hermann. Krisis der Musikerziehung. BOSSE/50TH 25–33
2408b Hauschild, Joseph. Erkenntnisse in der Behandlung der Kinderstimme, insbesondere der Knabenstimme. MÜNNICH/70TH [73–79]
2408c Holzknecht, Václav. Budapeštský zážitek [Budapest Experiences] PLAVEC/60TH 370–376
2409 Iseringhausen, Hermann. Gedanken zur Klavierpädagogik heute. WLH 45–53
2410 Jans, Franz X. Gedanken zur Chorerziehung. HILBER 87–89
2410a Koch, Johannes H. Chorsingen und Improvisation. EHMANN/60TH 90–102
2411 ——. Vorübungen zur Improvisation auf der Orgel. WLH 86–99
2412 Kraus, Egon. Der Musikant und die Schule. JÖDE 94–99
2413 Lange, Christian. Über die Anwendung des JALE-Silbensystems in der Lehrerbildung. MÜNNICH 77–80
2414 Lemacher, Heinrich. Das Musikseminar der Kölner Musikhochschule. MERSMANN 91–93
2415 Lipatti, Dinu. Une Lettre. LIPATTI 87–88
2416 Löbmann, Hugo. Die Gehörsbildung im Plane der Pestalozzischen Erziehungs-Idee. RIEMANN 122–133
2416a Lýsek, František. Amuzie a hudební výchova [The Unmusical Person and Music Education] RACEK/60TH 145–159, summary in German
2416b ——. Interpretační podmínky dětského pěveckého sboru [Conditions for the Interpretation of Children's Choral Singing] PLAVEC/60TH 57–67, summaries in German & Russian
2417 Marsop, Paul. Aphorismen zur Erziehung des Musikers. SEIDL/AR 118–127
2418 Martienssen, Carl A. Grundlage einer deutschen Klavierlehre. RAABE 171–181
2418a Michel, Paul. Die Bedeutung der ersten Lebensjahre für die musikalische Entwicklung. PLAVEC/60TH 19–31
2419 Mies, Paul. Der Musikerzieher. LEMACHER 50–53
2420 Moser, Hans Joachim. Kompositionsunterricht im Stilumbruch. MOSER/70TH 328–332; orig. in *Musikerziehung* 6 (1952)
2421 ——. Musikerziehung als Handwerk, als Wissenschaft, als Kunst. MOSER/70TH 335–344; orig. in *Musikerziehung* 9 (1955/1956)
2422 ——. Volksbildung und Musikerziehung. MOSER/70TH 306–311; orig. in *Zeitschrift für Musik* 114 (1953)
2423 Müller, Paul. Die psychophysiologischen Grundlagen des Zitherspiels. GRÜNWALD 25–30
2424 Neal, Heinrich. Lehrer und Schüler. GRÜNWALD 19–22
2425 Nuffel, J. van. L'Histoire de l'art à l'université. BORREN 327–335
2426 Oberborbeck, Felix. Grundzüge rheinischer Musikerziehung der vergangenen fünfzig Jahre (1900–1956). SCHIEDERMAIR/80TH 77–96
2427 ——. Musikerziehung als Gegenstand wissenschaftlicher Forschung. MERSMANN 97–99
2428 Pfannenstiel, Ekkehart. Aus der Wendezeit der Musikerziehung. JÖDE 46–52
2429 Preussner, Eberhard. Bild einer neuen Musikschule; Utopie und Wirklichkeit. MERSMANN 100–110
2430 ——. Musik und Menschenerziehung. PAUMGARTNER 87–101

2431 Reichenbach, Hermann. Zur Frage: Musik und Jugend. JÖDE 53–58
2431a Rossi-Vecchi, Enrico. La musica e i giovani. DESDERI/70TH 143–147
2432 Schäfer, Dirk. Het klavier. SCHÄFER 81–88
2433 Schneider, Albert. Die Kölner Musikhochschule nach dem zweiten Weltkrieg. MERSMANN 123–128
2434 Schneider, Norbert. Zur Situation der Musikerziehung an höheren Schulen. MERSMANN 133–134
2434a Schreker, Franz. Kompositionsunterricht. DAMDK 40–41
2435 Schroeder, Hermann. Der Kompositionslehrer in unserer Zeit. LEMACHER 27–29
2435a Schünemann, Georg. Die mechanische Musik an der Hochschule. DAMDK 41–44
2436 Schumann, Heinrich. Jugendmusik und Blockflöte. JÖDE 109–118
2437 Siukohen, Wilho. Erilaisia käsityksiä koulun laulunopetuksen peruskysymyksistä [Different Views concerning the Fundamentals of Teaching Vocal Music] KROHN 116–142 German summary vi
2438 Steinitzer, Max. Über den Nutzen des Gymnasialbetriebs. SEIDL/AR 97–117
2439 ——. Zur Methodik des Anfangsunterrichts für die Frauenstimme. RIEMANN 76–100
2440 Stone, David. Scholar-Musician as Teacher. DAVISON 337–340
2441 Thamm, Joseph. Carl Thiel—Theobald Schrems; zur Entstehung des Regensburger Musikgymnasiums. SCHREMS 170–185
2442 Thomas, Kurt. Zur Chorleiter- und Dirigentenerziehung. STEIN 129–134
2443 Übersicht der JALE-Schriften. MÜNNICH 152
2444 Waldmann, Guido. Einfluss auf die Privatmusikerziehung. JÖDE 99–109
2444a Weiss, Karl. Konzertierender Künstler und Lehrer. MÜNNICH/70TH [52–56]
2445 Wittelsbach, Rudolf. Zum Problem der Tonsprache im Theorieunterricht. MERSMANN 197–205
2446 Wölper, Ernst-Otto. Über den Sinn des Studiums an Musikhochschulen. MERSMANN 206–212
2446a Zecchi, Adone. La musica nelle scuole. DESDERI/70TH 187–201
2447 Zepf, Josef. Die Mundharmonika in der Jugend. JÖDE 172–175
2447a Zich, Jaroslav. Pedagogická práce na vysoké hudební škole [Pedagogical Work in the Conservatories] PLAVEC/60TH 33–43, summaries in German & Russian

THEORY & ANALYSIS: GENERAL

See also nos. 25a, 46b, 92, 274, 299, 337, 411b, 415a, 530a, 559a, 639, 747a, 1008a, 1302, 1321b, 1425, 1446, 1618a, 1652a, 1726, 1782, 1846, 1912a, 1959a, 2030, 2032, 2053, 2053a, 2322, 2345, 2351, 2357a, 2382, 2386, 2445, 2530

2448 Bengtsson, Ingmar. On Relationships between Tonal and Rhythmic Structures in Western Multipart Music. MOBERG 49–76
2449 Besseler, Heinrich. Musik und Raum. SEIFFERT 151–160
2449a Blanxart, Daniel. Consecuencias que se deducen del estudia minucioso de las distintas gamas y de la evolución de la tesitura. SUBIRÁ/80TH 109–121
2450 Blessinger, Karl. Versuch über die musikalische Form. SANDBERGER 1–20
2451 Blume, Friedrich. Fortspinnung und Entwicklung; ein Beitrag zur musikalischen Begriffsbildung. BLUME/S 504–525; orig. in *Peters Jahrbuch* 36 (1929)
2452 ——. Die musikalische Form und die musikalischen Gattungen. BLUME/S 480–504; orig. in *MGG* 4, col. 523
2453 Bücken, Ernst. Zur Frage des Stilverfalls. KROYER 164–168
2454 Chomiński, Jósef. M. Z zagadnień analizy formalnej [Concerning Formal Analysis] CHYBIŃSKI/70TH 146–197
2454a Clapham, John. Unorthodox Finales. HIRSCH 56–59
2454b Federhofer, Hellmut. Zur neuesten Literatur über Heinrich Schenker. MÜLLER-BLATTAU/70TH 69–79
2455 Fischer, Kurt von. Zur Theorie der Variation im 18. und beginnenden 19. Jahrhundert. SCHMIDT-GÖRG 117–130
2456 Flothius, Marius. Twaalf overwegingen. BERNET KEMPERS 35–37
2457 Fox, Charles W. Modern Counterpoint. a Phenomenological Approach. KINKELDEY 46–57
2458 Graf, Max. Musikkritik. UNIVERSAL 198–203
2459 Greissle, Felix. The Composer as Thinker. ENGEL 120–127

2460 Güldenstein, Gustav. Die Gegenwart in der Musik. NEF 72–101
2461 Handschin, Jacques. Der Begriff der Form in der Musik. HANDSCHIN 332–337; orig. in *Neue Zürcher Zeitung* 1088 (1932)
2462 Hartmann, Friedrich H. A Return to the Question of Atonality. SCHENK 246–251
2463 Herrmann, Joachim. Gibt es eine *schlesische Musik?* Eine stilkritische Problemstellung. SCHNEIDER /60TH 40–48
2463a Just, Martin. Musik und Dichtung in Bogenform und Reprisenbar. GERSTENBERG/60TH 68–77
2464 Keller, Hans. Key Characteristics. BRITTEN 111–123
2465 Klenau, Paul von. Streiflichter zum Problem "Aufgabe des Dirigenten." UNIVERSAL 130–132
2465a Krohn, Ilmari. Zur Analyse des Konsonanzgehalts. PIPPING 303–317
2466 Larsen, Jens Peter. Sonatenform—Probleme. BLUME/F 221–230
2467 Mahling, Friedrich. Das Farbe-Ton-Problem und die selbständige Farbe-Ton-Forschung als Exponenten gegenwärtigen Geistesstrebens. WOLF 107–111
2467a Moser, Hans Joachim. Beseelung der Musikgrundlagen. MÜNNICH/70TH [57–61]; also in MÜNNICH/80THM 153–157
2468 ——. Der Bildungshorizont des künftigen Musikers. MOSER/70TH 333–335; orig. in *Musikerziehung* 10 (1956/1957)
2469 ——. Diabolus in Musica. MOSER/70TH 262–280; orig. in *Musikerziehung* 6 (1953)
2470 ——. Das Gesetz der unabgebrauchten Tonstufe. MOSER/70TH 294–295; orig. in *Das Musikleben* 6 (1953)
2471 ——. Gleichgewichtserscheinungen in der Musik. MOSER/70TH 280–288; orig. in *Jahrbuch der Staatlichen Akademie für Kirchen- und Schulmusik* 4 (1932)
2472 ——. Das Schicksal der Penultima. MOSER/70TH 288–293; orig. in *Peters Jahrbuch* 41 (1934)
2473 ——. Stil-Lehre der Musik. OREL/70TH 121–126
2474 Nettl, Bruno. Notes on the Concept and Classification of Polyphony. BLUME/F 247–251
2474a Palmlöf, Nils Robert. Wie sind die Halbtonbenennungen Cis, Ces, usw. entstanden? Eine realetymologische Untersuchung. TEGNÉR 555–574
2475 Refardt, Edgar. Blasmusik und Blasmusiken. REFARDT 159–160; orig. in *Festführer zum Blasmusiktag* (Basel 1937)
2475a Rohwer, Jens. Systematische Musiktheorie. Anmerkungen zum Begriff einer wissenschaftlichen Disziplin. WIORA/60TH 131–139
2476 Sapp, Allen. The Record Review, Content and Purpose. DAVISON 313–323
2477 Schultz, Helmut. Das Orchester als Ausleseprinzip. KROYER 169–182
2477a Sychra, Antonín. Objektivní a subjektivní momenty v hudební analýze. RACEK/60TH 309–317, summary in German

THEORY & ANALYSIS: RHYTHM

See also nos. 409a, 417, 524a, 644b, 768a, 1209, 1254a, 1267a, 1406, 2015a, 2051, 2393

2478 Bárdos, Lajos. Éneklő hangszerek [Musical Instruments that Sing] KODÁLY/70TH 663–674
2479 Blümel, Rudolf. Die rhythmischen Mittel. SIEVERS 661–677
2480 Blum, Klaus. Zeitquanten als Struktureinheiten akustischer Kunstwerke. KAHL 140–146
2481 Hela, Martti. Rytminimet ja rytmianalyysimerkintä koulukäytössä [Rhythmic Terminology and Rhythmic Analysis for School Use] KROHN 41–49, German summary iv
2481a Jammers, Ewald. Takt und Motiv. Zur neuzeitlichen musikalischen Rhythmik. SCHMITZ 194–207
2482 Levy, Ernest. Von der Synkope; ein Beitrag zur Metrik und Rhythmik. NEF 150–156
2483 Lissa, Zofia. Die ästhetischen Funktionen der Stille und Pause in der Musik. SCHENK 315–346
2484 Lussy, Mathis. De la diction musicale et grammaticale. RIEMANN 55–60
2484a Machatius, Franz-Jochen. Dreiertakt und Zweiertakt als Eurhythmus und Ekrhythmus. GERSTENBERG/60TH 88–97
2485 Refardt, Edgar. Rhythmisches Empfinden. REFARDT 155–157; orig. in *Schweizerische musikpädagogische Blätter* (1939)

2486 Salazar, Adolfo. La Naturaleza del acento prosódico y del musical en la rítmica y la metrica. ORTIZ III, 1319–1328

2487 Scheiblauer, M. Die musikalisch-rhythmische Erziehung im Dienste der Heilpädagogik. HANSELMANN 94–103

2488 Schering, Arnold. Zur Entstehungsgeschichte des Orchester-allegros. ADLER 143–146

2489 Schieri, Fritz. Über das Dirigieren asymmetrischer Rythmen. MERSMANN 111–122

THEORY & ANALYSIS: MELODY

See also nos. 108, 349a, 508a, 1128, 1151, 2050, 2178

2490 Avasi, Béla. Tonsysteme aus Intervall-Permutationen. BARTÓK/S 249–300

2491 Bárdos, Lajos. Natürliche Tonsysteme. BARTÓK/S 209–248

2491a Boereboom, Marcel. "In melodia valete." BORREN/90TH 26–31

2492 Danckert, Werner. Melodische Funktionen. SCHNEIDER/80TH 343–346

2493 David, Hans T. Themes from Words and Names. ENGEL 67–78

2494 Eggen, Erik. Zur Entstehung und Entwicklung der Skala. SCHEURLEER 103–106

2495 Garms, J. H. Het maken van een inhoudsopgave van melodieën. SCHEURLEER 123–128

2496 Goddard, Pliny E. A Graphic Method of Recording Songs. BOAS 137–142

2497 Kolinski, Mieczyslaw. The Structure of Melodic Movement, a New Method of Analysis. ORTIZ II, 879–918

2498 Saygun, A. A. La Genèse de la mélodie. KODÁLY/80TH 281–300

2498a Schneider, Marius. Kriterien zur Melodiegestalt. ENGEL 331–334

2499 Szabolcsi, Bence. Dallamtörténeti kérdések [Problems concerning the History of Melody] KODÁLY/70TH 743–764

2500 Wiora, Walter. Älter als die Pentatonik. BARTÓK/S 185–208

THEORY & ANALYSIS: HARMONY

See also nos. 67, 693, 763, 770, 2028, 2331

2500a Albersheim, Gerhard. Die Rolle der Enharmonik in der abendländischen Musik. WIORA/60TH 149–156

2500b Apfel, Ernst. Probleme der theoretischen Harmonik aus geschichtlich-satztechnischer Sicht. WIORA/60TH 140–148

2501 Bimberg, Siegfried. Notwendiges Vorwort zur Harmonielehre. MÜNNICH 46–57

2501a Blažek, Zdeněk. Modulationen mit Hilfe von doppalterierten Dreiklangen. ŠTĚDROŇ/60TH 9–20, summary in Czech at end of article

2502 Borris, Siegfried. Hindemiths harmonische Analysen. SCHNEIDER/80TH 295–301

2503 Moser, Hans Joachim. Neapolitana. MOSER/70TH 324–328

2504 Münnich, Richard. Von Entwicklung der Riemannschen Harmonielehre und ihrem Verhältnis zu Oettingen und Stumpf. RIEMANN 60–76

2505 ——. Zur Theorie des Leitklangs. KRETZSCHMAR 101–104

2506 Piston, Walter. Thoughts on the Chordal Concept. DAVISON 273–278

2507 Reuter, Fritz. Über die Lage des musiktheoretischen Unterrichts an den Ausbildungsstätten für Musik. MÜNNICH 58–65

2508 Riemann, Hugo. Giebt es Doppel-Harmonien? PEDRELL 315–319

2509 Schmiedel, Peter. Einiges über Konsonanz und Tonverwandtschaft. BESSELER 489–494

2510 Tirabassi, Antonio. Complément à la note présentée au Congrès de Musicologie de Bâle en 1924. Histoire de l'harmonisation, les trois règles. BORREN 292–307

THEORY & ANALYSIS: OPERA

See also nos. 1678, 1701, 1708, 1742, 1745

2511 Abert, Hermann. Vom Opernübersetzen. KRETZSCHMAR 1–5

2512 Albright, H. Darkes. Musical Drama as a Union of All the Arts. DRUMMOND 13–30

2513 Auden, Wystan H. Reflexion über die Oper. STRAVINSKY/70TH 59–64

2514 Hassall, Christopher. Words, Words. NEWMAN 108–123

2515 Hörth, Franz L. Der Wendepunkt der Opernregie. UNIVERSAL 114–124

2516 Hoffmann, R. S. Die Operette. UNIVERSAL 204–211

2517 Middleton, Robert E. Opera Is Not What It Should Be. DAVISON 293–301
2518 Moser, Hans Joachim. Sciocchezze e saviezze del melodramma viste dal podio del direttore. MARINUZZI 113–138
2519 Vatielli, Francesco. L'Opera coi burattini. MÜLLER VON ASOW [222–225]

PERFORMANCE PRACTICE

See also nos. 97a, 104b, 130b, 175, 187, 402, 421, 573, 579, 746, 763a, 817, 851, 1012, 1121, 1201, 1230, 1361

2519a Carlson, Bengt. Klanger i svunnen tid. ANDERSON, A. 67–72
2519b Chomiński, Józef M. Kilka uwag o interpretacji dawnych utworów [Several Considerations Concerning the Interpretation of Early Music] FEICHT 198–209
2520 Daniel, Friedrich. Die Improvisation, eine versiegende Kunst. HILBER 70–75
2521 Fischer, Wilhelm. Die sogenannte *Werktreue*. PAUMGARTNER 12–16
2522 Gieseking, Walter. Intuition und Werktreue als Grundlagen der Interpretation. RAABE 154–157
2523 Göthel, Folker. Zur Praxis des älteren Violinspiels. SCHERING 96–105
2523a Greenberg, Noah. Early Music Performance Today. REESE/65TH 314–318
2524 Grout, Donald J. On Historical Authenticity in the Performance of Old Music. DAVISON 341–347
2525 Gui, Vittorio. La Funzione dell'esecutore. MARINUZZI 47–68
2526 Haas, Joseph. Über die Kunst der Improvisation in der Musik. RAABE 158–159
2527 Handschin, Jacques. Über das Improvisieren. HANDSCHIN 327–331; orig. in *Neue Zürcher Zeitung* 991 (1926)
2528 Hoffmann, Hans. La Pratica dell'esecuzione musicale. MARINUZZI 69–111 (Italian translation of his article *Aufführungspraxis* in *MGG* without the bibliography and many of the illustrations)
2529 Koczirz, Adolf. Über die Fingernageltechnik bei Saiteninstrumenten. ADLER 164–167
2530 Kornauth, Egon. Theorie und Praxis. PAUMGARTNER 128–133
2531 Kroyer, Theodor. Zur Aufführungspraxis. SCHEURLEER 191–200
2532 Langner, Thomas M. Darstellungs- und ausdrucksbetonte Werkbilder. MERSMANN 83–90
2533 Laux, Karl. Dirigent, Diener oder Diktator? KONWITSCHNY 53–56
2533a Levi, Lionello. Il destino del suggeritore. DESDERI/70TH 87–90
2534 Lohmann, Paul. Das Legato des deutschen Sängers. RAABE 182–186
2535 Malcolm, George. Boys' Voices. BRITTEN 100–103
2536 Meyer, Ernst H. Dirigent und Komponist. KONWITSCHNY 22–26
2536a Mueren, Floris van der. La compréhension historique d'une oeuvre implique-t-elle la connaissance du sens esthétique authentique? BORREN/90TH 219–233
2537 Raab, Peter. Über die Werktreue und ihre Grenze. STEIN 153–160
2538 Rubarth, Hermann. Gedanken zur Interpretation musikalischer Kunstwerke. KAHL 121–125
2539 Sittner, Hans. Wissenschaft und Praxis in der Stimmbildung. PAUMGARTNER 134–143
2539a Steglich, Rudolf. Zwei Beispiele "Manierlichen Musizierens" aus der Stadtkirche und vom ländlichen Tanzboden. BOSSE/50TH 133–138
2540 Stephani, Hermann. Orgelbegleitung in Chören? BIEHLE 38–39
2541 Strub, Max. Künstlerische Probleme im Alltag des Geigers. RAABE 229–234
2542 Thoene, Walter. Zur Frage der Artikulation im Cembalo- und Clavichordspiel. FELLERER/60TH 535–548
2543 Tutenberg, Fritz. Werktreue bei der Operninszenierung. STEIN 188–195
2544 Worm, Dieter Gerhard. Der Dirigent und die Schallplatte. KONWITSCHNY 87–90

INSTRUMENTS: GENERAL

See also nos. 1a, 21a, 54, 61, 363, 388a, 390–392, 393c, 394, 395a, 566, 569, 571, 572, 573a, 575b, 582, 1195, 1731, 2060, 2068, 2070, 2150, 2153, 2154

2545 Brenet, Michel. Notes sur l'introduction des instruments dans les églises de France. RIEMANN 277–286
2545a Goslich, Siegfried. Prolegomena zum instrumentenkundlichen Unterricht. MÜNNICH/70TH [80–95]

2546 Hornbostel, Erich M. von. Die Massnorm als kulturgeschichtliches Forschungsmittel. SCHMIDT 303–323
2547 Lehmann, Johannes. Beiträge zur Musikinstrumentenforschung; Literaturübersicht, Saiteninstrumente, Flöten. FGA 113–125
2548 Pericot, Luis. Instrumentos musicales en la cerámica ibérica de liria. ANGLÉS II, 647–649
2548a Racek, Jan. Hudební nástroje v dějinném vývoji lidské společnosti [Musical Instruments and the Historical Development of Human Society] NEJEDLÝ/75TH 180–200, summaries in English & Russian
2548b Scheurleer, Daniel F. Eene iconographie der muziekinstrumenten. BREDIUS 250–254
2548c Schrammek, Winfried. Gedanken zur Restaurierung historischer Musikinstrumente. WIORA/60TH 62–65
2548d Stockmann, Erich. Neue Beiträge zur Erforschung der europäischen Volksinstrumente. WIORA/60TH 512–519

INSTRUMENTS: ORGANS

See also nos. 1c, 387a, 393, 397a, 532c, 567a, 575, 575a, 583, 627, 797, 805, 815, 819a, 819c, 825b, 899, 925, 942, 959, 1048, 1092, 1145b, 1151a, 1435a, 1859–1861, 1986

2548e Dreimüller, Karl. Karl Straubes Sauer-Orgel in Wesel. Nachruf auf die im Zweiten Weltkrieg zerstörte Denkmal-Orgel des Willibrodi-Domes. FELLERER/60THS 55–70
2549 Dufourcq, Norbert. Autour des orgues de Notre-Dame de Poissy. LAURENCIE 19–27
2550 Enschedé, J. W. Oude en moderne orgels; sleeplade of pneumatische lade. SCHEURLEER 107–113
2550a Groszmann, Dieter. Zu einer Geschichte des Orgelbaues in Hessen. GUTBIER 174–184
2551 Handschin, Jacques. Die Orgelbewegung in der Schweiz. HANSCHIN 310–318; orig. in *Bericht über die 3. Tagung für deutsche Orgelkunst in Freiburg, 1927* (Kassel 1928)
2552 ——. Zeitgemässe Orgelfragen. HANDSCHIN 319–322; orig. in *Neue Zürcher Zeitung* 1885 (1926)
2552a Klusen, Ernst. Denkmalwerte Orgeln am Niederrhein. Ein Zustandsbericht. SCHNÜTGEN 271–277
2553 Kreps, Joseph. Le Tuyau à bouche, ses pression, longueur, diamètre, volume et matériaux. CLOSSON 110–138
2554 Mahrenholz, Christhard. Die Dorfkirchenorgel. MAHRENHOLZ 65–75; orig. in *Das Jahr des Kirchenmusikers* (1929)
2555 ——. Die Elektronen-Orgel. MAHRENHOLZ 90–91; orig. in *Hausmusik* (1954)
2556 ——. Fünfzehn Jahre Orgelbewegung. MAHRENHOLZ 46–65; orig. in *Musik und Kirche* 10 (1938)
2557 ——. Der heutige Stand des Orgelbaues. MAHRENHOLZ 28–45; orig. in *Gedenkboek van het Congres der Nederlandsche Organisten-Vereenigung* (Steenwijk 1932)
2558 ——. Zur Frage der Barockorgel. MAHRENHOLZ 88–89
2559 Mund, Hermann. Johannes Biehle und die modernen Orgelbauprobleme. BIEHLE 27–30
2560 Platou, Olaf. Nutidens orgeltyper og våre to domkirkorgler [Modern Types of Organs and Our Cathedral Organs] SANDVIK 184–200
2561 Raugel, Felix. Les grandes orgues de l'église Notre-Dame de Caudebec-en-Caux. LAURENCIE 33–38
2562 Reindell, Walter. Eine Orgelbauakte vom Niederrhein A.D. 1777. SCHIEDERMAIR/80TH 97–108
2563 Reuter, Rudolf. Die Grundlagen der Geschichte des Orgelbaues in Westfalen. FELLERER/60TH 439–453
2564 Schönstedt, Arno. Orgelbau in Westfalen. WLH 25–32
2565 Stephani, Hermann. Das Gesetz des Orgelanschlags. BIEHLE 36–37

INSTRUMENTS: STRING, INCLUDING KEYBOARD

See also nos. 26, 32, 35, 38, 395, 395b, 396, 398, 584b, 819d, 821, 1344a, 2219a, 2228a, 2529

2566 Andersson, Otto. Sträkharpan; en översicht [Bowed Harps; A Survey] HAMMARSTEDT 115–125
2567 Bjørndal, Arne. Felemakar Anders Askildson Heldal [Violinmaker A. A. Heldal] BJØRNDAL 130–134; orig. in *Fra Fjon til Fusa* (1949)
2568 ——. Nasjonalinstrumentet hardingfela, 1651–1951. BJØRNDAL

33–38; orig. in *Univ. i Bergen Arbok* (1950) Hist. Antikv. Rekke 3
2569 Boyden, David. The Tenor Violin, Myth, Mystery, or Misnomer. DEUTSCH/80TH 273–279
2570 Corrêa de Azevedo, Luis-Heitor. La Guitare archaïque au Brésil. BARTÓK/S 123–124
2571 Duhamel, Maurice. Les Harpes celtiques. LOTH 178–185
2572 Emsheimer, Ernst. Die Streichleier von Danczk. MOBERG 109–117; EMSHEIMER/60TH 99–107
2573 Fryklund, Daniel. Einige deutsche Ausdrücke für *Geige*. ERDMANN 120–125
2574 Handschin, Jacques. Das Klavikord. HANDSCHIN 323–326; orig. in *Neue Zürcher Zeitung* 258 (1929)
2575 Lorentz, H. A. De tonen van de aeolusharp. MENGELBERG 143–151
2576 Luithlen, Victor. Klaviere von Anton Walter in der Sammlung alter Musikinstrumente des Kunsthistorischen Museums in Wien. MÜLLER VON ASOW [128–131]
2577 Meyer, Josef. Über die physikalischen Grundlagen des Grünwaldischen Volltonsystems zur Resonanzverstärkung bei Saiteninstrumenten. GRÜNWALD 30–34
2578 Sachs, Curt. Der Ursprung der Saiteninstrumente. SCHMIDT 629–634
2579 Salazar, Adolfo. La Guitarra, heredera de la kithara clásica. ALONSO 118–126
2580 Schaeffner, André. Note sur la filiation des instruments à cordes. LAURENCIE 287–294
2581 Seewald, Otto. Die Lyredarstellungen der ostalpinen Hallstattkultur. OREL/70TH 159–171
2582 Simon, Alicja. Na drodze historycznego rozwoju gęśli słowiańskich; na marginesie odkrycia wczesnohistorycznego w Gdańsku 1949 r. [The Historical Development of the Slavic Gusle; On a Marginal Discovery in 1949 of its Early History in Gdańsk] CHYBIŃSKI/70TH 347–353
2583 Szulc, Zdzisław. Lutnicy polscy od XVI wieku do czasów najnowszych oraz ich karteczki rozpoznawcze; zbiór materiałow do słownika lutników polskich [Polish Violin and Lute Makers from the 16th Century to the Present Time and their Labels; A Collection of Materials Leading to a Dictionary of Polish Violin and Lute Makers] CHYBIŃSKI/70TH 354–379
2584 Väisänen, A. O. Eräs kanteletutkimus [A Kantele Study] KROHN 163–183, German summary vi
2585 ——. A vepsze kantele/Die Kantele der Wepsen. KODÁLY/60TH 337–342
2586 Viski, Károly. Hegedü/Hegedü, Geige. KODÁLY/60TH 43–54
2586a Wünsch, Walther. Zur Geschichte der Streichinstrumente des Südostens. WIORA/60TH 613–614
2587 Zingel, Hans J. Wandlungen im Klang- und Spielideal der Harfe; zur Geschichte des Instruments im 19. Jahrhundert. SCHNEIDER/60TH 147–153

INSTRUMENTS: WIND

See also nos. 26a, 29, 45, 64, 77, 394a, 397, 532c, 584a2, 827, 2192, 2202a, 2224, 2447

2588 Closson, Ernest. Un Facteur belge oublié, Nicolas-Marcel Raingo de Mons. BORREN 140–148
2589 Ehmann, Wilhelm. Neue Trompeten und Posaunen. WLH 58–63
2589a Göller, Gottfried. Das Rechnungsbuch des Holzblasinstrumentenmachers Eberhard Wünnenberg (1813–1877). FELLERER/60THS 71–85
2589b Kamiński, Włodzimeirz. Multanki z Przeczyc przyczynek do historii najwcześniajszych instrumentów muzycznych na ziemiach Polski [Bagpipes from Przeczyce. A Note about the History of the Earliest Musical Intruments in Poland] FEICHT 18–23
2590 Kollmann, J. Flöten und Pfeifen aus Alt-Mexico. BASTIAN 559–574
2591 Schmitz, Hans-Peter. Über die Verwendung von Querflöten des 18. Jahrhunderts in unserer Zeit. SCHNEIDER/80TH 277–284
2592 Schneider, Marius. Bemerkungen über die spanische Sackpfeife. MERSMANN 129–130
2593 Stumpf, Carl. Trompete und Flöte. KRETZSCHMAR 155–157

INSTRUMENTS: PERCUSSION, INCLUDING CARILLONS

See also nos. 28, 33b, 389, 393b, 397, 827, 2055, 2058, 2082a1, 2082b, 2082d, 2082e, 2202d

2594 Chapouthier, Fernand. Cybèle et le tympanon étoilé. DUSSAUD II, 723–728
2595 Denyn, Jef. Beiaardklavieren. DENYN 203–229

2596 ——. Technique et mécanisme du carillon/Inrichting en behandeling van het klokkenspel/Structure and Handling of the Carillon. DENYN 123–137/139–153/157–171
2597 ——. Wat zal de beiaard spelen? DENYN 67–79
2597a Dethlefsen, Richard. Glockeninschriften. BEZZENBERGER 14–23
2598 Graiule, Marcel. Symbolisme des tambours soudanais MASSON I, 79–86
2599 Kunst, Jaap. Honnan ered a gong?/Waar komt de gong vandaan? KODÁLY/60TH 84–87
2600 Mahrenholz, Christhard. Geläutedisposition. MAHRENHOLZ 91–100; orig. in *Musik und Kirche* 18 (1948)
2601 Márkus, Mihály. Jolsvai kolomposok/Bell-Making in Jolsva, County Gomor, Hungary. KODÁLY/60TH 245–264
2602 Ortiz, Fernando. La *Clave* xilofonica de la musica cubana. VARONA 171–209
2602a Sauermann, Ernst. Glockenwandlung in Schleswig-Holstein. PAULS 18–37
2603 Thiel, Carl. Über Kirchenglocken. KRETZSCHMAR 158–160
2604 Türnberg, Gerda. Afro-Cubano Rattles. ORTIZ III, 1419–1425

CHURCH MUSIC: GENERAL

See also nos. 1087a, 1746, 2100

2605 Beveridge, Lowell. Church Music. DAVISON 325–329
2606 Fellerer, Karl Gustav. Fragen um das auslanddeutsche Kirchenlied. SCHREIBER 379–394
2607 Goldammer, Kurt. Romantik und Realismus in der Liturgiegestalt. MAUERSBERGER 107–114
2608 Hamel, Fred. Kirchenmusik als Verlagsaufgabe. BOTE 61–64
2609 Handschin, Jacques. Die historische Stellung von Gesang und Orgelspiel im Gottesdienst. HANDSCHIN 161–165; orig. in *Die Tat* 10 & 17 (June 1941)
2610 ——. Vom Chorgesang in Russland. HANDSCHIN 300–304; orig. in *Neue Zürcher Zeitung* 276 (1928)
2611 ——. Vom russischen Kirchengesang. HANDSCHIN 291–295; orig. in *Neue Zürcher Zeitung* 906 (1933)
2612 Hatzfeld, Johannes. Vom Geheimnis der Musica sacra. HILBER 35–40
2613 Köhler, Johannes E. Die freie Improvisation und die Erneuerung der Kirchenmusik. MAUERSBERGER 152–157
2614 Mahrenholz, Christhard. Die Stellung des Credo im Hauptgottesdienst. MAHRENHOLZ 472–479; orig. in *Evangelisch-Lutherische Kirchenzeitung* (1956)
2615 Moser, Hans Joachim. Die Gestalt der deutschen Kirchenmusik. MOSER/70TH 224–234; orig. in *Walcker-Hausmitteilungen* (Aug. 1954)
2616 Saladin, Josef A. Die Bedeutung der Kirchenmusik im allgemeinen Musikleben. HILBER 55–59
2616a Schütz, Adalbert. Wort und Ton im Lied der Kirche. EHMANN/60TH 64–76
2616b Smith, F. Joseph. Church Music and Tradition. BUSZIN 3–14
2617 Sperry, Willard L. Church Music. DAVISON 331–336
2618 Wagner, Heinz. Kirchenmusik und Rundfunk. MAUERSBERGER 115–121
2619 Wiora, Walter. Zur Systematik und Geschichte religiöser Musik. SÖHNGEN 185–193

CHURCH MUSIC: PROTESTANT

See also nos. 492b, 671, 793a, 816, 1367b

2620 Adam, Theo. Die Gesangsinterpretation im geistlichen Raum. MAUERSBERGER 22–29
2621 Adrio, Adam. Die Komposition des Ordinarium Missae in der evangelischen Kirchenmusik der Gegenwart; ein Überblick. BLUME/F 22–29
2621a Andersson, Otto. Finlandssvenskt Koralarbete. BONSDORFF 150–157
2621b Barbour, J. Murray. The *Unpartheyisches Gesang-Buch.* BUSZIN 87–93
2621c Blankenburg, Walter. Kirchenlied und Kirchenmusik als Gegengewicht zur Predigt. EHMANN/60TH 32–42
2622 Böhm, Hans. Die evangelischen Kreuzkantoren; Notizen zu ihrem Leben, Wirken und ihrer historischen Situation. MAUERSBERGER 168–178
2622a Brown, Edgar S., Jr. Whither Church Music? BUSZIN 145–150
2623 Brück, Ulrich von. Dorfkirche—Stadtkirche. MAUERSBERGER 93–96
2623a Buszin, Walter E. Die West-

fälische Kantorei in der Oekumene. EHMANN/60TH 118–124
2623b Copes, V. Earle. Twentieth-Century Church Music—American Style. BUSZIN 151–156
2624 Ehmann, Wilhelm. Modell einer modernen Kantorei. WLH 33–39
2625 ——, & Arno Schönstedt. Die Ravensberger Kirchenmusiktage und die Orgelvespern im Münster zu Herford. WLH 43–45
2626 Fuchs, Carl. Metrik des Chorals; ernster Entwurf zu einem Landes-Choralbuch. RIEMANN 55
2626a Haeussler, Armin. The Struggle for Better Hymnody. BUSZIN 163–183
2627 Hofmann, Erna H. Wandlung und Bewahrung der Knabenchor-tradition im Dienst der evangelischen Kirchenmusik. MAUERSBERGER 142–151
2628 Kappner, Gerhard. Ausbildung der evangelischen Kirchenmusiker in der Deutschen Demokratischen Republik. MAUERSBERGER 158–167
2629 Mahrenholz, Christhard. Die Agende für evangelisch-lutherische Kirchen und Gemeinden, Band I. MAHRENHOLZ 430–471; orig. in *Jahrbuch für Liturgik und Hymnologie* (1957)
2630 ——. Die Aufgaben des Kirchen-chores im Gottesdienst. MAHRENHOLZ 229–239; orig. in *Zeitwende* (1948)
2631 ——. Entwurf zur Ordnung der Kirchenmusik in einer Landeskirche und in der deutschen evangelischen Kirche. MAHRENHOLZ 220–228; orig. in *Evangelischer Kirchengesangverein für Deutschland* 44 (1933) & *Musik und Kirche* 6 (1934)
2632 ——. 75 Jahre Verband evan-gelischer Kirchenchöre Deutschlands. MAHRENHOLZ 262–283; orig. in *Musik und Kirche* 29 (1959)
2633 ——. Ich danke meinem Gott allezeit. MAHRENHOLZ 3–10
2634 ——. Die Kirchenmusik in der neuen Lutherischen Agende. MAHREN-HOLZ 239–262; orig. in *Musik und Kirche* 25 (1955)
2635 ——. Kompendium der Liturgik zur Lutherischen Agende I. MAHREN-HOLZ 295–405
2636 ——. Die Liedauswahl des Evangelischen Kirchengesangbuches. MAHRENHOLZ 545–564; orig. in his *Das Evangelische Kirchengesangbuch; ein Bericht . . .* (Kassel 1950)
2637 ——. Liturgiegeschichtliches aus dem Lande Hadeln. MAHRENHOLZ 521–542; orig. in *Stat crux dum volvitur orbis* (Berlin 1959)
2638 ——. Die Melodien des Evange-lischen Kirchengesangbuches. MAHREN-HOLZ 592–608; orig. in his *Das Evangelische Kirchengesangbuch; ein Bericht . . .* (Kassel 1950)
2639 ——. Orgel und Liturgie. MAHRENHOLZ 13–27; orig. in *Bericht über die dritte Tagung für deutsche Orgelkunst* (Kassel 1928)
2640 ——. Die Textfassung des Evangelischen Kirchengesangbuches. MAHRENHOLZ 564–592; orig. in his *Das Evangelische Kirchengesangbuch; ein Bericht . . .* (Kassel 1950)
2641 ——. Zum Kirchenmusikergesetz 1932. MAHRENHOLZ 643–649; in *Begründung des Kirchenmusikergesetzes im Landeskirchentage. Protokolle . . .* (Nov. 24 & 25, 1932)
2642 ——. Zur Begründung des Agendengesetzes vor der Hannover-schen Landessynode. MAHRENHOLZ 421–430
2643 ——. Zur musikalischen Gestal-tung von Luthers deutscher Litanie. MAHRENHOLZ 169–195; orig. in *Luther-jahrbuch* (1937)
2644 ——. Zur neuen Gottesdienstord-nung der Agende I vor der Generalsynode in Braunschweig. MAHRENHOLZ 405–421; orig. in *Nach-richten der evangelisch-lutherischen Kirche in Bayern* (1954)
2645 Mauersberger, Erhard. Thuringia cantat. MAUERSBERGER 76–83
2645a Mrozek, Hans. Vom geistlichen Selbstverständnis der Posaunenchöre und ihrer Bläser. EHMANN/60TH 108–111
2646 Mudde, Willem. Brief aus Holland. SÖHNGEN 169–171
2646a Müller, Karl Ferdinand. Church Music Instruction in the Church Music Schools of Germany. BUSZIN 185–192
2646b Pettersson, Gustav. Kyrkliga sång- och musiksträvanden. BONSDORFF 251–257
2646c Pfatteicher, Helen E. The Dilemma of Church Music Today. BUSZIN 157–161
2647 Reindell, Walter. Gregorianik und evangelische Liturgie. JOHNER 101–104
2648 Schönian, Hans G. Das kirchenmusikalische Aufbauwerk. SÖHNGEN 162–168
2649 Schröder, Rudolf A. Die Kirche und ihr Lied. SÖHNGEN 61–74

2650 Smend, Julius. Was ist evangelische Kirchenmusik? SCHEURLEER 303–312
2651 Söhngen, Oskar. Die Entwicklung der neuen evangelischen Kirchenmusik seit dem Fest der deutschen Kirchenmusik 1937. MAUERSBERGER 32–41
2652 ——. Kirchenmusik und Theologie. SCHNEIDER/80TH 335–342
2652a ——. Das Lied der Kirche. EHMANN/60TH 13–31
2652b ——. Was heisst "evangelische Kirchenmusik"? Methodologische Überlegungen zur Kirchenmusik-Geschichtsschreibung. WIORA/60TH 120–128
2652c ——. What is the Position of Church Music in Germany Today? BUSZIN 201–218
2653 Straube, Karl. Kirchenmusikalisches Vermächtnis. MAUERSBERGER 132–134
2654 Thamm, Hans. Vererbung des Knabenchor-Ideals; Erziehung, Ausbildung, Leistung. MAUERSBERGER 138–141
2655 Voll, Wolfgang. Kirchenmusik und Schallplatte. WLH 53–57
2656 ——. Die Schallplatte im Dienste der Kirchenmusik. MAUERSBERGER 122–131
2657 ——. Das Wochenlied in katechetischer Sicht. WLH 67–75

CHURCH MUSIC: CATHOLIC

See also nos. 935a, 1404b, 1414c, 1415a, 1417, 1422b, 1428a, 1435b–1435d, 1580c, 1660a, 1737

2658 Drinkwelder, Erhard. Der musikalische Aufbau des Hochamtes. JOHNER 12–14
2659 Fellerer, Karl Gustav. Katholische Kirchenmusik und Musikforschung. SCHREMS 100–109
2660 ——. Kirchenmusik als Brauchtumsmusik. LEMACHER 30–37
2660a Haberl, Ferdinand. Zur Komposition volkssprachlicher Psalmen cum populo activo. DESDERI/70TH 79–85
2661 Jammers, Ewald. Choral und Liturgie. WAESBERGHE 89–99
2662 Köllner, George P. Der Mainzer Domchor als Träger der regensburger Tradition. SCHREMS 157–169
2663 Lueger, Wilhelm. Die geistige Situation der neuen katholischen Kirchenmusik. MERSMANN 94–96
2663a Madurell, Josep. Fundacions litúrgiques a Santa Maria de Mataró. BALDELLÓ 111–117
2664 Moissl, Franz. Von neuer Kirchenmusik, Reaktionäres und Fortschrittliches. UNIVERSAL 169–191
2665 Overath, Johannes. Die Enzyklika *Musicae sacrae disciplina* vom 25. Dezember 1955 und der Komponist. LEMACHER 9–19
2666 ——. Erwägungen über das Verhältnis des ACV zur regensburger Tradition. SCHREMS 8–13
2667 Schömig, Richard. Zur Theologie des christlichen Kultgesanges. SCHREMS 16–43
2667a Schuh, Paul. Der Trierer Choralstreit. FELLERER/60THM 125–138

PRINTING, PUBLISHING, ETC.

See also nos. 429, 432, 440, 510a, 1143a, 1368c, 1380a

2668 Berten, Walter. Komponist und Verleger, Ein- und Ausfälle. BOTE 38–43
2668a Bridgman, Nanie. La typographie musicale italienne (1475–1630) dans les collections de la Bibliothèque Nationale de Paris. FÉDEROV 24–27
2669 Davidsson, Åke. Isländskt musiktryck i äldre tider [Music Printing in Iceland in Olden Times] MOBERG 99–108
2670 Einstein, Alfred. The Gentle Art of Editing a Musical Magazine. ENGEL 95–102
2671 Elster, Alexander. Vom Einfluss des Urheberrechts auf die Musikpflege. STEIN 96–103
2672 Elvers, Rudolf. Datierte Verlagsnummern Berliner Musikverleger. DEUTSCH/80TH 291–295
2672a ——. Musikdrucker, Musikalienhändler und Musikverleger in Berlin 1750 bis 1850, ein Übersicht. GERSTENBERG/60TH 37–44
2673 Gilbert, Francis. Two Conflicting Theories of International Copyright Protection. ENGEL 106–114
2674 Hase, Oskar von. Zeitgenössischer Vertrieb deutscher Denkmäler der Tonkunst. KRETZSCHMAR 49–53
2675 Hitzig, Wilhelm. Ein berliner Aktenstück zur Geschichte des Notendruckverfahrens. WAGNER 81–86
2675a Hüschen, Heinrich. Rheinische Gesangbuchdrucker- und verlager des 16. und 17. Jahrhunderts. BOSSE/50TH 51–79

2675b King, A. Hyatt. C. G. Röder's Music-printing Business in 1885. FÉDEROV 53–59
2676 Lienau, Robert. Abschluss und Anfang. BOTE 75–79
2677 Moser, Hans Joachim. Aus den Erfahrungen eines Musik-Lexikographen. MOSER/70TH 234–242
2677a Müller-Blattau, Michael. Optionsbindungen zwischen Komponisten und Musikverlegern. MÜLLER-BLATTAU/70TH 201–211
2678 Oberborbeck, Felix. Original und Bearbeitung; Versuch einer Klärung der Terminologie. SCHNEIDER/80TH 347–355
2678a Quellenmalz, Alfred. Musikdarstellungen auf Flugblattbildern. SEIFFERT/70THA 15–28
2679 Refardt, Edgar. Vom Musikhändler Nägeli. REFARDT 24–27; orig. in *Schweizerische Musikzeitung* 71 (1931)
2680 Riemann, Hugo. Notenschrift und Notendruck; bibliographisch-typographische Studie. RÖDER app. 1–88
2680a Rohlfs, Eckhart. Gärtner und Garten der Musik. BOSSE/50TH 117–120
2680b Schulze, Erich. Ein Beitrag zur deutschen Urheberrechtsreform. STRAUSS, F. 117–120
2681 Waters, Edward N. The Wa-Wan Press, An Adventure in Musical Idealism. ENGEL 214–233
2682 Weinmann, Alexander. Zur Bibliographie des alt-wiener Musikverlags. DEUTSCH/80TH 319–326
2683 Wolf, Johannes. Antiquariat und Musikwissenschaft. FOCK 167–170
2684 Ziegler, Benno. Zur Geschichte des Privilegium exclusivum des Mainzer Musikstechers Bernhard Schott. LEIDINGER 293–305

MUSIC RELATED TO OTHER ARTS

See also nos. 21a, 49, 53, 60, 104b, 543, 760a, 764, 1406a, 2463a

2685 Amades, Joan. Danses rituals d'iniciació. ANGLÉS I, 11–26
2685a Anschütz, Georg. Das Verhältnis der Musik zu den bildenden Künsten im Lichte stilistischer Betrachtung. SEIFFERT/70THA 3–14
2685b Bernet Kempers, Karel P. Die Instrumentalmusik im Banne der Literatur. SCHMIDT-GÖRG/70TH 11–25
2686 Borren, Charles van den. Horace et la musique. HORACE 247–254
2686a Braun, Werner. Arten des Komponistenporträts. WIORA/60TH 86–94
2687 Coeuroy, André. Petites notes sur les touches musicales de l'impressionisme et du symbolisme allemand. ANDLER 109–113
2688 Cohen, Gustav. Musique et poésie. MASSON I, 15–19
2688a Grall, Franz. Volksspiele, Tanzspiele und ihre Stellung in der Volkstumsarbeit. MAIER/75TH 28–32
2689 Gurlitt, Wilibald. Über die Phantasie in den musischen und bildenden Künsten. BORREN/80TH 71–74
2689a Heinitz, Wilhelm. Musikalisch-dynamische Textauslese in faroischen und faroisch-danischen Reigentanzen (eine phonetische Studie). PIPPING 160–169
2690 Herescu, N. I. Le Sortilège des sons; remarques sur la structure musicale du vers latin. GRÉGOIRE III, 133–159
2691 Hohlbaum, Robert. Ton und Wort. RAABE 45–48
2691a Huffel, N. G. van. Analyse. BREDIUS 126–129
2692 Janzon, Åke. Vad hjälper musiken? [What Help is Music?] MALMBERG 58–62
2693 Kohler, Eugène. Historie d'un mot: farandole. HOEPFFNER 127–138
2693a Kross, Siegfried. Musikalische Strukturen als Literarische Form. SCHMIDT-GÖRG/70TH 217–227
2693b Kurath, Gertrude Prokosch. Dance in Modern American Culture. SACHS/C 343–367
2694 Lach, Robert. Sprach- und Gesangsmelos im Englischen. LUICK 23–31
2694a Langen, August. Zum Symbol der Äolsharfe in der deutschen Dichtung. MÜLLER-BLATTAU/70TH 160–191
2695 Maag, Otto. Musik und Sprache; ein Versuch zur Sinndeutung der Musik. NEF 165–173
2695a Madsen, William G. A Reading of "Musicks Duell." WILCOX 39–50
2696 Mendel, Arthur. Thoughts on the Translation of Vocal Texts. ENGEL 166–178
2697 Moser, Hans Joachim. Grenzen und Möglichkeiten der Querverbindung. MOSER/70TH 312–323; orig. in *Grundfragen der schulmusik* (Leipzig 1931)
2698 ——. Die Stilverwandtschaft

zwischen der Musik und den anderen Künsten. MOSER/70TH 295–305
2699 ——. Die Symbolbeigaben des Musikerbildes. SEIFFERT 35–52
2700 Newell, William W. Note on the Interpretation of European Song-Games. BOAS 404–409
2701 Peacock, Ronald. Probleme des Musikalischen in der Sprache. STRICH 85–100
2701a Rehnberg, Mats. Livgardisten han kommer till Gud. En studie i folkdiktningen kring de militära signalerna. SALÉN/70TH 133–198
2702 Rietsch, Heinrich. Sprachliches zur Tonkunst. KRETZSCHMAR 122–126
2702a Rödding, Gerhard. Der Teufel und die Musik. Einige Betrachtungen zur Music in Thomas Manns *Doktor Faustus*. EHMANN/60TH 125–136
2703 Sachs, Curt. Musik und bildende Kunst im Rahmen der allgemeinen Kunstgeschichte. SCHLOSSER 31–34
2704 Schellenberg, Ernst Ludwig. Gedicht und Lied. MÜNNICH 40–45; MÜNNICH/70TH [44–51]
2705 Schwenke, Paul. Die Buchbinder mit dem Lautenspieler und dem Knoten. HAEBLER 122–144
2706 Springer, George P. Language and Music, Parallels and Divergencies. JAKOBSON 504–513
2707 Stainton, Walter H. Color Music. DRUMMOND 60–77
2708 Steglich, Rudolf. Über die Wesensgemeinschaft von Musik und Bildkunst. SEIFFERT 23–34
2708a Vetter, Walther. Heinrich Wölfflin und die musikalische Stilforschung. ENGEL 433–441
2708b ——. The Image of Italian Music and Art Presented in German Literature. SACHS/C 313–327
2709 Vielhaber, Gerd. Der Präludiker, ein Porträt des Musikclowns Grock. NIESSEN 193–197
2709a Vogl, Franz. Volkstanzfeste. MAIER/75TH 20–27
2710 Wellek, Albert. Über das Verhältnis von Musik und Poesie. SCHENK 574–585

III

Author-Subject Index

WHEN BOTH author and subject references appear for the same person (e.g. Bartók), the subject references are given in italics after the author references.

B

C

D

E

F

G

H

K

L

M

N

O

Q

S

T

U

X

Y

Z